CLASSICS FOR THE MASSES

CLASSICS FOR THE MASSES

SHAPING SOVIET MUSICAL IDENTITY UNDER LENIN AND STALIN

PAULINE FAIRCLOUGH

YALE UNIVERSITY PRESS
NEW HAVEN AND LONDON

For Mum and Richard

For information about this and other Yale University Press publications, please contact:
U.S. Office: sales.press@yale.edu   www.yalebooks.com
Europe Office: sales@yaleup.co.uk   www.yalebooks.co.uk

Typeset in Minion Pro by IDSUK (DataConnection) Ltd
Printed in Great Britain by TJ International Ltd, Padstow, Cornwall

Library of Congress Cataloging-in-Publication Data

Fairclough, Pauline, 1970- author.
   Classics for the masses : shaping Soviet musical identity, 1917-1953 / Pauline Fairclough.
      pages cm
   ISBN 978-0-300-21719-3 (cl : alk. paper)
1.   Music—Soviet Union—History and criticism.   I. Title.
   ML300.F35 2016
   780.947'0904   dc23

                                                                        2015023659

A catalogue record for this book is available from the British Library.

10 9 8 7 6 5 4 3 2 1

CONTENTS

ILLUSTRATIONS

Figures

Tables

ACKNOWLEDGEMENTS

Research for this book has been funded by the Arts and Humanities Research Council, the British Academy, the Music and Letters Trust and the University of Bristol. For allowing me to use their reading rooms, libraries and archival holdings, I wish to thank the St Petersburg Conservatoire, the Institute for the History of Arts in St Petersburg and the St Petersburg Philharmonia, in particular its chief archivist Pavel Dmitriev and his wonderful colleagues Raisa Kuz'mina, Tatyana Znamenskaya and Nadezhda Stepanova. I also thank the staff at the Central State Archive of Literature and Art, TsGALI, St Petersburg. In Moscow I wish to thank the indefatigable librarians of the Composers' Union, Marina Saveleva and Tatiana Bresnitskaya, and the staff of the Russian State Archive of Literature and Art in Moscow, RGALI, especially Elena Chugonova and Dmitriy Neustroyev, the staff in the Russian State Archive of Social and Political History, RGASPI, and the State Archive of the Russian Federation, GARF and, especially, the staff of the Lenin Library and its music department. In London, I thank the staff of the Rare Books and Music Reading Room of the British Library and especially of the National Archives in Kew – truly an archival paradise on earth, where all weary researchers can find a comfortable seat and permission to use their digital cameras.

My biggest debt of gratitude goes to my friends in Russia, who made each of my research trips to Moscow and St Petersburg a pleasure. In particular, I thank Lyudmila Kovnatskaya for countless acts of kindness, not least lending me a wonderful place to live in St Petersburg, and Lidia Ader and Tanya Ader for their warmth and hospitality as well as for Lida's unfailingly swift responses to my questions and patient help with practical difficulties.

In Moscow, I have been privileged to have the support of two very dear friends, Olga Digonskaya and Levon Hakobian: their unfaltering generosity, stimulating company and practical assistance meant that I never once felt alone in their city, and I simply don't know what I would have done without them on many occasions. Levon offered many very welcome correctives and comments on my manuscript for which I am extremely grateful; I am of course entirely to blame for mistakes that remain. For their enjoyable company and friendly advice in Moscow, I would also like to thank Olesya Bobrik (who generously sent me several books on opera repertoire), Leonid Maksimenkov (who kindly assisted me with some biographical queries), Kiril Tomoff and Meri Herrala. I am grateful to colleagues back home who have helped me in various kind ways: David Fanning for his exceedingly long-term loan of microfilms (sorry, David – I will give them back, I promise); Gerard McBurney and most of all, Erik Levi, who has been unfailingly supportive and kind throughout, far beyond the call of duty. I cannot stress enough how grateful I am to Erik for his invaluable help in reading through the entire manuscript, saving me from many an embarrassing mistake and prompting new and illuminating lines of enquiry. My colleagues in the music department at Bristol University have been exceptionally generous in granting me extended research leave from 2009 to 2011 and I am truly grateful for their collegiality and kindness. I would also like to thank James Taylor for printing out a boxful of microfilm articles for me, thus saving me many hours of work, as well as checking some sources for me in St Petersburg.

Every academic experiences a certain amount of isolation when completing a major piece of research. Equally, every close relative knows the boredom of hearing all about the various travails and breakthroughs, and they are invariably extremely gracious in concealing it. My mother has racked up whole weeks, if not months, of dedicated telephone listening and shown nothing but the kindest encouragement and interest. Though I know she doesn't look for any thanks, nonetheless I want to thank her for being a constant source of support – remarkably engaged no matter how obscure my ramblings and an unfailingly cheerful presence at the other end of a Skype call from Moscow. What I would do without her I simply do not know. My husband Richard has lived with this project as long as I have and has never even got to the point where he would pull out a watch and time me when I began talking about it. More seriously, he has been incredibly supportive of my prolonged research trips to Russia, welcomed my Russian friends into our home, and waited for me faithfully as I sat, stranded, on a snowbound runway at Heathrow while the baggage handlers all went home. Thank you for everything! In return, I promise never to make you eat *grechka* or force you to read this book.

Bristol, March 2015

Extracts from Pauline Fairclough, 'Don't Sing it on a Feast Day: The Reception and Performance of Western Sacred Music in Soviet Russia, 1917–53', *Journal of the American Musicological Society*, vol. 65/1, 2012, 71–116, reproduced by kind permission of the University of California Press. Extracts from Pauline Fairclough, 'Wagner Reception in Stalinist Russia', in Luca Sala, ed., *The Legacy of Richard Wagner*, Speculum Musicae, Turnhout: Brepols Publishers, Centro Studia Opera Omnia Luigi Boccherini, 2012, 309–26 reproduced by kind permission of Brepols Publishers.

NOTE ON TRANSLITERATION AND ARCHIVAL SOURCES

I have used a slightly modified form of the *New Grove* convention for transliteration throughout the book, both for main text and for references. I have not retained the familiar spelling of certain names; thus, Tchaikovsky is rendered throughout as Chaykovskiy and Eisenstein as Eyzenshteyn.

Archival abbreviations and references are as follows: GARF: State Archive of the Russian Federation [*Gosudarstvennïy arkhiv rossiskoy federatsii*]; NA: The National Archives at Kew (FO: Foreign Office files); RGALI: Russian State Archive of Literature and Art [*Rossiskiy gosudarstvennïy arkhiv literaturï i isskustva*]; RGASPI: Russian State Archive of Socio-Political History [*Rossikiy gosudarstvennïy arkhiv sotsialno politicheskoy istorii*]; TsGALI: Central State Archive of Literature and Art, St Petersburg [*Tsentral'niy gosudarstvennïy arkhiv literaturï i isskustva*].

Russian archival abbreviations are given in the standard format of Russian and Soviet studies: f. – *fond*, or collection; op. – *opis*, or file; d. – *delo*, or item; ed. khr. – *edinitsa khraneniya*, or item; l. – list, or page.

SOVIET ACRONYMS AND ABBREVIATIONS

ASM. *Assotsiatsiya sovremennoy muzïki* [Association of contemporary music]

Glaviskusstvo. *Glavnoye upravleniye po delam khudozhestvennoy literat*ure i iskusstva* [Central administration for affairs in art and literature]

Glavrepertkom. *Glavnïy repertuarnïy komitet* [Central repertoire committee]

Narkompros. *Narodnïy komissariat prosveshcheniya* [People's commissariat of enlightenment]

NEP. *Novaya ekonomicheskaya politika* [New economic policy]

ORKiMD. *Obyedeniye revoliutsionnïkh kompozitorov i muzïkal'nikh deyateley* [Association of revolutionary composers and music workers]

Rabis/Vserabis. *(vse) rossiskiy professional'niy soyuz rabotnikov iskusstv* [(All-) Russian trade union of art workers]

RAPM. *Rossiskaya assotsiatsiya proletarskikh muzïkantov* [Russian association of proletarian musicians]

RAPP. *Rossiskaya assotsiatsiya proletarskikh pisateley* [Russian association of proletarian writers]

Vseroskomdram. *Vserossiskoye obshchestvo dramaturgov i kompozitorov* [All-Union society of dramatists and composers]

INTRODUCTION

When does tradition become appropriation, and when does biography become rebranding? The answer, of course, is that they don't – all that changes is cultural perspective. For Russians building up their musical life in the 1920s and 1930s – the formative years of Soviet musical culture that form the heart of this study – the concept of 'appropriation' never arose. There was simply no reason to think about repertoire that way: Russian and Western art music was a staple of early Soviet artistic life and no one thought in terms of its 'belonging' to any one culture or another – at least, not at first.[1] Nor did writers consider their scholarly work on composers to be a form of ideological marketing, though, as this book demonstrates, it was not long before more politicized writings appeared that do merit that label. Here the waters immediately grow murky because this marketing drive was not necessarily fuelled by a need to justify what I, following my Soviet pred-ecessors, will refer to as 'classical music' in the fledgling Soviet state. Rather, it was nearly always motivated by a wish to make composers – especially long-dead, bourgeois and foreign composers – seem interesting to the new mass audiences in the 1920s and 1930s. This is especially clear in the case of Beethoven, whom Soviet writers portrayed as a historical figure whose sympathy for the revolutionary cause gave him contemporary relevance. It is no exaggeration to call this marketing – the masses were being sold a cultural icon, not for money, but as part of their education.

The Bolsheviks' wish to instil in the urban proletariat and rural peasantry alike a love for culture was bound up with identifying the Soviet masses as inheritors of the greatest traditions of Western civilization. But not all artistic groups believed it was desirable to retain 'bourgeois heritage' and this iconoclastic strain of Russian culture actually pre-dated the 1917 revolution. Most famously, the Futurist movement wished as early as 1912 to 'throw Pushkin overboard from the steamship of modernity', but while this call was never in any danger of being heeded, it was a different matter when a delegate at the First All-Russian Conference of Proletarian Cultural Organizations (Proletkul't) in 1918 likened the weight of the cultural past on the new Soviet present to that of an 'overloaded camel' and called for it to be discarded 'like old rubbish.'[2] Some of the most talented and radical artists working in Russia after 1917 would have agreed with him: Lenin's wife, Nadezhda Krupskaya, took it on herself to purge Russian libraries of Pushkin's works throughout the 1920s, and one Soviet citizen interviewed in 1950 reported that 'up to 1935, you couldn't read Pushkin, you couldn't read Tolstoi, because they were considered the nobility.'[3] Lenin himself was not in favour of discarding past culture, insisting instead on the need to assimilate and respect great art of the past in order to build on the best of its traditions; and in fact, the year after his death, the Party published a resolution demanding an end to the 'frivolous and condescending attitude to the old cultural heritage.'[4] While Krupskaya's purge of Russian nineteenth-century belles-lettres reflected the hostility some of the more extreme political and artistic leaders felt towards the 'old rubbish' of the past, there is little evidence of similar moves against music during the 1920s. But, nevertheless, the cultural shift accompanying the transition from the 1920s to the 1930s – the era of mature Stalinism and Socialist Realism – made a clear mark on music writing. The marketing of classical composers became more urgently political as the decade wore on, and simultaneously, a creeping sense of 'appropriation' can be discerned in writings about Bach and Handel in the mid-1930s.

One reason for this shift may have been that it was precisely during this period that the creation of a new kind of citizen – a highly cultured Soviet 'Superman' – became an urgent preoccupation of the leadership.[5] It was at this time that the notion of *kul'turnost'* (the condition of being a cultured person) emerged as a vital ingredient to becoming an ideal Soviet citizen.[6] Another, closely related, reason might be that the rise of socialist realism – formally launched in 1934 at the First Writers' Congress – demanded a new canon of cultural and historical heroes, depicting classically 'noble' values of self-sacrifice, determination and faith in a higher purpose. Certainly, there was a powerful narrative of personal heroism in Soviet films and literature during this period, which spilled over into embracing artworks of the past that shared the same spirit – or at least could be marketed in a way that made them seem to share it. In tandem with this cult of heroism, composers' biographies assumed much greater importance to Soviet critics, who strove to present them in a way that could meet public expectations of especially noble characters or actions. We see this very clearly, for example, in the way that writers described Bach and Handel in the mid to late 1930s, where there is a clear move to distance them from their national identities and effectively make them 'Soviet'. Yet how effective such strategies were in shaping the Soviet citizens of the future is doubtful, especially where music is concerned. Evgeny Dobrenko has observed in relation to the Soviet reader that '[he or she] is not simply a recipient (or in the Western sense a 'consumer of books'): in accordance with the doctrine of "reshaping society" that lies at the heart of Socialist Realism, he is the *object* of reshaping, "molding." '[7] It is probably true that no Soviet listener was ever 'moulded' by exposure to Bach, Mozart, Beethoven and Chaykovskiy, though it would be nice to think that many of the recipients of Soviet cultural largesse enjoyed the music made available to them. Many, as we will see, were bored by it, just as many were bored by educational lectures and instructive books. Certainly, there is no concrete evidence of connections between the consumption of classical music and listeners' ideological development, either in audience responses to music or in the critical literature surrounding art music. Yet Dobrenko's point that the Soviet reader was not simply a passive consumer also holds for the Soviet listener: not all areas of reper- toire were available to them and they were given a quite carefully vetted 'canon' which, moreover, changed in accordance with broader cultural and political shifts throughout the 1920s and 1930s. The ideal Soviet listener was interested in classical music, but also interested in hearing about the political context in which it was written, and able to understand this from a Marxist-Leninist historical perspective. They were not supposed simply to soak up the beautiful sounds, but to engage intellectually with pre-concert talks and programme booklets, which could be extremely substantial. Yet when we read articles criticizing Shostakovich and praising Bach in 1936, or Andrey Zhdanov's criticisms of Soviet composers in 1948, the point most forcibly made is that older music – both Russian and Western – is simple, beautiful and easy to understand. Not a word is said about its educa- tive value – which certainly underlines the extent to which music's role in 'moulding' the public differed from that of other art forms.

However, it was certainly not clear to those at the front line of mass musical work in the earliest years of the Soviet Union that this would ultimately prove to be the case, and in fact how exactly the mass audience might be politically moulded was hotly debated in the 1920s – the idea that they *could* be moulded was taken as read. The most militant proletarian groups sought to use music merely as an indoctrination tool, seeing artistic worth only in the extent to which a song or piece of music could be politically instructive. Then there were those who sought primarily to educate and share culture – these were the people most likely to try to enthuse audiences with tales of Beethoven's revolutionary views as a means of reassuring them that classical music was not boring and irrelevant. There were also debates about the deleterious effect that Western 'decadence' might have on the 'healthy' Soviet listener in both the 1920s and 1930s. But when we look at Soviet musical culture in practice rather than in theory we see a far more pragmatic picture. Those with extreme views, by and large, did not exert far-reaching influence on concert programming. No matter how pointless much classical music seemed to the militant groups, it was played in the concert halls of Leningrad and Moscow every night, and for the most part, benignly reviewed in the major papers. And at the other end of the militant scale, no matter how much revolutionary modernists like Nikolay Roslavets hoped to raise the cultural level of the masses to appreciate radical new music, most Soviet listeners never really came to like music that sounded strange or difficult but continued to enjoy popular music, folk songs and familiar classics, much like audiences all over the world. No matter how critics from all sides fretted over the 'decadent' Mahler or Strauss, their music was still played, even if they never achieved full canonization as Soviet 'greats'. Even when musicians protested in 1932 about having to play music by such a mixed group as Saint-Saëns, Honegger and Richard Strauss on the grounds that it was 'hostile to the working class', their complaint fell on deaf ears – such accusations no longer had any credibility whatsoever.[8] After 1932, the aim of 'moulding' the listener was perhaps less urgent than that of creating a new image of Stalinist society: one that was rich in world culture, a socialist colossus towering over the declining West that would take its most treasured cultural figures and make them its own. Within this mighty macrocosm, the musical education of the Soviet listener was merely one more facet of their transformation into the ideal citizen that Hans Günther called the 'Soviet Superman'[9] – a necessary microcosm, to be sure, but a by-product rather than the goal itself.

The canonization of great figures of the past was crucially important to Soviet cultural arbiters, because they provided evidence that the Bolshevik Revolution was intellectually not only respectable, but more than that: it was the natural consequence of the most progressive and democratic European values. It was important not only for their international, but also for their domestic, image that the Bolsheviks would not be perceived as the barbarians storming the gates of culture – though in the turbulence of the civil war and the ransacking of estates that followed the 1917 coup, they seemed the personification of just that. Yet it would be wrong to conclude that Bolshevik support for cultural establishments and traditions was nothing but a cynical veneer. On the contrary, Lenin, Trotskiy and their cohorts considered themselves cultured, educated and enlightened and both Russian and Western history books are dotted with famous Lenin quotes about the value of preserving older culture (Krupskaya's literary purging notwithstanding). Their conscious decision to fund and support major musical establishments like the Bolshoy and Mariinskiy Theatres – though not instantly reached – underlined their commitment to a State model of cultural education. The Ministry of Education was given the much grander title of Ministry of Enlightenment – signifying its extraordinarily wide remit, from overseeing schools to every aspect of cultural life: publishing, art galleries, museums, concert organizations and mass education projects. Its first, and most distinguished minister (or Commissar in Soviet parlance) was Anatoliy Lunacharskiy, who has gone down in history as one of the most liberal of Lenin's inner circle. His liberalism was, of course, highly selective and relative, and the close relationship between the ministry and the secret police, or Cheka (later renamed the NKVD, the Narodnïy kommissariat vnutrennikh del [People's Commissariat for Internal Affairs]) meant that, just as some figures in the art world were protected, others were continually persecuted, arrested and even, in the case of the poet Nikolay Gumilev, actually shot.[10] Lunacharskiy's role in these events is not yet known, though Alexandra Tolstoy's distinctly unfavourable account of his behaviour towards her, her family and Tolstoy's estate at Yasnaya Polyana gives a very different picture of Lunacharskiy from that usually found in Western accounts of Soviet musical history.[11] Whatever the truth, he presided over the reforming of Soviet musical culture very firmly on the basis of the old, supporting new initiatives (new orchestras, choirs, mass work programmes) and giving his blessing to large and expensive projects like the Petrograd Institute for the History of the Arts and the Leningrad and Moscow Philharmonias.

As several writers have noted, the claims of totalitarian regimes on the European Enlightenment have been many and various. Régis Debray describes what he calls the 'totalitarian hijacking of the Enlightenment' in Eastern Europe during post-war communism in terms of an ossified museum culture:

> The process was frozen in the post-war period in Eastern Europe's huge conservatory of obsolete forms—a museum of the word, in which the living sources of the past lay fossilized. . . . To journey through those old-world provinces, where Western Europe's 19th century still lived on, was to witness a universal cult of books and an idolization of writers.[12]

For Debray, socialism – including its radical incarnation as communism – has historically been marked by an obsessive veneration of past culture, and his analysis draws almost causal links between Saint-Simonism in nineteenth-century France to Mao's regime in China. But Katerina Clark's analysis of the original process of cultural appropriation during the Soviet 1930s extends far beyond Debray's to observe a broader cosmopolitanism at work, taking in the old European and Russian past but also borrowing freely from the modern American and European present (especially in architectural trends melding classicism with skyscraper-building technologies).[13] This can clearly be seen in Soviet musical culture, where, between approximately 1926 and 1936, Western modernism – or more specifically, *European* modernism – was generously represented in Soviet concert programmes. But alongside new music, it was Western rather than Russian classics that held sway: Bach, Handel, Mozart and Beethoven were the icons of the mid to late 1930s, and their eventual replacement with Chaykovskiy, the *kuchka* and Glinka took place surprisingly late in the decade. Thus in music, the rhetoric of Enlightenment – incorporating revolution, social satire and nobility of the human spirit – was so strong in the mid-1930s that, when the dominant narrative became instead Russian nationalism, it actually overlapped with that of the Stalin-era 'Enlightenment' in the last part of the decade. With the two trends running concurrently, it is not surprising to find a degree of confusion in archival records about which composers should be championed and which not. In all likelihood, where actual bans or quasi-bans were involved, they were at the whim of individuals and were therefore subject to sudden change. For example, a senior bureaucrat might decide that a particular work is inappropriate repertoire; it duly disappears, only to resurface the moment the bureaucrat is replaced. This is exactly what happened with Rakhmaninov's *The Bells*, which was the subject of a hostile campaign by the proletarian lobby in the early 1930s and vanished from Philharmonia programmes, only to be restored after 1932; it was then attacked again in 1937 and its composer was once again scorned as a 'white-émigré'. Yet after the purges had resulted in sweeping personnel changes in arts administration, *The Bells* was instantly revived and, just a few years later, Rakhmaninov was being celebrated as a national treasure.

This book seeks to chart the evolution of the process of what, following Katerina Clark, I believe can truly be termed the 'appropriation' of older Russian and Western culture by the Soviet sphere, and the concurrent 'rebranding' or marketing of selected composers to the Soviet public. As I show in chapters One and Two, the 1920s was overwhelmingly the decade of education, sharing and discovery: though there were groups who wanted to use music to 'mould', most music workers did not share this aim, but simply wished to develop an educative Soviet musical culture along fairly conventional lines – to set up publishing houses, critical editions, scholarly journals, international exchanges, cycles of symphonies, composer jubilees and to build (or preserve) the institutions that would educate future generations of musicians and scholars. In this evolving situation, where different individuals and groups disagreed on the value of key figures such as Chaykovskiy, Rakhmaninov, Wagner and Mahler, it is not possible to speak of an overall consensus regarding individual composers, only to trace certain strands of argument and to pinpoint those writings that are particularly typical of one kind of view or another. Chapter Three addresses what I have termed the 'Stalinist Enlightenment' in music of the period 1932–41, while Chapter Four charts the rise of Russian nationalism towards the end of the decade. In both these chapters, the 'rebranding' of composers is dealt with head-on, as certain figures, both Russian and Western, were painted in far more tendentious colours than had been the case previously. I am not the first to describe the Soviet rebranding of Russian composers: the scholar Jiří Smrž has already addressed this phenomenon in Stalinist musical life in detail, but with a particular focus on political analysis of texts with reference to Socialist Realism.[14] Lastly, Chapter Five deals with the war years and the transition to the Cold War – a period that initially disrupted the 'iron curtain' that Stalinism had already closed around the Soviet borders at the end of the 1930s but which ultimately cemented that decade's emergent 'Great Russian Nationalism' and confirmed the anti-Westernism that was already emerging in the immediate pre-war years.

It is probably true that, at least outside Russia, there has been far greater interest in Soviet counter-culture than in the 'approved' public culture of the Stalin era. This book is perhaps unusual in taking as its subject the very visible nature of institutional music-making, without focusing either on individual Soviet musicians or on Soviet composers – the traditional heroes and heroines of Soviet musical history. Yet, when I first began to investigate the reception of Western music in the Lenin and Stalin periods (for which impetus I would like to thank Julian Horton), I became convinced that there was a unique story to be told that focused precisely on this public sphere of musical life. It was clear that certain works were being favoured at some times and not others, and there were evidently major cultural shifts influencing changes such as the discarding of European modernism after 1936, the strong emphasis on Russian nineteenth-century music after that date and the selective survival of Western sacred music throughout the whole period. This book is not just about repertoire, nor just about bringing music to the masses, nor is it primarily about bureaucracy or even the reception histories of specific composers, though at different times I touch on all of these areas. It is about how the first socialist regime in world history shaped its own cultural identity in musical terms: what it accepted, rejected and experimented with; and what the consequences of those decisions were. For the earliest musical pioneers of this gigantic social engineering project, seeing into a potentially infinite future of communism, the perspective was one of a blend of continuity and innovation. For the modern reader, seeing Soviet communism as a finite entity lasting just over seventy years, the whole period is stamped with the label 'totalitarian' and defined entirely by its political structures. In many ways, that is a crude historical perspective, and I welcome recent challenges to the standard approach of beginning Soviet music history at 1917, since there are clear continuities between the pre- and post-revolutionary years, not least of which was the Silver Age obsession with change, birth, death and renewal, from which sprang many classic Soviet tropes, including social improvement and self-overcoming, or the 'growth of a personality'.[15] However, as the reader will see, for this book I have retained the conventional boundaries that Soviet music historians habitually use to demarcate major policy and cultural shifts: 1917–32, 1932–41, 1941–8, ending with the early Cold War and the Soviet Union's retreat from the West, after which only the most familiar and accepted parts of Western classical repertoire could be retained.

Music-making under Stalin was not a fixed, unchanged phenomenon, either from the point at which he took over from Lenin as party leader in 1924 or from 1932, the year in which he pushed through the Resolution banning all factionalism in arts. Though in comparison with the 'thaw' years following Stalin's death, the whole Stalin era seems monolithic, in fact, when scrutinized more closely, musical life of that time shows many undercurrents of change and flux. The 'Enlightenment' of the early 1930s and the shift to Russian nationalism at the end of that decade are the most significant of those changes during the mature Stalin period, and their effect on musical life has been entirely unexplored until now. When put together with other events in musical life – the importance of foreign musicians, the influence of individuals like Mikhail Klimov, who introduced Soviet audiences to Bach in the 1920s, or of Ivan Sollertinskiy, who directed repertoire in the Leningrad Philharmonia from as early as the mid-1920s,[16] these overarching currents prove to be important guiding forces that both enabled and destroyed individual agencies. Klimov's pioneering work on Bach found favour in the 1920s because it was important to Lunacharskiy and others to retain major canonical works in the Leningrad capella's repertoire, even as they saw to it that Klimov had to remove Russian sacred works from his choir's concerts. In all likelihood, had it not been for Klimov's work in the 1920s, the Bach revival of the mid-1930s could not have taken place; yet within the context of the Soviet Union's positioning of itself at that time as a bastion of world culture, particularly in opposition to Nazi Germany, to be able to celebrate Bach's 250th anniversary was a major cultural coup in Soviet musical circles. A more destructive example of the power of these top-down forces, however, took place in 1936, when Shostakovich's opera *Lady Macbeth* found itself the focus of an arts-wide campaign against modernism (or rather, 'formalism' as it was then described): the Philharmonias abruptly removed Western modernist music from their programmes and contracts with foreign conductors were terminated. Yet just before these dramatic about-turns, Sollertinskiy and others had been building on the Stalinist ambition for cultural leadership to push through their own visions of world-leading musical centres in Leningrad and Moscow, with Arnold Schoenberg as their guiding spirit and mentor. It is through intersections of such top-down and bottom-up motivation that Soviet musical culture was formed, and better understanding of these processes should help us move ever further away from the temptation to look for top-down commands for every significant event in Soviet musical life.

Even within the constraints of a stifling dictatorship, such unpredictable human agencies as individual taste, career-building, friendships, loyalties and old animosities played significant roles.

By ending this study at 1953, I do not discuss the 'thaw' that character-ized the first decade after Stalin's death, although those years were, for many former Soviet citizens who remember them, the most exciting period of Soviet musical history. It was at this time that windows to the West were cautiously re-opened, and alongside global trends like post-war avant-gardism, the early music movement and the birth of electronics in both art and rock music, this combination was extremely potent. For the generation that still recalls those heady years, the contrast with what had gone before was remarkable. But how Soviet musical culture got to that point of stagna-tion is, of course, no longer remembered – very few people are still alive who could recall how concert repertoire changed between 1942 and 1952, let alone between 1932 and 1942. This study will help us better understand exactly why the post-Stalin era of concert life was such a breath of fresh air in the stale concert environment of the post-1948 years – it shows us exactly how repertoire under Stalin became as restricted as it did – but it also chal-lenges the easy assumption that, after 1932, concert life in the years of High Stalinism constituted two decades of anti-Western, anti-modern, provin-cial and dull music-making dominated by socialist realism. Though that did become largely the case after 1948, this applies only to the last five years of Stalin's rule, and it must be remembered that the sharp injection of American and British music during the wartime alliance had done much to open 'windows to the West' for Soviet musicians of Shostakovich's genera-tion. Just as importantly, this study shows how the fluctuating process of canonization operated under Stalin: what its limits were, how its priorities were changed according to geo-political policy, how the tastes and interests of the chief architects of Soviet musical life shaped its formation and ulti-mately, how the musical identity of the Soviet Union under Stalin was shaped by all these forces.

Postscript

As the manuscript of this book was undergoing review, an important new study was published: Marina Raku's excellent survey *Muzïkal'naya klassika v mifotvorchstve sovetskoy epokhi* [Musical classicism in the mythology of the Soviet epoch]. Our approaches differ chiefly in focus – my own study gives broad overviews of trends up to 1953, while Raku gives a lot of detail on the presentation of selected composers right up to the end of the Soviet period. It goes without saying that Raku's book is essential reading for anyone wishing to know more about this aspect of Soviet musical life. I wish to thank her here for kindly sending me a copy of her book and for her interest in my own work; if not active collaborators, we have indeed been fellow travellers.

CHAPTER ONE

PROPAGANDIZING THE CLASSICS
1917-1929

After 1917

To ordinary citizens of Russia in 1917 who had no part in the Bolshevik Revolution, October 1917 was a political coup that followed a number of momentous political changes: the 1905 'Bloody Sunday' shooting on peaceful protestors in St Petersburg's Palace Square, the abdication of Nicholas II and the formation of a Provisional Government in February 1917. There was no way of knowing if the Bolshevik takeover would hold; the Civil War lasted until 1920 and by the time it was over, the essential building blocks had already been laid for the administration and control of cultural life. There was no 'Soviet culture' as such: there was only pre-revolutionary culture that either continued after 1917 (as with many of the innovations and trends in theatre, art, literature and poetry) or was cut short by waves of emigration. Music was particularly affected by this: not only was their most famous young composer, Igor Stravinsky, ensconced in Paris with no apparent intention of returning, but Sergey Rakhmaninov also left Bolshevik Russia in 1917. Sergey Prokof'yev, their next rising star, left Russia for a concert tour in 1918 and did not return to live there permanently for almost two decades; meanwhile, their future bright hope, Shostakovich, was still a schoolboy. A great many musicians and pedagogues who had illuminated Russia's cultural life also left – as was the case with Prokof'yev, not necessarily intending never to return, but almost without exception, those who left in 1917 or 1918 did not come back. Many great musicians remained behind; but the loss of figures like Leopold Auer and his stupendously talented student Jascha Heifetz, the cellist Gregor

Pyatigorskiy and numerous others was a blow to the morale of those left behind. Others would follow them to America or Europe over the next decade, leaving Soviet musical culture seriously impoverished. With the catastrophic effects of the war economy established in 1917, where buildings went unheated in the hard Russian winter and food shortages were acute, it seems miraculous that cultural life proceeded in any form. Yet concerts went on: the Bolshoy Theatre remained open, Sergey Kusevitskiy's orchestra continued to give concerts (until he emigrated in 1920) and both Fëdor Shalyapin and Aleksandr Grechaninov have left memoirs of how they performed to audiences of workers and children in exchange for basic foodstuffs.[1]

It would be easy to form the impression that it was the Russian Revolution itself that produced a dedicated body of musicians who devoted their energies purely to the proletarian cause, while the more conservative wing of Soviet musical life tried their best to carry on under difficult circumstances, attempting to resist political pressures brought to bear on them by their more communist-minded colleagues. But the reality was far more complex: older musicians were not necessarily the ones most hostile to the Bolshevik regime, and even the most conservative among them often cared deeply about bringing 'music to the masses'. It would be utterly impossible to tease apart their dedication to keeping Russian musical life alive, their wish to share musical culture with those previously excluded from it, and their dedication to serving the regime. All those causes went hand in hand, and were balanced against the sheer need for survival during the lengthy Civil War period. The Russian musicologist Yekaterina Vlasova cautions against believing in what she terms the 'myth' of musicians' commitment to the revolution, noting wryly that, from a total of 150 professionals from Petrograd's intelligentsia contacted by the newly appointed minister of culture, Anatoliy Lunacharskiy in 1917, a mere five turned up to his first meeting.[2] Nonetheless, many applied themselves to their new circumstances with ingenuity, imagination and even zeal. Determination to share culture with those from social classes who were not traditionally exposed to it ran deep through the Russian liberal intelligentsia. Its roots were in the nineteenth century; Miliy Balakirev's 'Free Music School' had, after all, been set up in 1862 precisely as a counterweight to the more prestigious St Petersburg Conservatoire, which drew students from aristocratic and upper-middle-class backgrounds. This movement towards mass cultural education gathered strength after Aleksandr II's liberal reforms, including the emancipation of the serfs (1861), the formation of village councils or local self-government (*zemstva*) after 1864 and a raft of other measures, among which the rise of industrialization and the mass movements of rural peasantry into the new class of urban proletariat played a major role. As Lynn M. Sargeant has shown, the forerunners of early revolutionary mass music education were the People's Houses, initially founded by local *zemstva*, which assumed widespread importance after 1911, although the *Russian Musical Gazette* had printed calls for the elimination of 'musical illiteracy' from as early as 1899.[3] The People's Houses put on symphonic and opera concerts with heavily subsidized tickets, aimed at workers, and these, combined with the popular Moscow Sokolniki Park concerts (begun in 1884 as band concerts but switching to orchestras from 1892, including Kusevitskiy's orchestra after 1910), gave a very broad cross-section of the Moscow public cheap access to classical music concerts. Sargeant and Rebecca Mitchell both raise the issue of educated paternalism around the phenomenon of mass music education: as was so often the case with mass cultural projects (including those in contemporary Victorian and Edwardian England), the educators were motivated by, in part, a desire to distract workers from less enlightening pastimes such as drinking and carousing[4] (which went hand in hand with coarse urban songs rather than folk songs) and, in part, a desire to meet a genuine hunger for education and a share in elite culture that was impossible because of the expense of attending concerts. They had some wealthy aristocratic sponsors and educational venues could be very grand indeed: the Emperor Nicholas II house, sponsored by the St Petersburg Guardianship for Popular Sobriety, was so richly supported that it attracted more educated (and presumably significantly wealthier) audiences, although another aristocratically sponsored People's House (the Ligovskiy House in St Petersburg) took care to meet the educational needs of a wider socio-economic group.[5] The People's Houses were not the only means available to workers of cheap cultural education: Mitchell's research movingly uncovers the individual voices of workers attending the People's Conservatoire in Moscow, founded in September 1906 by a group of professional musicians and educators, including Aleksandr Gol'denveyzer and Nadezhda Bryusova. One student, Lyusiya Sokolova, wrote to Bryusova:

> I can ask you only one thing: give me the ability to develop musically, at least a little bit, to allow me at least a small but active participation in

singing and music . . . This question is the most painful for me. I cannot quietly listen to your lecture because every word of yours shows me my musical illiteracy, and awoke [*sic*] in me a thirst for knowledge . . . before me was the fateful question: why can't I play myself, when I love music, when music sounds in my ears at home?[6]

There was enough evidence that there was a ready audience for classical music among the working population for professional musicians to feel inspired to help them, or even just to entertain them. In his colourful auto-biography, related to Maksim Gorkiy and first published in Russian in 1917, Shalyapin described singing at one workers' concert in Kharkov in 1904:

Never did I have a more responsive and attentive audience than those workers. At first there had been terrible noise, laughter and shouts, and it seemed no power on earth could quench it. Yet they had their own discipline, and soon exacted it. . . . It was enough for me to appear on that stage surrounded by candles, and the entire hall was still.[7]

Given this powerful history, it is not surprising that the Bolshevik government chose to support, rather than crush, 'bourgeois' music-making, but it should be stressed that the fundamental concept of sharing art with the masses was not a Bolshevik one. Thus musicians who strove to do just that in the early revolutionary years were not necessarily politically allied to Bolshevism; rather, they were continuing a tradition with very deep roots and all that had really changed was that their work immediately became more difficult, as the culture of private patronage – the old system of *noblesse oblige* – was swept away and they were faced with uncertainty over future funding from the State.

The first group of musicians to act upon personal dissatisfaction with the new regime were those who chose to emigrate, either immediately (as was the case with Rakhmaninov; the conductor Albert Coates left soon after, in 1919) or within a decade or so of the October Revolution. Among these late émigrés who contributed valuable years of their energies and talents to the early Soviet cause are the conductors Emil Kuper (emigrated 1924) and Kusevitskiy (emigrated 1920), Shalyapin (emigrated 1921–2), the pianist Vladimir Horowitz (emigrated 1925) and the composers Nikolay Medtner (emigrated 1921), Aleksandr Grechaninov (emigrated 1925) and Aleksandr Glazunov (emigrated 1928).

Prokof'yev had already left the Soviet Union in 1918, with the permission and blessing of Lunacharskiy, and with every intention of returning; Stravinsky had left Russia much earlier to pursue a career with the Paris-based Ballets Russes and never showed the faintest whiff of interest in returning to Soviet Russia until he finally visited in 1962. An unfortunate mixture of premature death and old age claimed a further group of distinguished musicians: Aleksandr Skryabin had died in 1915 and Cesar Cui, the last surviving member of the *kuchka*, died in 1918. Anatoliy Lyadov had died in 1914, while Sergey Taneyev had died in 1915, shortly after attending Skryabin's funeral. Of those who were left in Soviet Russia, the most established talent during the first half of the 1920s was undoubtedly Nikolay Myaskovskiy, who had written five symphonies by 1918 and, in part thanks to his active relationship with Universal Edition, in part thanks to the efforts of Prokof'yev to persuade Kusevitskiy and others to perform his music, enjoyed a modest, but growing reputation abroad as well as at home.[8]

It fell to those remaining members of Russia's musical community to rebuild the culture that was under imminent threat, whether that threat stemmed from economic privation, hostile cultural policies, Civil War or sheer lack of organization. Lenin ordered the closure of both Bolshoy and Mariinskiy Theatres in 1922, deeming them 'bourgeois cultural heritage', and they were preserved only thanks to the efforts made by Lunacharskiy, who fought vociferously with Lenin over their planned closure.[9] As well as being supported by published documents in post-1991 sources, this fact was recorded in the much earlier testimony of the conductor Nikolay Mal'ko, whose son recalled that after the Bolshevik takeover, the Mariinskiy Theatre in Petrograd faced closure, and that it was indeed Lunacharskiy who, working with music professionals in the city, managed to save it.[10] Thanks to their combined efforts, both Leningrad and Moscow opera theatres remained open, and they were not alone in holding fast to pre-revolutionary performance traditions. Among the surviving choirs of the Tsarist era were the Imperial Court Capella in Petrograd–Leningrad, conducted from 1918 by Mikhail Klimov and the Synodal Choir in Moscow, directed by Aleksandr Kastal'skiy. One orchestra also continued from pre-revolutionary times: the former Imperial court orchestra in Petrograd–Leningrad led initially by Kusevitskiy until 1920, then by Emil Kuper until his emigration four years later.[11] First known as the 'State Philharmonia', it was re-launched in 1921 as the 'Petrograd [later Leningrad] Philharmonia'. There was no orchestra in Moscow at this time apart from that of the

Bolshoy Theatre and in fact Moscow would not get its first official symphony orchestra until 1928 when the Moscow Philharmonia (the umbrella title for the entire organizing body, encompassing several ensembles) formed its own orchestra in 1928, called the 'Symphony Orchestra of the (Moscow) Philharmonia', or 'Sofil' for short.

The first and most obvious point to make about these Tsarist survivors is that their repertoire was, to a considerable extent, chosen for them simply by the music they had available and by their own performance traditions. The scholar Stanislav Ponyatovskiy has published listings of the former Imperial orchestra's repertoire between 1909 and 1920.[12] It is almost certain that the vast majority, if not all, of this repertoire dated from pre-1917, since the practical difficulties of acquiring new scores and parts from abroad during the Civil War were considerable. What the listings show clearly is the pre-revolutionary presence of works that became Soviet-era staples: Berlioz's symphonies, popular excerpts from Wagner operas, Debussy's *La Mer*, *Nocturnes* and *L'Après-midi*, Dukas' *Sorcerer's Apprentice*, Liszt's symphonic poems, Mozart's Requiem, Richard Strauss's tone poems, Schubert's Fifth, Eighth and Ninth Symphonies and, of course, all of Beethoven's symphonies. But, as will be seen, even as fresh repertoire was added, substantial parts of the orchestra's earlier programmes were set aside for much of the Soviet period. With regard to the St Petersburg Imperial court capella (whose foundation year was 1703), among the most striking Soviet-era staples present from this pre-revolutionary period are Bach's B Minor Mass, Beethoven's *Missa Solemnis* and Mozart's Requiem – all sacred works. The peculiarity of retaining such repertoire in the stridently atheistic Soviet state will be discussed later in this chapter.

Shaping the Canon: The Russian Classics

Those faced with the task of building Soviet musical life during the 1920s were in a unique position. Most, if not all, of them had personal connections with the generation of composers that, in the Soviet period, would routinely be called the 'Russian classics' – the generation of the *kuchka* and Chaykovskiy. Those who came immediately after them would also be gathered into this category later in the Soviet period. Rimskiy-Korsakov himself had been dead for only nine years in 1917, and the pedagogical structures he established at the St Petersburg Conservatoire were still firmly in place, maintained by his former student Aleksandr Glazunov, who took over as

Director of the Conservatoire in 1905, and by his son-in-law Maksimilian Shteynberg (Shostakovich's future composition teacher), who became professor of composition at the Conservatoire in 1915. Rimskiy-Korsakov's son, Andrey Rimskiy-Korsakov, would continue a modest career as a musicologist in Leningrad until his death in 1940 and his grandson Georgiy was, at least at first, a radical innovator who founded a Society for Quarter-Tone Music in his student years.[13]

Therefore, the most immediate and urgent tasks facing the still relatively young Soviet musicologists like Boris Asaf'yev, Pavel Lamm and others included how to preserve the legacies of their cherished compatriots, many of them in imminent danger of loss or destruction, especially during the unpredictable Civil War years. Amid radical voices on the cultural left calling for the abolition of all past culture, the forcible requisitioning of apartments, instruments and property and an uncertain political environment where the value of pre-revolutionary art had still to be established, a small group of musicians and scholars made it their business to work closely with the new administration in order to preserve these precious legacies and to help build a new culture on the foundations of the old. Asaf'yev's role in these transitional years was of incalculable importance: he was one of the founders of the Petrograd (later Leningrad) Institute for the History of the Arts and helped the Petrograd–Leningrad Philharmonia make its transition from an Imperial orchestra to a fully functioning Soviet organization. I will not try to cover every single Russian 'classic' in this section, but will look at three major figures: Chaykovskiy, Musorgskiy and Glinka.

One of the first Soviet-era music books to be published in this transitional period was an important volume on Chaykovskiy edited by Asaf'yev (under his pseudonym Igor Glebov), which addressed the parlous state of Russian music scholarship head-on.[14] In his introductory chapter, 'Our Duty', Glebov observed that a huge amount of Russian music is still unpublished – even unpreserved – and that the journals in which it used to be discussed are now out of print with no hope of being revived:

> If, let's say, it turns out that someone would like to take up for study the works of some conspicuous Russian composer – he must be driven to despair from the hopelessness of the task of collecting primary sources. . . . There are almost no comprehensive collections, library guides or materials or any detailed literature to help answer your questions. . . . We don't need to go far to find an example: what do we know of Arenskiy

or Kalinnikov? Is it possible to think of popularizing Russian music if its personalities, its well-springs, spirit, everything that matters most about it is buried heaven knows where? . . . If we are to create less thankless conditions for the working out of the fundamentals of Russian musical history, then a significant role must be played by oral traditions: living composers from that milieu who can recount and disclose information about their close friends and musicians.[15]

This first book on Chaykovskiy was indeed just that: a first step in putting together important materials about the composer, still just a quarter of a century after his death. The composer's friend Nikolay Kashkin's early reminiscences about conversations with Chaykovskiy were included; there were documentary materials from the composer's recently established house museum at Klin and correspondence with his friend N. A. Gubert, and this was clearly seen as an ongoing task. None of the volume's contributions were in any way obviously political or ideological, and there is no mention at all of Soviet power. This set the scene for Chaykovskiy's steady and relatively uncontroversial place in early Soviet musical life: he was not initially a target for any influential militant attacks and his music maintained a steady and significant position in orchestral and operatic repertoire. From the earliest days of the Petrograd State Academic Philharmonia, as the soon-to-become Leningrad Philharmonia was called in 1922, Chaykovskiy's music was played every season, as were works by Glinka, Arenskiy, the *kuchka* and Russian composers of the Silver Age generation: Lyadov, Mikhail Ippolitov-Ivanov, Skryabin, Rakhmaninov, Grechaninov, even (for a time), Medtner. If we look at the repertoire (both opera and ballet) of the Bolshoy Theatre, it is clear that Chaykovskiy's major works were consistently a regular feature of every season, right through the civil war years, the 1920s and beyond.

However, it should come as no surprise that there were voices raised against Chaykovskiy from the more radical proletarian side. The journal *Muzïkal'naya nov'* [Musical virgin soil], founded by the new radical group that would soon become known as the Russian Association of Proletarian Musicians (RAPM = *Rossiskaya assotsiatsiya proletarskikh muzïkantov*) published a handful of articles of this type between 1923 (the year of the journal's foundation) and 1924, but it must be borne in mind that this journal was one of the most contentious of the early to mid 1920s. Its founder was David Chernomordikov, a middle-aged communist and party member who was then engaged in a bitter power struggle with Pavel Lamm in the Soviet music publishing house, *Muzsektor*. Though it is uncertain whether or not Chernomordikov was himself implicated in the fact of Lamm's arrest in March 1923 (he was allegedly present at the time), he undoubtedly benefited from his absence. While Lamm languished in Moscow's infamous Butïrka prison for two months, Chernomordikov effectively seized control of *Muzsektor* and co-founded RAPM, which would engage in increasingly aggressive polemics with ASM, the Association for Contemporary Music (*Assotsiatsiya sovremennoy muzïki*), throughout the decade.[16] He founded *Muzïkal'naya nov'* in October that year and used it to attack the whole Asaf'yev–Lamm wing of Soviet musical life. As Marina Raku has shown, between 1923 and 1924, the journal published several articles denigrating Chaykovskiy and calling for Soviet musicians to 'flee' from his music. One writer, 'Ignatovich Vyach', wrote in 1923: 'We must flee from Chaykovskiy's music. But to where? To the streets, to the light, to the burning bonfire, to noise, to the whirlwind, the maelstrom, the bustling life of our people, to the streets of revolution, and away from these sweet sounds, mystical motives, from concoctions of sick fantasies of fate ... Enough!'[17] And the following year, A. Bazilev, a representative of the workers' group Rabkor, declared that, 'All of Chaykovskiy's music just whines, and makes you feel as though he is inviting you yourself to whine about the untimely death of the bourgeoisie.'[18] Although the rhetorical punch of such writing cannot be denied, it was not terribly effective in terms of actually discouraging anybody from performing Chaykovskiy's music. During the 1924–5 season, the Leningrad Philharmonia performed his *Francesca da Rimini*, the *Nutcracker* suite, the Third, Fourth and Fifth Symphonies and Lenskiy's aria from *Yevgeniy Onegin*, while also devoting an entire concert to him in February 1925. In 1925–6 they programmed the Second, Fourth, Fifth and Sixth Symphonies, the 'Manfred' Symphony, *Romeo and Juliet*, *Francesca da Rimini*, *Capriccio Espagnol*, *Serenade for Strings* and arias from his opera *The Maid of Orleans*. During the same two seasons at the Bolshoy in Moscow, audiences were treated to the 1921 production of *Onegin*, the 1891 production of *Queen of Spades*, the 1922 production of *Swan Lake* and the repeated 1904 production of *Sleeping Beauty*. Although pronouncements about Chaykovskiy's 'whining' music would have struck many Soviet musicians as crass and offensive, and although they stand out so strongly that they may seem at this historical distance to be representative of this era, it is essential to bear in mind that they did not, in fact, represent a majority view, although when the RAPMovtsï were being criticized after 1932, this was precisely the picture that some Soviet musicologists offered as typical of the RAPM era. This was not really fair, since the principal reason for voicing such aggressive polemics against Chaykovskiy had been that he remained a core element of Soviet mainstream repertoire, and some (though not all) proletarian activists found this irksome. Thus, although it is certainly true that performances of Chaykovskiy's music increased exponentially in the mid to late 1930s, as will be seen, his status was so secure even in the early Soviet period that the huge rise in his popularity in the mature Stalin era merely built upon a performance tradition that had never gone away, rather than requiring a full-blown 'rehabilitation' of the composer.

Unsurprisingly, one of the most actively propagandized Russian composers during the 1920s was Modest Musorgskiy. Indeed, he was hailed from every conceivable side of the early Soviet musical spectrum as the ideal Russian composer for seamless transference to the Soviet sphere. This, of course, was due in no small part to the tireless propaganda of his friend and mentor Vladimir Stasov who, as Richard Taruskin has observed, effectively created Musorgskiy's identity both during his lifetime and even more actively after his death.[19] Stasov, who valued above all Musorgskiy's role as a musical equivalent to Ilya Repin and the wider phenomenon of Russian realism, harangued the composer in their correspondence to such an extent that it seems likely that Musorgskiy simply stopped taking him properly into his confidence (his substitute friendship with Count Arseniy Golenishev-Kutuzov is well described throughout Taruskin's book on Musorgskiy). In 1926, the journal *Music and Revolution* [Muzïka i revoliutsiya] of the Association of Revolutionary Composers and Music Workers (ORKiMD) published an article that tried to sum up the present state of Soviet Musorgskiy reception.[20] The author, Yefim Vilkovir, placed the Stasovians Vyacheslav Karatïgin and Ivan Lapshin on one side and Leonid Sabaneyev and Glebov on the other, with Karatïgin claiming that '*Narodnichestvo* [the quality of being "of the people"], realism and awareness of society (*obshchestvennost'*) were the pillars of Musorgskiy's creative foundation', while Lapshin called him a 'psychological realist'.[21] Glebov, on the other hand (in his *Simfonicheskie etyudi*, 1922), claimed that Musorgskiy's creativity was 'neither "idealist-classic" nor "realist-narodnik" but rather that of a visionary and dreamer', while Sabaneyev (in his *History of Russian Music*, 1924) [*Istoriya russkoy muzïki*] similarly rejected the *narodnik* label in favour of 'barin-slavyanofil' [roughly translatable as a 'Slavophile of the landed gentry class'] and, even less flatteringly, as a 'typical feudal-aesthete'.[22] Vilkovir himself clearly comes down on the side of Karatïgin and Lapshin, marshalling a host of citations from Musorgskiy's letters to Stasov from 1872–5 that stress his support for 'the people'. Eventually, he concluded that it was simply ideology that denied Musorgskiy's *narodnik* tendencies in the minds of his contemporaries (and, presumably by extension, in the writings of Sabaneyev and Glebov as well).

An especially important event for Musorgskiy's Soviet image was the Bolshoy Theatre production of *Boris Godunov* in January 1927, not in the original edition restored by Pavel Lamm (this was not published until 1928), but nonetheless making a modest claim to restoration by adding the St Basil's scene in a commissioned orchestration by Mikhail Ippolitov-Ivanov. This scene, as detailed by Taruskin in his chapter on the opera's revisions, had been cut by Musorgskiy when making his 1872 version of *Boris*, and it was Andrey Rimskiy-Korsakov who, with unparalleled access to his father's manuscripts, had first found the scene and published an article about it in the pre-revolutionary journal *Muzïkal'niy sovremennik* [Musical Contemporary] in 1917.[23] The book accompanying the production, edited by Yevgeniy Braudo and Andrey Rimskiy-Korsakov,[24] not only gives full details of the scene but also, in Braudo's article, sets out some of the earliest foundation stones for Musorgskiy's later Soviet identity. Braudo's description of Musorgskiy is not yet couched in Soviet-era rhetoric but sets out some crucial principles, all highly dependent on the Stasovian portrait of Musorgskiy: '[Musorgskiy was] an artist of the masses ... [he] began to distrust the systematic and scientific approach of his friend [Rimskiy-Korsakov] ... [he] dreamed that the divided fates of the revolutionary-*narodnik* and the masses would combine'.[25] There are three major ingredients here: first, there is Braudo's implication that Musorgskiy was overwhelmingly concerned with social problems and with the fate of the 'masses' (though, as Taruskin notes, Musorgskiy himself would invariably use the neutral plural term for 'people', *lyudi*, rather than 'the masses' or 'narod' which signified The People in the more romantic and emotive sense later evoked by Soviet writers);[26] second, he was suspicious of academicism and technique for its own sake and preferred to follow his instincts (thus keeping himself free from corrupting Western influences); and third, that Musorgskiy was himself a *narodnik* – a member of the (largely middle-class, landowning) movement who supported the interests of the peasant class in the 1860s and 1870s and who, in 1874, organized the famous but unsuccessful attempt to mobilize the peasantry itself to political action. Braudo goes further: 'Musorgsky could not endure any abstraction in art. He was an implacable enemy of any beauty for art's sake.'[27] In the years immediately following the unveiling of socialist realism in 1934, and especially during the anti-formalism campaigns of 1936 onward, this aspect of Musorgskiy's supposed creative ethos would become even more important: hostility to the notion of 'art for art's sake' or 'abstraction' in art was anathema to mature Stalinist culture, as will be seen later in this book.[28]

Though published in 1930, and thus falling slightly outside the parameters of this chapter, the weighty edited volume published by Viktor Belyayev, Glebov and Lamm belongs in this section, because it follows on from Lamm's 'restored' edition of *Boris Godunov*, which was published in 1928.[29] One chapter in particular lays vital foundation stones for Musorgskiy's image later in the Soviet period: Pëtr Kogan's short introductory chapter 'A social portrait of Musorgskiy', written in July 1929 and which is worth quoting at length:

> Musorgskiy still awaits investigation into his aesthetics, attention to those precious thoughts on art and its problems, which are still so wanting, which are scattered in such disorder throughout his letters and yet which ring so true with his everlasting music . . . Musorgskiy was a child of his time and, as with any artist, this was clearly expressed in his most basic inclinations. The dawn of his creative consciousness arose at the end of the 1860s and 1870s, that is, in the epoch of the . . . *raznochintsï*.[30] His aesthetic most fully responded to the ideas of Pisarev and Dobrolyubov and especially Chernyshevskiy. He had a negative attitude towards Nekrasov, and in fact his aesthetic view can to a significant degree be presented in this formula: 'You may not be a poet, but your obligation is to be a citizen' – this is a protest against the pointless glorification of 'sweet caresses' and the beauty of nature. As a theoretician he penetrated the spirit of utilitarian art, of course not in a simplistic way, but in the deepest sense of the word, that is in a spirit of enmity towards 'art for art's sake' to pure art, which also found expression in the ideas of militant *raznochintsï* of the 1860s and 1870s. When meeting with these 'worshippers of beauty' he 'felt a strange emptiness in his conversation with them'. He probably seemed a completely exceptional musician,

almost unique amid contemporary musicians, an early forerunner of our own day, when he announced: 'from Russian artists the public demands Russian things; it is shameful to play art for personal aims'. Yet this is not very far from our own idea, with which his words so warmly chime . . . 'The artistic representation of beauty in its material sense is crude and childish – the art of a child.'[31]

Though written in 1929, Kogan's description of this citizen-composer could easily have been written in 1939. It ticks a number of crucial boxes: Musorgskiy as enemy of 'art for art's sake' (later to be called 'formalism'); Musorgskiy as proto-revolutionary, drawn to the most radical Russian thinkers and finding the gentler aestheticism of Russian poets pointless and inartistic; and Musorgskiy as a supporter of 'utilitarian' art – art pressed into the service of the greater collective good. And finally, in a firm gesture drawing a clear, though only implicit, line between Musorgskiy and Chaykovskiy, Kogan asserts that Musorgskiy 'possessed none of the psychology of the "individual person" [lichniy chelovek]'.[32] Though most of the articles in this collection are nowhere near so tendentious, Kogan's chapter has pride of place at the very front of the book and, as will be seen in Chapter Four, his ideas eventually became the standard orthodoxy on Musorgskiy in the late 1930s.

As Albrecht Gaub has shown, Mikhail Glinka's acceptance into the canon of Soviet Russian classics was far from straightforward.[33] His opera A Life for the Tsar had opened every operatic season until 1916, but after 1917 its patriotic monarchist libretto could no longer be countenanced – hence the ill-fated (and short-lived) attempt in 1924 to recast it as Hammer and Sickle with a revised libretto by Nikolay Krasheninnikov, setting it as a Civil War drama.[34] Yet despite its removal from the Soviet stage, writers did not rush to criticize it. On the contrary, Igor Glebov described A Life for the Tsar in the most glowing terms:

[A Life for the Tsar] is the original realization and fulfilment of the culmination of Western-European musical creation on Russian soil through the achievement of a gifted and intelligent Russian composer, reared in the countryside on the sounds of folk poetry which established the beauty and strength of his vitality to the same standards as those developed in Western music. A Life for the Tsar created a songful poetic [pesennaya stikhiya], an awakening of Russian thought and social consciousness, the genius of Glinka itself and even – let us not hide the fact – the official proclamation of the time, the national doctrine of Nicholas I. *A Life for the Tsar* is the pilot book of Russian music [*korm-chaya kniga*] – and with this opera Russian canonic art was born.[35]

It was indeed the opera's indelible association with Nicholas I – the most autocratic and repressive of nineteenth-century tsars next to Aleksandr III – and its fulfilment of his 'doctrine' Orthodoxy, Autocracy, Nationality that meant that *A Life for the Tsar* (or *Ivan Susanin*, its alternative title) could not immediately be canonized. But Glinka himself did not attract particular hostility: although *Ivan Susanin* was not performed in the Soviet Union for over twenty years after the revolution, *Ruslan and Lyudmila* was performed nearly every season thereafter (it was omitted only in 1923, 1930, 1934, 1935 and 1936) at the Bolshoy between 1917 and 1939. 1939 was the year when *Ivan Susanin* was triumphantly given its Soviet premiere with a revised libretto written ostensibly by Sergey Gorodetskiy but in reality at least in part ghostwritten by Mikhail Bulgakov, apparently with input from the conductor Samuil Samosud and the director Boris Mordvinov, as will be discussed in Chapter Four.[36] The fact that *Ruslan* was so firmly established on the Soviet opera stage meant that Glinka was never cast out of the growing Soviet musical canon: indeed, he claimed a fundamental place within it from the start. All that was needed was a marketing strategy, and until the pre-eminence of the Russian classics was established from the late 1930s onwards, that strategy would be slow to proceed.

Gaub is right in noting that Glinka scholarship was scarce in the early Soviet period; indeed, until the exponential rise of Russian nationalism in the late 1930s, Glinka did not enjoy anything like the prestige of Musorgskiy, Chaykovskiy or Rimskiy-Korsakov. However, there were still a few attempts to assess his career in the 1920s: Gaub discusses Konstantin Kuznetsov's 1926 study, but this was preceded in 1923 by Nikolay Strel'nikov's volume.[37] Given that *Ivan Susanin* could not be performed at this time, Strel'nikov's glowing description of it is all the more astonishing: 'Glinka revealed all the beauty and dignity of Russian folk song; he placed it at a level of the highest cultural property of the people, compelling the West to recognize the fact of its existence. At the same time Glinka created Russian opera and a new Russian music.'[38] Later, Strel'nikov remarks that 'Glinka's music charms with his brilliant penetration into the people's [*narodniy*] soul.' This was a strong recommendation indeed in those years, and a clear attempt to align him with the more obviously 'acceptable' composers Musorgskiy or Rimskiy-Korsakov.[39]

Strel'nikov's confidence in describing the opera that had not been performed since 1916 in such canonizing terms seems astonishing: but it probably reflects more on the fact that the opera's music was less in dispute than was its libretto: though Krasheninnikov's attempt to reinvent it had failed, there was no reason to ignore its existence, even if such a tub-thumping spectacle of Tsarism had to be banished from the Soviet stage.[40]

Marketing the Western Classics

As we have already seen, early Soviet musical life was built on the core repertoire of the culture that immediately preceded it. It would not be until the creation of censorship bodies in the early 1920s that the 'selection' process began in earnest, as will be seen later in this chapter. Initially at least, the presence of key Austro-German, Italian and French composers in the repertoire of the first Soviet orchestras and choirs was a given. Major sacred works formed a natural part of early Soviet repertoire, too: Mozart's Requiem, for instance, was a staple ingredient in Soviet repertoire, having first been performed in a special concert commemorating fallen victims of the Revolution in the first of the so-called 'People's Concerts' in Petrograd that year.[41] Likewise, Beethoven's symphonies continued to be performed in complete cycles, with the Ninth – though in many cases just the finale – quickly becoming a particular favourite of Soviet festive and commemorative events. Wagner, too, was resurrected after 1917: Nicholas II had personally banned Wagner operas from the Mariinskiy Theatre in 1914, when Russia and Germany were at war. Lenin's personal enthusiasm for Wagner's music only became common knowledge on the publication of his widow's memoirs in 1935, but he immediately overturned Nicholas's ban on seizing power in 1917.[42] Wagner concerts were given in the very first Soviet musical events, Siegfried's funeral music from *Götterdämmerung* taking its place beside Mozart's Requiem as a mourning work for revolutionary heroes. It was played in the Field of Mars in a service commemorating those who fell in the revolution in 1920, prompting one critic to write: 'How could one fail to be moved, before the commemoration to those fighters for the ideals of the Internationale, by this amazing work of Wagner's very soul?'[43]

However, as the new Soviet state began the processes of censorship and cultural propaganda, retaining everything from the pre-revolutionary era became more complicated. The key to understanding why so many Western composers were drawn into the Soviet concert canon – and why others were not – lies in a grasp of basic Marxist-Leninist historiography. Essentially, European history was viewed through a Hegelian lens, whereby history proceeds through a series of phases marked by disruptive periods (the famous 'dialectic' of thesis–antithesis) before arriving at a glorious 'synthesis' – socialism. In the crudest terms, the goal of European history is socialism, which had been achieved in Russia through the Bolshevik Revolution – though the intention, until Stalin's support for 'socialism in one country', was for socialism to spread throughout Europe. As the final 'synthesis', socialism was the inevitable summation of all the social, economic, scientific, artistic and philosophical forces constituting the Enlightenment that had already led Europe away from medieval feudalism as far as the French Revolution. Within this historical model, a figure such as Bach, who lived and worked in early Enlightenment Europe, is essentially a victim of history – if he was religious he could not help it – but he at least belonged to the proto-democratic Lutheran faith rather than to Catholicism, and so symbolized the nascent move away from feudalism to democracy. The musicologist Sergey Chemodanov claimed in the RAPM journal *Muzïkal'naya nov'* that Bach's music actually spearheaded the cultural movement away from Catholic 'gloom' [*mrachnost'*]. Though writers would later go to extraordinary lengths to justify retaining Bach's music later in the 1920s and 1930s, this was a very early attempt to place Bach in the Marxist timeline of 'progress'. Similarly, Haydn and Mozart, in their own time, may have been dependent upon aristocratic patronage (for which they could hardly be blamed), but they should be regarded as members of the so-called 'Third Estate' – the title given to those in pre-revolutionary France who were not members of the clergy or the aristocracy. In other words, they were members of the rising eighteenth-century bourgeoisie, who overturned medieval feudalism and laid the foundations for republicanism and democracy. In Chemodanov's argument, the period of tension between feudalism and the ascent of this class is represented in the music of Bach, Haydn and Mozart, no matter to whom their music was dedicated. As he put it, 'the whole atmosphere of the pre-revolutionary epoch was saturated with the psychological struggle of two cultures, the obsolete feudal and the rising Third Estate'.[44] Even Haydn and Mozart's music, with its salon elegance, anticipates the victory of the bourgeoisie 'over the dying culture of the feudal classes'; eighteenth-century heroism lies behind Gluck's tragic operas, while Beethoven's 'titanic protests against the power of fate in the name of the free spirit' were sustained by the

Enlightenment philosophy which itself was that of the Third Estate, 'already close to the storm of the French Revolution'.[45]

With regard to Western composers, the Soviet appropriation of Bach during these early years is very interesting. His music was not especially well known in Russia at the time, and it was revived largely because of the efforts of Mikhail Klimov, conductor of the Leningrad Capella, who gave the first Soviet-era performance of the St Matthew Passion in 1923 and the St John Passion the following year. The reviewer for *Zhizn' iskusstva* [Life of art] responded to the St Matthew premiere with undisguised delight:

> With regard to the Bach cult in the West, Russia has always been at something of a disadvantage: one the one hand, the lack of a suitably and appropriately trained choir and director, and on the other hand, a serious lack of actual music has always made performing Bach almost impossible. This year, the indefatigable efforts of Petrograd's academic capella has given us the chance to hear a wonderful work of Bach's – the St Matthew Passion – which hasn't been heard here for over ten years. We cannot but greet this remarkable event in our musical life without declaring that this enormous expense of strength and energy witnessed in this concert took the capella to a new artistic stage which must be noted first and foremost.[46]

But when the Passions were performed again in 1927, the proletarian movement was properly established, and not all its reviewers welcomed such an open display of sacred music. A critic for the *Moscow Workers' Gazette* [*Moskovskaya rabochaya gazeta*] wrote ironically:

> I hear of a great and glorious event: in the *Dom Soyuzov* [House of Unions, a favourite location for workers' concerts] there will be the 'Passion' of our Lord Jesus Christ, a composition by Bach ... I rubbed my eyes, looked at the calendar and ... couldn't believe it! Then I heard that, though the 'Passion' is spiritual music, at the same time it is interesting in this or in that way. In the end I just couldn't understand why we have to have 'The Passion of Our Lord'. When the Passion ended it was 'And now listen to Sleeping Beauty.'[47]

Other, more sympathetic, critics bent over backwards to justify Klimov's choice of repertoire: also in 1927, the critic Anton Tsenovskiy defended

Bach's sacred works on the grounds that, because they were music, they posed no ideological threat whatsoever:

> Church-ness, sanctimony, unctuous going on your knees before 'god' — the poison gas of religion in all this is considerable . . . [but] it is only music. It is the creative thought of a genius, a deep and enriching artistic work with choir, soloists and orchestra—a concert the like of which we have not heard before.[48]

But Anton Uglov, the critic of *Izvestiya TsIK*, posed an even more radical approach to the 'Bach problem', arguing that Bach's religion was a mere coincidence of history and may not even have been genuine:

> In our day has arisen the 'problem of Bach'. Usually this great composer of theory is treated as a mystic and church-follower, who must be kept far from the Soviet stage. Such an understanding of Bach is only half right. If he was a mystic and religious man, then it was only by education, against his will, and later it was just a matter of habit. Two marriages and nineteen children testify to his totally different 'real' nature. . . . The majority of his works speak of this, even those written on religious subjects that are filled with the deepest expressive content. Now it is necessary to have a 'coming back to' Bach in order to make him contemporary, which he certainly can be, if we reveal his potential merit and cast off the mystical robes which cloak his works. There is basically no religious 'danger' in performing the Passions – these are just the same as Prokof'yev's *Oranges* in their musical illustration of a fantastic legend, separated by time, subject and objective; it is important in order to interpret it as new, strong, and 'anti-mystical' as possible.[49]

This reading prefigures the later Soviet canonizing of Bach in the 1930s and his rebranding as a dramatic, rather than a sacred, composer. As will be seen in Chapter Three, writers went to great lengths to achieve this, and in fact, Bach did need to be re-launched as a 'Soviet' composer in the mid-1930s. Though Klimov repeated the Passions several times, pressures from RAPM later in the 1920s and his own poor health in the 1930s meant that they were not performed as often as he might have wished, as will be seen later in this chapter.

These arguments were a crucial element of the Soviet's canonizing of major Western composers whose music could otherwise have been discarded as simply relics of a previous class that were now irrelevant to the proletariat. Analyses like Chemodanov's turned this repertoire into the rightful inheritance of Soviet culture. Whether placing Bach in a Marxist view of cultural history or simply asserting (like Uglov) that a man with so many children could not be as religious as all that, such arguments helped to cement Bach's (and others') places in Soviet repertoire throughout the 1920s. The 'humanistic' depiction of Bach as a musical eighteenth-century equivalent of Shakespeare sank deep into the Soviet mindset and even had a direct effect on the evolving Soviet Bach performance tradition.[50] Klimov made his own performing editions of the Bach Passions, and the capella's performances were, according to contemporary witnesses, markedly more dramatic than any within living memory. Their Soviet premiere perform-ance of Bach's St Matthew Passion in 1923 was sensational precisely because it presented Bach in a new light: not dull or academic (as some critics had evidently been expecting), but dramatic and full of expression.[51]

Although the status of Beethoven and Mozart as classics was always stable, and the desirability of performing their music in the post-revolutionary era was never seriously disputed, a certain amount of marketing was required in order to build up their Soviet identities. Unsurprisingly, Beethoven's life furnished writers with a rich supply of anecdotes illustrating his 'democratic' or 'revolutionary' inclinations, while little could really be claimed for Mozart personally. As will be discussed in Chapter Three, in the 1930s, writers would focus on the romantic image of Mozart as abandoned by his former wealthy employers and left to die a pauper's death as a way of obliquely painting him as a victim of history, but in the 1920s, although performances of his orchestral music were not espe-cially frequent, his Requiem was quickly established as an essential classic. Despite this, however, not a single Mozart opera was staged at the Bolshoy after 1917 until the new Russian-language performance of *The Marriage of Figaro* in 1926.[52] Be that as it may, in 1927, Igor Glebov explained why Mozart was so popular in the Soviet Union: 'all of our music from a short time before Glinka up to our own time has been penetrated by Mozartian culture. Chaykovskiy and Taneyev were Mozartians. The Rimskiy-Korsakov school also traced a connection through Glinka to Mozart. Glazunov gravi-tated more towards a Mozartian texture than to Beethoven.'[53] Thus, while not appropriating Mozart as somehow Russian, Glebov argued that Russian music itself was so strongly influenced by Mozart's music that it sounds familiar to Soviet ears. Further, he claimed, 'this music sounds at once as simple as Schubert's and as the best music of Prokof'yev. This is not simplicity in the sense of simple life, nor in the guise of uneventfulness. I am speaking of . . . simplicity as a high artistic ideal, as the result of a complete mastery, when mastery itself does not protrude.'[54] Therefore, Mozart can be regarded as a potentially important element of Soviet musical culture even in the 1920s, thanks to the popularity of his Requiem and proselytizing efforts on the part of major music writers, but his music was never a high priority for opera and concert organizations in the 1920s.

Beethoven enjoyed a status in the Soviet Union that can best be compared to that of Shakespeare – the dramatist *par excellence* who would always be held above any criticism. Since there was enough anecdotal and documentary evidence to paint Beethoven as a true revolutionary, he was feted by all sides of the ideological spectrum and was, along with Musorgskiy, one of the very few composers of the past to be consistently approved by RAPM later in the decade. Beethoven's close relationships with aristocratic patrons were not concealed – that would hardly have been possible anyway, given the many dedications of his compositions to them – but Soviet critics stressed his tempestuous relationship with them, and revelled in his refusal to bow and scrape before dignitaries. Famous incidents such as Beethoven's refusal to stand aside for the Imperial family at Teplitz, his angry rejection of Napoleon after he became Emperor, his angry flight from Prince Lichnowsky's castle and the letter which followed it ('Prince! What you are, you are by birthright. Of princes there have been and will be thousands. Of Beethovens there is only one'[55]) were repeated *ad nauseam* in programme notes and lectures in the 1920s. It was not difficult to create the Soviet image of Beethoven as an artist whose music was directly inspired by the French Revolution and the rhetoric of personal freedom and fraternal equality that surrounded it. Beethoven made an obvious role model for Soviet composers, encapsulating the ideal blend of popular appeal and detectable ideological content – at least, for those wishing to detect it. As Chemodanov put it: 'Is Beethoven necessary today? What can the revolution gain from him? Can he aid the education of the masses in the spirit of revolutionary ideology? These are legitimate questions, so far as we can paint Beethoven as a musical ideologue of the third estate. And to all the questions we categorically reply "yes".'[56]

Lunacharskiy's article 'Great Sisters' of 1926 was typical of this early phase of constructing Beethoven's Soviet identity: 'Not for nothing did Beethoven's music come out of the French revolution; it was saturated with it. . . . Such a demigod of the musical world as Beethoven . . . is able to plunge into the deepest musical poetry which, being expressed in the language of human consciousness, raises mountainous problems, struggles, and victories.'[57] In the Beethoven centenary year 1927, specialist music journals devoted whole monthly issues to the composer.[58] *Muzïka i revoliutsiya* [Music and revolution], the journal of the Association of revolutionary composers and music workers (ORKiMD), ran a special issue in March, headed by Lunacharskiy's article 'How Beethoven Lives for us'; Yevgeny Braudo's article 'Beethoven-Citizen' claimed that in the *Eroica* 'the musician and social activist is revealed in all his depth and breadth. . . . Revolutionary rhythms run through [the *Eroica*] like a red thread; its rhythm is of the electrified crowd rushing to storm the Bastille.'[59]

Beethoven, as a figure of known revolutionary sympathies and composer of quintessentially 'heroic' music, was perhaps bound to be adopted as a fellow traveller. His later Austro-German contemporaries were a less straightforward proposition. In the Marxist-Leninist view of history, Romanticism was seen as a decline and a process of disillusionment among the European intelligentsia. However, some writers regarded the Romantics in a more positive light. In his 1928 article 'Romantika', Lunacharskiy posited two alternative views of romanticism, one negative, reflecting the despair of the fallen aristocracy and their supporters, who supposedly turned to mysticism and pessimism, and the other positive, reflecting the aspirations of the bourgeoisie and the 'stormy rise of the revolutionary class'. Beethoven, of course, is identified as a part of this, though his later contemporaries are firmly excluded:

> In my opinion it is impossible to deny the romanticism in Beethoven, though only Beethoven's romanticism is that of the bellicose progressive. . . . The romanticism of later composers – Schubert . . . Schumann and Chopin – offers its own transfer to romantic despondency and pessimism. . . . Individualism proved to be their portion. The isolation of this individualism compelled them to search for refuge in folklore in order to find the essence of nationalism, some kind of native order.[60]

Yet not every writer felt that the early Romantics (those after Beethoven) should be seen in this way. Mikhail Pekelis's article marking Schubert's centenary in 1928 set out arguments for embracing him as the most democratic of composers, writing for friends and family in a new style of domestic music-making that Soviet writers could convincingly point to as the prototype for their own amateur activities. Moreover, he marked the shift from revolutionary heroism to the celebration of intimacy and family as an integral part of Romanticism, affecting all major figures including Goethe, Schiller and Lessing: 'They idealized their own everyday lives, the intimacy and cosiness of the family home. . . . Interest in everyday life, in nature provoked the broad dissemination in art – especially in music – of programmatic and illustrative principles.'[61] Schubert, in Pekelis's view, was a 'new social type' who encapsulated the new democratic citizen and appealed to the new kind of listener as well as to a new 'democratic audience'. As a composer, Schubert was of the same social type as his audience, and so was able to reflect their tastes and interests more successfully than if he had been part of an aristocratic court. It is easy to see how this portrait of Schubert, the modest Biedermeier citizen, who wrote symphonies for his old orchestra and songs for his friends, could be regarded as a model for Soviet composers: he is the antithesis of the remote genius, patronized by the aristocracy. In addition, Pekelis argued, Schubert 'often saturated his songs (and his other works too) with a strong living current, with a realistic sensation of reality. A thirst for observation, the echoing of nature and the attempt to capture it sonically in his works, an inquisitiveness of psychology.' Schubert as realist, chronicler of the natural world and of human emotions is also an idealized Soviet type; in drawing attention to this part of his legacy, Pekelis aligned Schubert with the acknowledged master of realism – Musorgskiy. And the comparison with Musorgskiy did not end there, for Pekelis also pointed out that Schubert's music closely reflected German folk songs and culture: 'This realism, truth, compels us to regard Schubert in the light of programme-illustrative principles in music.'[62]

Of the later Romantics, Franz Liszt was probably the most popular figure in Russian musical life before the revolution. He had visited Russia in 1842 and 1843 and had close connections with Stasov, Balakirev and the Russian National School and with Anton Rubinstein, whom he knew and admired as a pianist, composer and conductor. Virtuosic Romantic piano repertoire was a staple of Conservatoire pedagogy and of concert life in both Moscow and Petersburg, a tradition, in which Chopin, Liszt and Schumann featured prominently. Liszt's symphonic poems were extremely popular in the 1920s, and Philharmonia listings regularly show performances of the 'Dante' and 'Faust' symphonies, *Mazeppa*, *Les Preludes* and other orchestral works (including, of course, the piano concertos). As with Beethoven, there was enough revolutionary lore around Liszt to preserve ideological credibility and his reputation remained stable during the whole Soviet period. But Schumann was a more difficult composer to market. During the 1920s, his orchestral music was not performed with anything like the regularity of Liszt's or Berlioz's and some critics felt that he needed careful re-branding to emphasize that his music was not just 'abstract' and self-indulgent. In 1926, Mikhail Ivanov-Boretskiy asserted that 'Every bar of Schumann's music is far from formalism . . . and is saturated with a genuine, deep romanticism understood as the reflection in music of the composer's spiritual life.'[63] Later, in the early 1930s, Mikhail Cheremukhin would paint Schumann very definitely as a dreamer in the type described by Lunacharskiy in 1928, writing that '[Dichterliebe] is already akin to a narcotic hashish.'[64] There would always be some writers who would see Schumann in that light, but in 1930, Ivanov-Boretskiy struck a powerful blow for Schumann the proto-revolutionary: he published an important article on his recently-discovered revolutionary choruses, reproducing Schumann's unpublished 1848 song 'To arms!' in his own handwritten manuscript and arguing that only those little acquainted with Schumann's biography would describe him merely as a dreamer who was sunk in his own creative work.[65] Schumann never rose to the status of Beethoven or Schubert, but his music retained a modest position in Soviet concert repertoire, not only in the 1920s but right through the Stalin years as well.

Hector Berlioz – whose revolutionary sympathies were far better documented than those of Schumann – fared much better than his German contemporary, which perhaps reveals the importance in those early years of having an ideologically respectable biography, or at least some track record of revolutionary sympathies. His 'Funeral and Triumphal' Symphony commemorating those who died in the 1830 revolution is obscure in the West today, but was frequently performed in the Soviet 1920s, as was his *Symphonie fantastique*. The first recorded Soviet performance of the 'Funeral and Triumphal' Symphony took place on 8 November 1918, at the second of Lunacharskiy's 'People's Concerts' in Smolniy, Petrograd, and it remained a sporadic repertoire piece through the 1920s and 1930s. Much later, in the 1940s, Berlioz's *Grande Messe des Morts* actually became a major repertoire piece as the cult of the 'monumental' that went hand in hand with Stalin's cult of personality took hold of Soviet cultural life: after Klimov performed it with the Leningrad capella in the 1928–9 season, his successor Aleksandr Sveshnikov revived it on 8 January 1940 and repeated it twice more that season. *Lelio*, the rarely performed sequel to *Symphonie Fantastique*, had also been revived in Leningrad (1934–5 season, conducted by Pierre Monteux), but it was not repeated thereafter.

The early Soviet reception of Wagner is especially intriguing. Even before the Civil War ended in 1921, *Parsifal*, *Lohengrin*, *Die Walküre* and *Die Meistersinger* had been staged in Petrograd/Leningrad and Moscow (at the Theatre of Musical Drama and former Mariinskiy, Petrograd and at the Zimin Opera and Bolshoy Theatre in Moscow). Championed initially by pre-revolutionary leaders in the music/theatre world like Fyodor Kommisarzhevskiy (*Lohengrin* at the Zimin Theatre in 1918) and the critics Karatïgin and Sabaneyev, Wagner's music was also supported by major artists in the modernist sphere. A few years before the Revolution in 1917, the Constructivist Vladimir Tatlin had been working on set designs for *Der fliegende Holländer*; sadly, because of the ban on Wagner imposed by Nicholas during the First World War, the production was never staged. Until the mid- to late 1920s, a few notable pre-revolutionary Wagnerians still worked in Petrograd/Leningrad and Moscow, including Kuper at the former Mariinskiy Theatre in Petrograd/Leningrad, the famous Wagner tenor Ivan Yershov and the veteran critic Karatïgin (who died in 1925). Rosamund Bartlett is largely correct in saying that during this early period, Wagner the revolutionary was championed, while Wagner the reactionary was 'summarily and conveniently overlooked'.[66] There was indeed a Wagner Silver Age cult that had its roots in Russian *fin de siècle* mysticism, dreams of a 'superman', immortality, the death of an old world and the birth of a new, and the replacement of Christian faith with belief in mankind's potential for greatness. Although the Silver Age could be said to have ended after the Civil War in 1921 (the year of Blok's death), several major proponents of Symbolism and Futurism continued to be active well until the end of that decade and even beyond. Even those only peripherally involved with either movement, such as the theatre director Vsevolod Meyerkhol'd, the writer Maksim Gorkiy or the politician Lunacharskiy, were strongly influenced by some of its ideas: Gorkiy's 'God-building' project (to which Lunacharskiy is known to have been sympathetic), for example, was intended as a religious substitute for Christianity, based on a sacred love for humanity and art. It is not hard to see how Wagner's music and writings chime with Silver Age/ early Soviet culture: art not as entertainment but as a sacred ritual for the benefit and edification of mankind; the advancement of humanity to an emancipated, enlightened future; the need to destroy the 'old' society and its ways in order to build a new one. Small wonder, then, that 'Wagner the reactionary' was of secondary importance to writers like the poet Aleksandr Blok, who pragmatically regarded the conflicts in Wagner's own creative and intellectual makeup as a 'useful poison' rather than as a major existential hurdle.[67]

One of the curiosities of Wagner's reception in the Soviet Union is the unpopularity of his only overtly revolutionary opera, *Rienzi*. According to Bartlett, it was performed three times between 1920 and 1923 then dropped, while *Lohengrin* – potentially problematic because of its Christian theme – was the most frequently performed, right up to 1940. Writing in 1923, Karatïgin pondered this apparent anomaly, concluding that, in the end, it was *Rienzi*'s relative immaturity and lack of interest that made performing it a less exciting prospect than, for example, a new production of *Parsifal* might be. When Kuper put *Parsifal* into rehearsal in 1918, the production was withdrawn, and thereafter it was never performed for the entire Soviet era.[68] Since *Lohengrin* comes from the same literary source as *Parsifal*, its popularity seems puzzling, although it may be that its mixture of Christianity and paganism placed it sufficiently close to Russian nineteenth-century operatic traditions, in particular to Rimskiy-Korsakov's fairy-tale operas and the State/Orthodox pageantry of Musorgskiy's *Boris Godunov*, or the ritualism of *Khovanshchina*. In some contexts, Christianity on stage was acceptable, and *Lohengrin* was seen as primarily a tragic love story rather than a journey towards redemption, with its Grail references part of the background to the plot rather than its driving force.[69]

Gustav Mahler and Richard Strauss both had difficult receptions in the 1920s, and it would not be until the 1930s that Soviet critics began the process of canonizing Mahler. Strauss never received that honour, partly because he was still living and could therefore not be regarded as a 'classic', and partly because of his prominent role in Goebbels's *Reichsmusikammer*, which had a serious negative effect on his Soviet reputation. Despite the prominence of German musicians and composers in early Soviet musical life, there was a discernible anti-Western slant to some Soviet music criticism, and while this did not affect the appropriation of more established Austro-German repertoire, it did affect Soviet perceptions of newer music, and the charge of 'decadence' is never very far away in some of these reviews. Yevgeny Braudo's 1922 article 'On Expressionism in Music' claims that, though Mahler was antipathetic to the Russian listener, he was popular with the German public. This in itself is recognizable in the rhetoric of the time as an insult, which Braudo immediately expands upon: 'It is impossible to ignore the sign of the times in the fact that Mahler holds such sway over the soul of the contemporary West.'[70] In other words, Mahler's popularity was a symptom of the decline of Western culture into decadence; by implied contrast, it was only in the Soviet Union that the more spiritually robust Beethovenian symphonic tradition could be renewed. Those features of Mahler's music that had always been the most controversial – his juxtapositions of the serious and the banal – registered with Braudo as equally objectionable, and he complained bitterly of its 'unexpected transitions from . . . gloomy pathos to artificial lightness and gaiety . . . fairy-tale craft alongside the most philistine gutter taste. In a word, [it is] a total rejection of that which until now was considered the chief object of a symphonic composition: self-possession, balance and refinement of artistic material.'[71] The Moscow ASM critics Viktor Belyayev and Leonid Sabaneyev were also Mahler sceptics; in 1924 Belyayev echoed Braudo's suspicion of Mahler's German popularity, sarcastically linking him with Strauss as 'the apparent idols of German lands'.[72] Compared with the 'dazzling' Skryabin, of whom Belyayev was an established supporter, Belyayev described both Mahler and Strauss's music in typically anti-German terms as 'dry classicism', 'abstract from life'.[73] Indeed, when Bruno Walter visited Leningrad and performed Mahler's First Symphony, the *Sovremennaya muzïka* [Contemporary music] reviewer sniffed that it was 'uninteresting and trivial to the last degree'.[74] Rather more thoughtfully, Braudo pondered the question of why Strauss did not seem more popular in Soviet Russia: 'Most unusually for contemporary German symphonists, [Strauss] doesn't receive great sympathy from Russian audiences. His invariable striving for superficial inventiveness, melody that, in the view of influential Russian critics is awkward, even trivial . . . is not to the taste of Russian audiences, who are exasperated by his linearity and prosaism.'[75] And in 1926, the reviewer of Kuper's performance of *Ein Heldenleben* accused the German composer outright of 'dilettantism', complaining that 'German contemporary music . . . stubbornly ignores ours without any foundation.' In comparison with the Russian melodic style, the reviewer continues, 'the melos of the German national [style] could define the very word "banal" '.[76]

Mahler's Soviet reception would improve dramatically in the 1930s, thanks largely to the efforts of Ivan Sollertinskiy, who published a monograph on him in 1932. As Sollertinskiy's writings on Mahler demonstrate, it was relatively easy to paint him as a fellow traveller, broadly in sympathy with the proletariat. Such anecdotes as Mahler's joining the Vienna May Day parade in 1905 and his Dostoevsky-inspired expression of fraternity, 'How can one be happy when a single being on earth still suffers?', enabled Sollertinskiy to stress Mahler's democratic credentials.[77] But this was still some way off and certainly, Mahler and Strauss were anathema to the older generation of Soviet critics, for whom their music seemed to fall between two stools: it was neither 'romantic' in the old established sense, nor was its modernism of the type that these Russian critics were prepared to accept.

Narkompros

As discussed above, the working populations of Russia's industrialized cities were, even before the Revolution, involved with musical life, whether through singing in choirs, running their own concert series, or even playing in amateur instrumental groups. All this activity would expand in scale under the Bolsheviks, and after October 1917 the overall responsibility for running and monitoring all these organizations fell to the newly formed government department, the People's Commissariat for Enlightenment [*Narodniy kommissariat prosveshcheniya*], or 'Narkompros'. The term 'Enlightenment' conveys a slightly archaic flavour for a state department that was simply responsible for education and research (in both arts and sciences), but it also suggests to non-Russian readers something of the totalizing nature of the endeavour as well as its idealism. Narkompros answered directly to the Ministry of Internal Affairs [*Narodniy kommissariat vnutrenikh del'*], otherwise known as the NKVD. In overall charge of Narkompros was its Commissar, Lunacharskiy. Educated, cultured and relatively liberal (by the standards of the time), he has been generally lauded by cultural historians for his light touch and supportive attitude to the arts organizations under his jurisdiction. There were certainly no-tolerance zones even in Lunacharskiy's concept of how mass enlightenment should be conducted. Those who held to ideologies running counter to Bolshevism, such as religious beliefs or any alternative faith system, were not permitted to 'propagandize' them in public events, meetings or within education. Yet even these restrictions took a few years to become an accepted reality, and musical activities linked with Russian Orthodoxy continued until 1922, as will be seen.

Composer Societies in the 1920s

A call to arms published in the journal *Artist-muzïkant* in 1918 stated: 'All music activists, from composers to soloists, from choirs to orchestral players, are obliged to work via the state for the people . . . alongside artistic duties, they are at liberty to found free music collectives and societies.'[78] As the Russian scholar Yevgeniy Dukov drily notes, this promise of liberty was not actually fulfilled until the 1980s and Mikhail Gorbachev's *perestroika*, but the fact remains that the 1920s saw a plethora of amateur and professional music societies springing up throughout Leningrad and Moscow.[79] Among them was the Beethoven Society, founded in the composer's centenary year of 1927 with a membership including some of the best musicians, scholars and music workers of the period.[80] An especially notable detail about this society was its range of membership: among the professional names listed, that of the young proletarian music activist Lev Lebedinskiy and other RAPM colleagues sit innocently alongside those of musicians whose dedication to musical culture took a very different course: the 'establishment' composers Nikolay Myaskovskiy, Reyngol'd Glier and Aleksandr Glazunov, flanked by the heavyweight (and defiantly traditionalist) Soviet pianists Aleksandr Gol'denveyzer and Genrikh Neygauz. The Beethoven Society's aims were typical for their time, including the desire to 'acquaint the broad working masses and peasantry with Beethoven's work and artistic ideas', 'to carry out scientific research on Beethoven's music and his epoch' and 'to explore the evolution of musical culture and Beethoven's role within it'.[81]

Another such society was the Bach Society, registered formally with Narkompros and the NKVD in October 1928. Its membership was broader in scope than that of the Beethoven Society, being drawn from musical professionals and students alike, especially from the Moscow Conservatoire. Its professional members included the cellists Svyatoslav Knushevitskiy and Viktor Kubatskiy, the organists Aleksandr Gedike and Mikhail Starokadomskiy, the pianists Samuil Feynberg, Grigoriy Ginzburg and Neygauz and the musicologists Pavel Novitskiy and Mikhail Ivanov-Boretskiy.[82] Its aims were no less laudable than those of the Beethoven Society: 'to bring the broad working masses close to both classical and contemporary serious music; the dissemination of musical-artistic knowledge to society and to assist in any way the development of artistic musical culture; to put on lectures, give concerts, open music studios, schools, courses and institutes, publish work, organize exhibitions and competitions, keep a library, form international links and open sister departments within the RSFSR'.[83]

Founded much earlier than the Beethoven and Bach Societies, the 'Society for Wagner's Art' began in 1923 (though was only fully ratified with Narkompros in 1925).[84] It was a perfect example of an amateur society that, by being well run and supported by high-profile professionals, managed to achieve results that were astonishing by any standards. Founded by an engineer, Konstantin Khmelnitskiy, the society's chief aim was to produce Wagner's operas in chamber music versions, so that they could be presented in as accessible a form (both artistically and financially) as possible to mass listeners and students. Performing operas in chamber versions, even with just piano accompaniment, was a well-founded tradition of amateur music-making in Russia, stemming from the People's Houses of the pre-revolutionary years. Their project addressed a real need in Russian musical life: critics already bewailed the lack of experienced Wagnerian singers, and pre-revolutionary audiences not previously acquainted with Wagner's operas were unlikely to appreciate them when only hearing them once, with little or no prior knowledge of either the plot or the composer. The society was known to Cosima Wagner, who had met at least one of its members (Professor A. V. Sapozhnikov) at Bayreuth, and sent over a portrait of Wagner as a gift. Khmelnitskiy himself had attended Bayreuth until the outbreak of war in 1914, so not only did he have the benefit of personal experience of seeing Wagner's operas staged in as ideal an environment as the composer was able to realize in his lifetime, but he was also clearly a determined and resourceful organizer.

Khmelnitskiy's society began modestly, but it still managed to put on *Das Rheingold*, on 11 June 1924 at the chamber music hall on Nevskiy Prospekt. The orchestral parts were performed in a two-piano reduction and a small group of singers took multiple roles. As he would for every performance mounted by the Society, Khmelnitskiy himself gave the introductory lecture. Critical success and the acceptance of the Society by Narkompros gave them credibility when seeking new members and advisors prior to its next big production; the pianist Mariya Yudina (Leningrad Conservatoire) and the celebrated tenor Ivan Yershov (by now People's Artist of the USSR) agreed to act as advisors and give general support. All performances were given in Russian, as was the norm even in the major opera houses.[85] In their ambitious project to perform the whole *Ring* cycle in the 1925–6 season, the Society sadly never got further than repeating *Das Rheingold* and *Die Walküre*: both were performed in May 1925 in the hall of the Leningrad capella. The reasons for not completing the tetralogy seem to have been a mixture of financial difficulties and problems with singers. The 'mass' concerts in the capella hall brought in only 200 roubles per concert which, when spread over the forty or so performers, barely covered their costs. Tickets for the 'Friends of Chamber Music' concerts on Nevskiy Prospekt started at a mere twenty-five kopecks (just over half the cost of the cheapest ticket at the capella) and these concerts yielded even less income. Singers – who were presumably paid next to nothing – complained that the rehearsals were too time-consuming; gradually they began to make their excuses and drop out of further productions. But the Wagner Society was a heroic short-term project rather than an out-and-out failure; until it was dissolved in 1930, it gave performances of Acts One and Three from *Die Walküre* and the Prologue to *Das Rheingold*, sometimes with just a single piano part. The demands made on both pianists and singers must have been incredible, and the fact that reviews were, on the whole, positive, testifies to the commitment and energy of such groups.

Mass Work in the 1920s: Amateur Groups

The efforts and achievements of those working in the amateur sphere have not been much studied by Western scholars, who have tended rather to focus exclusively on professional art music practitioners. The two pioneers in this field have been Neil Edmunds and Amy Nelson, whose books dedicated to the 1920s remain indispensable to anyone interested in this field.[86] Nelson focuses chiefly on the structures underpinning the mass musical work rather than on the work itself, and her book is the fullest account available in English of the complex and shifting music bureaucracy of the 1920s. Edmunds goes into far more detail on the practical application of RAPM's mass work, describing concerts, repertoire and the activities of workers' clubs. I do not want to repeat their findings here, but rather try to fill a gap in the pictures that both scholars have given us. Scholars whose work encompasses the late pre-revolutionary period and the early 1920s are Lynn M. Sargeant and Rebecca Mitchell, who have carried out research on amateur and local music-making and early mass education movements, and their work is of major importance to anyone wishing to understand the pre-revolutionary background to the Bolshevik programmes to bring music to the masses.[87]

There are several good reasons why oral testimony from those who participated in amateur music-making is almost entirely absent in scholarship on this period. At the most basic level, there is a dearth of sources. Archival materials for this period tend to fall into two categories: the personal *fond* and the institutional *fond*. For a major archive like the Glinka Museum or the State Russian Archive of Literature and Art to accept a personal *fond*, it would normally be one from an arts professional; that is, a practitioner rather than a participant. Therefore, those accounts of these activities that remain, both published and unpublished, tend to come only from the perspective of those delivering art to the 'masses' rather than from those on the receiving end. Institutional *fonds*, it goes without saying, fail almost entirely to provide the researcher with perspectives outside the professional and political sphere; the rare exceptions are stenographic reports of meetings where workers were invited to attend and speak, and a few attempts during the 1920s to capture workers' responses to music, which will be discussed below. In all these accounts, invaluable as they are, the voices of those for whom the vast edifice of mass musical work was ostensibly intended – the Soviet working man and woman – remain almost completely silent.

This section will present a few of those lone post-revolutionary voices, captured in stenographic reports, published books and articles from the period, but there is no doubt that this is a field requiring a lot more research. The major difficulty, of course, is the frailty of oral testimony – occasionally an opinion or reaction is captured for posterity after a concert, but even when, as in the 1930s, the Leningrad Philharmonia actually distributed questionnaires to audiences asking for their response to symphonic works in the programme, it seems likely that the majority of listeners would have left without returning the form. Finding samples of these questionnaires in archives raises the tempting possibility that completed slips were kept; but it seems that neither the Moscow nor Leningrad Philharmonia made any special effort to retain them. So far as I have been able to establish, the whole Leningrad Philharmonia *fond* in TsGALI (St Petersburg) retains just one batch of questionnaires, printed on small slips of flimsy paper, invariably completed in soft pencil or crayon and difficult to decipher.[88] It is certainly ironic, given the immense expenditure of effort and the reams of rhetoric devoted to the project of 'music for the masses', that the masses themselves should be so silent and invisible to historians researching this period now. But ultimately, they were no more than guinea pigs for a giant socio-cultural experiment in which the winners and losers were not so much the recipients of cultural largesse as those fighting to be the ones to deliver it. This is underlined by the fact that the wider public's musical tastes and preferences were so often swept aside: as will be discussed below, workers bored with singing the same mass songs over and over again were exhorted to glean satisfaction from their political content, while attacks on jazz and dance music in the proletarian journals could be extremely vicious. Looking back at this period through journals and archival records, one's overriding impression is that during the time of the 'Great Break' (1929–32), when proletarian militancy was at its height, the notion of workers' entertainment, pleasure and even education for its own (rather than ideological) sake was of little or no concern to those who were supposedly dedicated to mass music-making, in stark contrast to the idealism of the earlier revolutionary years.

The sheer numbers of workers involved in amateur musical activities during the 1920s even just in Moscow and Petrograd–Leningrad goes well into the tens of thousands. For details of their activities, the best source is Edmunds's *The Soviet Proletarian Music Movement* and I will not dwell excessively on the details he provides here. Suffice to say that every factory in Moscow and Leningrad had its own music club, which could be a very modest affair (a string band or a choir) or could be remarkably ambitious. To give some idea of the range of these clubs, the Putilov Factory in Leningrad had its own opera studio (founded 1927) as well as a choir; the 'Red Triangle' factory in the same city also ran an opera group, led by the Conservatoire-trained Ivan Arkad'yev. They successfully produced scenes from Dargomïzhskiy's *Rusalka* and the whole of Glinka's *Ruslan and Lyudmila* in 1926.[89] But not all factories could muster such impressive forces: Leningrad's factory 'Red Dawn' had a chamber orchestra of twenty-four players (founded 1926), but the music club of the Moscow–Kazan Railway workers (founded 1924) could, by 1927, only find eight violinists, two violas, a cello and an upright piano. Their plight was described in their brief report 'We Dream of a Symphony Orchestra' in which they explained that, despite their difficulties, they still managed to perform Wagner and put on free concerts for workers – a sad reflection on the perhaps less than ideal structure imposed on workers' club activities, which seemed to prevent them from joining forces for more ambitious projects.[90]

In 1927, the conductor Nikolay Mal'ko tried to account for what had gone awry in some of these club groups. Though claiming that after the Revolution a wave of enthusiasm propelled music activists into organizing music-making and concerts for workers, he reflected that a lack of material resources – chiefly shortage of instruments as well as music – had hampered their efforts.[91] Yet though this was evidently a real problem for many groups, the journals chronicling their music activities – *Rabis*, *Muzïka i bït* [Music and everyday life], *Muzïkal'naya samodeyatelnost'* [Amateur Music] – show an incredible level of achievement among clubs with strong music sections.[92] Following from this, however, it should be remembered that the membership of these clubs was not necessarily particularly lower class or poorly educated. Many of the most successful music clubs were full of doctors, engineers and academics: one example was the Leningrad Orchestra of the House of Engineers and Technicians led by N. A. Sass-Tisovskiy, like Arkad'yev, a graduate of the St Petersburg Conservatoire and an old student of Rimskiy-Korsakov. They performed advanced repertoire, including full symphonies and opera excerpts. Sass-Tiskovskiy's Engineers' orchestra accompanied Shostakovich in his own First Piano Concerto as well as playing his First Symphony, so they were clearly playing to a very high standard indeed.[93] But amateur music clubs were only one manifestation of the many and varied projects to bring art music to the masses. Since all aspects of professional musical life were involved, directly or indirectly with such projects, the range of events created for workers was bewildering, as will be discussed in relation to the Leningrad and Moscow Philharmonias below.

One of the best sources for charting the evolution of music work among the proletariat was the journal *Muzïka i revolyutsiya*, created by ORKiMD, a proletarian group led by Lev Shul'gin that broke away from RAPM in 1924. Far less militant than RAPM's journal *Muzïkal'naya nov'*, it began publication in 1926 and folded in February 1929 when ORKiMD was subsumed back into RAPM. Its articles offer a mixed snapshot of music educational events and contain real evidence of new audiences eagerly consuming art music for the first time. Sometimes the earnest tone of its writers masked what were probably enjoyable social events as drearily educational: in the October 1928 Schubert-themed issue, the reviewer of a workers' concert intoned:

> Schubert is for us not only the author of superb songs and the 'unfinished' symphony, but also a significant cultural–historical influence; the substance of this influence was revealed before an audience of workers at an evening of Schubert at their club. When experiencing the character of Schubert as a definite stage in Western European social development, it is essential for such an evening to convey an educational character.[94]

This does not sound like much fun; though the performances of Schubert transcriptions for balalaika, mandolin and guitar (F minor *Moment Musical*), and *Rosamunde* for an orchestra of folk instruments would have been the product of many hours' club rehearsals and were probably very enjoyable for the players involved.[95]

Descriptions of workers' concerts are usually mundane, but occasionally a review appears that indicates genuine success and originality. In 1928, the Kommunal'shikov's [society of *kommunalka* workers] amateur production of *Fidelio* impressed the critic of *Rabochiy i teatr* by introducing a contemporary twist to Beethoven's romantic rescue opera. Using modern day props like brooms and shovels and altering details of staging (one scene featured a quartet of tram-drivers playing cards), the production's standard of musical performance was not especially high, but the originality of the staging impressed the reviewer, who thought it could have been the first genuinely original amateur opera production. The main curiosity of this production was the ending: instead of finishing with the final scene where Don Fernando announces his general amnesty of prisoners, the opera concluded instead with a placard reading: 'Later in the play the king [*sic*] frees the prisoners. Class consciousness does not allow us to continue the play, and we throw off our masks.'[96] One can only read this as a refusal to cast the high-ranking Don Fernando in a positive light, since the real villain of the piece is supposed to be the much lower-ranking official (and prison governor) Don Pizarro. It seems safe to guess that the opera therefore ended with Leonore's dramatic rescue of Florestan and the lovers' reunion.

Perhaps unsurprisingly, there is evidence of lack of audience enthusiasm at the larger venues like the Philharmonias and the Bolshoy. As early as 1920 – before the end of the Civil War, but also during the period of supposedly maximum discovery of 'high art' by the masses – Nikolay Roslavets wrote an article for the art workers' journal *Vestnik rabotnikov iskusstv* [Art workers' bulletin], in which he paints a picture of utter failure:

Are workers in clubs worn out by back-breaking rounds of rehearsals for 'khaltura' productions, or do the spectacles extend [stretch] actors, musicians, poets and people with refined, sensitive tastes? . . . In these clubs you see a concert of Haydn, Mozart, Chaykovskiy. Try it and you will feel all the horror of your own isolation in the empty hall.[97]

Another brutally honest assessment of engagement levels was given by the anonymous reviewer 'D' in the Moscow monthly journal *Rabochiy zritel'* [The worker-listener] in 1924, who reported that, though each month the Bolshoy Theatre put on concerts for workers (serving an estimated 9,000 members of the professional unions), workers themselves simply did not come:

> If we ask ourselves what elements of Profsoiuzï [the professional unions] consists of 'mass' visitors to these concerts, then the answer must be that the concerts are for the staff of Profsoiuzï and their families. Machine workers just don't come to these concerts; or, when they do come, they simply do as they please (read libretti, the papers, chat and so on) but don't actually listen to the music, no matter how well it is performed. Speaking with comrades who deal with giving out tickets to union members, it seems clear that workers stubbornly refuse to accept tickets for symphony concerts. Why is this? The basic reason is our musical illiteracy, which remains our legacy from the Tsarist regime.[98]

This issue of *Rabochiy zritel'* (and the two issues after it) contained a sample questionnaire for workers, requesting information on their job, their theatre-going habits (though not their concert-going habits), what they liked and didn't like and why. It seems perverse that the same effort was not made on music's behalf: perhaps it seemed self-evident to musicians from all persuasions that light music was *de facto* bad for workers, who instead needed to be uplifted and inspired by 'great art'. Where ideological content could be demonstrated – in films, plays and literature – battle lines could be more clearly drawn between factions, but in the musical sphere, it seemed beyond question that 'classics' were what the proletariat needed: all that remained to be decided was which ones were most suitable. It is not surprising to find those on the proletarian side striking an authoritarian note on this subject: in a lengthy critique of the Soviet Philharmonia in 1929, the critic Lev Kaltat insisted that it must:

> decisively remove from its programmes all *tsïganshchina* [gypsy music], philistine and hack culture. The basic principle guiding repertoire for all workers' concerts is that the worker-listener must receive from the concert a cheerful, healthy emotional impression and that the concert must enrich the worker's psyche, and play a part in raising the general vigour of the listener.[99]

There were to be no short cuts to justifying repertoire via sleight of hand from a crafty pre-concert speaker either:

> Introductory talks must put an end to general phrases like 'the bourgeoisie is in decay, but . . .', 'an epoch of cruel reaction reigned, but music . . .', 'as the storms of the great revolution thundered, music responded . . .'[100]

Yet the self-interest in such demands is made immediately obvious when Kaltat goes on to complain that only 'bourgeois flowers' of Soviet music are exported abroad rather than proletarian works; that not a single professional choir had performed the collectively composed oratorio *The Path to October*, and finished up with a sneer at the International Society for Contemporary Music (ISCM), with its membership of 'white émigrés'.[101] Though such articles certainly give the impression that RAPM was overwhelmingly concerned about power and influence for its members, they also show that they felt frustrated by their perception that the balance of power still lay with their mainstream opponents, who largely controlled the Philharmonias and major musical institutions, as well as enjoying international reputations and associated publishing royalties.

Even by 1924, whatever novelty there may initially have been for workers sampling high art for the first time was evidently wearing off rapidly in some quarters, much to the consternation of the critic Anton Tsenovskiy in his article ' "Them" and "Us" ':

> Why should it be so? [that is, 'Them' and 'us'] How many concerts are given in Moscow, orchestral concerts, evening concerts, matinee concerts, concerts for children, to which people might willingly go. There is Persimfans – the First Symphonic Ensemble! There are concerts at the Bolshoy Theatre! There are orchestral concerts by the Revolutionary Theatre! There are concerts given by children's organizations! There are so many concerts, so much wonderful instrumental music! And yet workers are never seen at any of them! And this is all because of disorganization and indifference to culture on the part of the masses and the old prejudice 'they won't understand it'.[102]

With pained inevitability, he concludes, 'they prefer accordion, couplets, balalaikas, gypsy romances . . . And serious culture – is for "us"'. Yet there is also evidence to suggest that workers in these club music groups were themselves frustrated by poor leadership, inadequate supply of instruments and sheet music, and even with the physical conditions of the club accommodation. Some even complained about the repertoire offered them by visiting ensembles, while others simply disliked the conditions offered by the club itself: one correspondent to *Muzïka i revoliutsiya* in 1926 had this to say about how his music club was run:

> As for the club, it is filthy, it has cobwebs in the corners and the floor hasn't been cleaned in a hundred years. The benches are rotten and there's not much light. It's dingy and it's cold. My home is much nicer. They need to get the clubs so that they are nicer than home. As for the concerts, it's the ninth year they've been singing and playing and they still haven't figured out that we have grown up in that time and begun to demand more. They give us any old rubbish. . . . For the day of the October Revolution we got 'Love is an entrancing dream' . . . what does that teach us? . . . I was at the Conservatoire, at a concert. The orchestra played without a what d'ya call it – a conductor. It was very good and I understood it well. Those playing were masters who loved and cared about what they did. . . . We need to look to our club; it needs cleaning up and a proper society establishing . . . we need more music by real masters.[103]

Another writer to *Muzïka i revoliutsiya* noted that access to decent instruments was patchy to say the least; no new instruments had been manufactured in the Soviet Union until 1927 (orchestras bought new instruments from foreign suppliers), and those used by clubs tended to be pieced together from old separate parts and frequently fell apart. Further, he complained that the system put in place by the State shops for selling instruments, especially in groups (for a wind or string band, for example) made the price prohibitively expensive and therefore acted as a block on improving conditions for amateurs.[104]

In addition to these practical difficulties, there was plenty of evidence that workers continued to evade the educational efforts of RAPM. In an article published in *Rabochiy i teatr* in 1931, M. Korotkov lamented that the wind orchestras proliferating in Leningrad's musical clubs continue to play 'hackneyed waltzes' and even music like Albert W. Ketelbey's *In a Persian Market*. Not only that, but the orchestras freely mixed up 'suitable' and 'unsuitable' repertoire in a way that signalled indifference to its alleged ideological content. Worse still,

> proletarian journals such as *Proletarskiy muzïkant* and *Za proletarskuyu muzïku* aren't even known about in these clubs. Workers don't embrace this political work. They don't know about VAPM [=RAPM]. In one club they play foxtrots and the 'Dollar Waltz' and excerpts from operettas.[105]

Clearly, programmes to teach basic music literacy had been popular enough for workers to form their own groups and play music together; what they then chose to play – if given a free hand – was up to them, availability of sheet music permitting. Another writer (N. Kudryatsev) in *Proletarskiy muzïkant* noted that workers' choirs always wanted to sing well-known popular songs and even sacred music (probably because they knew it already, or it sounded familiar to them), making the obvious practical point that in many cases, those leading them had little or no knowledge of repertoire themselves.[106] Music club leaders, especially outside the major cities, were often former church regents, and while many were probably fine choral conductors and musicians, some workers felt that they were insufficiently trained. One worker from Minsk in 1929, writing in to *Muzïka i revoliutsiya,* voiced his frustration at the weak leadership in the provinces and the impossibility of their leaders attending the training courses that ran in Moscow.[107] Two issues later, the writer A. Koposov wrote to the same journal, calling for properly trained group leaders to replace those whose training was of the Tsarist past, who have, he claims, an 'aesthetic-intelligentsia ideology. . . . Such leaders play into the hands of the bourgeoisie, considering themselves to be pure, neutral, apolitical workers.'[108] Brass bands were apparently not in much better shape according to these proletarian critics: in reports of the activities of military bands in Moscow, the frustrated reviewer of *Proletarskiy muzïkant* fumed: 'In Moscow's parks and gardens you can hear sugary, mouldering, Philistine, salon repertoire. Conductors of military wind orchestras never even think of playing any serious classical pieces.'[109] The fact is that amateur music-making was taking place on such a vast scale that the paltry membership of RAPM was completely unable to exert the level of influence on the hundreds of workers' ensembles and choirs active in Moscow and Leningrad that it wished to, let alone the many more that existed outside the major Russian cities.

Monitoring the Masses

Given the Russian background of trying to break down class barriers to music education, it is not surprising that music professionals, as well as officials in Narkompros and in the government, worked from the fundamental assumption that cultivating an appreciation of art music in the Soviet working class was socially and culturally desirable. Issuing free tickets and organizing special orchestral concerts for workers acknowledged the fact that there had been an economic barrier to their sharing fully in musical activities before the Revolution, and the new Soviet regime wanted to eliminate this. Musical illiteracy was not, of course, so urgently addressed as was the need for workers and peasants to learn to read and write. But an appreciation of culture – including culture of the past, and of Western countries, not just Russia – was widely encouraged in musical circles. Emphasis was not on the entertainment value of art music; rather, it would provide a counterweight to the lively popular culture that flourished – without any official assistance – in towns and cities of folk song, jazz bands, popular Russian song and dance styles (*chastushki*, gypsy romances and so on). Any pre-revolutionary distaste for these light, popular forms of entertainment became, if anything, even more puritanical after 1917, especially in the ranks of proletarian music activists such as RAPM. Opposition to light music was chiefly the province of the proletarian militant wing, since their notion of educational value was guided by not what workers liked, but what was supposed to be politically good for them. For those music activists, nothing was more destructive than workers' clubs performing light music, whether they featured jazz bands, gypsy singers or any other popular music of the time, which they dubbed *khaltura* (hack-work) or *makulatura* (pulp). Once workers had begun to consume and even perform such repertoire, they reasoned, it would be far harder to inspire them with the mass songs proletarian composers were writing for them.

One element of pre-revolutionary culture that prompted a clash between genuine popularity and ideologically driven disapproval after 1917 was the performance of Russian folk culture. Initially, for ensembles like the Leningrad capella, traditions of singing folk song actually provided a concrete example of their 'relevance' and popular appeal. But it is not hard to see why some officials and musicians may have been suspicious of this celebration of Tsarist-era culture, despite its popular roots. As we have seen, popularity was no indication of ideological correctness, and since one of the chief Bolshevik objectives was to eliminate vestiges of historic remnants of serfdom such as illiteracy, political disengagement and belief in Orthodoxy, the whole notion of fetishizing village culture carried with it the danger of sentimentalizing the past and obscuring Soviet achievements in education and urban/industrial expansion. RAPM became increasingly militant on the question of whether amateur groups should be singing pre-revolutionary Russian culture of any kind. The Pyatnitskiy Choir, formed in 1911 by Mitrofan Pyatnitskiy, was originally formed entirely of peasants, many of whom were illiterate. By almost any measures, one would imagine this to have been regarded as a model of Soviet musical integrity, and so it was for a long time; yet it came close to dissolution when not only RAPM, but also other figures in the musical world began to attack it publicly in the early 1930s. In her PhD dissertation on the choir, Suzannah Lockwood Smith has shown how popular the choir was with radio listeners in 1929–30, the years when it came under attack. But one change its new director Pëtr Kaz'min (nephew of its founder who took over in 1927) made would have instantly antagonized RAPM: he introduced *chastushki* into the choir's repertoire. Audiences loved them, but these fast-paced, often witty, songs belonged in RAPM's category of *khaltura*.[110] Further, the Russian folk songs that had always made up the choir's core repertoire fell foul of RAPM in the 1930 All-Russian Choir Conference, where the delegates voted to liquidate peasant choirs, deeming them 'alien, harmful, corrupting to the class consciousness of [their] participants and listeners'.[111] Even the academic study of folk culture was questioned at this late stage of proletarian dominance, defined in one conference as 'relict culture'.[112] But RAPM was not the only organization hostile to the choir or to the Soviet phenomenon of 'peasant culture' more generally; nor did ideological suspicion of 'village culture' originate wholly in the years of 'cultural revolution' from 1929 to 1932. Asaf'yev (under his pseudonym Igor Glebov) pondered the 'problem' of its popularity as early as 1926, in an article for *Muzïka i revoliutsiya*. His main argument was that the urban proletariat and the village peasant required quite different types of folk song:

> Everyday peasant song, by the specific historical conditions and social position of the *narod* [the people] in former Russia, is strongly alienated from the musical life of cities . . . Between the archaic *bïlinï* and 'bridal laments' and the cheeky *chastushka*, there is a chasm. They are two different worlds . . . The old 'folk' song, which summoned up the old

[life], is hateful to the young contemporary life of the village, and is irrevocably disappearing, for it does not correspond with our own tempo, the dynamic of our new life. It follows then that in our towns we have a complex problem: how to cultivate in the musical consciousness contemporary village musical culture of the contemporary age and realize within it the riches of earlier *narodnïy* [folk] creativity.[113]

Asaf'yev's article may have been written in response to a letter from a peasant two issues (months) earlier, in which the writer, born in the 1870s, recalled his early experience of folk song in his village: 'The music of our folk songs fascinated me from earliest childhood. The songs awoke my consciousness; through song I began to understand myself, and to under-stand that I lived in the light.'[114] One can easily see how this simple state-ment could ruffle Bolshevik feathers: pre-1917 the peasants were supposed to be in darkness, not in the light; post-1917 they were supposed to be grateful to the Soviet state for liberating them from this darkness, and, moreover, they were not supposed to believe in God any more, but to place their faith in communism instead. Asaf'yev's claim that the old folk song culture was 'hateful' to village youth may have been partly true in some quarters, but the popularity of Russian folk culture even in urban centres like Leningrad and Moscow indicates that it was far more widely loved and cherished. This lingering affection for old peasant tradition is what saved the Pyatnitskiy choir in the end, when ideological hostility to it grew to the level of public attacks.

After the choir had suffered a string of bureaucratic persecutions, the critic Vladimir Blyum, who was closely linked with the ASM, published an outright attack on it in the journal *Radioslushatel'* [Radio Listener] in May 1930, accusing it of 'kulakism' and undermining the building of socialism. In response, the journal's editors invited their readers to submit their own views, both positive and negative. The positive response – letters defending the choir – was overwhelming and, if the journal had planned to openly call for its liquidation, its editors stepped back from that position as a result.[115] Nevertheless, the prevailing political conditions of 1930 were unfriendly to all organizations of 'peasant culture' and the choir was banned from the radio and from further touring. In the end, they were probably saved from destruction by the appointment of the more politically astute Vladimir Zakharov as co-director.[116] He transformed the choir from a pre-revolutionary model of folk preservation to a fully Sovietized institution that was able to survive into the mature Stalin period, even becoming an official State Choir in 1940.

If music professionals were genuinely interested in sharing culture with the 'masses', then it would have made sense to have monitored their reactions to music from the start to see what they did and didn't like. Yet, although workers' and peasants' views on literature were surveyed and preserved, this did not really happen with music. When, in December 1928, the musicologist Roman Gruber wrote his pioneering article charting the fruits of research conducted by the *Dom Kul'turi* [House of Culture] into the responses to music of a workers' audience to concerts held in the Leningrad Institute of Arts History, he admitted that it was one of the very few pieces of research carried out on the subject.[117] The research was of very limited scope, surveying only 178 people over the course of two chamber concerts in March and April 1928. Its aims were never clearly stated, nor is there any evidence that its conclusions had any effect on programming policy. But what their research did achieve – and at a time when all musicians not belonging to RAPM were beginning to feel pressure from their growing power – was a range of extremely positive responses to music that was emphatically 'bourgeois': nineteenth-century instrumental works and romances.

Workers made up 40 per cent of Gruber's audience, students 16 per cent, housewives 5 per cent, office workers 20 per cent, and 'individuals' (!) the rest. The audiences were asked if they regularly listened to 'serious music': the standard term for what, in English, would be 'art music' or – as is more commonly used – 'classical music'. Most did not; at least 50 per cent were hearing such music for the first time, and only 15 per cent of the remaining half said they listened to classical music regularly (mostly workers and students, apparently leaving housewives and 'individuals' trailing behind). But of those who did listen, some responses were noted: 'Yes, but it demands a lot of attention and intensive work' (a worker); 'Yes, but I don't understand everything, especially new music'; 'Yes, but only what I like'; 'Yes, but when I feel like something lighter I listen to romances'; 'Only at weekends, but on weekdays when I get in from work I prefer something lighter and jollier'.[118]

Responses to the question of whether they got any pleasure from listening to serious music were reasonably gratifying. Figures reveal that the concerts had been very well received, with 85 per cent of the audience saying they found the music enjoyable, and 9 per cent unsure (only 5 per cent said they hadn't enjoyed it at all). Some memorable personal opinions must have touched Gruber as he made his survey: 'Music elevates the soul of man and takes you to another world' and, best of all, 'Till this evening I didn't really enjoy playing the piano ... but now, when I listen to "La Campanella" I am in rapture from it all. For me it has opened up a new world.'[119] This would surely gladden the heart of any music worker seeking to expand the cultural range of the Soviet working class. Gruber's conclusions were practical, noting that good work was clearly being done, but that everyone needed to do more – something no one would be likely to argue with. But he did draw some factual conclusions too: the favourite piece by far had been the showiest and most virtuosic (also short) – 'La Campanella' – and the audience's firm favourites were Liszt, Chopin and Grieg. Chaykovskiy was generally liked: audiences listed other popular composers as being Glinka, Dargomïzhskiy, Beethoven and Rakhmaninov, but only weak enthusiasm was voiced for Bach, Schubert and Schumann.[120] Also, in the light of the worthy-but-dull comments offered on Schubert's educational value, a few of the listeners' more negative comments on the pre-concert lectures are revealing: 'In order to understand the lecturer you have to study the music in detail, which is impossible', and 'I don't really like the introductory talk, it's a waste of time.'[121] Clearly, the level of audience engagement depended entirely on the lecturer; some, such as Sollertinskiy, were famously inspiring, but it is inevitable that not all would manage to engage their audiences, especially if they chose to explain Marxist-Leninist theories of cultural history in order to justify playing the music at all.

A rather more tendentious survey was carried out by Lev Lebedinskiy and his then wife, Sarra Krïlova, both RAPM activists, in 1925–6. Their ensuing book, *Rabochie o literature, teatre i muzïke* [Workers on literature, theatre and music] is the most significant source I have found from this period for workers' responses to art culture, though most of the really colourful statements relate to literature and drama. For music and drama, the authors did not conduct their own survey but reviewed past issues of the workers' periodical *Rabochiy zritel'* [The worker-listener]. Their introduction to the section on music is combative from the start: 'There are those who say that only musicians are able to hold opinions on music ... that music is for a narrow circle of "initiates".'[122] Needless to say, it is impossible to find such a view expressed in the pages of journals and papers of the 1920s, and the very concept of music being only for the few is utterly out of step with the overwhelming majority of opinion from all sides of the cultural arena; but it suited RAPM to overstate their case in order to discredit other musicians. Most of the views expressed in the collection relate to opera and ballet. One worker praised the singing, the staging, scenery and costumes of a production of *Onegin*, but wondered 'why it is necessary to show us, workers, things that are over and done with, and which don't teach us anything? All those aristocrats (Onegin, Lenskiy, Tatyana) lived off the peasants, they did nothing themselves and simply didn't know what to do with themselves from all their loafing around! For us workers life is more interesting, but no one writes operas about that – even in drama, pretty much everyone ignores the real life of workers.'[123] Perhaps surprisingly, no worker recorded here (in the journal *Rabochiy zritel'*) complained of the famous Act One scene from *Onegin*, where joyfully singing serfs present their landowner, Madame Larina, with her harvest and bow down before her and her household. In fact, that very scene fell foul of a Glavrepertkom censor in 1925 who ordered its removal on the entirely accurate grounds that this episode 'conveyed a false impression of a serf idyll'.[124] Some of the most derogatory comments were aimed not at Chaykovskiy, however, but rather at Rubinstein's *Demon* (whose characters 'whined') and Verdi's *Aida*: 'What use is this to us [workers]? What about those who *built* the towers, pyramids and Sphinxes?'[125] (my italics). Instrumental music provoked less colourful responses, but the authors took as representative a letter from the Komsomol member Vladimir Edel'man published in the journal *Muzïkal'naya nov'*: 'Very rarely indeed do you meet the proletariat, or brother-komsomols [at orchestral concerts]. When you do, they are either yawning or stuffing themselves. From this you can conclude either that workers are bored at concerts, that they are just ignorant, they simply don't like it, or that the music doesn't connect with them. . . . Why do our workers love choruses and songs that are close to us and our lives, or folk melodies? . . . I think it is because we are a real, practical people. For us a work of art only has value if it helps us understand the world around us.'[126] Krïlova and Lebedinskiy do not discount the value of what they call 'academic' concerts here, but it is inevitable, given their political beliefs, that they sympathize with Edel'man's conclusion. Observing that Rosfil (the then name for what became the Moscow Philharmonia) put on concerts in working-class areas and in clubs, they called for the invitations to foreign conductors and virtuosi to cease and for them to organize more widely accessible concerts with cheaper tickets, performing concerts of Russian music from folk music to composers of the present time.[127] They mocked the fact that Russian music to Rosfil appeared to mean Stravinsky, Prokof'yev, Rebikov, Feynberg and Roslavets, all figures who, in their eyes, 'don't respond to the revolution in any way. . . . Where are the composers active in recent years, those songs sung for the last ten years by a hundred thousand members of the Komsomol and Red Army? Where are Lazarev, Buglay, Kastalskiy and others?'[128] Even in 1926, this is a clear pitch for greater inclusion of RAPM-affiliated composers and the concurrent pushing out of 'old' (meaning irrelevant) composers who may be Russian, but who do not, in Krïlova and Lebedinskiy's view, serve the needs of the proletariat. The inclusion of Roslavets was an especially sly dig, given that he still worked as a Glavrepertkom censor, was one of the foremost avant-gardist composers in Russia and had devoted his musical career to serving the new regime.[129]

Krïlova and Lebedinskiy's final call is for a sea change in the type of work done in music clubs. Declaring that workers did not need a single 'serious song', they instead advocated their own brand of humorous, satirical and cheerful songs of both anti-religious and political stripe. At the same time they damned *khaltura* – roughly definable as foxtrots, other dances, operetta and other light music, and even Soviet-era popular songs. Without appropriate ideological content, they argued, all musical culture was essentially pointless from a worker's perspective: it did not educate them or help to build socialism, while its entertainment value was merely deceptive and potentially harmful. They concluded with a brutal assessment of the appeal of classical music to workers: 'It is highly unlikely that, after a day of hard physical labour, plus demanding voluntary [or civic] work, a worker seriously wishes to sit still for five hours, straining his ears and giving himself up to daydreams. But if he . . . could choose suitable extracts from Beethoven and adapt them for playing in a club for some revolutionary festival, then we can certainly say that Beethoven can be useful.'[130] This is an extreme conclusion to draw even for Lebedinskiy, who went on record elsewhere listing numerous Western and Russian composers whose music could be judged suitable for workers' audiences, including Schubert, Chopin, Bach and Verdi – not composers traditionally associated with revolutionary fervour.[131] Yet here – and not even in the most militant period of RAPM – he and Krïlova find no use for Beethoven other than as a source of excerpts for revolutionary celebrations. There is no doubt that many workers would have agreed with their unflattering picture of tedious orchestral concerts – and after all, the authors had Edel'man's testimony to bolster their case. But the voices of all those who found solace and inspiration in those allegedly five-hour concerts find no place in this biased account. Over the next five years they would continue to be inaudible as RAPM concentrated their efforts on controlling both professional and amateur music-making.

The Modernism Question: Repertoire Politics in the Leningrad and Moscow Philharmonias, 1921–8

Alongside Russia's two main opera houses, the Bolshoy and Mariinskiy, the old Imperial orchestra and capella in Petrograd–Leningrad were the two most visible survivors from the Tsarist era. Therefore, both institutions felt under pressure to show that they were not just hoping to carry on as before, with no change: they recognized the urgent need to reach out to the widest possible audience and to show that they were fully cognisant of their political responsibilities. The Leningrad Philharmonia in its Soviet incarnation was not just an orchestra: from 1921 it became an umbrella organization comprising an orchestra, an orchestra of folk instruments, a string quartet, a mass music work department, a concert hall, music library, finance and accounts, planning department, administration and director. The structure of the Moscow Philharmonia was similar, but this is complicated by the fact that, contrary to the situation in Leningrad, Moscow had no established symphony orchestra until the founding of the Symphony Orchestra of the Soviet Philharmonia in 1928; orchestral concerts were given by the orchestra of the Bolshoy. Moreover, although the Moscow Philharmonia was, like the Leningrad Philharmonia, an umbrella organization, its name changed five times between its foundation in 1920 and 1936. Figure 1 shows the evolution of what finally became known as the Moscow State Philharmonia:

Figure 1.1: Titles of the Moscow-based Philharmonia[132]

Rossiyskaya filarmoniya (ROSFIL)	1920–8
Sovetskaya filarmoniya (SOFIL)	1928–31
Moskovskaya filarmoniya (MOSFIL)	1931–34
Gosudarstvennaya filarmoniya (GOSFIL)	1934–6
Moskovskaya Gosudarstvennaya Filarmoniya	1936–

As with the Leningrad Philharmonia, Rosfil comprised multiple departments, including a mass work department, music library, advertising and publishing, accounts, tickets, management of all the concert halls (the Great and Small Halls of the Conservatoire, later also the Chaykovskiy concert hall), planning and programming and artistic department and concert bureau. The concert bureau and mass work department worked in tandem, with the concert bureau (or 'club bureau' as it was called until 1950) arranging lectures in clubs, parks and schools, and the mass department taking care of introductory lectures and exhibitions.

The Moscow Philharmonia

In its first incarnation as ROSFIL, the Moscow Philharmonia presented its concerts at the Great Hall [*Bolshoy zal*] of the Conservatoire. Their records between its foundation and the change of name to Sofil in 1928 are almost non-existent, which makes it impossible to draw a fair comparison between the orchestral cultures of Moscow and Leningrad in these early years.[133] The little that survives in Moscow between 1920 and 1929 suggests parity between the two cities, with visits by Klemperer and Andre Segovia in 1925–6, Josef Szigeti, Ernest Ansermet, Oskar Fried and Roland Hayes, the American tenor, in 1927–8. A fair amount of new Soviet music was played in Moscow: for one thing, Rosfil put on special concerts at the *Dom Soyuzov* (House of Unions) that were openly 'proletarian' and aimed at workers. Again, the records are incomplete between 1928 and 1930 (the years which survive in the file), but these concerts show a strong orientation towards nineteenth-century Russian classics in bite-sized chunks, together with new works composed by members of RAPM. The programme for a typical, largely nineteenth-century, concert at the *Dom Soyuzov*, given on 17 November 1928, runs as follows: Borodin Nocturne [presumably from the Second String Quartet] and Polka, Donizetti aria, Alyab'ev song, assorted folk songs, Bezïmenskiy poems (reading), Red Army march, Bizet 'Habanera', gypsy song, Wieniawski Mazurka, Brahms Hungarian Dance, Chopin Waltz no. 7, Grieg, 'Anita's Dance' (from *Peer Gynt*), Glier 'Yablochko' (Sailors' Dance from *The Red Poppy*). Works by the proletarian composers Viktor Beliy, Boris Shekhter, Dmitriy Vasil'yev-Buglay, Lev Shul'gin and others featured regularly in the programmes alongside a variety of 'easy' Western and Russian miniatures and single movements. Therefore, though without gracing the concert stage of the *Bolshoy zal*, Soviet composers had a prestigious public forum for performance, organized by Rosfil. Certain names are conspicuously absent from these concerts: Myaskovskiy is nowhere to be seen, nor (unsurprisingly) are Roslavets, Mosolov, Knipper or any of the other 'modern' Soviet composers of those years; but older figures such as Glier, Kastalskiy, Grechaninov and Aleksandr Kreyn do appear regularly.

When it came to the Conservatoire programmes, the picture looks very different and arguably more 'elite'. Proletarian composers are completely absent, while Skryabin, Rakhmaninov, Myaskovskiy and Prokof'yev feature regularly. Any common ground between the two Moscow-based concert series is occupied chiefly by nineteenth-century Russian music: the *kuchka*, Chaykovskiy, Glinka and so on. Apart from that, it is not really possible to say that the Moscow Philharmonia performed more Russian and Soviet music than did their Leningrad counterpart: what patterns there are seem chiefly confined to narrower trends like a slightly higher proportion of Bruckner and Mahler in Leningrad – nearly all the performances recorded by Sollertinskiy between 1921 and 1941 took place in Leningrad.[134]

The Leningrad Philharmonia

From 1921, the Leningrad Philharmonia's archival records show that its concert programmes were carefully balanced to showcase several repertoire strands, each considered vital in its own right. There was 'Revolutionary' repertoire, which was almost wholly Western, starting with composers of the French Revolution like Étienne Méhul and François-Joseph Gossec, and revolutionary sympathizers like Beethoven (and occasionally Schumann, Liszt and Wagner). Then there was the Russian School, embracing Glinka, Dargomïzhskiy, Rubinstein, the *kuchka* and Chaykovskiy and the last pre-Revolutionary gener-ation of Taneyev, Arenskiy, Rakhmaninov, Skryabin and their contemporaries (including the still-living Glazunov, Shteynberg and Medtner). Alongside these Soviet/Russian-orientated repertoire zones, the orchestra presented standard Western classical and romantic works, extending into the twentieth century only as far as Debussy and Ravel at first (in the 1921–2 season), though this would soon change as conductors became more adventurous.

Before the start of NEP in 1921, the Leningrad Philharmonia was still being led by pre-Revolutionary figures such as Kusevitskiy, Kuper and Glazunov. Until Kuper's emigration in 1924, Russian composers still had an active champion; though Kuper regularly performed Austro-German repertoire – chiefly Beethoven, Schubert, Liszt, Brahms, Wagner and Strauss – he performed Russian repertoire in equal balance. A representative example of his programming practice is an all-Strauss programme (*Ein Heldenleben, Salome's Dance, Till Eulenspiegel*) on 9 January 1924, followed on 16 January by a programme of Myaskovskiy, Tcherepnin and Lyadov. And the fact that Glazunov was then still active as a conductor also meant that a lot of Russian repertoire from the last half-century was performed: works by Skryabin, Chaykovskiy, Rakhmaninov and Rimskiy-Korsakov were all regular fixtures in the Leningrad schedules.

After Kuper's departure in 1924 and Glazunov's steady withdrawal from conducting, the Leningrad Philharmonia's programming culture began to change. A consequence of losing Kuper and Glazunov was that replacements urgently needed to be found: Oskar Fried, who would eventually settle in the Soviet Union, began to guest conduct the orchestra in the 1922–3 season; in 1924–5 he was joined by Otto Klemperer, Heinz Unger and Hermann Abendroth, and from this point until 1928 visiting foreign conductors began to predominate in the Leningrad Philharmonia concerts. The shift in balance from the era of Kuper and Glazunov to that of the late 1920s to early 1930s, where Russian music was matched – even overshadowed – by Western repertoire, took place over a number of years and depended largely on who was visiting. The general trend among visiting conductors was to perform Western music (in which category Stravinsky can be included), with very rare exceptions: Unger, for example, conducted Skryabin and Prokof'yev in 1925, but this was highly unusual. By 1926, Nikolay Mal'ko had begun to conduct the orchestra regularly, and he followed Kuper's tradition of combining Russian and Western repertoire, though he took his programmes in a markedly more contemporary direction than Kuper ever did. From the first, Mal'ko championed young Soviet composers like Prokof'yev (mostly *in absentia*) and Shostakovich; but he was also the Soviet conductor who did most in the 1920s to introduce Soviet audiences to modern music from Europe. In addition to the efforts of both Soviet and guest conductors, the establishment of cultural relations between the Soviet Union and Western nations in 1926 produced an influx of curious composers and musicians, eager to see the new 'revolutionary' society for themselves. The earliest visitors included Alban Berg, Alfredo Casella and Darius Milhaud: Milhaud and Casella came in 1926, with Berg following a year later and Béla Bartók coming in 1929.

Table 1.1 below shows the increase in Western modernism (defined here as music composed outside Russia after 1910) in the Leningrad schedules between 1922 and 1929:

Table 1.1: Western modernism in the Leningrad Philharmonia programmes and (where possible) conductors, 1922–9[135]

1922–3
—

1923–4
Respighi, Violin Concerto, *Fountains of Rome* (Schmuller)
Schoenberg, *Verklärte Nacht* (Schmuller)
Reger, *Variations on a theme by Mozart* (Schmuller)

1924–5
Stravinsky, *Pulcinella* (Klemperer)

1925–6
Schreker, Chamber symphony, Vorspiel zu einem Drama *Die Gezeichneten*, Five Songs
Pfitzner, Preludes to Acts 1, 2 and 3 of *Palestrina* (Gauk)
Stravinsky, *Ragtime* (premiere, Dranishnikov), *Rite of Spring*
Strauss, *Ariadne* (premiere, Gauk)
Honegger, *Pacific 231* (Monteux)
*Milhaud, Symphony No. 3, *Five etudes for orchestra and piano*, *Creation du monde*, Sonata for flute, oboe and clarinet
*Satie, *Gymnopédies*
*Poulenc, *Mouvements perpetuels*
*Jean Wiener, *Deux Blues*, *Concerto Franco Américain*
*Georges Auric, *Sonatina*

1926–7
Stravinsky, Suites 1 and 2 for chamber orchestra (Stiedry), Suite from *L'Histoire du Soldat*
Schoenberg, *Five Pieces for Orchestra* (Stiedry), *Pelleas und Melisande* (Kleiber)
Reger, *Romantic Suite*
Berg, *Three scenes from Wozzeck* (Kleiber)
Casella, *Pupazzetti*, *Partita for Piano and Orchestra*, *Tre Canzoni Trecentesche* (Casella)
Castelnuovo-Tedesco, *Cipressi* (Casella)
Malipiero, *Pause del Silenzio*
Pfitzner, Violin Concerto (Stiedry), Preludes to Acts 1, 2 and 3 of *Palestrina* (Gauk)
De Falla, *Nights in the Gardens of Spain*
Ravel, *La Valse*
Krenek, Violin Concerto, Piano Concerto (Mal'ko, with Yudina)
Honegger, *Pastorale d'été* (Mal'ko)
Hindemith, *Concerto for Orchestra*

1927–8

Schoenberg, *Gurrelieder* (Mal'ko), *Five Pieces for Orchestra* (Mal'ko)

Honegger, *Pacific 231* (Mal'ko), *Le Chant de Nigamon*, *Pastorale d'été*, Nocturne from *Judith*, Concertino for Piano and Orchestra,
Horace victorieux

Milhaud, Dance Suite (Ansermet)

Auric, *Nocturnes* (Ansermet)

Bartók, Dance Suite No. 1

Stravinsky, *Mavra* (Ansermet), *Symphonies of Wind*, *Rite of Spring* (both Ansermet)

Krenek, Symphony No. 2

Hindemith, *Concerto for Orchestra*, *Kammermusik No. 2*

1928–9

Franckenstein, *Variations on a theme by Meyerbeer* (Knappertsbusch)

Reger, *Variations on a theme by Mozart* (Abendroth), *Serenade*, *Romantic Suite* (Busch), *Ballet Suite* (Busch)

Stravinsky, *Les Noces* (Klimov), *The Rite of Spring* (Ansermet), *Oedipus Rex* (Ansermet), *L'Histoire du soldat* (Ansermet), *The Nightingale*, *Apollon Musagete* (Klemperer), *Mavra* (Klemperer), *Pulcinella*, *Three Pieces* (string quartet), Piano Concerto (Ansermet)

Krenek, *Pot-pourri* (Abendroth)

Ravel, *La Valse* (Ansermet)

Honegger, *Rugby* (Ansermet), *Pacific 231*

Hindemith, 'Viola Concerto'[136] (Mal'ko)

Kammermusik no. 5 (Mal'ko)

Bartók, Piano Concerto no. 1 (Gauk, with Bartók)

Janacek, *Sinfonietta* (Busch)

De Falla, *L'amour sorcier* (Ansermet)

Modarelli, *September* (Sheydler)

Berg, *Seven Early Songs* (1908)[137]

Bliss, *Songs and Dances for Strings*[138]

*These French works were all conducted by either Milhaud or Wiener, who travelled to the Soviet Union together in 1926.

The three seasons between 1926 and 1929 must have been some of the most exciting and varied Leningrad had ever experienced, and this period certainly marks the high point of Western modernism in the Soviet Union under NEP. Set alongside this was a very similar picture in opera: as Schwarz noted, the Leningrad premieres of Schreker's *Der ferne Klang*, Berg's *Wozzeck*, Stravinsky's *Pulcinella* and *Renard* and Prokof'yev's *Love for Three*

Oranges all took place between 1925 and 1927 at the Leningrad Mariinskiy,[139] while its 'rival' opera theatre the Malïy staged Krenek's *Der Sprung über den Schatten* (1927) and *Jonny spielt auf* (1928).[140] Boris Schwarz cautions against believing that these years were nothing but an unchallenged success for modernists, noting that several other operas (including Hindemith's *Neues vom Tage*) had to be cancelled due to 'increasing agitation' from the proletarian side, though he does not provide details, and I have not found evidence of this in any journal or archival record of the time.[141]

Debates in the Music Press

Although we might assume that RAPM would be bitterly opposed to Western modernism, there is in fact very little evidence to suggest that it was a major target. This can easily be gauged from the music journals of the time as well as from archival records; attacks from the extreme proletarian side tended to be more focused on personal enemies and particular bête-noirs (Skryabin, the jazz entertainer Leonid Utësov, Rakhmaninov, Roslavets, Aleksandr Mosolov, church music) than on Western modernism or on the proliferation of Western conductors. Reviews of Ansermet's three May 1929 programmes in the moderate journal *Rabochiy i teatr* were glowing in their praise for Ansermet and the novelty of the music he performed.[142] Even RAPM's hostility towards Krenek stemmed from the perceived jazz content of *Jonny* rather than his modernism per se (or his foreignness), just as when they railed against 'NEPman music' it was the light and dance genres they objected to, rather than European modernists specifically.[143] Nor did they generally object to foreign conductors on the Moscow and Leningrad stages: writing in the RAPM journal *Za proletarskuyu muzïku*, Anatoliy Groman-Solovtsov and V. Voloshnikov gave a moderately favourable review to Beethoven concerts in January 1932 given by Oskar Fried and Eugen Jochum in Moscow. Their objections focused chiefly on the poor quality of the orchestral playing, on the programme essay by Sergey Chemodanov, which they disliked, and on Fried's 'bloodless and formal' interpretation of the Fifth Symphony, in which he allegedly downplayed precisely those elements of Beethoven's style that Soviet audiences warmed to the most: his heroic and revolutionary voice rather than his 'mystical' or 'religious' tendencies. Of the two conductors, the reviewers expressed strong preference for Jochum, who was only twenty-seven at the time – a whole generation younger than Fried. Jochum's 'deeply emotional' conducting was clearly far more appealing to Soviet tastes, at least in the opinions of these reviewers.[144] Bartók's visit to Moscow in January 1929 drew rather grudging praise from the reviewer (Anatoliy Groman again) for *Proletarskiy muzïkant*, who opined that his earlier works, though much cruder, won more enthusiastic applause than his more polished, but much less folk-inflected later ones; he also sniped at Bartók's pianism ('not first-rate'), and suggested that his music would probably sound a lot better 'in the hands of a real master'.[145] There is little sense in these journals of a blanket hostility to European modernists on the part of the RAPMovtsï – they were much more preoccupied with attacking perceived cultural malaise in their own backyards, antagonizing and bullying their rivals, ensuring that workers were being properly supplied with suitable music and not dancing to foxtrots and tangos, and calling for tighter restrictions on church music. In this respect, the old Imperial capella – renamed the Leningrad Capella – did find itself a target, and proved less able to defend itself than the more powerful Philharmonias.[146] However, more covert hostilities were sometimes voiced: an unsigned editorial in the June 1929 edition of *Proletarskiy muzïkant* accused those 'six or seven people who hold all the levers of our musical life' of a gross failure to protect Soviet audiences from harmful Western influences, in which category the writers explicitly include Prokof'yev and implicitly the whole of the 'urban' school (in which they certainly included Honegger, and possibly also Milhaud). Under the pretence of speaking not only on behalf of RAPM (though the writer does complain that music by Koval' and Davidenko is overlooked), the writer claims to be speaking for fellow travellers and even ASM, all of whom suffer from what the anonymous author, with heavy sarcasm, calls the 'benevolent neutrality' of those whose undue influence in Soviet musical life champion this Western decadence and neglect their own composers. Finally, the writer makes a formal charge: 'In the area of musical creativity we can observe a tendency to insinuate under the pretence of formal and technical "progress" the clearly harmful creativity of the modern-day bour-geoisie, which reflects the period of social degeneration and emotional devastation of the ruling classes.'[147] This is about as close as RAPM get to open complaints about the proliferation of Western new music in the major concert programmes, and even here the only composer 'denounced' is Prokof'yev. The archival record also does not show that, even behind the scenes, RAPM tried, in any organized or concerted way, to stop Western contemporary music being performed by the Philharmonias.

However, there is no doubt that the proliferation of Western contemporary music on the Soviet concert stage – and even the perceived domination of ASM in the mid-1920s – was a cause for concern to many, and not only on the hard-line proletarian side. While this should not be interpreted as ideological hostility to the West, or to modernism *per se*, several writers and composers were evidently concerned that Soviet composers were being squeezed out; or even that musical institutions were supporting the 'wrong' composers. Inevitably, it was the proletarian composers who felt the most grievance in this regard: they already felt that the musical 'establishment' merely tolerated their music and gave it the absolute minimum of publicity, and that is principally why it was RAPM members (and, before 1929, ORKiMD members too) who tended to write openly in the music press about weaknesses in Leningrad and Moscow concert life. But we should not leap to the conclusion that all such writers were merely concerned with seizing power and dominance, nor should we regard individual statements as necessarily representative of collective views. For one thing, the tone of several important articles expressing concern about trends in Western contemporary music is not one of philistine militancy, but rather of a much milder – even old-fashioned – conservatism. Second, there is no doubt that many on the proletarian side – whether from ORKiMD or RAPM – had first-hand experience of workers' dislike of modern music, and found it incredibly frustrating that, in the 'new' Soviet age, state-funded institutions continued to cater for minority 'elite' tastes. *Muzïka i revoliutsiya* published an anonymous attack on the young composer Mosolov in 1927, which was almost certainly written by its editor Lev Shul'gin. Shul'gin was an interesting figure: one of the few older members of RAPM and indeed one of its founders in 1923. He broke away from the group in 1925 and formed ORKiMD (Association of Revolutionary Composers and Music Workers), a far more inclusive organization whose journal (*Muzïka i revoliutsiya*) welcomed a mixed range of opinions, including those on contemporary Western and Soviet music. Asaf'yev, for example, was a regular contributor despite being the founder of ASM and an active supporter of much of the kind of music Shul'gin himself disliked.

The article in question, '"Levïy" flang sovremennoy muzïki' [The 'left' wing of contemporary music], castigates Mosolov's *Children's Songs* and *Four Newspaper Advertisements*, both of which were written in a self-consciously avant-garde style that blatantly set out to shock. As though wishing to demonstrate that the author's distaste for Mosolov's brand of modernism was not motivated by a spirit of anti-Westernism or anti-modernism, the author cites Alfredo Casella's own deprecation of aggressive avant-gardism ('Woe to the composer who uses last year's chords in his works of today. He will be told: "This is not the done thing." ').[148] Later that year, the journal published a translation of an article by the Berlin music critic S. A. Liberson written in response to the recent (1926) contemporary music festival in Donaueschingen in which music for an early electronic piano had been performed that, in his opinion, was less art than industry, an illustration of 'speculative theory' – a path not taken, he asserts, by the greatest talents, whose music genuinely enriches the 'treasury of art'. The Alois Habas, Schoenbergs and Stravinskys of the present, he concludes, do not represent the music of the future: rather, the future of true music still awaits its real master, who will lead it once again to its former heights.[149] Obviously, views of this sort expressed by foreign writers gave valuable support to Soviet musicians who had little patience with radical avant-gardism on their own soil. A more considered protest in this vein was voiced by the moderate composer Aleksandr Veprik, a former Red Professor[150] who travelled to Europe in 1927 and met Schoenberg, Hindemith and Ravel. Though a passionate admirer of Schoenberg's earlier, more romantic, music, when Veprik realized the full extent of his idol's preoccupation with 12-note technique (presumably – as Veprik saw it – at the expense of expressive content, or of any desire to reach out to listeners) he was horrified. It was just as much the intention behind the music he heard as its sound (which he found disorientating and 'revolting') that appalled him. Shocked and disappointed, he wrote to his friend and colleague Nadezhda Bryusova that:

> For us, music is first of all a revelation: we expect to find a Weltanschauung there, an attitude towards the world. Here it's very different. They *make* music over here, and that's all. Full stop. Music is seen as the use of timbre or rhythm only as the solution to a structural problem. . . . That is the principal distinction between contemporary Germany and what we do, all that is dear to us.[151]

Two years after his trip to Europe, Veprik published an article in *Muzïka i revoliutsiya* protesting at what he regarded as a misguided appropriation of the terms 'left' and 'right' in contemporary Soviet music criticism. In the West, he argued, composers either use avant-garde techniques or they don't – but there was nothing inherently 'left' or 'right' about their aesthetic choice. It was only when those advanced techniques were in the hands of composers like Hindemith (a composer of 'a-emotional' music) that they became reactionary. Pressing his point, Veprik noted that, if Soviet writers took this terminology to its logical conclusion, Schoenberg would be 'left' and Rakhmaninov 'right', yet both were equally alien to Soviet musicians precisely because of their 'reactionary' views, and not because of their music.[152] This was an original position, and a rather uncommon one: Veprik seems to be saying that no technique, no matter how avant-garde, was inherently out of bounds for Soviet composers. Rather, the critical question would be the ideological orientation of the work produced. But the essential point for Veprik was that there must *be* such an orientation: simply to produce 'pure' music would be to echo what was – for him and for several others – the same heartless, socially disengaged aesthetic of the West. More hard-line proletarian colleagues would have scoffed at this argument, since they believed that Soviet composers should be writing music that appealed to mass audiences, and mass audiences would never learn to love avant-garde music.

Veprik may have been in part responding to an article – again anonymous, again very probably written by Shul'gin – published a year earlier, in which the author freely uses the terms 'left' and 'right' in relation to both Western and Soviet contemporary music, in particular that of the 'industrial' versus the 'folk' type. Into the 'industrial' camp go, predictably enough, Milhaud, Poulenc, Honegger, Antheil, Deshevov and Mosolov. Chiming sympathetically with Veprik's comments to Bryusova in 1927, the author objects to their 'machine music' thus: 'In their glorification of "things" and "mechanization", the human being, with all his emotions and strivings, is totally bypassed; he has somehow fallen from view from these [supposedly] "revolutionary" composers.' The 'revolutionaries' the author scorns here had been championed by the writer Orest Tsekhovnitser, whose article 'Novaya muzïka i proletariat' [New music and the proletariat] in the ASM journal *Sovremennaya muzïka* [Contemporary music] in 1927–8 argued that those resisting the passive continuation of the 'narodnicheskiy' trend in art were the real revolutionaries in contemporary Soviet music. The author particularly takes umbrage at Tsekhovnitser's allegation that workers were bored with older classical music ('even Beethoven's "Appassionata"') and at his dismissal of practically every single distinguished name in Russian music of the time as representative of 'academicism, impressionism, psychologism, Skryabinism', including Myaskovsky, Gedike, Rakhmaninov and Medtner.

'Alone in composing "deeply felt, joyous music"', huffed the author, were apparently only 'Mosolov, Deshevov, Schillinger, and several other young composers'.[153] It is clear that Shul'gin – the likely author of this editorial – was venting his frustration at what was, to him, a positively slavish emulation of the very worst Western trends in the name of 'revolution'.

Fundamentally, this anonymous author and Veprik are in agreement over the absolute necessity for Soviet music to contain expressive content and an appropriate ideological message. Their position is underlined by the collective protest issued by ORKiMD in May–June 1928, when they publicly objected to ASM's choice of Schillinger's 'October' rhapsody to represent Soviet music at the ISCM festival in Siena. Although it used revolutionary and everyday songs (the Internationale, 'Bravely, comrades' and others), ORKiMD argued that its portrayal of the revolutionary theme was ambiguous at best and trivial at worst. They listed works that in their view would have been far more suitable: Gnesin's *Symphonic monument*, Kreyn's *Funeral Ode* or Shostakovich's 'October' Symphony, which all took the revolutionary theme much more seriously.[154] What is admirable in this protest is the lack of obvious partisanship: the signatories knew perfectly well that Shostakovich was linked with Asaf'yev's Leningrad branch of ASM, who had sponsored the premiere of his First Symphony, while neither Gnesin nor Kreyn were members of ORKiMD.

These early critics of Western modernism, therefore, were relatively mild and were certainly not powerful, as the programmes of the Leningrad Philharmonia make abundantly clear. Their animosity stemmed not from personal resentment so much as from exasperation on behalf of the worker audiences that ORKiMD in particular were committed to, and from a belief that to neglect the mass listener and to aim one's work solely at a small educated elite was against the spirit of the times. There were no militant voices calling for the total banishment of these composers from the Philharmonia programmes or from the opera stages: a blanket 'ban' (and then a tacit one) would not come until much later, and I will return to this in Chapter Four.

The Church Music Problem

The third major organization discussed in this chapter was the old Imperial capella in St Petersburg. The Imperial capella was initially renamed the Petrograd People's Choral Academy (1918), gaining the appellation 'Academic' in 1922 and becoming the Leningrad State Academic Capella.

Its fortunes in the early years were inextricably bound up with its director, Mikhail Klimov, whose training, personal interests and musical tastes shaped its repertoire over the crucial years of the choir's transformation from a relic of the Imperial age to a fully fledged Soviet ensemble. He took over direction of the choir in 1918 and continued in his post until he was forced to step down by serious illness in 1935, from which he died two years later.

Klimov had been a student at the St Petersburg Conservatoire, where he was taught composition and conducting by Rimskiy-Korsakov, Lyadov and Tcherepnin. In addition to this, he was a gifted administrator and an astute diplomat, traits that were valued highly in the changeable years of the 1920s, when the choir's future existence was in question. From the time of their first concert in 1918, Klimov's good relationship with Lunacharskiy proved critical to the capella's survival during the turbulent 1920s. He supported them as a first-rate choir with a unique role to play in bringing bourgeois culture to the masses, and he valued Klimov as a talented professional who could be entrusted with the capella's Soviet 'perestroika'. Moreover, Klimov's talents as an administrator were useful to Lunacharskiy beyond his work in the capella. From 1925, Klimov – at Lunacharskiy's behest – joined the administration of the Leningrad Philharmonia, and the two organizations maintained a close relationship, with the capella acting as the Philharmonia's official choir.[155]

The capella's repertoire before 1917 was not confined only to sacred works; it had never been only a chapel choir, and this is largely what enabled it to adapt to the new conditions. Among the secular pieces performed before 1917 were nineteenth-century romances (by Arenskiy, Glinka, Gounod and others), choruses from Russian and Western operas (*Prince Igor*, *Khovanshchina*, *Orfeo*, *Tannhäuser* and others) as well as major Western sacred works like Palestrina's *Missa Papae Marcelli*, Handel's *Messiah* and others.[156] Both sacred and secular repertoire would be retained and further developed after 1917, but initially Klimov had no assurance that the capella's sacred repertoire would be acceptable to the new Soviet government. Their first post-revolutionary concert – at which they sang sacred music as well as Russian folk songs – was in February 1918, at the House of the Worker-Peasant Army, prefaced by a lecture by Lunacharskiy on 'The separation of the Church from the State and the art of church singing'.[157] The essence of Lunacharskiy's argument was that Russian church singing had a cultural value completely independent of its religious context, and this position – though certainly not left unchallenged – paved the way for the development of the capella's Soviet-era identity.[158] A number of reforms were put in place, including formalizing Klimov's position as manager and artistic director from 1919 and the introduction of women in the choir from March 1920.

Table 1.2 shows a list of major sacred works performed by the capella between 1918 and 1932, indicating which works were added after 1917:[159]

Table 1.2: Major sacred/biblical works in the capella repertoire, 1918–32

Mozart, Requiem (pre-1917)
Beethoven, *Missa Solemnis* (pre-1917)
Rakhmaninov, *All-Night Vigil* (added post-1917)
Chaykovskiy, *Liturgy of St John Chrysostom* (added post-1917)
Berlioz, Requiem and *Te Deum* (Requiem pre-1917; *Te Deum* performed only once, in 1921–2
Verdi, Requiem (added post-1917, first performed 1928)
Bach, St Matthew Passion, St John Passion and B Minor Mass, Cantata no. 80 (only B Minor Mass pre-1917)
Handel, *Samson*, *Judas Maccabeus* (all pre-1917; note that *Messiah* was in their repertoire, but not performed in the Lenin–Stalin period)
Brahms, *German Requiem* (added post-1917; performed in 1929, once only, conducted by Otto Klemperer)

The retention of older classics like Mozart's Requiem and Beethoven's *Missa Solemnis* remained uncontroversial throughout the 1920s; in fact, Mozart's Requiem was adopted as a key work of the Soviet era, never leaving the Philharmonia schedules, even during the most insular years of Stalinism when Western repertoire was kept to an absolute minimum. It was performed in the very first of the 'People's Concerts' – a series organized by Narkompros for proletarian audiences – and took place in the Winter Palace on May Day 1918, as a memorial to those killed in the revolution.[160] It was also the Requiem of choice when Lenin died in 1924; Klimov conducted it with the Leningrad Philharmonia in special Lenin memorial concerts that year (25 January and 8 February), paired with Chopin's Funeral March (from the B flat Minor Piano Sonata op. 35) and the old (pre) revolutionary song 'You fell as victims'. Beethoven's *Missa Solemnis* had a special St Petersburg history; Beethoven himself had requested a performance of it in March 1824 and therefore during the centenary years of its premiere – 1924 – it was played again in celebration of the fact, though its Soviet premiere had actually taken place the year before. Soviet performances of Bach's Passions were pioneered by Klimov; the last pre-revolutionary performance of either of them that I have been able to trace was the Russian Musical Society's concert of 9 December 1913 in the Moscow Conservatoire Great Hall, where the St Matthew Passion was sung in a new Russian translation (possibly for the first time in Russia).[161] It seems that the Passions were not widely known to Russian audiences until Klimov championed them, performing both in the 1920s with the capella and Leningrad Philharmonia. Writing in the early Khrushchev period, the Soviet musicologist A. Anisimov recalled that these Bach performances were truly memorable, prompting students who were used to thinking of Bach as 'boring' to revisit their prejudices. Klimov made his own performing editions, heavily marked up with expression marks and, Anisimov claims, no other Soviet choir made Bach seem so accessible.[162]

From September 1922 the capella came under the direction of the newly created Glavprofobr and had to submit repertoire plans for inspection to Glavnauka (Narkompros),[163] which immediately impacted upon their repertoire plans. Klimov began to submit programmes for inspection with themed headings such as: Russian folk song (four concerts), Russian choral music (eleven concerts), Russian choral literature of the fifteenth to seventeenth centuries (one concert), Western choral literature (five concerts), works for choir, soloists and orchestra (five concerts).[164] But the single concert devoted to fifteenth- to seventeenth-century Russian choral music was not allowed to go ahead.[165] On the Narkompros repertoire committee that year were three highly respected cultural and musical figures: Lunacharskiy himself, the music education specialist Nadezhda Bryusova and the theoretician Boleslav Yavorskiy. All evidently respected Klimov and the capella, but felt unable to permit them to perform what was self-evidently Orthodox choral liturgy. Klimov's justification for retaining old Orthodox chant was that it gave, as he put it, 'unsurpassed examples of musical thought and creativity from unique documentary materials that show us some idea of the sources . . . of Russian professional choral song'.[166] He was backed by no less a figure than Asaf'yev, who asserted that its 'ancient sacred melos is no less significant than the monuments of ancient Russian [icon] painting'.[167] But their historical arguments could not stand up against what was evidently – to the repertoire committee – a step too far towards propagandizing church music in a State that had made the propaganda of religion a criminal offence.

Tension would simmer over the capella's retention of sacred works, both Russian and Western, over several years. Whether to allow the capella to programme sacred music at all was a sensitive question, batted back and forth within various Narkompros bodies over the next decade. Lunacharskiy intervened quickly when Glavrepertkom went so far as to ban religious works completely in December 1923.[168] After his intercession, an outright ban of Western sacred music would not be broached again. This distinction between Russian and Western sacred repertoires became a turning point in the presentation and reception of Western sacred music and its subsequent re-branding as effectively secular. Once its identity had been properly formed and justified in the context of Soviet cultural policies, it could freely maintain its position as a bastion of civilized culture while posing no religious threat.

However, the formation of that neutralized identity took time, and censors would still raise objections to Western sacred works well into the 1920s. In the middle of the 1923–4 season, Glavrepertkom aggressively demanded to know for whom this demonstration of 'religious emotion' was intended, citing works by Lassus, Bach, Beethoven and others as examples.[169] And in July 1924, at a meeting of the music section of the scientific-artistic sector of the State Academic Council [Gosudarstvennïy uchënïy sovet, or GUS], Bryusova presented a critical evaluation of the capella, after which GUS passed a resolution that recognized the capella's 'enlightening' role but demanded that it strengthen its ideological credentials. As a result of this resolution, Klimov's plans for a concert of Russian choral art of the fifteenth to the seventeenth centuries were again dropped. They would be revived (albeit briefly, and then only in private concerts) only after Narkompros lost its power in 1932.

Bryusova's hard-line attitude towards the capella's sacred repertoire caused friction in Narkompros, but she never managed to have it banned altogether. Counter-arguments in its defence, coming from Klimov himself and endorsed by Lunacharskiy, were founded on the cultural value of such repertoire to the audience, and on the professional value of retaining them for the capella's singers.[170] Clearly, the argument that sacred repertoire was essential for maintaining professional standards carried a lot of weight. But whereas Lunacharskiy had publicly defended the capella's retention of 'classical' repertoire, no one cared to endorse Russian sacred music, and it rapidly became a lost cause.[171] A directive from Glavrepertkom in July 1928 stated that, while there was no objection to the inclusion in the capella's work plan of Bach's Passions and B Minor Mass, they must not be performed more than twice a year, and not on any day coinciding with the church calendar. In the same directive, Russian seventeenth- and eighteenth-century choral music was explicitly banned.[172] Chaykovskiy's *Liturgy* had already vanished from the capella's schedules four years earlier, and after various attempts to oust Rakhmaninov's *All-Night Vigil* from the capella's repertoire, it was finally dropped after 1928. Neither work would be sung by a major state choir again until the mid-1960s.[173]

Though we might suspect militant proletarian groups of being behind vetoes of sacred music, Glavrepertkom documents from 1928 show that the censor's hand at this time was apparently that of the modernist composer and innovator Roslavets, an avowed enemy of the 'mass song' representatives of the proletarian cause who were soon to play an invasive role in Soviet musical life. Roslavets was fairly militant in his own way: he passionately supported the Soviet avant-garde and considered advanced music essential for forming the tastes of the Soviet masses. In this he was bitterly opposed by those proletarian musicians who favoured mass songs, marches and other simplified genres. But he was no enemy of Western music, nor even of sacred music per se. There is no evidence that Roslavets wanted to ban Western sacred music; it is more likely that he wished to avoid the capella or the Philharmonias being charged with religious propaganda. This sense of caution, probably, is what lay behind his injunction to remove either one of the Requiems of Mozart or Verdi from the capella's proposed work plan for 1927–8.[174] Roslavets passed every one of the capella's requests to perform Bach's Passions and B Minor Mass, the Mozart and Berlioz Requiems, and Beethoven's *Missa Solemnis*. The proposed concert of Russian seventeenth- and eighteenth-century choral music, however, was prohibited outright as 'unsuitable'.[175] But Glavrepertkom nonetheless cautioned the capella not to perform any of the sacred works on a church feast day and forbade the performance of Beethoven's *Missa Solemnis* and Mozart's Requiem in workers' clubs.[176] In consequence, the only religious work presented at the Leningrad Philharmonia with the capella in the two seasons between 1928 and 1930 was Brahms's *German Requiem* (1929), in its one and only performance during the Stalin period, conducted by Otto Klemperer (with Stravinsky's *Apollon musagète* as the partnering work).

On the eve of the so-called 'Cultural Revolution', then, Soviet musical life had taken major defining steps. Its evolving canon accepted key Western and Russian classics and, with the exception of Russian sacred music, no works or composers had been targeted as suitable for outright bans. What can be broadly defined as Western contemporary music – chiefly Central European music – had established a firm place in the Philharmonias' repertoire, and music by Soviet composers, though present, did not yet occupy a significant place in orchestral programmes. This would change significantly in the 1930s, as will be seen in Chapter Four, but first the chief agents of Soviet musical life – established composers, pedagogues and musicologists – had to negotiate the most difficult period of their new history – the years of proletarian domination that threatened to overturn all they had worked for.

CHAPTER TWO

CULTURAL REVOLUTION, REPERTOIRE POLITICS AND THE CLASSICS

The 'Great Turning Point' [*Velikiy perelom*, also often translated as the 'Great Break'] was announced as a formal change of direction in Soviet economics in 1929 and marked the end of the New Economic Policy (NEP) period, which Lenin had introduced in 1921 as a way of enabling the new Soviet economy to stabilize and grow after its disastrous start under war communism. Since NEP was acknowledged to be an intermediate stage towards full socialism – Lenin called it 'state capitalism' – when Stalin scrapped it in favour of policies that directly contradicted NEP's, such as agrarian collectivization and grain requisition, he was effectively returning the USSR to the more radical economic model of the immediate post-revolutionary period (1917–21). The impact of such a massive change of socio-economic policy on cultural life is often discussed in terms of the more aggressive 'cultural revolution as class war' period coinciding with the First Five-Year Plan (1928–32).[1] But Katerina Clark and Evgeny Dobrenko argue that the cultural climate started to become more hard line as early as 1927, with attacks on the 'Left Opposition' headed by Leon Trotskiy within the Politburo itself, and mirrored in LEF, a group that drew in avant-garde artists such as the poet Vladimir Mayakovskiy, Aleksandr Rodchenko and Sergey Eyzenshteyn.[2] Though all three artists named here were successful in the Stalin period too (Mayakovskiy mainly posthumously, after his death by suicide in 1930), the whole LEF movement in the arts was harnessed to 'Trotskiyism' by its opponents in the proletarian art movements.

Soviet music during this period found itself, therefore, in what seems a paradoxical situation: artists wholly devoted to the communist cause became divided along lines of avant-garde versus 'proletarian' art. Thus the most bitter opponents of the early Soviet serialist, and committed communist, Nikolay Roslavets were not the 'soft' modernists such as Asaf'yev and Myaskovskiy, nor the traditionalists in the Conservatoires who believed in bringing Bach and Beethoven to the workers, but rather Lev Lebedinskiy and other members of RAPM, precisely because they were fighting over the same territory – how to compose new music for the masses. Roslavets believed in 'raising' the general cultural level and not 'writing down' to people unfamiliar with modern music; RAPM believed in educating the masses only to the level required for political indoctrination, and hence demanded an alarmingly restricted musical diet. They did not limit their antagonisms to fellow art music composers: RAPM was just as hostile to the light music entertainer Leonid Utësov as it was to all kinds of popular music-making, especially the Western dance crazes for tangos, foxtrots and so on; gypsy romances and popular songs were all perennial targets for RAPM.[3] Equally in RAPM's sights, though usually less aggressively targeted, was the less radical wing of musical modernism, as represented by the Associations of Contemporary Music (ASM in Moscow, LASM in Leningrad), organiza-tions run by the musical elite of the time such as Asaf'yev and Myaskovskiy, who worked closely with international colleagues (publishers, music socie-ties, festivals and individual musicians and composers) in order to foster a strong, international cultural base for Soviet music and musicians.[4]

Although the classics had always been part of RAPM's approved reper-toire for the proletariat – Beethoven and Musorgskiy were their two staple composers – it is clear that certain composers and works were judged to be more desirable than others. The future leader of the Committee for Arts Affairs in the late 1930s, Platon Kerzhentsev, was a Proletkul't activist in the 1920s and promoted to head of Agitprop around 1928. He quickly weighed in with public criticism of the Bolshoy's conservative choices of opera in *Pravda* which, as Marina Frolova-Walker and Jonathan Walker point out, had the unintended result of initially leading Soviet modernists to believe that they had found a new supporter.[5] In fact, Kerzhentsev's position proved to be relatively hostile to musicians: in a speech made in 1929 he denounced *The Queen of Spades* and *The Demon* as 'not simply unpleasant but actually harmful' and opined that opera theatres that staged such repertoire should no longer exist.[6]

Although RAPM had from the first included Musorgskiy in their unof-ficial canon of approved composers, their image of him as a proto-revolutionary composer depended on a very selective reading of his operas.

Khovanshchina – never an easy work to be quite sure of, not least because Musorgskiy never finished it – eventually became an RAPM target by virtue of its very ambiguity. Perhaps following in the direction signalled earlier by Kerzhentsev, Lev Lebedinskiy added his voice to Agitprop's in denouncing the staging methods of the opera houses and found inappropriate propagandizing of 'class enemies' even in Musorgskiy's opera:

> Why, the devil take it, when we see an opera by Musorgskiy, Rimskiy, Bizet or Beethoven, do we not see this 'great past' that they tell us about, but the rather dull, petty contemporary bourgeois or kulak? Take for example Khovanshchina. . . . Think of the Act Three finale. They sing a real prayer; the chorus approaches the footlights, the tempo slows, achieving a pure church sound. And not only that, but the chorus is the most encored part, twice repeating to the joy of the sons of priests in the audience. Marfa in Khovanshchina is not what Musorgskiy intended, tender and feminine, but a type of Russian merchant's wife, vulgar and gypsy-like, singing with unrestrained portamento. And Dosifey sings like a Russian deacon: not the political leader Musorgskiy wished to depict. . . .
>
> And when we see the Tsar's Bride, it is the same: we know what Rimskiy intended – to show the terrible conditions of women in old Rus and even in his own time – . . . But what do we see in the production? In the first place, a lovers' tiff, the petty merchant ideology of the Sobakin's house, the idyll of the fat kulak baker.[7]

More horrors were to come Lebedinskiy's way: on seeing *Carmen*, he saw 'not the young working girl, mainly simple, even naïve, spontaneously relating to other people and to nature, but a fat, dull, well-drilled *nepmansha*, the contemporary kept woman who lounges around Petrovka, gross, stupid and boundlessly trivial [*poshliy*]'.[8] Finally, he concluded that this wasn't a problem with Russian musical heritage as such, but rather with contemporary Soviet 'class enemies' who propagandize the kulaks and merchants instead of seeking directly to serve proletarian ideology. In short, he was not saying that *Khovanshchina*, *The Tsar's Bride* and *Carmen* should not be staged: he was only criticizing the way in which Soviet directors were interpreting them. Though after 1932 writers were quick to denounce RAPM for their alleged condemnation of great masters of Russian music, in fact hostility to the *kuchka*, Chaykovskiy and others was not a constant preoccupation of RAPM, who devoted relatively little energy to criticizing them in comparison with their campaigns against Rakhmaninov, Roslavets and their perennial targets, *khaltura*, religious music and jazz.

The All-Union Conferences, 1929–31

Towards the end of the 'proletarian' era Glaviskusstvo held a number of All-Union conferences dedicated to various branches of art workers. It is chiefly from stenographic reports and minutes that we can gauge some of the problems that amateur music groups encountered, though as usual, most comments come from activists rather than participants. By 1930, choral conductors working in schools and factory clubs were reporting high levels of hostility from workers, pointing to a lack of decent resources and flagging motivation.[9] Reasons for this can easily be gleaned from the minutes of other, similar, meetings. At one of the June 1929 meetings of the All-Russian Music Conference (spread out over several days), a representative of Profsoiuzov insisted on the necessity to protect the working class from the harmful influence of decadent Western music, or any tendency that might 'stir religious feelings'.[10] In another meeting, the speaker Chicherov expanded on a favourite RAPM theme: 'Comrades, we await decisive action against that perverted art, in which our bourgeoisie take such pleasure – against foxtrotism, charlestonism [which] have regrettably infected the evening parties of our young people . . . we must find them something better, healthier.'[11] On the third day of the conference Robert Pel'she[12] added his voice to this chorus of disapproval: 'The power of the foxtrot, shimmy and Charleston is persistently knocking at the doors of art clubs', but adds that, though 'Muscovites know that Dom Soiuzov [House of Unions] is a great place to go to for gypsy concerts, decadent singing and dance . . . [the authorities] have . . . begun to organize concerts for workers . . . to sow real musical culture and not . . . musical depravity.'[13] With such grim-faced intolerance of light music now regarded as entirely consonant with building socialism through mass musical work, it is hardly surprising if the appeal of singing in amateur choirs or playing in ensembles was wearing thin for some club musicians.

Another target of RAPM was the surviving remnants of church music, whether that was art music derived from the Russian Orthodox tradition or songs sung by non-denominational worshippers. This had never been the province only of RAPM – the Glavrepertkom censor had excised most

Russian sacred music from the Leningrad Philharmonia repertoire plans in the early 1920s – but Narkompros had never maintained a particularly strict policy on monitoring remnants of church music activity. When another speaker at the conference, Nikitin, called for an end to the direction of village choirs by ex-church singers who may exert a parlous influence on young singers, Lunacharskiy – still in his post at this point – chose to respond directly to this point in his own speech, in a way that was probably not congenial to the overwhelming majority of delegates. Acknowledging that having ex-precentors direct village choirs was probably not ideal and may 'objectively' even be harmful, he nevertheless defended the practice:

> They [certain practitioners] encourage art of a religious character, which they clutch hold of as the sole rope of assistance in the stormy sea of life. Objectively, they are to some degree harmful, but perhaps not entirely so, for in searching for these vague metaphysical sensations they truly produce real art. They [church singers] can be very talented. In this search they find peace and comfort; they find all those elements that are useful for genuine art, which then gives us the possibility of approaching those heights of joy, in the highest sense of the word.[14]

Clearly, this particular problem was not resolved quickly, because at the 1931 All-Russian Conference on Amateur Art, the speaker Okushko called for urgent action on this very topic: 'We still have to pose the question of liquidating musical illiteracy as a political issue. Because this illiteracy is used by our class enemies – priests, precentors, popes and vermin who shove their own art at us because we are not literate enough.'[15] If, as it sounds, this is a genuine voice of the 'people', it tells us that militant propaganda was, at least in some quarters, very successful.

Returning to the quality of music available to amateur groups, a Leningrad delegate (Anisimov) reported that a choir member had complained to him that they had nothing to sing except for Davidenko's mass song 'They Wanted to Defeat Us'. In response, Anisimov reported, 'I said, "Let's do 'Ekh, tï dolya moya', then 'Komsomolskiy March'" ... then the same member said "Let's sing 'They Wanted to Defeat Us'"'. The picture Anisimov paints is of singers utterly bored with the same songs, yet his solution is not really to expand the range of songs but rather to urge the choir to appreciate them better: 'Don't say "They Wanted to Defeat Us" is boring ... When songs have a real political meaning, they're not boring.'[16]

This picture of jaded workers and dogmatic choirmasters is a far cry from the more vivid picture of amateur music-making of the earlier revolutionary period, and even from that of the immediate pre-revolutionary years, where workers' choirs sang folk and classical repertoire at People's Houses and factories. Under the deadening hand of militant proletarianism, the life-blood of mass music-making – good music that people loved and wanted to sing and play – was drained from the very people whom the militant activists claimed they wished to help and inspire.

Repertoire Politics during the 'Great Break'

One of the Leningrad Philharmonia's duties, right from its earliest post-revolutionary years, was to provide educational concerts for workers. They did this in a number of ways, but by far the most common was to put on special concerts for them, featuring less demanding repertoire (single movements, works with an obvious revolutionary subject) and putting on special introductory lectures. When planning repertoire, the Philharmonia's committees typically drew up cycles of concerts from different categories of music, divided by nationality and/or by historical epoch. A typical lecture plan drawn up by members of the Leningrad Philharmonia repertoire and planning committee for a cycle of chamber music concert-lectures in 1925 ran as follows:

> The musical life of France and Germany in the eighteenth century and music of the Great French Revolution. Content of lecture: the eighteenth century from a socialist point of view. The general musical types of the epoch. What were the connections to the previous period? Enlightenment absolutism and music. The general significance of opera. Influence of the commercial bourgeoisie and development of opera and chamber music. The social position of musicians. Haydn and Mozart as a musical expression of the eighteenth century. For which social strata did Haydn and Mozart compose? Music in Revolutionary Paris. The role of music as a social-educational force. Music festivals and songs of the Great French Revolution. The significance of revolutionary music for the further development of art. Music played: Michael Haydn D major Quartet, Couperin Sarabande, Rameau Two Dances for Clavecin, Mozart Violin Sonata in E major, old French songs, opera arias.

The driving force behind this kind of Enlightenment-focused planning can be summed up in two words: inheritance and education. Long before what Régis Debray has termed the 'totalitarian hijacking of the Enlightenment' of the early Cold War,[17] Soviet musicians were working to present the history of music to their new audiences as an unbroken stream of rationalization from the first stirrings of emancipation from the Church (to which end Bach and Handel were appropriated) to the full flowering of Enlightenment symphonism in Beethoven. A recurring Soviet truism that was very quickly established painted Western music beyond that point as charting a lengthy process of decline and decadence as Europe rejected revolutionary change and capitalism gained the upper hand; but nonetheless, the notion that major achievements of Western bourgeois culture should be presented to the Soviet proletariat and preserved within Soviet culture was absolutely taken for granted. Problems with certain sections of that culture – in particular with its sacred music – were acknowledged, as will be discussed below. At the height of RAPM's influence these became more acute and affected other areas of repertoire as well; but overall, the period 1917–32 was one of a very broad embrace of 'bourgeois' repertoire. Some of the best minds in Russian musical culture applied their extensive knowledge of repertoire, history and aesthetics to marketing that repertoire to its greatest advantage; and it is probably true to say that most of those directly involved in the Philharmonias' work during these years were sincerely motivated as much by the wish to share culture with the proletariat as by the desire to maintain professional standards and preserve that culture at a time when its future – in terms of funding, ideological approval and state support – hung in the balance.

Though the Leningrad Philharmonia lecturers were obviously attempting a long-range politicization of the Western canon, the 1925 lecture plan discussed above pales in comparison with those for 1931. Here, at the highest point of RAPM's influence, the planned lectures were far more overtly political and far less well structured, trying to cover a dizzying amount of ground:

1. Music as ideology. The role and significance of music. Epoch of socialist construction. Music's place in the arts. Music in everyday life; music as organism of class consciousness. Origin of music as process of labour/rhythmic declamation of workers' songs. Music as instrument of class struggle, church music, rise of bourgeois class etc. Understanding

of elements of melody, harmony, rhythm and timbre. Musical genres. Vocal, instrumental and theatre music. Chamber music and symphonism. Understanding of the symphony orchestra.

2. Our musical front. Positioning of class strength on the music front. Residue of aristocratic music. Chaykovskiy and his school. Music of the ascendant bourgeoisie. Glazunov, decadence, Skryabin and his followers, anarchism, mysticism, individualism in music. Westernism, urbanism, music of the large capitalist city. Mechanization and machines in music. Jazz bands. Honegger 'Pacific', Stravinsky, Prokof'yev, Mosolov 'Zavod', Deshevov 'Rails' etc.

3. Academicism. Rimskiy-Korsakov tradition, Shteynberg, Gladkovskiy, Pashchenko. Shostakovich speaks about his own work, 'October', 'First of May', 'The Nose', 'The Golden Age', his work with TRAM. VAPM, Koval, Beliy, Shekhter, Davidenko and others. Problems of mass song. Struggle against church music, foxtrot and gypsy music. Soviet symphonism and Soviet opera.[18]

Though the names of RAPM activists are not usually found on minutes of these planning meetings, it is obvious that the Leningrad Philharmonia was trying to placate them, or at least, their members in Glavrepertkom, the body that would scrutinize the Philharmonia's plans for the forthcoming season. Their approved reading list for music study includes several scholarly tomes by Western and non-RAPM Soviet musicologists – Paul Bekker's *The Symphony from Beethoven to Mahler*, Igor Glebov's (Boris Asaf'yev) *Russian music in the 19th Century* – but also features Lev Lebedinskiy's *On Proletarian Mass Song* and Semën Korev's *Music and the Contemporary Age*.[19] Bizarrely, the only two music journals recommended in this list were RAPM's own tendentious *Proletarskiy muzïkant* and *Za proletarskuyu muzïku* – more obvious (and better quality) choices might have been *Rabochiy i teatr* or *Zhizn' iskusstva*. Yet those attending these meetings included illustrious names from Leningrad's music scene: Shostakovich's close friends Ivan Sollertinskiy and Isaak Glikman, the German-trained musicologist Konstantin Kuznetsov, the conductor Aleksandr Gauk, the composers Arseniy Gladkovskiy and Andrey Pashchenko and the critic Nikolay Malkov. Not all were present at every planning meeting in 1931 but it seems likely that a finely judged balance of appeasement and intelligent programming lay behind what otherwise seems to be a puzzling imperviousness on the part of the Leningrad Philharmonia during this difficult period. No matter how viciously the battles between the militants and the moderates raged in the press and how much hostility was shown towards the Philharmonia in the All-Union meetings of 1930–1 (see below for further discussion), the Philharmonia remained remarkably unaffected in terms of its repertoire. Admittedly, as will be seen, changes were made to their practices during these years, but the Philharmonia, unlike the Leningrad capella, never performed music by proletarian composers even at the very height of their power.

It was not only public lectures that were subjected to political strategizing. Repertoire plans – for musical institutions as for all cultural bodies in Moscow and Leningrad – had been submitted to Glavrepertkom for approval since 1922. A meeting of a Glaviskusstvo subcommittee in June 1929 gave itself the task of studying the Philharmonias' concerts in order to establish what kind of concerts they put on for workers, what the 'ideological point of view' of their concerts might be, which foreign artists they were inviting and how concerts were reviewed in the press.[20] The membership of the committee included several RAPM members and those involved in mass music work: Lev Kaltat, Anatoliy Groman, Nadezhda Bryusova and Nikolay Sherman. Later meetings that year show that Lebedinskiy, Valerian Bogdanov-Berezovskiy, Yuriy Keldïsh, Yevgeniy Braudo and Aleksandr Davidenko were also present, making the committee a mixture of those on the militant and moderate sides of musical life, but with an overall weighting towards mass musical activism. What effect the committee really had on the Philharmonias' repertoire is not quite clear. In May 1929 the committee had held a discussion of Lebedinskiy's 1926 proposal on 'Principles of concert work in workers' auditoriums', a verbose and almost entirely content-free document in which Lebedinskiy criticized repertoire that stimulated the wrong kind of emotions (especially 'sentimental mysticism') and called for 'healthy activity . . . [and] an emotional charge of a clear-cut kind'.[21] Groman's response on behalf of Narkompros had a distinctly ironic tone: 'There were eight western composers missing from the category [of composers whose music should be propagandized]: Beethoven, Mozart, Wagner, Liszt, Schumann, Schubert, Rossini and Bizet. Undoubtedly, we should plan programmes that are interesting and sufficiently valuable in ideological content . . . and the quantity of composers and works selected for performance should, of course, show adequate breadth. If, for example, we perform Verdi, then why not also Meyerbeer? If Bach, why not also Handel?'[22] There the archival record stops, and the only way to try and gauge the effect any of these discussions had on real programme planning is by looking at what was performed rather than what was talked about. But the Leningrad Philharmonia archive shows that concert planners could draw up very ambitious plans, doubtless for submission to Glavrepertkom, which were not then carried through. A list of planned themes for the season 1931–2 runs as follows (Table 2.1):

Table 2.1: Plans for themed programmes (from minutes of Leningrad Philharmonia meeting held on 21 April 1931)

[Present: Popov, Gauk, Pashchenko, Glikman, Malkov, Livshits]

Musorgsky and VAPM	National musics of the USSR
Beethoven	Music as class awakening (proletarian and bourgeois)
Schumann, Schubert and Koval'	
Russian song and dance music	Humour and satire in music
Italian song and dance music	First of May
Spanish song and dance music	Anniversary Soviet Constitution
French song and dance music	Anti-Easter
German song and dance music	Pushkin
Scandinavian song and dance music	Lermontov
Polish song and dance music	Shakespeare
The French Revolution in music,	Schiller
music from comic operas up to our	Goethe
own time	RAPM and VAPM[23]

Yet the actual programmes from that season suggest that most of these themes were quietly dropped. The song and dance programmes are nowhere to be seen, and no member of RAPM featured in the schedule at all. Of the literary programmes the only survivor was a big Goethe-themed day on 31 March 1932, with music by Schubert. Wagner – entirely absent from the themed plan – was honoured with a mini-festival in January, when Carl Bamberger visited Leningrad. It is entirely possible, even likely, that late substitutions were made following the April Resolution: Mikhail Gnesin, a declared foe of RAPM, had his Symphony-fantasy op. 40 performed in May, and Mosolov's *Three Songs for Soprano and Orchestra* op. 33 were performed in the same concert.[24] Since both had been sharply criticized by the proletarian wing, this would have been provocative if RAPM had still been peering over the Philharmonia's shoulder. Another striking feature of this season conspicuously absent from the planning meetings in early 1931 is the continued – indeed increased – presence of foreign guest conductors, though it should be noted that, so far as I have been able to ascertain, RAPM never seriously tried to pressurize the Philharmonia into formally ceasing to invite them, nor do their published articles call for such a move. It is possible that ending the practice of inviting foreign artists was never a strong concern of RAPM, though minutes from another meeting on 27 January 1931 reveal that discussion did take place about whether to continue inviting them, and the conclusion was that invitations would be sent as normal.[25] Tables 2.2 and 2.3 below show that, although there was a small drop in the number of invited guest conductors and composers during the height of RAPM's influence (1928–32), the Leningrad Philharmonia managed to retain a remarkable level of internationalism and modernism during this extremely difficult period in Soviet musical history:

Table 2.2: Contemporary (post-1910) non-Russian/Soviet music in the programmes of the Leningrad Philharmonia, 1928–32.

1928–9	1929–30
Franckenstein, *Variations on a theme by Meyerbeer*	Honegger, *Pacific 231*
Reger, *Variations on a theme by Mozart, Romantic Suite, Ballet Suite*	Hindemith, *Concert Music for Wind*
Stravinsky, *Les Noces, The Rite of Spring, Oedipus Rex, L'Histoire du soldat, The Nightingale, Apollon Musagete, Mavra, Petrushka, Pulcinella, Three Pieces* (string quartet), Piano Concerto	Franz Schmitt, *Variations on Theme by Beethoven*
	Ravel, *Boléro*
	Hindemith, *Kammermusik No. 5*
	Respighi, *Roman Festivals*
	R. Strauss, *Panathenäenzug*
Hindemith, 'Viola Concerto'[26]	
Krenek, *Pot-pourri*	**1930–1**
Ravel, *La Valse*	Honegger, *Pacific 231*
Honegger, *Rugby suite, Pacific 231*	Nielsen, *Pan and Syrinx*
Hindemith, *Kammermusik No. 5*	Stravinsky, *Petrushka*
Bartók, Piano Concerto No. 1	
Modarelli, *September*	**1931–2**
Berg, *Seven Early Songs* (1908)[27]	Busoni, suite from *Turandot*
Bliss, *Songs and Dances for strings*[28]	Stravinsky, *Pulcinella*
	Franz Schmitt, Symphony No. 2
	Hindemith, 'Organ Concerto'[29]

Table 2.3: Foreign guest conductors of the Leningrad Philharmonia, 1922–32

1922–3	1928–9
Oskar Fried	Hans Knappertsbusch
	Fritz Busch
1923–4	Otto Klemperer
Oskar Fried	Hermann Abendroth
Alexander Schmuller	Ernest Ansermet
	[NB visit of Bartók in January 1929]
1924–5	
Otto Klemperer	**1929–30**
Hermann Abendroth	Emmanuel Rhené-Baton
Heinz Unger	Rudolf Ziegel
	Heinz Unger
1925–6	Ernst Vendel
Franz Schreker	Hans Knappertsbusch
Otto Klemperer	Vladimir Savic
Fritz Stiedry (new chief conductor)	
Oskar Fried	**1930–1**
Pierre Monteux	Heinz Unger
Felix Weingartner	Joseph Rosenstock
Darius Milhaud [visited 1926]	Fritz Stiedry
	Julius Erlich
1926–7	Johan Mowinkel
Fritz Stiedry	
Bruno Walter	**1931–2**
Erich Kleiber	Bruno Walter
Alfredo Casella	Julius Erlich
Otto Klemperer	Heinz Unger
Albert Coates (Russian, but	Alexander Zemlinsky
emigrated in 1919)	Oskar Fried
	Carl Bamberger
1927–8	Erich Paul Stekel
Ernest Ansermet	Václav Talich
Clemens Krauss	Gertrude Herdlichka
Otto Klemperer	Georges Sébastian
Bruno Walter	Albert Coates
Hermann Abendroth	Heinz-Wilhelm Steinberg
Arthur Honegger	
Fritz Stiedry	
Alexander Zemlinsky	

Clearly, since the Resolution was not announced until April 1932, the likelihood is that the Philharmonia had already invited all these guest conductors for 1931–2 right at the peak of RAPM's influence. This might suggest that in early 1931, musicians were already beginning to sense that RAPM's power was waning, and other factors do bear this out, but the situation seems to have changed several times during the course of 1931. As Marina Frolova-Walker and Jonathan Walker claim, RAPM's dominance actually increased in the first half of 1931; Asaf'yev finally delivered himself into their hands in March ('to work solely under their control . . . There is no other way out').[30] Yet it is possible that the Leningrad Philharmonia planning committees may have hoped for RAPM's downfall by the fall of 1931. Pavel Lamm wrote gleefully to Asaf'yev in October that he believed RAPM's downfall was imminent in the wake of newly confident attacks on them from within Narkompros after Stalin's speech, delivered in June 1931 to an audience of economists, which hinted that the end of class war was in sight.[31] Yet despite Lamm's optimism, RAPM's position was still strong at the end of 1931: the new arts head of Narkompros, Feliks Kon, was a supporter in a powerful position and it looked as though the proletarians might still retain their status. In short, nothing was predictable during 1931: the mood among RAPM's foes and victims must have been changeable, while it was clear that the RAPMovtsï themselves were not going to go without a fight. The Leningrad Philharmonia probably gambled on the success of their appeasement strategy, while concurrently actually increasing the number of foreign performers and – it seems very likely – drawing up a politically correct repertoire plan that they had little intention of following through.

The gaps left in the Leningrad Philharmonia's repertoire between 1929 and 1932 once Western contemporary music was thinned out were not, as might be thought, filled by Russian classics or by a new wave of Soviet proletarian compositions. For example, the Leningrad Philharmonia's 1929–30 season was strikingly short on Russian music, even though nearly all of its concerts were conducted by the foreign (but resident chief conductor) Fritz Stiedry and the Russian Aleksandr Gauk. There were six all-Russian concerts that season in total, most of them a blend of Russian and Soviet music, such as Gauk's 15 March programme of Chaykovskiy's 'Manfred' Symphony and Shostakovich's Third, or Georgiy Sheydler's 19 October programme of Chaykovskiy's Third and Shostakovich's First Symphonies together with Mosolov's ever-popular *Zavod*. There was only one concert featuring only nineteenth-century Russian music, and that was the 11 January programme: Chaykovskiy's *Francesca da Rimini* and Fifth Symphony with arias from Borodin's *Prince Igor*.

The fact that a drop in the performance of Western contemporary music did not coincide with a rise in Russian music suggests that the Philharmonia's directorate in these years felt they had no reason to make a special effort to programme Russian music as part of its strategy. At that time, it had few champions, since RAPM chiefly supported its legacy of folk-inspired song rather than its symphonies or operas. The Philharmonia's 1929–30 season is therefore well stocked with Western classical and romantic repertoire, from Bach, Handel and Rameau to Bruckner, Mahler and Strauss. The same is true of the 1930–1 season, where, as with the previous year, more Russians than foreigners were conducting and repertoire is accordingly more conservative, probably largely because the relative lack of visiting foreign conductors meant a drop in the introduction of newer music. Most of the concerts were conducted by Gauk, and occasionally Vladimir Dranishnikov or Aleksandr Pavlov-Arbenin. Both Dranishnikov and Pavlov-Arbenin (principally an opera conductor) were schooled in nineteenth-century Russian repertoire and so one might expect to find them conducting it here; but in fact it was Pavlov-Arbenin who conducted *Pacific 231* – in a concert (3 November 1930, introductory lecture by Sollertinskiy) devoted to revolutionary music and including Vladimir Deshevov's Suite from *Bolsheviki*, Mosolov's *Zavod*, Henri Litolff's *Maximilien Robespierre* and the finale of Beethoven's Ninth Symphony. He conducted an almost identical concert three days later, this time with Chopin's Funeral March (from the B flat Minor Sonata) and the March from Prokof'yev's *Love for Three Oranges*, but without the Beethoven. As for Dranishnikov, after an all-Chaykovskiy concert on 26 October (*Romeo and Juliet* overture, Violin Concerto, Fifth Symphony, arias from *Queen of Spades*), his only other concert was all-Wagner. In fact, 1930–1 was not a dull season at all. It featured Shostakovich's Second Symphony, Mahler's First and Second, Mendelssohn's *Midsummer Night's Dream*, Bruckner's Seventh and Ninth, Brahms's Second, Third and Fourth, First Piano Concerto and Violin Concerto (so much Brahms was still a novelty for Soviet audiences), Nielsen's *Pan and Syrinx*, several Strauss tone poems and a good sprinkling of nineteenth-century Russian and Western classics: Beethoven symphonies, Chaykovskiy symphonies and concertos, excerpts from Wagner's operas, a Haydn symphony ('Military'), Schubert's Eighth, a Mozart Piano Concerto (unspecified), Borodin's *Polovtsian Dances* and Liszt's *Faust* Symphony.

For both the 1929–30 and 1930–1 seasons, the relative absence of music composed post-1910 makes them appear far duller than they actually were. Both seasons were fully international and not devoid of novelty, even if they were rather conservative overall. Pre-revolutionary Russian repertoire is mixed in alongside Western classical and romantic music in a way that suggests a total absence of anxiety over how it should be programmed. Concessions to RAPM can be discerned in the concerts of revolutionary music, which were probably aimed at workers (the Philharmonia records often specify this, but not for these seasons) and in other mixed-genre concerts where single movements and songs take the place of longer works, such as that on 22 January 1931, featuring various Glinka songs, the second movement of Beethoven's Seventh Symphony, the finale of his Fifth and the first movement of his Fifth Piano Concerto. But RAPM's composers never managed to encroach onto the programmes themselves, and they may even have felt some resignation over their lofty neglect, since stenographic reports of their meetings in the late RAPM period invariably reflect negatives (selecting works that they wished the orchestra would ban, like Rakhmaninov's *The Bells*) rather than positives (selecting their own best compositions and agitating to have them performed). Their attack on Rakhmaninov came in March 1931, at the All-Russian Conference on Amateur Art in Moscow, where the conference passed the following resolution:

This conference considers that the works of Rakhmaninov are reactionary, reflecting a decadent mood of the petit bourgeoisie, and that this work is particularly harmful in the bitter conditions of class struggle on the musical front. This conference proposes that the well-known group of music specialists who propagandize Rakhmaninov's music under the guise of consideration for the value of formal technical training are actually propagandizing a class of alien ideology by means of music. Members of this conference pledge:
1) To lead a ceaseless struggle against the propagandizing of Rakhmaninov's music through concerts, schools, published collections, the press etc.
2) This conference appeals to all music societies to lead this struggle against the work of the white-émigré Rakhmaninov
3) This conference proposes a broad-ranging discussion of Rakhmaninov's music with musicians, societies and professional organizations

4) This conference proposes that Muzgiz ceases publication of Rakhmaninov's music

5) This conferences demands that Glavrepertkom bans the performance of Rakhmaninov's music

6) This conference demands the removal of Rakhmaninov's music from libraries.[32]

Why the conference passed such aggressive motions against Rakhmaninov is puzzling on the face of it, because he was not an especially fashionable composer in Leningrad or Moscow at that time. The Leningrad capella had not performed his *All-Night Vigil* since 1928, and the Philharmonia did not perform his music very often either. In the two seasons preceding the conference, 1929–30 and 1930–1, there is not one work by Rakhmaninov programmed; nor does he make a dramatic comeback in the immediate wake of the April 1932 Resolution, when the militant groups lost their power – during the 1932–3 season, once again, Rakhmaninov is totally absent. *The Bells* was performed in the 1928–9 season (conducted by Mal'ko, and partnered with Prokof'yev's *Steel Step* and Hindemith's Kammermusik No. 5) but it was certainly not an established repertoire piece; his piano concerti were occasionally performed (Leningrad 1923–4, 1927–8 seasons) but again, these did not really gain widespread acceptance in Soviet orchestral programmes until the late 1930s, when they became extremely popular. Therefore, the conference was simply pushing on an open door, and this makes some sense in the light of the proletarians' comparatively negligible influence on the Philharmonia. The resolution against Rakhmaninov was quite possibly never in any real danger of staunch opposition; no collected works had been mooted in any case and his music was simply not core repertoire at this time. Calling for bans sounded impressive and intimidating, but no organization was in any real danger of censure, since *The Bells* had not been repeated since Mal'ko's 1928 performance anyway.

As the 1932 Resolution approached, the programming culture of the Leningrad Philharmonia was firmly set to Western eighteenth/nineteenth-century repertoire. Although there was no significant increase in European modernism, the gap was not filled with a turn towards programming more Soviet or Russian music. The visiting German conductors brought programmes of Wagner, Viennese classics, Berlioz, Brahms, Strauss and Mahler and, with a single exception, not one of them performed anything Russian (unless it was by Stravinsky) or Soviet. The exception was Carl

Bamberger, who included one of Chaykovskiy's piano concertos in two of his three programmes – and that was all. It fell to Gauk to perform almost every concert that included Russian or Soviet music in the whole season – an especially sobering thought when one reflects that Gauk had taken the lion's share of concerts in the preceding two seasons as well. Without Mal'ko to assist him, Gauk was now almost single-handedly promoting the few Soviet composers whose music ever made it to the Leningrad concert stage in those years – Shostakovich, Myaskovskiy, Mosolov, Pashchenko, Shteynberg, Deshevov, Polovinkin and Gladkovskiy; and Pashchenko and Gladkovskiy were, as we have seen, involved in concert planning and so could be perceived as having unfair leverage. Therefore, when after 1932 Philharmonia minutes begin to record increased levels of concern for Russian and Soviet repertoire, it is easy to understand the source of that concern: it may have been growing steadily throughout the NEP period, as European conductors championed the music they knew and loved, while the wave of emigrations in the 1920s (seeing the departures of Kusevitskiy, Coates and Kuper) had left the Leningrad Philharmonia without the champions of Russian music that had given the orchestra its core repertoire in its very earliest years. Then, when Nikolay Mal'ko's defection in 1929 also left Soviet composers without an important and influential champion, it must have seemed to many Soviet musicians that the void those departing conductors had left had never really been filled; only after 1936 would a new school of Soviet-trained conductors come to replace them at last, and if fewer foreigners visited in consequence, then it would be understandable if some calculated that this redressed some sorely needed balance. The apparently seamless timing of this replacement – the rise of genuinely brilliant conductors like Yevgeniy Mravinskiy and later Kirill Kondrashin at the same time as foreign musicians ceased to visit the USSR – makes it impossible to draw a chicken-and-egg conclusion about the change in culture simply by looking at the concert programmes. However, as will be seen in Chapter Three, accusations that the Philharmonias neglected Russian and Soviet music and showed undue reverence for foreigners rose to a hysterical pitch after 1936, after which Soviet concert culture changed irrevocably.

Final Attacks on Church Music

After RAPM began to claim more power and influence over Soviet musical life from around 1929, Klimov was forced to alter the capella's programming to fend off more severe criticism. In a way, it is surprising to find that RAPM did not target the capella more aggressively, since church music was one of their regular targets in the journals they published between 1929 and 1932, *Proletarskiy muzïkant* and *Za proletarskuyu muzïku*.[33] That being said, minutes from meetings of Glaviskusstvo (main administration of arts affairs) between 1929 and 1931 show clearly that the capella and Leningrad Philharmonia were in RAPM's sights. In a meeting dedicated to antireligious propaganda on 9 April 1929, the Mass [work] Department of Glavisskustvo included among their aims to 'ban the sale of religious musical literature', to 'examine concert, opera and radio repertoire with the aim of banning religious music and any works saturated with religion' and 'to exclude any operas saturated with religion'.[34] Though it would be reasonable to assume that RAPM felt just as strongly about Bach's Passions as they did about Rakhmaninov's *All-Night Vigil*, this seems not to have been so, though that is not to say that some hostile critics did not attack the Philharmonias' performances of sacred music. After the All-Russian Music Conference of June 1929, the writer 'Muzrabotnik' [music worker] responded to the conference's discussion of the pros and cons of performing works like Brahms's Requiem and Bach and Mozart masses:

> If their 'academic value' up to now justified the performance of sacred musical works, then this opens up immense scope for decadent works of the past and present which hide their true essence under an innocent, indifferent title of symphony, quartet, sonata and so on! This loophole for smuggling through contraband is like a narcotic abyss, essential for maintaining cheer as class barriers melt away![35]

There was undoubtedly pressure on the Philharmonias to show that they responded to such complaints, and sympathetic critics tried hard to market sacred or biblical works in a worker-friendly manner. During the five years or so that RAPM exerted real influence on musical life, there is a perceptible drop in the numbers of sacred works performed by the capella, which was more visibly affected by hostile press campaigns than the Philharmonias were. In response to RAPM's insistence on the importance of mass songs, Klimov's work plans show a marked increase in popular Soviet song repertoire as early as the 1929–30 season. His plans for 1931–2 included the major themes 'Songs of the Peoples of the USSR' (five concerts) and 'Russian choral literature' (four concerts);[36] other themed concerts included 'Humour and satire', 'Lenin memorial concert' and 'Antireligious choral literature'.[37] This last category is clearly extraordinary for the capella, and it was in fact never to be repeated, since pressure to gratify RAPM's demands vanished after the 1932 Resolution that was issued during that very season.[38]

End of an Era

Changes wrought in the leadership of Narkompros at this time had a strongly negative effect on musical life: Lunacharskiy was sacked and replaced by the less liberal Andrey Bubnov in 1929 as overall Commissar, while the arts section of Narkompros was headed by Feliks Kon from 1930, an Old Bolshevik revolutionary and Comintern official best known today for the undeserved honour of having the Moscow Conservatoire temporarily named after him between 1930 and 1932. Though this period is rightly regarded as an intensification of the proletarian factions' seizure of power and influence over the arts sphere, it is nevertheless clear that, in its intolerance of multiple interest groups and its desire for a much stronger, more interventionist central control of the arts, Narkompros, guided by the NKVD, initiated a process that strongly prefigured the 1932 Resolution; indeed, might be said to have guided it. It is not yet clear, from the archival records studied by researchers, exactly why the purge of arts societies began: on the one hand we can see that it was initiated by an NKVD investigation of Glaviskusstvo, with Kon merely the instrument by which higher political movers achieved their goal. Members of RAPM were commissioned to write reports on the activities of music groups, including those of a proletarian nature. Needless to say, those groups were permitted to survive, while all the others were liquidated; yet it would be too hasty to conclude that powerful members of the proletarian wing presided over the entire purge. On the other hand, as matters currently stand, we do not know why the NKVD began to investigate Glaviskusstvo (other than a report stating that their work was unsatisfactory) or which, if any, figures in the proletarian arts world carried any influence in higher political circles. What is clear, though, is that only proletarian groups stood to gain anything by the ensuing purge of arts organizations, as will be seen.

The auditing wheels began to turn early in 1930, with an NKVD inspection of Glaviskusstvo's monitoring activity, which had been judged unsatisfactory with regard to its tolerance of multiple arts groups. In a report from M. Aleksinskiy (Secretary to Narkompros) sent to Narkompros and copied to Kon and the NKVD on 13 April 1930, it is evident that Kon himself did not initiate the purge of arts groups, but that it came about as a result of a higher-up investigation of Glaviskusstvo's leadership by the NKVD: 'Bring to the notice of comrade F. Kon about the complete absence of leadership on the side of Glavisskustvo on the work of voluntary arts societies and recommend to him that he should ask questions about the provision of permanent control and leadership of their activities. [We are] to hear within 3 months a communication from comrade F. Kon about the fulfilment of his decision.'[39]

Kon duly wrote to all arts groups on 15 November 1930, giving them a single day to respond to his request:

> To all Artistic Societies:
> The Arts and Literature Sector of Narkompros requires you, no later than the 16th of this November, to report to us information about planned convocations in 1931, congresses and conferences, indications of their duration, location, orientation, agenda and number of participants. At the same time we ask that you send us a production plan for a specific quarterly period and separately for 1931. Also, accounts for the year 1929–30.[40]

Just a week earlier, on 9 November, he had already tabled a draft resolution on a report of the Arts and Literature Sector of Narkompros concerning voluntary societies: 'To recognize as essential the rapid creation of a Federal [administration] for all musical societies, to propose a re-examination of all existing musical societies, and to liquidate those which lack either artistic or practical significance.'[41] Clearly, he expected the results of his audit to be grim, which strongly implies a presumption of guilt before it had even taken place. The list of societies preserved in RGALI and examined under Kon's report includes the following groups: The Ostrovskiy Society, The Chekhov Society, Friends of Soviet Cinema, Friends of Radio, Union of Revolutionary Dramatists, Society of Proletarian Writers, Society of Peasant Writers, Society of Chamber Music, Society for Jewish Music, Music for the Masses, Bach and Beethoven Societies and the Association of Contemporary Music (ASM). In later reports, the Society for Wagner's Art and the German Music Society were also mentioned. Some were deemed 'essential to preserve and re-register', while others were to be liquidated. Those considered 'essential' included the Society of Proletarian Writers, Society of Peasant Writers,

Friends of Soviet Cinema, Union of Revolutionary Dramatists, and Music for the Masses. The remainder were judged expendable.

Regardless of its impeccable aims and broad membership, the Beethoven Society fell victim to Kon's purge. It was not only very distinguished, but it was also one of the very few groups where proletarian and non-proletarian musicians could profess to work together – but it was still considered expendable. Semën Korev, the RAPM activist and musicologist, was commissioned to write a report on the activities of the music groups; his final paper cited the Beethoven Society as an especially parlous example:

In autumn of this year the Arts Section of Narkompros began a broad and profound inquiry into the conditions of musical societies. . . . This inspection showed an extremely deplorable picture of existing musical society life. First of all, a picture emerged of an extraordinary atomization, a splintering of our musical strengths . . . revealing a . . . quantity of 'on paper' [in theory], but in reality, lifeless, societies. They seemed clearly unhealthy, groups hostile to us with anti-proletarian, anti-Soviet activities. . . .

Here is a concrete example. In Moscow, at least in theory, in the course of the last few years, there has been a Beethoven Society. It came about at the time of the Beethoven celebrations (centenary of his death) in 1927 and had the aim of propagandizing the work of this great composer. At its foundation it had a number of prominent musicians, and it was very well organized and financed. The inspection established that in the course of the last two years, neither the society or its leadership have once had a meeting, not even a hint of one. The Arts Sector liquidated the society, and turned its running over to the membership and funds of the Society 'Music for the Masses'. When it was liquidated it was found that upwards of 3000 roubles remained unspent. This was at the same time that, until this very year, the greatest subsidy of any organization did not exceed 2000 roubles![42]

Though the lack of organized activity and the alleged over-funding didn't look good, Korev's charges of the 'anti-proletarian' and even 'anti-Soviet' nature of these music groups were vicious; a formal charge of anti-Soviet activity was a serious criminal offence. Yet why should such music groups have been so perceived? Beethoven was a bona fide RAPM-approved composer, declared by all sides of the political spectrum to be suitable for mass musical work. Sense can only be made of these hostile reports by noting who is making them (RAPM members) and for whose benefit. This could only be RAPM's, since by systematically persecuting all other music groups they inched towards total power themselves. Narkompros's directions on its closure concluded that: 'The Beethoven Society is to be liquidated, by order of the relevant government department and by decision of the All-Russian Society Congress'; 'upon liquidation by order of the All-Russian Society Congress, the [Beethoven] Society must deliver a speech at Narkompros and Narkomvnudel justifying [the closure], guided by instructions'; 'the liquidation of the Society must be undertaken by a liquidation commission comprised of members of Narkompros and Narkomvnudel. All of the Society's property remaining after its liquidation is to be passed over to Narkompros.'[43]

The Bach Society inevitably suffered the same fate, though it put up a robust fight. When it was alerted to threats of closure by Glaviskusstvo (either late in 1929 or very early in 1930), it made an official protest to Narkompros. In its favour, they argued, the majority of their concerts were for workers; they worked in 'political campaigns' as well as organizing music events; it had opened a sister branch in Novgorod and its membership (of over one hundred) wished the Society to continue.[44] They asked Narkompros/NKVD to 'consider our protest as the expression of a will and strong desire of musicians and music workers united by the Bach Society, to address those cultural and political issues before society, the Party and the State.'[45] In a letter to Narkompros/NKVD sent on 24 January 1930, the Society fought for its survival using language and arguments intended to persuade Narkompros/NKVD of their dedication to the cause of building socialism:

> At this moment of socialist reconstruction, in the life of the Union, when both Party and State are conducting an intensive struggle for maximal collectivization of mass activities, when all those participating in socialist construction undertake courses on maximal exposure and development of social initiatives in amateur activity, this attempt to liquidate such initiatives seems to oppose this basic principle of socialist construction.[46]

It should have been a convincing argument, but in reality, the Society's fate was sealed. And in fact, its position within Narkompros and the NKVD had never been as secure as that of the Beethoven Society. Its president, the pianist E. Gol'dsheyn, seems to have been perceived as hostile to the reform of the

Moscow Conservatoire under the new direction of Boleslav Pshibïshevskiy, when it was notoriously re-named the Feliks Kon Higher Music School in 1930. Vlasova notes that, from autumn 1929, the Bach Society – by now in existence for only one year – was pressurized to 'strengthen [its] communist influence' and 'recognize as essential the inclusion in its future structure of Pshibïshevskiy, namely in regard to its leadership and presidency. In the event of producing a politically negative response and support from the majority around Gol'dsheyn . . . the question of liquidating the Society should be raised.'[47] In the end, it shared the fate of the Beethoven Society and, by order of Narkompros, from 1 July 1930 the Bach Society was abolished completely. Korev's report was just as damning as that of the Beethoven Society had been:

> The Bach Society existed for over a year. It brought together c. 100 musicians, among whom were some highly qualified members. The tasks of this society were both broad and respectable: mass work and education of society members, the propaganda of Bach's music and many other such aims. It was only when the inspection began that it quickly became evident that, in the first place, all its activities had come down to a few symphonic and mixed concerts, everything proceeded with no plan at all, with no aims or purpose, with no connection with the given aims of the society. In the second place, this society had no principal aims, no programmes, no objective team leaders for its great number of members and in the third place, its members were members on paper only, and all the 'activities' of the society were expressed in energetic activities of doubtful value, of one single member, the society's organizer.[48]

Turning his attention to the Society for Wagner's Art (thirty-three members, founded 1925), Korev merely remarked that 'The ideological foundation is obscure, but is evidently expressed in the double-edged words of its president, which appear in the inspector's report – "Wagner cannot be associated with Marxism."' The Society's founder, Konstantin Khmelnitskiy, had, it seems, given his opponents all the ammunition they needed. Korev's comments on the German Music Society (founded 1922, eighty-nine members) were more seriously xenophobic: 'The inspectors of this society found a cultivation, in the main, of sacred music of a chauvinistic character, unnecessary and harmful for the working masses, and that this society had tendencies to participate in activities harmful for youth.'[49]

In what must have been part of Kon's interim report to Narkompros (there is no date preserved on the document in the file), he writes:

> Artistic societies until recent times have been found to be in such conditions, that there was no serious ideological leadership to speak of; in view of this the Arts Sector, after its inspection of them, had put in place a whole raft of measures. . . . On the musical front there has been until now complete chaos. There have been, and still exist, societies which have neither artistic nor practical significance, in connection with which the Arts Sector, recognizing that it is essential to – as soon as possible – create a Federation of all musical societies and to liquidate those which do not have any artistic significance.[50]

This shows that already, before 1932, Narkompros officials judged the whole arts sphere to be rambling out of control and in urgent need of streamlining. What Stalin's Resolution finished off, therefore, the NKVD had initiated, at whose instruction we still do not know. The mechanisms of the purge – the financial audits and requests into activities – established the nature of future purges in the mid to late 1930s, when all the major musical institutions would be subjected to detailed scrutiny, scapegoats found and severe punishment – including execution in some cases – meted out. For the time being, however, no one was arrested or executed for their allegedly dubious affiliation to a music society. The societies themselves were deemed unsuitable and ineffectual and – whatever the truth of Korev's reports into their non-activity – the archival record has preserved officially accepted reasons for their liquidation. A brief report on these mass liquidations in *Rabochiy i teatr* in 1930 underlines Korev's reports in accusing the German Music Society of 'anti-Soviet' activity, presumably because of its alleged 'clerical' nature.[51]

The Campaign against RAPM

As discussed above, by March 1931 Asaf'yev had resigned himself to working under RAPM, feeling that they were set to become the dominating force in Soviet musical life. But some of his colleagues were less easily defeated; and those more urgently under threat, such as Mikhail Gnesin (who was the target of a sustained RAPM campaign) were precisely the ones who led the fight back. Even before the April Resolution declared

RAPM finally routed and defeated, it was under attack from Gnesin and others. As Frolova-Walker and Walker have shown, prominent voices began to be raised against them from various quarters, including the Vseroskomdram meetings of October 1931–January 1932, at which Levon Atovmyan, Mikhail Gnesin and Shostakovich (among others) gave speeches that signalled a new surge of confidence that RAPM's days were numbered. In the December 1931 meeting, Shostakovich delivered a speech that would permanently cut any friendly ties with RAPM. Beginning with exaggerated praise for the interest and importance of the journals *Proletarskiy muzïkant* and *Za proletarskuyu muzïku*, Shostakovich continued with a feigned inno-cence that swiftly turned into deadly mockery:

> We, composers, who try to cultivate a proletarian world view, follow everything that goes on in the proletarian musical front. And recently we see a sizeable rift within it, which has already been exposed to 'serious criticism' . . . In fact the music [of proletarian composers] is utterly help-less. Davidenko's 'Derailed' [*Pod otkos*] is technically, a completely help-less work. It is necessary to sharply criticize RAPM for the helpless, illiterate things that they are publishing and spreading around. RAPM must answer for the works of its members and must not churn out pulp like the opera 'Derailed'.[52]

If Shostakovich felt confident enough to cut his ties with RAPM in such vicious terms, he was not alone: Atovmyan openly mocked RAPM at the meeting, while Gnesin – who proved to be at this time a far more powerful critic than they had bargained for – not only criticized them publicly at the meeting and in print but wrote privately to Stalin as well, complaining of RAPM's banal approach to selecting appropriate repertoire (arbitrary 'bans' on Chopin for being a salon composer and so forth) and other affronts to musical intelligence and integrity.[53] Further attacks on RAPM followed swiftly from this point: *Rabochiy i teatr* published a highly critical (unsigned) article in January 1932, 'Cleansing RAPM from its dangerous vulgar theo-retical expressions', based on the previous Vseroskomdram meeting. It sharply criticized writings by RAPM members on Beethoven and Musorgskiy for drawing simplistic parallels between, for example, tonic/dominant proc-esses in sonata form and Marxist theories of historical dialectic. A last gasp from the proletarian side was published in a February 1932 issue of the same journal from the 'revolutionary society of Philharmonia workers', protesting at the lack of vigilance in programme committees in allowing works 'hostile to the working class' to be played, citing Saint-Saëns' Third Symphony, Honegger's *Pacific 231* and Strauss's *Also Sprach Zarathustra* as examples.[54] Needless to say, the letter had no effect whatsoever. After the Resolution had drawn a line under the whole affair, there remained only for RAPM's members to recant, meekly seek integration into the new structures created after the Resolution and silently accept the volley of criticism that was inevitably coming their way. In June later that year, the same journal printed an article by Vladimir Iokhelson and V. Tobol'kevich on 'The Musical Front and the Party's Decision', setting the scene for what proved to be a fairly substantial campaign against RAPM:

> It is absolutely essential to broaden our cultural heritage, both in performance and education, and at the same time for musicologists to turn their attention to analysing the works of Bach, Handel, Chopin, Wagner, Debussy, Skryabin, Scarlatti, Rameau, Stravinsky, Prokof'yev and others whom RAPM supplied with 'yellow cards': the greatest masters of classical musical culture.... Without the critical study of music of the past and even [music] of classes hostile to us from contemporary Western Europe and America, we cannot achieve the highest level of the development of musical culture.[55]

The authors do not reject the concept of 'music from hostile classes' but maintain that Soviet musicians still need to know it and learn from it. This fundamental position of openness to the West while simultaneously aiming to take first place in world culture would typify both the internationalism of this next period up to 1936 and its emerging narrative of Russian cultural dominance.

CHAPTER THREE

INTERNATIONALISM, MODERNISM AND THE 'STALINIST ENLIGHTENMENT' 1932-1941

With Stalin's Resolution 'On the Reconstruction of Literary and Artistic Organizations' of 23 April 1932, it seemed that an era in Soviet cultural life had come to an end. For the majority of musicians, the liquidation of RAPM came as a huge relief and a vindication of their own more moderate positions. But just how much of a cut-off point the Resolution marked in terms of how musical life was being conducted is open to question. As we have seen, private arts societies were being closed down by Narkompros on the eve of the Resolution, so cultural life was already moving towards a centralised model. Narkompros itself continued to oversee cultural life until 1936, underlining the extent to which the 1932 Resolution sought to stabilize cultural life rather than to transform it overnight. Another particularly uncongenial legacy from pre-1932, the harassment of composers and institutions by those who positioned themselves as strongly ideologically committed, continued into the post-Resolution era. Although RAPM itself was publicly discredited after 1932 and then again later in the decade following the attacks on Shostakovich and 'formalism', its tactics of public denunciation and political slander became thoroughly normalized during the purge years. Moreover, some officials who had gained power during the height of the proletarian era (Platon Kerzhentsev being just one) rose to even greater positions of influence at that crucial time, and became far more dangerous as a result.

Narkompros was wound down several years after the Resolution, and by January 1936 it was fully replaced by the Committee for Arts Affairs, with Kerzhentsev invited to take up a position as first leader of the Committee. Additionally, the Moscow branch of the newly formed Composers' Union, which was run on a local branch basis and overseen by Kerzhentsev's committee, was also headed by a bureaucrat (Nikolay Chelyapov) but after he was purged in 1937, the leadership of the Union would always be in the hands of composers.[1] It is probably accurate to say that, though the silencing of RAPM in 1932 had a dramatic and immediate impact on Soviet musical life, the most fundamental changes did not occur until early 1936, when Narkompros was disbanded, the leadership of the Composers' Union attacked, and a far-reaching campaign against the Soviet art world was launched by *Pravda*'s aggressive critique of Shostakovich's opera *The Lady Macbeth of Mtsensk District* and his ballet *The Limpid Stream* in January–February 1936.[2] Although this event had an immediate effect on concert programming generally, as will be seen, it would be a full year before the wider investigations into musical institutions began.

In many ways, this nine-year period in Soviet cultural history is the hardest to interpret retrospectively, because it was a period of extremely intense flux. First, there was the issue of a power-struggle within the government itself. From 1932, Stalin worked to fully consolidate his position and ensure that those in his Central Committee who may have challenged him – above all Nikolay Bukharin – were publicly discredited and removed. Over fifty leading politicians would be shot, or meet other, equally gruesome, fates over the course of the decade. The Leningrad Party chief Sergey Kirov was assassinated under suspicious circumstances in December 1934; two other Politburo members, Grigoriy Zinoviev and Lev Kamenev, were arrested in 1935 and they, along with their colleague Nikolay Bukharin, were placed on public trial in three 'show trials' presided over by the procurator Andrey Vishinskiy between 1936 and 1938. All were charged with terrorism, vilified in the media, and shot.[3]

Second, there was the question of relations with the West. Britain had suspended diplomatic relations with the Soviet Union in 1927 but restored them in 1930; America did the same in 1933, though their suspension went back further, to 1917. It is not surprising that Stalin turned away from the fascist leaders of Germany and (to a lesser degree) Italy at this time and chose Western democracies, rather than other totalitarian states, as his cultural allies: the enmity between fascism and communism within Europe and Russia was deeply-rooted and still passionately nurtured in the Soviet press. The spectacle of Soviet solidarity and cultural friendship with France, Britain and America during the 1930s may be surprising in retrospect: certainly, the history of Soviet music as written so far has had little to say about this brief period of internationalism between 1932 and 1936. Yet it was during these crucial years that the Soviet Union truly began to craft its image as inheritor supreme of Enlightenment values. Much valuable research has been done on this in relation to literary exchange during the period, in which the work of the All-Russian Society for Cultural Relations Abroad, or VOKS,[4] played a particularly important role. Katerina Clark's study, *Moscow: the Fourth Rome*, focuses on this climate of cosmopolitanism in the 1930s, and sets its boundaries between 1931–2 (note the overlap with the April Resolution of 1932) and 1937, the year when a shift towards Russian nationalism became dominant.[5] For Clark's study, which focuses on literature and drama, these boundaries are wholly convincing. But in music, the groundwork for what she has aptly termed the 'Great Appropriation' of Western culture had already been securely laid in the 1920s. In fact, I would contend that in the arena of music, the process of appropriation began far earlier than it had done in literature, for a number of simple practical reasons. First, there was the well-established concert culture of symphony orchestras and opera houses which, as elsewhere in Europe, functioned on the basis of a more or less accepted canon of older musical works which were mostly Western, and as we have seen, Western music formed the core of early Soviet repertoire. Second, the steady exodus of Russian conductors before and during the 1920s meant that Soviet orchestras were badly in need of foreign expertise, which is why conductors like Eugen Szenkar, Oskar Fried and Heinz Unger gained long-term contracts to work within the Soviet Union. Third, there was the tradition, already established by ASM, with their keen interest in the ISCM and contemporary music festivals in Europe, of sending Russian musicians abroad to experience Western contemporary culture for themselves. Although this practice was waning by the late 1920s due to ever more restrictive policies on Soviet citizens travelling abroad, Soviet music journals like *Sovremennaya muzïka* (the ASM journal) and *Muzïkal'noe obrazovanie* (which ran till 1930) had carried a lot of information on musical life abroad, including reviews of concerts and of new scholarly publications.[6] There were enough Soviet musicians determined not to allow Soviet musical life to become insular and second rate to have ensured an extremely lively international culture during the 1920s, and the 1930s would build on this. In other words, where music was concerned, the post-1932 era did not so much effect a cultural shift as allow an established tradition to continue.

Between 1932 and 1941 – the year in which Nazi troops invaded the Soviet Union – Stalinist cultural policy went through several stages, each affecting major musical institutions and the repertoire they performed. Though it is tempting for music historians to assess that whole nine-year period retrospectively as a gradual, even deliberate, move towards totalitarian control of the arts, the fact is that the repressions of 1936 and 1937–8 could not have been foreseen by either artists or bureaucrats in 1932, and there is no evidence in any case to suggest that they were pre-planned from such a distance. As the historian David Hoffmann notes, the phenomenon that Western historians since Robert Conquest have widely termed the 'Great Terror' – the years of purges and arrests throughout the Soviet Union between 1936 and 1939 – was not a single pre-planned event so much as 'a series of related yet discrete operations' or, in Nicolas Werth's description, 'the convergence of several repressive lines'.[7] In particular, the investigations launched into the conservatoires, Philharmonias and other musical institutions in 1937 appear to have been instigated by Kerzhentsev's newly formed Committee for Arts Affairs and more particularly by his senior music administrator, Sergey Shatilov, both of whom were presumably keen to show how assiduously they were addressing 'problems' in Soviet musical life. Though repercussions were extremely severe for those affected by their investigations (including dismissal, arrest and execution), some of the consequences – such as the cessation of invitations to foreign musicians – might have been short-lived had it not been for the intervention of war. However, there is an alternative interpretation that is equally plausible: the fact that the Soviet Union was forced to join the Western Allies in 1941 actually put a temporary stop on the withdrawal of cultural relations with the West and thus could be said to have extended the period of 1930s internationalism to the start of the Cold War in 1946–7. Archival evidence suggests the second interpretation is more accurate. As will be seen in this chapter, some highly placed officials believed that once the 'excesses' of the repressions were over, there could be a return to normality, and musical life could pick up from where it had left off in 1936. But once we look back on published and archive documents from those years, there is very little evidence to suggest that their hopes would have been vindicated. Indeed, when a similar situation arose after the war, with cultural officials wishing to continue cordial relations with the West, only to have all inquiries rejected, it seems certain that it was Stalin personally who did not wish to continue the friendly practice of inviting foreigners to the Soviet Union to participate in cultural life, either before the war or after it. Therefore we might safely suppose that the source responsible for the freezing over of international relations in the late 1930s was also Stalin: in short, this was a truly top-down cultural shift that took a good many cultural professionals entirely by surprise, as will be seen. Had it not been for the outbreak of physical war on Soviet territory, Stalin's cultural cold war would almost certainly have begun in 1938 instead of a decade later.

The End of RAPM?

Perhaps not surprisingly, the most vociferous members of RAPM did not publish statements in the months after the April Resolution. As the new organizational structures were being formed, they retained some influence simply by virtue of their membership of the Composers' Unions in Moscow and Leningrad. Lev Lebedinskiy, one of their most outspoken members, worked more or less quietly on mass and folk music for the rest of his career (and became one of Shostakovich's more unlikely friends), though certain RAPM composers – chief among them Marian Koval' – would exact their revenge on Shostakovich and other major Soviet composers in 1948.[8] But 1932–3 was not the time to begin to defend RAPM's work, and when the new Composers' Union journal, *Sovetskaya muzïka*, was launched in January 1933, it contained an assault on RAPM in its very first issue. Its author, Pavel Veys, dismissed RAPM's narrow focus on the definition of 'art for the people' as mass songs, to the exclusion of almost everything else. One special focus of Veys's criticism, Boleslav Pshïbïshevskiy, was an especially soft target in 1933 – dismissed from his post at the Moscow Conservatoire, he now retreated to the fringes of musical life, and his work on Beethoven in particular was roundly mocked. Veys singles out his 'canonization' of Beethoven and Musorgskiy as composers whose music 'shares a class-proletarian content' as particularly 'vulgar'.[9] Clearly, some of the more moderate members of RAPM felt tarnished by their association with militant members of the group, and wished to distance themselves from the kind of work, which, in the post-1932 era, was often described as 'vulgar-sociology'. Yet the former RAPMovtsï did not all go out quietly. One of the few significant attempts to defend aspects of their work is the article 'Fighting for a Heritage' by Lev Kaltat and David Rabinovich, published in *Sovetskaya muzïka* in March 1933.[10] Its authors publicly agreed with the main gist of the criticism meted out to them and, far from defending

Lebedinskiy, actually cited at length his speech from the March 1929 Glaviskusstvo meeting, where he had reeled off an impressively long list of 'suitable' composers for mass audiences that actually included most major nineteenth-century figures, both Russian and Western. They did not point to the long list of 'approved' RAPM composers in order to counter accusations that RAPM held to an unreasonably narrow circle of composers and genres (namely, Beethoven, Musorgskiy and the mass song) because, the authors note, in practice, RAPM's activities never used music by most of these composers.[11] Theoretically, RAPM could have pointed to Lebedinskiy's speech (and indeed several other public statements) as evidence that their range of musical interests was not as narrow as their opponents claimed. But Kaltat and Rabinovich seem to take special care to ensure that this flimsy plank of RAPM's defence should be demolished. Even RAPM's understanding of Beethoven was limited, they claim, to anchoring him only to the French Revolution, instead of showing a fuller grasp of the equally vital influence on his music of the Napoleonic era, or indeed of the *Sturm und Drang* movement in Germany. However, at the conclusion of their article, Kaltat and Rabinovich urged caution in throwing out the baby with RAPM's dirty bathwater: they argued that it was essential to retain anything positive that was achieved by RAPM (for instance, its vigilance against light music) rather than to immediately reject everything about its work, and reminded readers that the move from one phase to another (from the RAPM age to the post-Resolution age) was all part of the move from immature to mature socialism, in which RAPM played its part, albeit one that contained elements of the 'disease of leftism'. At this point, Kaltat and Rabinovich could not have foreseen the coming wave of enthusiasm for precisely the kind of light music RAPM had always attacked, and so their belief that on this front at least, RAPM's activity had been a good thing, was entirely reasonable. Nor would anyone be quick to shout this argument down, any more than they would suddenly criticize RAPM's fight against church music: it was not yet clear, in early 1933, that light music would go on to play an essential role in propagating the illusion of a happy Soviet society under Stalin's fatherly care, or that monuments of Western sacred music were about to be reinstated on the concert stage.[12] But it was clear that, from Veys's article onwards, throughout the rest of the decade, the standard frames of reference for denigrating RAPM were set: their musical tastes were absurdly narrow; they indulged in 'vulgar' sociological arguments and rejected vast swathes of valuable musical heritage on the grounds that it was 'bourgeois'. Worse, Russian composers and folk music were part of the heritage that they had rejected, and this was to provoke especially harsh criticism later in the decade, as will be seen.

Kaltat's and Rabinovich's defence of RAPM's practices was, therefore, rather mild, and was not followed by any substantial supporting voices. But RAPM was not finished yet. In 1936, when Shostakovich was publicly criticized in *Pravda*, former RAPMovtsï re-emerged to assert aspects of their earlier ideology. Sheila Fitzpatrick has shown how the Moscow Composers' Union discussions – in contrast to those in Leningrad (Shostakovich's own city) – featured several hostile speeches from their ranks. Lebedinskiy seized the opportunity to regain status by praising the *Pravda* article as 'a searchlight shining into the formalist fog' and named Davidenko (who had died in 1934) as the inspiration for the opera that was now held up as a shining example for Soviet composers to follow: Ivan Dzerzhinskiy's *Tikhiy Don* [The Quiet Don]. Now repaying Shostakovich for his public slandering of Davidenko's music as 'illiterate' and 'pulp' five years earlier, Lebedinskiy defended his former colleague and publicly blamed Shostakovich and other 'formalists' for the decline in Davidenko's prestige after 1932.[13]

A year later, the Composers' Union was battling with the Committee on Arts Affairs as Kerzhentsev made the first steps towards eliminating the Union's leader, Nikolay Chelyapov, and consolidating his Committee's position in the musical sphere.[14] Now the tables were turned so comprehensively against RAPM's former ideological positions that the situation for old RAPMovtsï became frightening. In effect, they became the most convenient musical scapegoats in an atmosphere of State terror, all the more so because, as we shall see, their anti-nationalist, anti-bourgeois ideology ran counter to the imminent glorification of the entire body of pre-1917 Russian musical heritage. Old scars were again re-opened as Moysey Grinberg (a senior music bureaucrat who would become leader of the music section of the Committee between 1938 and 1939) launched an investigation into the Union's deficiencies. First of all, he supported Kerzhentsev in his denigration of Chelyapov by accusing the Union of weak and ineffective leadership. Petty infighting soon emerged within the Union's ranks as the threat of purges hung over them; as Kerzhentsev did his best to keep pace with the shifting nature of statements from Stalin on liquidating 'Trotskyites' and 'saboteurs', the situation moved from unpleasant to critical and RAPM found themselves in the alarming position of being the favoured scapegoats for problems in the musical world.

Internationalism and Modernism

The Soviets' rationale for embracing Western culture in this short period was twofold: on the one hand, Soviet musicians on the progressive wing had always seen themselves as part of a pan-European culture, just as Russian Imperial musical life had historically been. As we have seen in Chapter One, Soviet musicians and critics visited major Western music festivals in the mid-1920s and took a keen interest in contemporary music. On the other hand, Western composers from previous historical periods were also co-opted and given new Soviet-approved identities in the 1920s, generally drawing upon narratives of Enlightenment, the French Revolution and the rise of European revolutions in the mid-nineteenth century. This twofold embrace extended well beyond musical culture: it was equally visible in literature and other art forms. New translations of Western classic authors and dramatists such as Dickens, Shakespeare, Goethe, Molière and Rabelais were commissioned and published in the 1930s, but the Soviet Union also welcomed living artists and writers to the Soviet Union and even published their work in translation. *Literaturnaya gazeta*, for instance, ran positive articles on left-wing avant-garde figures while they were still accepted as 'fellow travellers' (such as Picasso and James Joyce), while *Internatsional'naya literatura* printed a Russian translation of a part of *Ulysses* in 1935 – though this was already right at the time limit of when such liberality was permitted.[15] Courtesy of VOKS, prominent Western writers visited the Soviet Union frequently, right through the years of collectivization, famine and purges.[16] As Nailya Safiullina has shown, the canonization of living Western writers during the 1930s was wholly directed by Stalin's perception of their attitude towards Soviet power. Because France was in an anti-fascist alliance with the Soviet Union in 1935, and the Comintern was then pressing for a similar alliance with the American government, French and American writers were especially (though not exclusively) favoured. Of the numerous writers who were initially 'approved' and translated – including J. B. Priestley, H. G. Wells, George Bernard Shaw, James Joyce, Upton Sinclair, Ernest Hemingway, Erich Maria Remarque, Thomas Mann, Johannes R. Becher, Lion Feuchtwanger, Romain Rolland, Andre Gide and Henri Barbusse – many were later judged inadequately politically driven and were omitted from any further canonization.[17] Indeed, Andre Gide fell spectacularly from grace (after the publication of his book *Return from the USSR* in 1937[18]) while others, like Rolland, were raised to unprecedented levels of acceptance: Stalin even presented him at a Red Square parade in 1935 – official approval could scarcely get any higher.[19] Moreover, the xenophobia that became such a prevalent trope of the later 1930s and of the post-war era was absent in this short period between 1932 and 1935: the first Soviet Film Festival of 1935, for example, awarded prizes to Disney films, and in the same year Moscow hosted an international theatre festival, attended by Brecht and Eisler.[20] The First Writers' Congress of 1934 was attended by many foreign delegates along-side their Soviet colleagues, and in the spring of that year, Leningrad hosted its first 'Intourist' music festival. The musician and critic Valerian Bogdanov-Berezovskiy wrote a glowing review in which he stressed the fact that Leningrad was keeping pace with new musical developments from Europe; and not only keeping pace, but new Soviet music was itself attracting inter-national interest.[21] Boris Schwarz notes that American and Soviet musi-cians at this time began a serious, if in retrospect short-lived, process of acquainting themselves with each other's music, citing Henry Cowell's 1934 article 'Music in the United States' in the Composers' Union journal *Sovetskaya muzïka*.[22]

On the musical front, Soviet culture had of course for a long time been rich in foreign musicians, who both brought over new scores and intro-duced Soviet audiences to the latest trends in Western modern music. From at least 1928–36, concert life in Moscow and Leningrad was thoroughly international in scope. As Soviet musicians watched Germany's cultural pre-eminence as the leading centre of new music trickle away after 1933, some began to hope that here the Soviet Union might truly achieve domi-nance on the world cultural stage. The loudest voice in this respect was that of Sollertinskiy, who, in a 1935 piece for the journal *Rabochiy i teatr*, set out what Leningrad and Moscow needed to do to secure that pre-eminence. In the first place, he stated, their orchestras are already fully international in range and able to tackle difficult contemporary works (the Leningrad Philharmonia had performed Schoenberg's *Variations for Orchestra* that season). But the city's chamber music culture, he alleged, was negligible, the capella was seriously under-performing and in short, only when both these deficiencies had been addressed could Leningrad successfully compete with cities like Vienna or Naples.[23] Sollertinskiy had already tried – and failed – to persuade Narkompros to invite Schoenberg to come and take up a post at the Moscow Conservatoire as early as 1932: clearly, he had seized on the opportunity offered by the liberalization of the post-Resolution cultural climate to set in motion events that would, so far as he was concerned, guarantee the Soviet Union's cultural pre-eminence.[24]

As discussed above, Leningrad and Moscow had already established close ties with musical circles in the West, and several of the foreign conductors working in Leningrad and Moscow in the 1930s had first visited in the 1920s. In this respect, musical 'internationalism' was not a new feature of the 1930s, though it did require a new influx of energy after the last two years of RAPM's campaigns. But after 1933, foreign conductors working on longer-term contracts in the Soviet Union included several Jewish exiles from Hitler's Germany, instigating a significant transfer of talent from central Europe to the Soviet Union. These included Fritz Stiedry (chief conductor of the Leningrad Philharmonia 1933–7), Oskar Fried (the first foreign conductor to visit the Soviet Union – in 1922 – and who became a permanent Soviet citizen from 1934), Eugen Szenkar (Moscow Philharmonia, 1934–7), Heinz Unger (Leningrad Radio Orchestra, 1934–6), the Hungarian-French Georges Sébastian (chief conductor of the All-Union Radio Orchestra, Moscow, 1931–7) and Kurt Sanderling (from 1936 conductor of the Moscow Radio Symphony Orchestra and from 1942 joint principal conductor of the Leningrad Philharmonia orchestra with Yevgeniy Mravinskiy). Otto Klemperer, a regular visitor in the late 1920s and 1930s, was also forced to leave Hitler's Germany but only ever visited the Soviet Union briefly and did not take up any longer-term post there.

It may look at first glance as though this wave of exiled musicians signalled that the Soviet Union was a refuge where cultured musicians could travel and conduct repertoire that was in the process of being banned in Hitler's Germany. That holds true for the proliferation of Mahler, especially in Leningrad (though Bruckner was popular in the 1930s there too). Yet if we look at the repertoire these exiles and visitors brought with them, it is not, by and large, representative of the most 'advanced' avant-garde European trends. Music by the Second Viennese School, for example, is almost entirely absent. What the visiting programmes represent, therefore, is not so much a festival of unlimited avant-gardism on Soviet soil as a showcasing of far more moderate European trends: music by Paul Hindemith, Bohuslav Martinů, Alfredo Casella and Ottorino Respighi. Thus, while the Soviet Union accepted a small number of highly talented Jewish musicians into its top ranks after 1933, it did not extend this show of cosmopolitanism into a wholesale acceptance of repertoire banned under the term 'Entartete Musik', a category that did not just include music written by Jewish composers, but which extended far beyond that to include jazz and atonal music as well. In fact, after 1936, the Soviets would themselves use similar terminology (especially 'degenerate') to denounce exactly the same repertoire, as will be seen later in this chapter. But between 1926 (see Chapter One Table 1.1) and 1936 (see Table 3.1 below), music by Schoenberg, Berg, *Les Six*, Honegger, Hindemith and Krenek was openly performed and positively reviewed in Leningrad, at least: sadly, large gaps in the Moscow Philharmonia's archival record means that it is not possible to see whether the two cities were broadly comparable in terms of performance of post-1910 Western modernism.

The short period between 1933 and early 1936 is of special interest here, for it is during this time that the Soviet Union had – in theory – time to respond to Hitler's cultural repressions before its own cultural climate became oppressive. There is no evidence that the Soviet Union made any deliberate attempt to showcase music that was banned in Germany; indeed, though there is no doubt that a considerable amount of the repertoire presented in the schedules below could not have been performed in Nazi Germany (because it was too modern, or composed by Jews, or both), two figures who made successful careers under Mussolini – Adriano Lualdi and Alfredo Casella – visited the Soviet Union between 1932 and 1934 and performed their own music there, suggesting that a coherent cultural response to fascist musical repression was never seriously mooted in the Soviet Union.[25] It was manifestly not the case that Soviet musical establishments made any concerted effort to snub composers tainted with fascism, at least not before 1937. Although prestigious Jewish musicians were welcomed as guests to the Soviet Union, the wholesale import of contemporary European music did not follow automatically from that, and some – Fritz Steidry in particular – were only able to continue their championing of modern composers to the extent that they really wanted to after they had left the Soviet Union.

Tables 3.1 and 3.2 below present scheduling trends for what I will loosely call 'contemporary non-Russian music'. As with Chapters One and Two, this is defined here as any music composed outside Russia after 1910, no matter who the composer was (Debussy, Berg or Stravinsky). We can see that, at least in Leningrad, there is a strong continuity from the mid-1920s up to 1936 in terms of composers represented. Paul Hindemith, Max Reger, Krenek, Maurice Ravel, *Les Six*, Arthur Honegger and Stravinsky appear quite regularly, as do the sometime neo-Baroque specialists Respighi, Gian Francesco

**Table 3.1: Contemporary non-Russian/Soviet music in
the programmes of the Leningrad Philharmonia 1932–41
(conductors given where possible)[26]**

1932–3
Hindemith Concert music for strings and wind (Stiedry), *Variations for Orchestra* (Paul Breisach)
Ravel, suite from *Daphnis*, *La Valse* (Fried)
Korngold, suite from *Much ado about nothing* (Egor Pollak)
Reger *Variations and fugue* (unspecified) (Pollak)
Krenek, *Symphony* op. 58 (Pollak)
Rathaus, *Prelude for trumpet and strings* (Horenstein)
Vogel, *Ritmica ostinato* (Horenstein)
Respighi *Ancient airs and dances*, *Fountains of Rome* (Lualdi)
Lualdi, *Adriatic Suite*, *The King's Daughter* (Lualdi)
Kozaku Yamada, *Suite* (Yamada)
Debussy, *Six Antique Epigraphs* (Ansermet)
Honegger, Symphony (1930), *Pacific 231* (Ansermet)

1933–4
Szymanowski, Symphony No. 4, scenes from *Harnasie*
Janáček, excerpts from *House of the Dead* (Breker)
Hindemith, *Konzertmusik* for piano and wind

1934–5
Stravinsky, *Petrushka*, *Pulcinella* (Stiedry)
De Falla, *Night in the Gardens of Spain*
Honegger, *Pacific 231*
Janáček, *Sinfonietta* (Stiedry)
Schoenberg, *Variations for Orchestra* (Stiedry)
Kodaly, *Hary Janos* suite, *Dances of Galanta* (Paul Breisach)
Ravel, *Daphnis et Chloe* (Rodzinski)
Malipiero, *Sinfonia* (Casella)
Casella, *Introduction*, *Scarlattiana* (Stiedry), *La Giara*, *Serenade*, Symphony for Bloch, Piano Quintet (Casella unless indicated)
Krenek, Suite from *Karl V* (Stiedry)
Weinberger, Polka and fugue from *Schwanda the Bagpiper* (Stiedry)

1935–6[27]
Berg, *Lulu* Suite
Milhaud, Suite from *Maximilian*
Honegger, *Pacific 231*
Hindemith, excerpts from *Mathis der Maler* (Stiedry – concert December 1935)
Martinů, *Half-time* (concert 22 February 1936)

1936–7 (data available from 5 March 1937)
—

1937–8
Stravinsky, *Pulcinella*
Ravel, *Boléro*

1938–9
—

1939–40
—

1940–1
Honegger, *Pacific 231*
Ravel Piano Concerto (unspecified), *Boléro*
Stravinsky, *Pulcinella*
[season interrupted by the start of the blockade; orchestra evacuated from the city]

Malipiero and Casella, all of whom featured on Leningrad programmes in the 1920s as well. Especially interesting from the viewpoint of comparison with Nazi Germany is Stiedry's performance of Schoenberg's *Variations for Orchestra* in the 1934–5 season – a work no longer played in Germany – and the performance of Berg's *Lulu* suite the following year. Stiedry's championing of Hindemith in his December 1935 performance of the *Mathis der Maler* symphony may also have been a deliberate act of solidarity following the composer's denunciation by Joseph Goebbels in 1934 (Hindemith's music would be banned in Germany in early 1936). After these strikingly pro-modernist events, a drastic change in programming comes in early 1936, following *Pravda*'s attack on Shostakovich. This can be seen despite the five-month gap in the record from October 1936 to February 1937, though the gap prevents us from forming a complete picture of how seriously programming was affected by the fallout from *Pravda*. As it stands, it looks as though nothing of the pre-January 1936 modern repertoire survives in the Leningrad and Moscow schedules from the start of the 1936–7 season until the end of the 1937–8 season other than *Petrushka*, *Pulcinella*, Ravel's *Boléro* and *Rapsodie Espagnole*.

It is absolutely clear from these tables that the attacks on formalism marked a watershed in Soviet concert programming and, though there were seasons when chinks in the anti-Western armour did appear (most notably during the war, but also in the Moscow Philharmonia's 1938–9 season), it is

Table 3.2: Contemporary non–Russian/Soviet music in the programmes of the Moscow Philharmonia 1933–41 (conductors given where possible)[28]

1933–4 (incomplete record)
Schoenberg, *Verklärte Nacht* (Horenstein)
Roussel, Symphony No. 2 (Horenstein)
Vogel, *Ritmica ostinato* (Horenstein)
Szymanowski, Symphony No. 4, Concerto for voice and orchestra, Three songs from *Harnasie* (Fitelberg)
Roman Palester, *Polish Dance*
Ravel, *Boléro*, *La Valse*

1934–5 (incomplete record)
Stravinsky, *Pulcinella*
Kodály, *Hary Janos* (Szenkar)

1935–6 (incomplete record)
Kodály, *Hary Janos*

1936–7
Ravel, *Boléro* (Szenkar)
Weinberger, Polka and fugue from *Schwanda*

1937–8
Ravel, *Rapsodie Espagnole*

1938–9
[single concert, cond. Nebolsin]
Ravel, Piano Concerto (unspecified), *Rapsodie Espagnole*
Roussel, Symphony No. 4
Auric, overture (unspecified)
Honegger, *Pastorale d'été*
Elsa Barraine, Symphony No. 1 (finale)
Henri Sauveplan, *Jeanne d'arc*

1939–40
Ravel, *Tsigane* (Lev Ginzburg)

1940–1
Ravel Piano Concerto (unspecified), *Boléro*

---

broadly true to say that, for the rest of the Soviet era, the Leningrad Philharmonia never recovered the pan-European focus of the pre-1936 period. As already indicated, it is not possible to make an accurate comparison between the Moscow and Leningrad schedules due to gaps in their archival records, though Tables 3.3 and 3.4 below do suggest a strong connection between visiting foreign conductors and contemporary Western repertoire. This seems particularly clear for the Leningrad Philharmonia: removing foreign names would have a dramatic effect on how much new Western music was played, and it is for this reason that, when they stopped coming (from 1937), the only contemporary (and not necessarily all that contemporary, either) Western music left in the orchestras' repertoire that Soviet conductors either had access to (in terms of scores) or felt able to perform, for whatever reason, was *Pulcinella*, *Pacific 231* and a few works by Ravel. The fact that Vasiliy Nebol'sin conducted the Moscow all-French concert in 1938–9 (see Table 3.2 above) strongly suggests that the issue was one of score availability and likelihood of securing official permission rather than a matter of personal disinclination to conduct foreign or modern repertoire on the part of Russian conductors.

Tables 3.3 and 3.4, despite gaps in the records, do at least suggest that there was no immediate drop in foreign conductors visiting Leningrad and Moscow after the January 1936 *Pravda* attacks until the cut-off point in late 1937. It seems scarcely believable that with Erich Kleiber, Georges Sébastian, Eugen Szenkar, Otto Klemperer, Ernest Ansermet and Fritz Stiedry all conducting the Moscow orchestra in the 1936–7 season, the only music they performed composed outside the Soviet Union post-1910 was Ravel's *Boléro*, Stravinsky's *Petrushka* and Weinberger's Polka and fugue from *Schwanda the Bagpiper*. Nevertheless, it was so; and there are multiple reasons why, not all of which can realistically be covered here: factors such as broad international scheduling trends and the preferences of touring conductors, publication of new works and the commercial practices of different orchestras worldwide undoubtedly play a role but all lie well beyond the remit of this study. Political repression is not necessarily the only driver in such cases, though it is surely true that the first and most obvious reason for the conservatism of their repertoire choices is that, post-*Pravda*, the very first strand of repertoire to be cut was that of Western post-1910 music. If those visiting conductors had wished to present new repertoire, or even repeat post-1910 European works that had already been played, they could quite possibly not have done so without seriously compromising the safety of the orchestra's leadership. That season (1936–7), Klemperer performed nothing newer than Debussy's *Nocturnes*, while Ansermet opted for Berlioz's *Harold in Italy*, Schumann's Cello Concerto, Debussy's *La Mer* and Franck's Symphony in D minor. The 'retreat' – if it

Table 3.3: Foreign guest conductors of the Leningrad Philharmonia, 1932–41

1932–3	**1935–6**
Fritz Stiedry	Fritz Stiedry
Oskar Fried	Eugen Szenkar
Egon Pollak	Desire Defauw
Jascha Horenstein	Pierre Monteux
Paul Breisach	Oskar Fried
Adriano Lualdi	George Szell
Václav Talich	
Kozaku Yamada	**1936–7** (data available from 5 March)
Ernest Ansermet	Heinz Unger
	Fritz Stiedry
1933–4	Otto Klemperer
Fritz Stiedry	
Oskar Fried	**1937–8**
Gregor Fitelberg	—
Gustav Brecher	
	1938–9
1934–5	—
Fritz Stiedry	
Pierre Monteux	**1939–40**
Albert Coates	—
Georges Sébastian	
Vittorio Gui	**1940–1**
Artur Rodziński	—
Alfredo Casella	
Eugen Szenkar	
Paul Breisach	

really was a retreat – to safe Western harbours mirrored that of the Leningrad Philharmonia's programmes in the RAPM era, where despite having plenty of visiting foreign conductors, levels of new Western music dropped, only to be replaced not by new Soviet, or even nineteenth-century Russian music, but simply by more pre-1910 Western repertoire. Another reason for the drop in post-1910 Western repertoire is that a frequent visitor, Szenkar, had begun to conduct Russian and Soviet music – a very unusual practice for a foreign conductor. In October–November 1936 he performed Myaskovskiy's Symphony No. 16 and conducted the premiere of Prokof'yev's *Russian Overture* and Kabalevskiy's Piano Concerto No. 2, works which, alongside nineteenth-century Russian standards like Chaykovskiy symphonies and

Table 3.4: Foreign guest conductors of the Moscow
Philharmonia, 1933–41[29]

1933–4 (incomplete) Jascha Horenstein Gregor Fitelberg 1934–5 (incomplete) Albert Coates Desire Defauw Eugen Szenkar Oskar Fried Stefan Strasser Jascha Horenstein 1935–6 (incomplete) Eugen Szenkar Oskar Fried	1936–7 (start of complete record)[30] Erich Kleiber Georges Sébastian Eugen Szenkar Otto Klemperer Ernest Ansermet Fritz Stiedry 1937–8 — 1938–9 — 1939–40 — 1940–1 —

piano concertos, he repeated several times that season. This accounts for at least half of Szenkar's appearances that season, though other visitors like Kleiber, Klemperer and Ansermet stuck firmly to older Western music.

We can take the temperature within Philharmonia circles after the *Pravda* attacks in two ways: by looking at repertoire, and by examining evidence of meetings with officials. The first meeting to take place between Kerzhentsev and the Moscow Philharmonia was in March 1936, at which major musicians and composers were present: Sergey Vasilenko, Aleksandr Sveshnikov, Aleksandr Gauk, Aleksandr Alexandrov, Nikolay Kulyabko (the Philharmonia's chief director), Lev Knipper, Aleksandr Gol'denveyzer and a few others. There are no negative comments voiced here about contemporary Western music, but Vasilenko put in a plea for more archaic repertoire: 'It is necessary to pay more attention to the works of old masters . . . there is a fear of Palestrina, Orlando Lasso . . . that they don't appeal to the public, but this just isn't the case. I was at a concert where the audience was packed with workers and they were absolutely unfamiliar with music like Orlando Lasso and Handel oratorios – yet they made a great impression.'[31] Kulyabko was still in his post in December 1936 when, at another meeting with Kerzhentsev, he admitted failings in the orchestra's programme of pre-concert lectures, although even then he was confident enough to strike a semi-humorous note, joking that 'one lecturer on Russian folk song said that it was born in the age of the boyars and launched into a panegyric. Another regaled the audience with anecdotes about Beethoven's syphilis and the number of bedbugs in his mattress.'[32] At this December meeting, again no word was mentioned of repertoire: focus instead was on the usual Holy Grail of orchestral aspiration: drawing in the 'mass listener'. It seemed that no orchestra could ever be judged adequate in this field; or rather, whenever orchestras were required to cite their failings, this was the least harmful point to make, and certainly a lot safer than drawing attention to their repertoire choices.

So, then, even in the immediate wake of the *Pravda* attacks, the Moscow and Leningrad Philharmonias were neither under aggressive scrutiny, nor were they scrambling to eject foreign conductors and all modern Western music from their programmes. Admittedly, their repertoire choices did immediately become a lot more conservative; but that was probably a safety measure, and there is no evidence to say that any directive was imposed on them at this point. Nor was Kerzhentsev himself hostile to every facet of internationalism, nor even to cultural exchange per se. What happened after January 1936 was that modernism and internationalism became regarded as entirely separate entities: modernism – now dubbed 'formalism', or music that was considered complex, atonal or jazz-inflected – was to be judged inappropriate for Soviet audiences and misleading for the Soviet composers who were supposed to serve them, but internationalism was a marker of cultural esteem, of the Soviet Union's right to participate on the world stage. Therefore, it makes sense to find Kerzhentsev writing to Andrey Andreyev and Nikolay Yezhov of the Central Committee of the Communist Party in July 1936, requesting permission to send Soviet musicians to Salzburg and to invite a number of high-profile Western artists to tour the Soviet Union. Kerzhentsev writes:

> The most significant events in the musical life of Europe are showcased at the annual festival in Salzburg, Austria, where musicians gather from all over the world. At these festivals the best European conductors appear: Toscanini, Bruno Walter, Weingartner and others. I consider it very valuable to send a group of our own conductors, composers and musicians to the next festival in Salzburg at the end of July this year . . .

Apart from that, I consider that professional connections which would result from this trip would be established with the most distinguished conductors, opera singers and musicians of world importance. I have in mind the possibility of inviting a few of them to tour the USSR, not on the basis of accidental recommendation, but after concrete acquaintance with them by our own specialists.[33]

The letter has written on it in red pencil 'issue unresolved' [*Vopros ne reshën*], but it is clear from the Philharmonia records that these visits did not take place: there are no foreign guest conductors in the 1936–7 season at all and I have not found any record of Soviet musicians travelling abroad to such events at this time. Kerzhentsev would not have made such a request if he had not imagined he stood to gain from it, both in terms of personal prestige and in the security of his position. Such evidence of internationalism even fitted well with his later discrediting of Chelyapov as a supporter of the RAPMovtsï, which will be discussed below. Indeed, high-level policy on internationalism was changing so fast at this point that very few at Kerzhentsev's level would have been aware of the tidal wave of Russian national pride that was about to engulf Soviet cultural life.

Narratives of Enlightenment, 1932–41

Where Western 'classical' music was concerned, the post-1932 period was in part a continuation of the canonizing tendency of the 1920s, but also in part a period when certain aspects of that repertoire were singled out for attention and praise. Some works, such as Mozart's Requiem, Beethoven's Third, Fifth and Ninth Symphonies and Bach's B Minor Mass, had already become an accepted part of Soviet concert repertoire in the 1920s; others had been performed in that decade, but had to wait until the 1930s to come to the forefront of public attention. The precedent for marketing classical and romantic composers for Soviet audiences, however, was essentially set by 1932; the only significant change would be that genuine disagreement over whether certain composers should be performed at all (recalling some of the concerns over Bach in the 1920s), would – on the whole – cease, and be replaced by a critical consensus on the selection of past geniuses. In fact, as will be seen, Soviet consensus over the greatness of Bach, Mozart, Haydn and others in the Austro-German pantheon was an effective tool in attacks on Soviet composers for undue complexity and 'formalism' in the wake of

Shostakovich's mauling in *Pravda* in January–February 1936. Hostile Soviet critics required a canon of accepted geniuses in order to castigate peers whom they judged to have fallen short of those high standards, and so, for the first time, a substantial body of both Russian and Western composers was placed beyond criticism, even as some of their major works were silently removed from concert repertoire.

Clark argues that the Stalinist co-option of Enlightenment artworks was a feature chiefly of the period 1932–5 and that thereafter Stalinist culture veered towards a more Romantic and nationalistic form of 'imperial sublime'.[34] In the musical sphere, the change in emphasis from championing past European masters to Chaykovskiy and the *kuchka* was fluid, and stretched out over a longer period of time. Soviet musical culture was noticeably reluctant to relinquish its embrace of the eighteenth century; the high point of such performances was as late as 1938–40, and this is why the chronological boundaries for this chapter overlap with those of the next. In reality, there is no tidy cut-off between the 'Stalinist Enlightenment' and the aggressive rise of Russian nationalism: the two phenomena existed simultaneously for several years between 1937 and 1941, and this overlap is even more pronounced when the importance of the monumental and epic style that typified the move to what Clark calls the 'Imperial sublime' was, in music, so visibly dependent on large-scale choral works of the Baroque and Classical periods as well as those of the Romantic era. Haydn's *The Seasons* joined the list of Enlightenment works given repeat performances in the 1939–40 season, and only after that point is there a definite move away from the eighteenth and early nineteenth centuries towards more Romantic repertoire, with only occasional classical concerti and symphonies remaining.

One of the most curious aspects of this canonizing tendency was the way in which Soviet critics dealt with major repertoire that musicians wanted to retain, but which was rendered potentially problematic by its sacred nature. As I have already shown elsewhere, there was a move between 1935 and 1940 to incorporate several major Western works of this kind: the Requiems of Berlioz and Verdi, for example, became repertoire staples during this period. Verdi's Requiem reappeared in the Leningrad schedules in the 1935–6 season, after an absence of five years, and Berlioz's Requiem was revived in early 1940, after a gap of just over a decade.[35] Both works fitted entirely with the Stalinist trend of monumentalism in art, both in terms of scale and in their epic spirit. It is the notion of 'epic' – encompassing concepts such as the

grandeur of the human spirit, the focus on lofty ideas, heroes and courageous acts – that typifies Stalinist culture of this period, both home-grown
and appropriated. Fortunately for Soviet music-lovers, the Western classical
canon was richly endowed with works of exactly this epic type, but what
emerges from the pattern of selection and Soviet-style branding is a very
carefully vetted and marketed canon indeed. In Western culture, and especially in eighteenth-century music, religious themes featured in a significant
proportion of such epic works, not only in settings of liturgical texts like
the Requiem mass, but also in subject-matter. By emphasizing their epic
character, Soviet critics moved attention away from their sacred or biblical
subjects and instead focused on their portrayal of more universal themes
such as the people's struggle against oppression, the heroism of a noble leader
and the honest reflection of human emotions.

In 1935, the musicologist Yevgeniy Braudo showed how this could be
done even in relation to Berlioz's *Requiem*, reminding readers that it was
originally written to commemorate victims of the 1830 French Revolution
and asserting that, on hearing it, the listener is reminded of Shakespeare
and Michelangelo – both standard-bearers of the appropriated Soviet epic
type.[36] An even more successful example of Stalinist rebranding can be seen
in an anonymous review of Verdi's Requiem in 1935. The writer, 'Musician',
describes the work as a 'civic panikhida' that was both 'healthy and vital' (as
opposed to mystical and dark, as Catholicism was supposed to be), adding
further: 'The glorious success of Verdi's Requiem always poses a challenge
to sputtering catholic clericalism. His [Verdi's] dissatisfaction with them
is quite clear. Verdi's Requiem continues on the same lines as Berlioz's
Requiem, a great civic lament left over from the revolutionary uprising.'[37]
More radical still was the anonymous author of the programme note for the
performance of Verdi's Requiem in Leningrad on 27 May 1937, after noting
how though the premiere of the work was given in church (because it was
composed for the poet and writer Alessandro Manzoni), it was quickly
moved to the concert hall. Catholic clerics, the writer claimed, were shocked
by the work, because they felt it did not express genuinely religious feelings
and Verdi himself did not deny the 'impossibility of "holiness"' in his mass.
Moreover, the author continues, the 'best representatives of the leading
Italian bourgeoisie in the nineteenth century can clearly be called atheists
and [Verdi] completely ignored all the ritual dogma of religion and avoided
the Catholic church.' Ultimately, the author concludes, Verdi's Requiem is
about the conflict between heaven and earth (between the real and ideal)

and therefore it expresses tragedy in the form of 'cosmic cataclysm', giving voice to the 'gigantic protest of mankind'.[38] Verdi's Requiem, thus re-branded as essentially secular, was performed in Leningrad and Moscow almost every season after 1935 until its last pre-war performance in Moscow in May 1941 and thus became a true Stalin-era classic.

But perhaps the best example of marketing classical music in epic terms can be found in the critic Ivan Sollertinskiy's reviews of Handel oratorios in 1938–9. *Samson*, *Israel in Egypt* and *Judas Maccabeus* were all performed in Leningrad during that season and Sollertinskiy's review of *Maccabeus* makes much of the secular reading of this biblical work:

> Handel's biblical oratorios are not in any way church pieces. They have been performed in the Anglican church very rarely indeed. Indignant pastors even called them 'religious farces'. The oratorio *Judas Maccabeus* ... portrays with emotion the heroic struggle of the Jewish people against their Syrian enemies. The people [narod] are the focal point of the action. Herein lies their birth in classical drama such as *Fuente Ovejuna* [The Sheep Well] ... by Lope de Vega, or Schiller's *William Tell* ... we find the same idea of the people in Handel's choruses. The people's grief, awakened in protest, becomes a destructive fury, a stormy triumph after its victory—all this is clearly delineated in Handel's *Judas Maccabeus*. Here is a true leader, connected in his blood with the people, embodying the best of their qualities: manliness, valour, moral courage, hatred of oppressors.[39]

Sollertinskiy here evokes many of the standard tropes for the musical epic: courage, heroism, clearly defined heroes and villains, the theme of popular uprising and righteous moral and civic anger. Such tropes were, of course, already deeply embedded in revolutionary mythology and by transferring the same concepts and language to music criticism, Sollertinskiy clearly seeks to draw Handel into the Soviet pantheon of greatness. Sollertinskiy's booklet note for this concert further stresses that Handel used the biblical theme only to illustrate timeless points about the people's struggle, asserting that the main hero of *Maccabeus* is in fact the people. In a litany of epic terminology, Sollertinskiy lists its attributes as 'joyfulness, melodic simplicity; children's and women's voices are the victorious hymn of the people ... [its features are] greatness, power, optimism'.[40] In an earlier piece for *Izvestiya*, Sollertinskiy had asserted that: 'For the Soviet listener,

Handel is one of the examples of grandiose musical heritage of the past. His dramatism, his great heroic pathos, his connection with folk culture . . . all draw us near to the great 18th-century master.'[41] Roman Gruber's monograph on Handel from the anniversary year stressed the composer's 'moral-ethical centre of gravity' and placed him firmly within the musical equivalent of what Friedrich Engels had termed the 'breathing-space' between the first and second phases of the French Revolution: 'This was a period of collection, drawing together strength, substance, thorough preparation for the approaching offensive of the bourgeoisie, the break with the absolutist regime, for revolutionary combat; this epoch aided the foundations for the future political-economic and cultural leadership of the bourgeoisie. . . . Without Handel there could have been no Gluck, nor the composers of the French revolution, Beethoven or Berlioz.'[42]

The Soviet Bach Revival

The timing of Handel's Soviet revival in the 1930s was not coincidental, nor was it an isolated phenomenon. On the most practical level, major anniversary celebrations could be held for both Bach and Handel, since 1935 marked the 250th anniversary of their births and both composers were very conspicuously celebrated in Hitler's Germany that year – something Soviet critics were acutely aware of.[43] Reclaiming Bach for the Soviet listener was a major concern at this time; although Mikhail Klimov had introduced both Bach Passions into the Leningrad capella's repertoire in the 1920s (the first Soviet-era performance of the St Matthew Passion was in 1923 and of the St John Passion in 1924), the St John Passion was revived in the 1934–5 and 1935–6 seasons in order to mark the anniversary year. Reviewing the April 1935 performance of the St John Passion, the critic Viktor Gorodinskiy emphasized Bach's own personal striving to reach beyond 'chilled' Protestantism to something much warmer, more personal and more vivid. We also see here another popular tactic of Soviet critics: the deliberate adoption of a cultural figure to render them effectively 'Soviet' – to make them *nashi* (ours), no longer 'theirs':

His music . . . directly flows from the *idea* of his text and from his penetration of that idea. That is why it is not possible to speak of Bach's indifference to religion. He was a son of his times and he could not cross over the threshold of his own boundaries. Though an artist of genius, he could not find room within the bounds of the chilled academicism of Protestantism, in his own creative consciousness, and his unconscious invariably resided in the deepest . . . personal conflict with his own environment. In his works, Bach outstripped his own epoch by more than a hundred years and this was never appreciated by his contemporaries. He is dearer to us than he was to them. We have solicitously preserved the legacy of this great master.[44]

Sollertinskiy tried more specifically to wrest Bach away from his parallel canonization by the Nazis: 'Mongrel "theories" of fascist stripe have seen Bach made up as the "true Teuton" or the "expression of North German spirit" – but the remarkable creative heritage of this peerless master will now be taken up in Soviet musical practice. Like all the other great achievements of old European culture [Bach's music] belongs to the proletariat.'[45] Indeed, Sollertinskiy was far from alone in making Soviet claims for Bach, notwithstanding his Christian faith. Citing Friedrich Engels as her authority, the musicologist Tamara Livanova described the theme of Bach's 'Eine Feste Burg' as 'the Marsellaise of the 16th century' and argued that Bach's understanding of the 'Christian legend' was predominantly 'earthly', even that Protestantism as a movement was a social phenomenon: 'Bach always understood religion as a philosophy . . . [the questions that occupied him] were questions of life and death, of ethics . . . Bach's particular attitude to religion is shown in that, he realizes images realistically, regardless of the spiritual context or thematic and in this he rejects religion.'[46] In her assertion that Bach's music 'refutes mysticism and church-ness'[47] Livanova was repeating an old argument from the 1920s – that religion was not especially important to Bach, or if it was, he should not be blamed for failing to transcend the customs of his native culture. At the very least, critics contended, Soviet audiences should not be deprived of Bach's music simply because of its religious content, since the real essence of it was profoundly human and emotional – the very opposite of 'religious mysticism'. If we recall Anton Uglov's call for a re-branding of Bach in 1927 – 'Now it is necessary to have a "coming back to" Bach in order to make him contemporary, which he certainly can be, if we reveal his potential merit and cast off the mystical robes which cloak his works' – it is clear that Livanova was fulfilling Uglov's call for the mature Stalinist era. Gorodinskiy's more reasonable argument of 1935 – that Bach could be torn from his own historical epoch and made into something that he was not – would be swept away in a tidal wave of aggressive Bach re-branding in the later 1930s. The urge to 'make him contemporary' now meant that the religious content of Bach's music would be relegated to the background as historical context and nothing more.

Ivan Martïnov's programme booklet for the 1935 Moscow performance of the *Magnificat* set the bar high for Livanova's subsequent bold negation of Bach's religious sensibilities. He claimed the work as 'one of the foremost treasures of world art' in which the 'church topic' [*tserkovnost'*] is 'only its external casing' because the 'core of Bach's creative work was not religion but real life. [The *Magnificat*] is not a pious conception, but rather a nerve-racking picture of human life unfolding before us.' Martïnov's description of each movement conspicuously failed to acknowledge the sacred text at all, focusing instead on details of instrumentation and vocal parts as well as highlighting Bach's use of popular tunes and dance styles which, in a bold gesture of adding two and two and making five, he asserted, 'underlines the worldly nature of Bach's oratorio'.[48]

Later writings would take Livanova's line of argument much further. Georgiy Khubov was, like Livanova, a politically well-connected scholar who made a specialism of Bach and the eighteenth century in the 1930s and 1940s. He wrote a monograph on Bach in 1937 which developed the idea that the 'philosopher Bach' image that was being forcibly created in Soviet writings was inevitably in direct opposition to the 'churchman' Bach and that therefore, because of what Soviet writers kept describing as the 'deep emotional content' and 'philosophical conception' of Bach's music, it was actually impossible for his music to be regarded as religious in any way:

> We must not forget that the 'creators' of the Protestant chorale broadly used folk melodies and subtexts, putting them with the religious 'wisdom' of the 'language of the fatherland' in order to pursue essentially only one aim: the ideological capture of the masses through music . . . This was its chief demagogical aim . . . But [Bach's works] acquired a new abstract-philosophical meaning. The boundaries of the 'sacred' and 'holy' in music were destroyed. Sacred forms became essentially 'religious robes' in which to conceal new content – content that was living and real, but which was inaccessible at once to the understanding of the church ortho-doxy, to the dilettante lord, or to the bigoted, drowsy *meshchanin*.[49]

In this reading, Marxist historiography is given pride of place in the new Soviet appropriation of Bach. Khubov had already set out a Marxist potted history in his programme note for the B Minor Mass two years earlier, in which – citing Engels on Germany's social and political history after the Thirty Years War – he argued that Bach's music contained the seeds of coming revolution: 'the protracted and determined struggle already conveyed an "explosive idea" that matured within German culture leading to a new epoch, a new class [the bourgeoisie], breaking up the teleological basis of feudalism.'[50] Bach's music is that of 'the rationalist-philosopher, who reveals in his work the constrained, secret strength of the rising class'. These are the foundations for what became a Soviet truism of the late 1930s and beyond: that Bach's sacred music was not actually sacred at all. Khubov goes so far as to blandly state that the St Matthew Passion was not 'tserkhovnïy' [church music] because the 'deep philosophical content of this work smashes the boundaries of sacred music'.[51] And of the B Minor Mass, Khubov asserts that 'Bach's High Mass, like his Passions, are above all representative of the monumental high symphonic style. This work is least of all a church composition, even though its theme is religious.'[52] And when, for each work, he describes each movement in turn, like Martïnov, Khubov chooses not to mention the text itself, instead describing technical and expressive details for the listener to take note of, guiding them away from any inappropriate curiosity as to what the words may actually mean. A slightly later booklet, again written for the Leningrad Philharmonia, this time for the 1939 performance of the *Magnificat*, repeats the fundamentals of Khubov's arguments:

> As often as was appropriate for Bach, he fulfilled his service and duty to compose music on various sacred texts. But he never went so far as to create specifically sacred musical images. In all of his sacred music there is not one image of holiness, spirituality, ineffability or any other similar religious concepts. Therefore, in the sacred text belonging to heaven, Bach brings us to earth. The incorporeal he gives flesh, the invisible he gives visual tangibility, the inaccessible becomes close, earth-bound, real.[53]

Yet even supported by arguments such as these, after 1940 both Passions disappeared from Leningrad and Moscow schedules for the remainder of the Stalin period.[54] The concurrent revival and spectacular success of the *Magnificat* performed by the Leningrad capella in 1938 and 1939 was also short-lived, vanishing as soon as it had appeared, despite winning its conductor (Aleksandr Sveshnikov) the Order of the Red Banner of Labour. The only remaining major choral work by Bach permanently to win a place in the concert programmes of mature Stalinism was the B Minor Mass, and this was probably because it was both in Latin (the vernacular Passions were sung in Russian translation, making their sacred texts comprehensible to every audience member) and large-scale, unlike the more modest *Magnificat*. Moreover, there was already an established tradition of performing Latin Requiem masses, and since translations of these were phased out in the early 1920s, and the ability to understand Latin was very limited in Soviet concert audiences, their continued performance could not possibly be construed as religious propaganda.[55]

Pergolesi, Mozart and Beethoven

The revival of Giovanni Battista Pergolesi's comic opera-intermezzo *La Serva Padrona* (1733) in 1933 was part of the Hermitage's series of historical concerts. Between 1933 and 1934, the Leningrad Hermitage Theatre, together with the museum itself, supported a number of concerts and exhibitions with a political theme, including: 'French music in the epoch of the decay of feudalism and bourgeois revolution' and 'German music in the epoch of imperialism'; 'Paganini and the problem of virtuosity in romantic music'; 'The origins and development of instrumental music in Italy'; 'The struggle for realism in French music of the 18thC'; 'History of the forte-piano in connection with the development of piano music'.[56] Semën Ginzburg, in his booklet accompanying the Hermitage series *Music in the museum*, explained the importance of preserving 'museum culture' for the Soviet masses. Opening with a quote from Lenin – 'in order to claim victory it is necessary to understand the entire history of the old bourgeois world' – Ginzburg continues:

> The proletariat create their own culture on the basis of historical continuity, the path that is widest in its use of those cultural values which humanity has accumulated in the course of its previous evolution. One such, active in the hands of the proletariat, is the mastery of the cultural heritage serving the museums of culture and art. Soviet museums have for a long time played an important role in mass-cultural-political work. An enormous quantity of excursions and visitors every day fills the exhibition halls of the entire Soviet Union.[57]

Ginzburg's reasoning forcibly asserts the value of preservation, assimilation and continuity – building the new on the foundations of the best of the old. It was a view that gathered strength during the 1930s, which was, perhaps more than any other period in Soviet history, the decade of reclaiming the past for the present. Pergolesi's miniature opera-buffa *La Serva Padrona*, fully staged, with historical costumes, was part of a Hermitage series celebrating 'Italian bourgeois music theatre of the 18th century' and shared a programme with instrumental works by Domenico Scarlatti and Pergolesi, and an opera aria by Leonardo Leo (from *La clemenza di Tito*, 1735). As far as I have been able to establish, the music was played on historical instruments: at least, we know that the keyboard used for the performance was a clavecin.[58] Ginzburg also wrote the booklet note for *La Serva Padrona* and, given that the theme of the opera was a bossy maidservant tricking her master into marrying her (whereupon he realizes his love for her), it made a suitably 'democratic' spectacle for a Soviet audience, even if its gentle social satire was hardly on the same level as that of *The Marriage of Figaro*. Ginzburg notes that it had been done at the Hermitage before (though he doesn't give a date), in a concert entitled 'Voyna Buffonov' [Battle of the comic actors], a reference to the 1752–4 'Guerre du Bouffons' disputes between the relative merits of French and Italian opera sparked by a performance of *La Serva Padrona* in Paris. No clumsy attempt was made to present the work as proto-democratic or revolutionary: Ginzburg points out that Italian music theatre at this stage was an aristocratic pastime. However, the comic opera-intermezzo would, he argued, eventually play an 'explosive role on French soil' because of its overt opposition to 'class ideology' in music, which is why, Ginzburg argued, 'we must be aware of it as we create our own Soviet musical comedy'.[59]

Mozart's Soviet image during the mid- to late 1930s was broadly that of a brilliant composer who faithfully reflected a particular stage in the European Enlightenment and was thus part of the movement which (in Marxist historical thinking) provided the necessary philosophical conditions for the French Revolution. Although *The Marriage of Figaro* was revived in a new production at the Bolshoy from 1936 (the previous Soviet production of 1926 had been shelved since 1931), the Bolshoy did not stage any other Mozart opera during this period. However, the Leningrad Philharmonia put on several concert performances of his other operas, including *Don Giovanni* and *The Magic Flute* in the 1937–8 season (*Don Giovanni* was repeated in the following two seasons). The modest upsurge in Mozart performances coincided with the Soviet peak of Baroque and Classical Western repertoire in the mid- to late 1930s and it was only at this point that Mozart received a proper 're-branding', however mild in comparison with that of Bach. While, as Boris Shteynpress observed in 1935, for Soviet listeners, 'the composer of the "Jupiter Symphony" must give way to that of the "Eroica" and the "Appassionata" ',[60] Mozart may have been obliged to work for the aristocracy, but his music still had much to offer the Soviet listener:

> Mozart wrote in the epoch of the Enlightenment . . . which arose from the soil of the struggle for freedom of bourgeois democrats against the feudal regime and which enveloped the whole area of public life and culture. The distinctive features of that world view . . . are a deep and steadfast optimism based on a solid faith in the victory of the ennobling force of the human intellect, in faith in progress, in a better future for humanity.
>
> In replacing constrained and abstract religious content . . . and the superficial hedonism of the salon and court, the classical style advanced a new ideo-emotional musical content. Its source was on the one hand a striving for real, earthly life, for the 'natural state' of man, to a spiritual life of idealized simplicity and on the other, the approach of a whole, harmonious world view.[61]

Conspicuously absent from Mozart's Soviet reception in the 1930s was any attempt to recast him as a champion of the masses, in the way that Handel's oratorios made it easy for Sollertinskiy and others to position him on the side of the downtrodden. But Sollertinskiy took care to challenge the old childlike image of Mozart, arguing that this *naif* sketch of the composer was ideologically motivated:

> Bourgeois musicology of the 19th century created its own myth of Mozart. According to this myth Mozart was a 'child of the divine', a musician of genius, with supernatural gifts, not a scholar in his craft, but one who wrote music as the birds sing – a naïve artist, not given to pondering philosophical thoughts, not applying himself to any 'accursed questions', not admitting to his music – in contrast to Beethoven and Wagner – any world problem, only happy feelings and the unmeasured play of music itself . . . In the light of this point of view there arises an absolutely clear class meaning of this legend about Mozart. Its function

is to remove responsibility from bourgeois-aristocratic Europe for one
of its greatest crimes in the sphere of culture – Mozart's poverty-stricken
life and premature death.[62]

These were harsh words, themselves based on the nineteenth-century 'myth'
of Mozart's burial in a pauper's grave and his abandonment by former
friends and patrons. But Sollertinskiy, if he wished to create maximum
distance between Mozart and his aristocratic employers, and draw attention
away from the fact that so much of his music was written for court orchestras, was forced to make much of Mozart's death in order to paint him as a
victim, rather than a beneficiary, of aristocratic patronage. Certainly, the
Mozart who 'composes as the birds sing' and whose music was free from any
kind of serious social content was not a figure that could find a credible
place in Soviet scholarship, and by sweepingly dismissing 'bourgeois musicology of the 19th century', Sollertinskiy created further distance between
earlier writers and a Soviet critic like himself, who endorsed Mozart as a
serious, socially engaged artist who was limited by his professional and
financial dependence on the aristocracy through no fault of his own.

It was inevitable that Soviet scholars should lay more stress on some
parts of Mozart's legacy than others: Beaumarchais' satirical plays, though
famously enjoyed by Marie Antoinette and her private court, were deemed
by Soviet critics such as Sollertinskiy to be funny but nonetheless destructive to the French monarchy, whether in their original incarnations or as
Mozart's adaptions of them in his operas. Perhaps because of the diluting
effect of humour in *The Marriage of Figaro*, Sollertinskiy wrote about *The
Magic Flute* with a much stronger sense of its political significance to Soviet
audiences. For this opera, he claimed, cast Mozart himself as the wise
Sarastro, ruler of a kingdom that personified an Enlightenment idyll that
could only have been envisaged by a generation 'not yet tempered by the
flames of the French bourgeois revolution' and who still believed in the
possibility of a 'painless reconstruction of the world'.[63]

> The dying away of feudalism came about under the influence of the men
> of reason ... The monarchy symbolized the world of prejudice and
> superstition, old ideas, which would lead to bloodshed and enmity – and
> already Mozart's contemporaries saw in it the embodiment of feudal
> reaction, religious fanaticism, clericalism, hysteria and, above all,
> Jesuitism. The monarchy [of Mozart's day] opposed that of the wise

Sarastro – the quiet palm grove, where three monuments are erected: to Wisdom, Nature and Reason. Sarastro was Mozart himself – a native brother of Lessing's Nathan the Wise or the Marquis of Posa in Don Carlos of Schiller. His characters speak of tolerance, Enlightenment philosophy, European humanism and liberalism.[64]

Despite the rhetoric linking the European Enlightenment with Stalinism between 1932 and 1936, it was still fairly unusual to see such a litany of bourgeois values as tolerance and liberalism presented as so admirable, even in the context of explaining that they were 'deluded'. Sollertinskiy concluded, 'This is why The Magic Flute can be considered not only as a conclusion to a creative path of Mozart's, but also as a brilliant epilogue to the whole musical-philosophical culture of the 18th century, as the summit of musical thought of the European intelligentsia.'[65] Sollertinskiy's evocation of this noble but vanished age of bourgeois values was not entirely isolated: Yuliy Kremlëv's earlier study of Mozart had described The Magic Flute in terms Sollertinskiy would surely have sympathized with: 'At first glance it is a pure fairy tale. . . in reality, it is the abstract expression of a definite social idea. All the content of the Magic Flute relates in the strongest possible way to Freemasonry, and through that canvas shows very clearly the idealistic conception of cleansing, purification through trial.'[66] This positive endorsement of Freemasonry – outlawed in the Soviet Union – is as striking as Sollertinskiy's praise for tolerance and liberalism, although Kremlyëv's book was at least published in 1935 and so was written right in the midst of the most liberal and Western-facing period of Stalin's regime.

Soviet interest in Beethoven had not abated during the 1930s: he was still, along with Musorgskiy, the composer of the past who could be most persuasively marketed to Soviet audiences as proto-revolutionary. The famous incidents in Beethoven's 'revolutionary' biography – his angry letter to his patron Prince Lichnowsky and his refusal to join Goethe in stepping aside for the Royal family at Teplitz – are rehearsed in literature of the 1930s as frequently as they had been in the 1920s. Beethoven's vaunted sympathy for the French revolution, his disgust at Napoleon's seizure of power and his 'love for mankind' as evidenced in his setting of Schiller's Ode to Joy in the Ninth Symphony were all by now very well-established elements in his Soviet reception. Fidelio, as we have already seen in Chapter One, had been produced by a workers' music group and hailed as the first true 'Soviet' production of a historical opera – though it had still never once been performed at the Bolshoy by 1941. It was put on in concert performance, however, by the Leningrad Philharmonia in 1931 and by both Leningrad and Moscow Philharmonias between 1936 and 1939 as a further boost to the orchestras' classical credentials during that period. Both Philharmonias frequently performed full cycles of Beethoven symphonies and the *Missa Solemnis* was also performed in this late 1930s period (Leningrad Philharmonia, 1939–40 season).

One of the most popular books published on Beethoven in this 'Enlightenment' period was Aleksandr Shaverdyan's *Simfonii Betkhovena* [Beethoven's symphonies], published in 1936. Its tracing of Beethoven's career from 'dutiful' pupil of Haydn and Mozart to a broken figure in Metternich's Vienna abandoned by friends, was absolutely textbook for this time: during Beethoven's last years, Shaverdyan claims, 'Inspiration and fantasy had long since forsaken the composer and he did not compose any significant works. . . . There is a reduction of scale, tension and dynamic thought and emotion. We can observe in the late works only a narrow personal experience and meditation. Religious and mystical motives occupy a place here.'[67] The late sonatas and quartets – the works cherished precisely for their 'mysticism' and *Innerlichkeit* by Schumann and his contemporaries – are rejected here for those same qualities. The Beethoven most cherished in the Soviet Union during this period (and for most of the Soviet period up until that time) was the heroic Beethoven of the middle period: the composer of the 'New Way', of the 'Eroica' and Fifth Symphonies. The Ninth Symphony had been part of the revolutionary musical canon since the earliest Soviet years and so, though a late work, cannot possibly be written off in the same way, though here Shaverdyan claims that, despite Beethoven's sincerity, its expression of 'revolutionary ideas, thoughts of a free humanity . . . the highest degree of freedom and happiness' was flawed:

> In this symphony we find the expression of the best ideas of the genera-
> tion of artists of the democratic-bourgeois intelligentsia. . . . But with
> tragic force it rejects and totally opposes the world view of this intelli-
> gentsia.
>
> Aiming to glorify all-embracing human joy, which has had no place
> in the historical reality of his epoch, returning to the 'millions' who were
> not accustomed to art in the conditions of those times, Beethoven was
> not able to avoid a certain vagueness and lack of clarity. . . . We see
> this in his choice for the finale of Schiller's Ode to Joy – a particularly

idealistic work. Further, it sounds distinct notes of doubt, weariness and religious humility which can be heard in several of the finale's episodes. In its basic tragic elements the Ninth Symphony . . . seems to be the last will and testament of the brilliant composer.[68]

In other words, Beethoven's sincerity was utterly real, but his awareness of the deaf ears on which his masterpiece was falling, and his disillusionment with the collapse of revolutionary ideals – those very Enlightenment ideals running through the music of Bach, Handel and Mozart – meant that the Ninth Symphony could not be the triumph it was intended to be. By implication, its 'doubt' and 'tragic elements' were an accurate reflection of Beethoven's own *milieu*; the French revolution and the European Enlightenment were together understood in Marxist–Leninist historiography as only milestones on the path to socialism – unfinished business, not an end in themselves. In 1936 Stalin unveiled the Soviet Constitution and declared socialism achieved in the Soviet Union; and only these conditions – certainly not those of Metternich's Vienna – could, Shaverdyan implies, inspire art that truly reflected, in execution as well as in intention, 'all-embracing human joy'.[69]

Anti-fascism and Wagner

Wagner's reception in the Soviet Union had been politicized in anti-German rhetoric from as early as 1923, when Asaf'yev commented negatively on the 'trivial, self-congratulatory German nationalist egoism' that he perceived in *Lohengrin*.[70] And when the correspondent from *Muzïka i revoliutsia* visited Bayreuth in 1926, he was disgusted by what he felt was its appropriation by a resurgent German imperialism. Wagner's connection with the rise of fascism – and more especially his full-scale appropriation by Hitler as the prime musical mouthpiece for his repellent views on German expansion and racial superiority – could not escape negative echoes in Soviet Russia, though sympathetic writers worked hard to rescue him from his ignominious association with fascism. Inevitably, politics affected the extent to which opera directors felt confident enough to stage his operas, and between 1936 and the November 1940 staging of *Die Walküre*, the only Wagner opera to be performed at the Bolshoy or Mariinskiy was *Lohengrin* in 1936 (at the Bolshoy). After the signing of the Nazi–Soviet pact in August 1939, Eyzenshteyn's *Aleksandr Nevskiy* was withdrawn from further distribution and the director was quickly charged with the task of staging a new production of

Die Walküre. This was duly staged at the Bolshoy in November 1940, only to be withdrawn again (and *Nevskiy* reinstated) after the Nazi invasion of the Soviet Union in June 1941.

Yet if Wagner's popularity on the opera stage waned in these years, in the concert hall he remained a firm favourite. Indeed, performing Wagner was extremely important to the wave of exiled Jewish conductors who worked with Soviet orchestras up to 1937. Every year between 1930 and 1940, the Leningrad Philharmonia performed sizeable extracts of his operas: Siegfried's funeral music from *Götterdämmerung*, the overtures for *Meistersinger, Die fliegende Holländer, Rienzi, Tannhäuser*, the Introduction and entr'acte of Act Three of *Lohengrin*, Wolfram's arias from *Tannhäuser*, excerpts from *Parsifal* (1936–7 season), Act Two from *Parsifal* (1935–6 season), excerpts from *Die Walküre* (Sieglinde and Siegmund's duet).

But although Wagner was punished for his popularity with Hitler after 1933 by appearing far less frequently on the Soviet stage, he is not reviled in the musical press. Instead, critics show awareness of the unpleasant sides of the Wagner cult, while trying to argue that Wagner's music should be considered independently. In any event, Wagner was certainly not formally banished from the opera stage just yet, since in 1933, the Leningrad Hermitage Theatre embarked on the *Ring* cycle. In his article for *Rabochiy i teatr* connected with this production, Sollertinskiy tackled head-on Wagner's connections with Imperial Germany, his negative image in parts of nineteenth- and twentieth-century progressive culture and his appropriation by the Nazis. For Wagner's 1933 jubilee, he notes, books and pamphlets have been printed, fascists praise his 'Teutonic' style and he was proclaimed the 'premier German man after Bismark'.[71] He explicitly links Wagner and the *Ring* cycle to German and British imperialism and even to contemporary fascism, blurring the boundaries between Wagner's own intentions and his reception in Bismarck's Germany and subtly pointing out a connection between Bismarck's imperialism and the Nazi obsession with race in the character of Siegfried:

> When, after *Tristan*, Wagner returned to the *Ring* cycle, Siegfried was far from the 'socialist-atoner' that he was before. He was now a superman, something like the 'white beast' of Nietzsche, a conqueror of life, with a poetic, strong nature, a projection of the Aryan-colonizer, the imperialist prototype for the conquistador type of Cecil Rhodes. And so Siegfried became the symbol of the new united Germany. . . . The issue of revolution had been replaced by that of 'regeneration' and the rebirth of humanity.[72]

Sollertinskiy squared up to the facts of Wagner's life and philosophy with a directness that could have come from a hostile repertoire censor rather than a writer who wished to see more Wagner on the Soviet stage. But the purpose of his brutal honesty becomes clear in his conclusion, where Sollertinskiy essentially sought to create distance between Wagner and Wagnerism. The Soviets may observe the spectacle of Nazi-era Bayreuth with distaste, but to deprive themselves of such great music would be a self-defeating response:

> Wagner did not retain his place in the history of bourgeois uprising. But he did not express Imperialist ideas in his music. Imperialism was only one of the dialectic threads of the time in Wagner's complex ideological development. Aspects of petit-bourgeois utopianism are preserved in his work right to the end. They are there in the very construction of Bayreuth ... intended as an oasis of serious art in the midst of vulgarity. The irony is that it became the haunt of the fashionable, of American tourists and ... a centre of the national German establishment, with chauvinistic overtones.
>
> It seems to us that the problem of Wagner for Soviet musicologists is not to diminish Wagner or to see him as a precursor of militant fascism. Wagner must be understood with all his gaping oppositions ... The logic of the development of German capitalism was discarded by Wagner's first dreams, compelling him to serve that very capitalism and imperialism which was no less repulsive to him. Wagner is a deeply tragic figure. But his music outlives his philosophy. His works will for a long time remain in the memory as grandiose ideological struggle and capitulation, and Wagner himself turned out to be one of the greatest musical innovators at the dawn of the new imperial age.[73]

In all these arguments about Wagner's transformation from revolutionary to reactionary, the *Ring* cycle looms largest of all. It was arguably the work that was most widely discussed and which Wagner connoisseurs longed to see established in Soviet operatic repertoire. To Soviet Wagnerians, not only did the tetralogy scale such heights of artistic genius that it simply had to be part of Soviet musical life, but it was also a good illustration of Wagner's personal journey over his mature adult life – an instructive example of the dead-end of bourgeois utopianism. Where Marx had been pragmatic, focused on the proletariat and the economic details of industrial capitalism, Wagner had been a bourgeois dreamer – an impractical utopianist. From a Soviet perspective, this was socially and politically useless, but

that did not mean it could not be admired as a worthy aim given its historical context. By seeing him as a tragic figure, writers of the 1930s faced up to
his 'reaction' but underlined the humanitarian principles that lay behind
Wagner's disillusionment. As for the meaning of the *Ring* cycle, Soviet
writers took Wagner at his word.[74] As an anti-capitalist allegory, the *Ring*
was entirely persuasive, even if it failed to usher in a brave new world at its
end. In 1934 the critic Dmitriy Gachev continued this line of argument thus:

> [The character] Siegfried was the most complete realization of
> Feuerbach's writings: a being from Nature, free from any social class,
> never knowing fear or sorrow, ego-less and never craving wealth: a very
> tsar of love and 'communism'. . . . [But this changed with the continua-
> tion of the *Ring*.] Its predominant theme is of doom and reconciliation.
> In 'Götterdämmerung' it is not the gods who perish, but the whole idea
> of revolution, its 'shining truth'. . . . Wagner after 1848, with hanging
> head, genuflected before both heavenly and earthly gods: Ludwig II of
> Bavaria, Wilhelm I of Prussia, Bismark.[75]

As a man who rejected revolution outright, Wagner was in a position to be
heavily censured; but as a man to be pitied, a noble victim of historical
forces, he gained a measure of protection.

One of the last to write publicly in defence of Wagner before the signing
of the Nazi–Soviet pact made it unnecessary was D. Baksan, who published
a lengthy piece in *Izvestiya* in 1937. Here, Baksan tried to wrest Wagner's
music and his personal image from the hands of the by then Nazi-infested
Bayreuth and its supporters:

> They [the Nazis] have in recent years falsified the heroic epoch of the
> 'Ring of the Niebelung'. The heroes and gods that Wagner took from folk
> German myths and which he used to present his humanistic ideas, the
> German fascists try to turn into their own sacred image. Siegfried, the
> hero-bogatïr who must, in Wagner's conception, free humanity from
> slavery and exploitation, they have turned into a blond Aryan beast.[76]

Wagner's legacy – like that of the European Enlightenment – was thus the
heritage of the Soviet proletariat. Invoking the Soviet veneration of those
years for folk culture, Baksan emphasizes that Wagner's art stemmed from
folk tradition and further links him to Russia with his emotive use of the

term 'bogatïr'; Siegfried the Russian knight of ancient lore, who bravely fights the evils of capitalism, is deftly transformed into a proto-Soviet (and very Russian) hero – the antithesis of the Nazi's Aryan 'beast'. It was a very brave attempt, connecting with several contemporary strands of Soviet music criticism: the idea of proletarian heritage, of the importance of folk roots and countering Nazi appropriation of great composers. It had worked for Bach and Handel, but it would not work for Wagner. After this article, there were no further attempts to canonize Wagner until his brief, politically motivated revival on the eve of war.

Classics versus Moderns

Among all the canonizing of Western composers during these years, it is easy to forget one of the major driving forces of the whole post-1936 period: the need to hold up models to Soviet composers in the wake of Shostakovich's disgrace over *Lady Macbeth*. As we have seen, the canonization processes – even in the context of 'revived' works like the Bach Passions – went further back than the post-*Pravda* anti-formalism campaign. But since this campaign was launched right in the middle of the Stalinist 'Enlightenment' it dovetailed neatly with the anti-formalism rhetoric; indeed, the lauding of classical composers in the Soviet press fed directly into the public castigation of Shostakovich and others. Articles published at this time extravagantly praising eighteenth- and nineteenth-century Russian and Western composers at the expense of their Soviet counterparts consistently make the point that while composers of the past wrote in clear, comprehensible language that appealed to the mass public, Soviet composers were still entranced by the decadent modernism of the West. After the immediate furore of composers' discussions in Leningrad and Moscow about Shostakovich's opera and the now-urgent question of 'formalism' in Soviet music, Vladimir Iokhel'son called for Soviet Rimskiy-Korsakovs, Beethovens, Chaykovskiys, Musorgskiys and Bachs – 'great geniuses of humanist culture'.[77] The pianist Genrikh Neygauz publicly validated *Pravda*'s criticism of Shostakovich's *Lady Macbeth* for its over-complexity and lauded the works of Mozart and Beethoven as free from the 'poverty of content' found in modern music.[78] But the most hard line of these articles was an unsigned piece in *Sovetskoe iskusstvo* entitled 'Classical music in the land of the Soviets', which launched a vicious attack on Shostakovich, Gavriil Popov and contemporary Western composers at the same time as lauding the 'classics', both Russian and Western:

We know and understand where the great strength of Beethoven and Mozart, Musorgskiy and Glinka, Chaykovskiy and Rimskiy-Korsakov lies; it consists precisely of this: they draw from the same source of all music – from folk art. . . . The Leningrad musical formalists, headed by Sollertinskiy, grovel before Alban Berg, Hindemith, Krenek, Schoenberg and other sacred idols of German expressionism, the most perverted of all the modern musical schools. They turn away from 'Tikhiy Don' [Ivan Dzerzhinskiy's song-opera] because Dzerzhinskiy writes comprehensible music, namely '19th century music'. They scornfully dismiss and mock Chaykovskiy. Chaykovskiy, in his whole creative legacy, did not achieve as much as Popov, in just one symphony, did. But then the young composer Popov proclaims himself a genius because he composed a gigantic work filled with elephantine roars and all sorts of rattling and howling noises but quite original music.[79] If our young composers would actively respect the classics . . . they would remember the great self-sacrifice and modesty distinguishing those people. The glorious Christoph Willibald Gluck, composer of French dramatic music, gathered around himself the leading lights of the glorious 18th century: Diderot, Rousseau, Melchior, Grimm, D'Alembert . . . Nearly 100 years before Wagner, Gluck proclaimed the high principles of dramatic truth and created classical images of musical purity and beauty.[80]

Having been named as one of the classical 'greats' in these discussions, Gluck's *Orfeo* duly reappeared in the late 1930s, being repeated three times in concert performance in the 1939–40 Moscow season. Yet attempts to rebrand him in the way that Bach and Handel had been claimed for the Soviet listener were decidedly lacklustre. When the German-trained musicologist Konstantin Kuznetsov wrote an anniversary article on the composer in December 1937 (marking 150 years since Gluck's death), he concluded with only the mild observation that *Orfeo* was 'profoundly consonant with our own epoch' owing to the fact that it draws upon the 'living stream' of folk song for its inspiration.[81] This claim could have been made for almost any composer of the eighteenth or nineteenth centuries (and frequently was): the important point to emphasize is that such 'credentials' did not need to be as substantial in the late 1930s as they had been in the 1920s, when constructing an ideological identity for composers and their music was more sincerely expected. Handel, Bach, Gluck, Haydn and Mozart were canonical at this time, regardless of their personal views, affiliations with aristocracy, religious convictions or anything else. They were valued for their status as key icons of the Enlightenment, and performing their major works on the operatic and concert stages signified the Soviet Union's embrace of those political and aesthetic values: additionally, claims that their music was 'democratic', written 'for the people', 'simple', 'clear' and drawn from folk traditions all underlined demands that Soviet composers should follow their example. Marking the high point of the Soviets' appropriation of the musical Enlightenment, Aleksandr Shaverdyan speculated on the rise in popularity of eighteenth-century music in Soviet concert life:

After Bach's Magnificat, Handel's Samson, Gluck's Orfeo, Haydn's The Seasons, we have Mozart's Requiem! Music from the 18th century has become an increasingly organic part of Soviet concert practice. I suspect that the reasons for the rebirth of monumental works of classicism and for the broad recognition of Shakespeare and Rembrandt is the sheer gravity in [their] philosophy of art; [it is] art of great ideas and feelings, their forms are irreproachable and clear. The rebirth of these great examples of cultural heritage has not accidentally occurred in the period of a great upsurge in Soviet musical creativity, in the period when all the most distinctive features of the folk-roots of the Soviet musical classics can be observed and when there is a remarkable rise in demand for work by Soviet composers.[82]

It is easy to see why the Stalinist 'Enlightenment' narrative was so useful. On the one hand, as we have seen, it provided the means of subsuming great works of art into the Soviet canon. But it had its darker function too, and post-*Pravda* reviews typify the Enlightenment's co-option for the purposes of criticizing contemporary Soviet artists. As we will see in the next chapter, however, the old masters of the European Enlightenment – though never formally rejected – would lose their high ranking in Soviet concert programmes as they gave way to nineteenth-century Russian music. As the new culture of 'Imperial Sublime' began to spread into musical life, the old Enlightenment narrative was quickly replaced by one of Russian supremacy, and a new flurry of anniversary celebrations – above all, Chaykovskiy's in 1940 – would permanently cement their new dominant position.[83]

CHAPTER FOUR

TURNING INWARDS: THE RISE OF RUSSIAN NATIONALISM
1937-1941

Coinciding with the end of Katerina Clark's boundary for 1930s cosmo-politanism, 1937 marked the beginning of a new phase in Soviet historiography that explicitly placed Russia in a position of national authority over all the other Soviet republics. The historian David Brandenberger has described the rationale for this change in terms of a need to consolidate popular opinion in the wake of the First Five-Year Plan, with its traumatic enforcement of collectivization and attendant famine:

> Distancing themselves from fifteen years of idealistic, utopian sloga-neering, Stalin and his colleagues gradually refashioned themselves as etatists and began to selectively rehabilitate famous personalities and familiar symbols from the Russian national past. . . . This new catechism came to play a central role in public schools and party educational insti-tutions for almost twenty years. Textbooks published in 1937 replaced all competing curricular materials and established a historiographic orthodoxy over almost a thousand years of Russo-Soviet history. Serving as obligatory handbooks for students and adults alike, the new texts also scripted the depiction of historical events and personages in the works of A. N. Tolstoi, S. M. Eisenstein, and numerous other great names of the period.[1]

As Brandenberger also makes clear, the fact that such major ideological changes were taking place can be seen more easily retrospectively than at the time, and the drastic nature of the change meant that even Soviet histo-rians in the 1930s were not necessarily aware of the way in which history was being rewritten to fit this new Russo-centric model. He cites the letter to Stalin from the theatre critic V. I. Blyum, written as late as January 1939, in which the writer protested that

> the character of Soviet patriotism has . . . been distorted and nowadays is sometimes beginning to display all the characteristics of racial nationalism . . . [Our people] don't understand that we ought to beat the fascist enemy not with his own weapon (racism) but with one that is far superior – internationalist socialism.[2]

Needless to say, Blyum would hardly have written such a letter had he suspected even for a moment (recalling that January 1939 still falls within the period of the purges) that Stalin would not sympathetically agree with him and possibly even act on his prompting. Yet 'internationalist socialism' was far from dead in the minds of many who had ardently believed in it; as we shall see, musicians and music officials continued to believe in it even after the purges had taken place and indeed, they may even have felt that a fresh start – after the removal of Kerzhentsev and his deputy for music Shatilov – was the ideal time to begin reinstating past practices.

The Philharmonia Purges

Alongside shifts in geopolitical ideology and the resultant swing towards Russian nationalism, the Stalinist purges of the late 1930s had a major impact on musical life. They began with the systematic removal of political rivals, spread to the cultural sphere after early 1936 (spearheaded by *Pravda*'s attack on Shostakovich and subsequent attacks on visual arts and literature) and eventually swept through the entire Soviet population in a tidal wave of denunciations, arrests, penal sentencing and executions. Though Shostakovich avoided the tragic fate of his colleague, the great theatre director Vsevolod Meyerkhol'd, who was arrested in 1939 and shot in prison in 1940, the musical world was caught up in a frenzy of investigation and scapegoating. Initially at least, the process of investigation (for our purposes, encompassing the Philharmonias and Leningrad capella in 1936–8) was initiated by the Committee on Arts Affairs under its president, Kerzhentsev. The first phase of the investigation – from approximately February 1936 (straight after his Committee was formed) to the summer of 1937 – sought chiefly to stamp Kerzhentsev's authority over musical affairs and 'weed out' allegedly under-performing bureaucrats in the Composers' Union and in the Philharmonias. But Kerzhentsev did not personally instigate the more serious second phase, which began in October–November 1937 and continued into early 1938. Within the Moscow Philharmonia, at least, this seems to have been started by its own Party activists, and was far more deadly: Kerzhentsev himself ended up being a target for criticism, finally resigning in early 1938.

Purges were typically characterized by a number of factors: archival records often show a combination of 'unsolicited' complaints about a person or body (which may in reality have been solicited in some form), a 'response' to grass-roots complaints, an official investigation, including a financial audit, serious failings 'discovered' and culprits dismissed or otherwise punished, and their replacement by politically approved people. All these things happened during the investigations and purges of the Moscow Philharmonia in 1937. In late 1937, a trio from the Moscow Philharmonia Party group (or 'cell') comprising Lazarenko, Smirnov and Nikolayev[3] complained over Kerzhentsev's head to Vyacheslav Molotov about his failure to correct the Moscow Philharmonia's political failings. Among various charges, the most serious accusation levelled at Kerzhentsev was that he had not taken proper action over Nikolay Kulyabko, its director. This was both opportunistic and incorrect. Kulyabko was known to have been a close friend of Marshal Mikhail Tukhachevskiy, who was arrested in May 1937 and shot in June. As invariably happened after a prominent figure was arrested, a circle of associates and friends quickly became implicated in the alleged 'plot' that formed the initial trumped-up charge. Kerzhentsev dismissed Kulyabko in June 1937 and explained his actions to Andrey Andreyev (of the Central Committee of the Communist Party) on the grounds that he was an associate of Tukhachevskiy's.[4] Kulyabko's case was now closed so far as Kerzhentsev was concerned; but then the composer Nikolay Zhilayev – another close friend of the Marshal – was arrested on 3 November that year. It seems to have been immediately after this that the complainants Lazarenko, Smirnov and Nikolayev contacted Molotov, and this intervention prompted a serious purge within the Philharmonia.[5] Kulyabko was arrested, probably in early November 1937, and was almost certainly sent to the Gulag. He was in fact a prime target for elimination: though he was an Old Bolshevik and a Party member since 1918 whose family had supported Lenin during his exile, it was precisely this category of politicians that Stalin was purging most ruthlessly at this time.[6]

Fortunately, he survived whatever sentence he received and was rehabilitated in the late 1950s, writing a brief testimonial of Tukhachevskiy after the Marshal's own rehabilitation in 1957.[7]

Lazarenko's reign as Kulyabko's replacement was brief. Almost immediately, complaints were made about his leadership, some by highly placed figures in musical life.[8] In the January 1938 issue of *Sovetskoe iskusstvo*, Lazarenko was denounced by the Presidium of the Moscow branch of the art workers' union, *Rabis*, as a leader who did not even stop short of flouting Soviet law, who made up his own rules as he went along, woefully mismanaged the Philharmonia's artists and was insufficiently self-critical.[9] Further indications of Lazarenko's poor leadership appeared in the February issue, when he was criticized for the 'mixed' programmes he had brought in which combined symphonic repertoire with, for example, a second half of accordion music and dance. In one concert, finding the audience restless during Beethoven and Wagner, the conductor had allegedly turned around and said, 'Don't worry, there will be accordion music and dance in the second half.' The author of this article rebuked the Moscow Philharmonia for cultivating a bad taste in 'low estrada' in the audience. Finally, he added, if anyone dared to complain, Lazarenko's response was invariably very severe.[10] Kerzhentsev – or his music deputy Shatilov – had foisted Lazarenko onto the Moscow Philharmonia, and his disgraceful behaviour instantly reflected poorly on them. They would both be dismissed early in 1938 and Lazarenko was swiftly replaced by S. N. Preobrazhenskiy.[11]

If Kerzhentsev was not the prime mover in the second wave of Philharmonia purges, then an alternative candidate may have been his music deputy, the Committee for Arts Affairs senior music bureaucrat, Sergey Shatilov, who ended up conducting the investigations. Certainly, Shatilov worked, apparently harmoniously, with the Party cell trio who had complained about his superior, Kerzhentsev, in the purge that followed. A vicious document dated in the archival folder as September–December 1937 makes it clear that the purge was intended to eliminate key figures in Soviet musical life: those named as 'enemies' included Mikhail Arkad'yev of Narkompros, Boleslav Pshibïshevskiy (former director of the Moscow Conservatoire), the director of GOMETs, GOSestrada, the Moscow Philharmonia (Kulyabko and his deputy, Mel'nikov) and of the Composers' Union, Nikolay Chelyapov. Of these, we know that Arkad'yev, Pshibïshevskiy and Chelyapov were shot in 1937, Pshibïshevskiy in August and Arkad'yev in September, so this list was almost certainly drawn up after their arrest, and quite possibly after their execution. Other names listed here are further directors of Conservatoires and Philharmonias across the Soviet Union, choir directors, folk bands and orchestras.

Shatilov also led investigations into the work of the Leningrad Philharmonia between September 1937 and January 1938, though I have not found evidence that this was prompted by Party activists in the organization. In fact, the Leningrad Philharmonia had been under financial scrutiny for some time; it managed its own finances until 1 August 1936, when it came under the jurisdiction of the Committee for Arts Affairs. There were four basic areas of responsibility: concert organization, club work, publishing and educational work. In addition to the symphony orchestra, the Philharmonia had an orchestra of folk instruments and a quartet, both of which were engaged in club work. From the moment Kerzhentsev's Committee was formed in January 1936, a financial investigation was launched into payments, which lasted until August 1937, including an audit by the art workers' union, *Rabis*, and all these investigations eventually culminated in Shatilov's report to Kerzhentsev in January 1938. Among Shatilov's many criticisms of the Philharmonia's leadership under their then director, the pianist Isay Renzin, was the claim that ticket sales were catastrophically low due to poor marketing, with the capella hall left almost empty for some concerts. The criticism that the Philharmonia's chamber music organization was particularly poor rather bears out Sollertinskiy's critical comments on this sphere from 1935; and the result had been a slump in ticket sales overall. Shatilov accused the director of club work, Merovich, of having made a loss of over 78,000 roubles during his eight-month term of office and charged him with favouritism towards his own students. Renzin was dismissed in 1937 and replaced by Mikhail Chulaki, though he himself was then dismissed in January 1938, having apparently failed to right Renzin's wrongs.[12] Chulaki's deputy, Chernobïlskiy, was dismissed at the same time. No one is listed in the documents from the investigation as having been arrested apart from a certain Shur, a former worker in the club concert section, though that certainly does not mean that nobody suffered this fate: it may be simply that archival records were not preserved, or that the document trail between Shatilov and Kerzhentsev is intact, but makes no mention of arrests.[13] The inspector who actually did the auditing work, Belyayev, reported to Shatilov that although the Philharmonia's repertoire plan for the 1937–8 season was 'acceptable', 'it included works by such composers as Krenek, Hindemith, Schoenberg, the formalists Casella and

Respighi, who are fascists and of dubious worth'.[14] Needless to say, all these composers were removed from the orchestra's programmes for that season, and this document is the only piece of extant evidence of the direct effect these purges undoubtedly had on the Philharmonia's programming of modern Western music (and incidentally, the only real evidence of a 'ban', however short-lived, on composers believed – even if erroneously – to be favoured by Nazi Germany and Fascist Italy). Finally, in April 1938 A. Ponomaryev was appointed Director, a post which he successfully held for just under twenty-five years.[15]

Nationalism and Repertoire

Among the charges levelled at both Philharmonias – both specifically by Shatilov and possibly by other, more senior, bureaucrats – is one concerning repertoire that sheds further light on the sudden preponderance of eighteenth- and nineteenth-century Western and Russian repertoire from 1938 onwards. Both organizations were accused of inadequately propagandizing 'heroic' music (including Russian music, Beethoven, Berlioz, composers of the French Revolution and Wagner) and music based on folk-lore. This indicated an important new strand in official criticism of the Philharmonias and it is possible that the driver was not Shatilov at all, but someone far above him, perhaps even within the Central Committee.[16] An unattributed and undated document in the Committee on Arts Affairs file relating to the investigations of the Moscow Philharmonia (with an archive date range of 10 November–29 December 1937) goes into far more specific detail on repertoire. The tone of this document is very different from Shatilov's other letters; it is written from a more expert perspective, both in terms of political and musical literacy. It was very probably not the work of a single person, and certainly benefited from some relatively expert musical input, though there is no evidence as yet to suggest who that musician may have been. It began with a bold political statement and went on to flesh out, in considerably more detail, and with far greater authority, the failings listed elsewhere by Shatilov:

> The Communist Party has repeatedly shown workers on the ideological front the necessity for close attention to the study of the heroic past of the peoples of the USSR, their histories and cultural richness. These have been given clear expression in the works of comrades Stalin, Kirov

and Zhdanov regarding the question of a textbook on the history of the peoples of the USSR.

The vile attempts of the Trotskyites, Bukharinites and vulgarizers from the Pokrovskiy school who have discredited the great past of the Russian people and defamed the significance of Russian national culture have received a cruel rebuff. The bourgeois nationalists have been destroyed without mercy, having attempted to thwart the cultural development of the national republics of the Union.

The fruits of these enemy activities, however, are not yet comprehensively rooted out. This is strongly evident in the musical sector of our ideological front. Enemies, sitting on the apparatus of regional management in the arts, in the leadership of the Philharmonias and music schools, carry out their undermining, enemy work, setting the mass of Soviet musicians on a false path.

Amid a well-known section of musicians there are still enemies who believe in our inferiority, with provincial narrow-mindedness towards the musical art of the peoples of the USSR regarding the West, and especially of German music. Worship of German composers goes together with an intolerable undervaluing of the achievements of Soviet creativity and that of the national peoples of the USSR.

The enemy character, the bourgeois-reactionary nature of these tendencies is absolutely clear.

The repertoire of our symphonic and chamber concerts is restricted to a small circle of foreigners, in the main German authors. Of Russian symphonies, only those that are recognized abroad, that are popular with Western bourgeois audiences, are propagandized. Chaykovskiy's early symphonies are not played, Taneyev's symphonies hardly at all, nor those of Kalinnikov, Balakirev or Glazunov; many of Rimskiy-Korsakov's works are forgotten – Sadko, Antar, Glinka's Prince Kholmskiy, Spanish Overture, Borodin's First Symphony.

From the West's heritage we do not sufficiently make use of works with a heroic character, of Handel and Gluck, musicians of the epoch of the French bourgeois revolution. Berlioz, Wagner and such works filled with a popular [narodniy] melos of Haydn, Schubert, Grieg, Dvořák and Smetana.

The same thing is found in the repertoire of our performers and soloists. Here there is an aspiration to endure a style that is peculiar to the bourgeois concert hall. Pianists stubbornly limit their programmes to a narrow circle of a few works of Bach, Beethoven, Chopin, Schumann, Liszt and Debussy. Of the Russian piano repertoire we hear only the music of the émigrés Rakhmaninov and Medtner – the major piano works of Arenskiy are ignored as 'second-rate'.[17]

The document goes on to criticize the teaching of Yuriy Keldïsh, a former RAPMovets now working at the Moscow Conservatoire, for insufficiently recognizing the importance of Russian music and disproportionately focusing on the 'White-émigrés' Stravinsky and Rakhmaninov. Georgian and Azerbaijanian musical institutions are accused of failing to explore their folk heritage, although in Kirghizia musicians are accused of 'trying to separate the development of national music from Jewish and especially from Russian influences'.[18] On the one hand, the Soviet Republics were supposed to study their own folk culture attentively; but if that study seemed to be leaning too far away from Russian influence, they could be censored for that too. Russian national music was now to take centre stage: Soviet republics should study their own culture, but should acknowledge the central importance of Russian music at the same time, and all the while, the 'valuable instructions of Stalin, Kirov and Zhdanov on questions of history' must be used as the fundamental basis for teaching Russian music. RAPM is dealt a glancing blow for its 'vulgarizing, enemy articles and brochures' but a more bizarre target is the holdings of old 'German' teaching materials in the conservatoires: textbooks by Ebenezer Prout (not German but English), Ernst Kurth and Ludwig Bussler must now be replaced by those by Sergey Taneyev, Aleksandr Kastal'skiy, Georgiy Katuar and others. The State music publishing house Muzgiz was not exempt from criticism either; the document goes on to protest against the fact that 'after twenty years of Soviet power we don't even have a vocal score of "Ruslan and Lyudmila" or "Ivan Susanin"'.[19] Parts of this document – those that object to the lack of older Russian music in the concert halls and of Russian opera scores – read as though they were penned by a disgruntled musician, but the reference to the 'German' Prout reveals that it was probably not the joint effort of a bureaucrat and a properly trained musician; or if it was, the musician played only a minor initial role in its preparation. The reference to *Ivan Susanin* – the opera which had not yet received its Soviet premiere at the time this document was being circulated – also provokes the suspicion that this document was primarily the work of a bureaucrat, and an uninformed one at that, since a musician would have known that a vocal score of this opera could hardly have been produced with a libretto that had been banned since 1917. As will be discussed in the next chapter, the minister for arts, Andrey Zhdanov, took advantage of both musicians and letters from the public when drafting his own report on composers in 1948, and there is every reason to suspect that this document is similarly constructed from a medley of personal and official sources.

We do not know either who wrote this document, or to whom it was sent. But its appearance in the Committee for Arts Affairs file suggests that it was not a draft, but a finished report that was probably circulated from the Committee on Arts Affairs to all musical institutions in the Soviet Union. If it was not circulated, but functioned as guidance for Kerzhentsev and Shatilov, then this would certainly explain why Shatilov's reports on the Philharmonias highlight the lack of this repertoire (taking his cue from the document); but on the other hand, Shatilov's reports do not contain anything like so much specific detail on performance trends. Assuming it was circulated to at least the Moscow and Leningrad Philharmonias at the end of 1937, its greatest impact would have been on the following season, from 1938–9. Its specific demands were that Russian and Soviet music should occupy a much more prominent role than it had previously enjoyed; also, that more works by Handel, Gluck, Berlioz, Wagner, Haydn, Schubert, Grieg, Dvořák and Smetana would be welcome. Handel and Gluck are named for their Enlightenment-epic status; Wagner and Berlioz are the token 'revolutionaries', while Haydn, Schubert, Grieg, Dvořák and Smetana are all lumped together for their alleged folk-inspired style, or *narodnïy melos*. Sure enough, the Moscow Philharmonia performed Handel's *Samson* in February and April 1939, Haydn's *Seasons* in March 1939 and Gluck's *Orfeo* in April 1939; *Judas Maccabeus* was performed in Leningrad in February 1939, Bach's *Magnificat* in the same month, and a concert of Smetana, Dvořák, Chopin, Berlioz and Saint-Saëns in April 1939. In the following Leningrad season, the Russian works named in the document all dutifully made their appearance: excerpts from Glinka's *Ivan Susanin* were played at a workers' concert, while the standard subscription series included *Prince Kholmskiy* and his Spanish Overture No. 1, 'Aragonskaya Khota', Rimskiy-Korsakov's 'Antar' Symphony, *Mozart and Salieri* and *Boyarïnya Vera Sheloga*, Kalinnikov's First Symphony, Balakirev's First Symphony and *Islamey*. A complete concert performance of Dargomïzhskiy's *Stone Guest* was also given in the 1939–40 season, cementing Leningrad's commitment to nineteenth-century Russian classics. There was a *dekada* of Soviet music in November 1940 (at which Shostakovich's Sixth Symphony was premiered). In Moscow, the 1939–40 season also included Gluck's *Orfeo* (three times in the season, in October 1939 and in January and April 1940) and Haydn's *Seasons*, but overall, Moscow's season was more Russian-focused than Leningrad's. Borodin's Second Symphony was chosen for the opening concert; there was an all-Lyadov concert, a parallel *dekada* of Soviet music (also given in November), and practically all of Chaykovskiy's orchestral music: his complete symphonies, plus *Francesca da Rimini*, *Romeo and Juliet*, *Hamlet*, *Rococo Variations*, ballet music, piano and violin concerti, orchestral suites, *Serenade for strings*, *Andante and finale* for piano and orchestra and excerpts from *Onegin*. This was not, of course, a coincidence, since Chaykovskiy's centenary year was 1940, and the Soviet Union celebrated it with all the pomp it could muster. I will return to the Chaykovskiy centenary at the end of this chapter, but it is seems extremely likely that this document – whoever wrote it – played an important role in the shift from musical cosmopolitanism to Russian nationalism from the end of 1937, a process that was fully established by 1939.

The demand for more Handel and Gluck in this document provides a chilling backdrop to the upsurge of Enlightenment-era repertoire in the Philharmonia schedules between 1938 and 1940. It does not, of course, fully account for it – the Leningrad capella and other choirs had been performing Bach and Handel since the mid-1920s, and there is the 250-year anniversary and comparison with Nazi Germany to consider – but this does partly explain why in music, in contrast to Katerina Clark's observation that the Soviets' embrace of the Enlightenment was switching towards the 'imperial sublime' and Russian nationalism after around 1937, both trends were juggled simultaneously, at least until 1940. There was in fact noticeably more Enlightenment-era music on the Philharmonia programmes at this time, a state of affairs which lasted until the onset of war in 1941: the revival date of Berlioz's Requiem in the post-1932 years was as late as January 1940 (Leningrad Philharmonia under Sveshnikov).

Although it is undeniable that the proportion of Soviet music performed in the Leningrad and Moscow Philharmonias increased after the purges, it is important to acknowledge that both orchestras had not neglected Soviet composers prior to those events. Accusations that they had played insufficient quantities of nineteenth-century Russian and contemporary Soviet music should not be taken at face value. Indeed, all charges – those of financial mismanagement included – must be regarded sceptically, since just because no defence is preserved in the archival record, this does not mean that investigators' accusations were correct. It is in the nature of committee documents only to record one side of a case and where scapegoats are so transparently being sought, to leave investigators' charges unquestioned risks perpetuating unjust accusations that in several cases led to punishment that by far exceeded what was morally justifiable, even if those charges had been accurate. In the minds of those more sympathetic to Western modernism, there was already far too much nineteenth-century Russian music being performed in Leningrad and Moscow: Sollertinskiy made exactly this point in his address at the Composers' Union conference convened in February 1935 to discuss the future of Soviet symphonism. Arguing, as he often did, that Soviet musicians did not have enough knowledge of modern Western music, he joked that 'in the [Leningrad] Philharmonia Schoenberg's "Variations" have been heard in full only once, whereas we have been given Chaykovskiy 190 times this year and Rimskiy-Korsakov 189 times'.[20] The notion that nineteenth-century Russian music was under-represented in the orchestras' programmes could only hold true for those who believed that the orchestras should not be playing so much Western music, and especially not Western contemporary music. In short, the claim that nineteenth-century Russian music was not sufficiently played could not have been made were it not for the cultural shift of 1937 towards Russo-centricism and the very public idealization of Tsarist-era figures such as Pushkin and Tolstoy.

Table 4.1 lists performances of Soviet music between 1934 and 1937 with as complete data as are available, but gaps in the Moscow record mean that it is far from representative. One thing the data do tell us, though, is that both orchestras supported new Soviet music and had done so from 1933 at least, without any threats from Narkompros to force them to do so. Though it is true that after 1937 the increase in Soviet music (including *dekadas* celebrating works written by composers from the Soviet Republics) was exponential, these data show that Soviet contemporary music had not been neglected in favour of Western contemporary music – in fact, it played an equal role within schedules that were notably balanced between different repertoire strands. All that happened after 1937 was that Soviet and nineteenth-century Russian music utterly dominated repertoire, with even Western classics eventually coming to play a subservient role.

Hand in hand with calls for more Soviet music went increasingly anxious demands for more nineteenth-century Russian music as well. But this move

Table 4.1: **Performances of Soviet repertoire in the Moscow and Leningrad Philharmonias, 1933–7**

Moscow	Leningrad
1933–4 Shostakovich, Piano Concerto No. 1, suite from *The Bolt* Prokof'yev, Symphony No. 1, Piano Concerto (unspecified), suite from *Ala and Lolly*, March from *Three Oranges* Gladkovskiy, *Memorial to the fallen, Twenty-six* Shebalin, *Introduction* (premiere) Myaskovskiy, Symphony No. 9 Shaporin, Two songs from *Dekabristï* Knipper, Third Tadjik song Rogal'-Levitskiy, *Chopiniana* Burshteyn [*sic.* – should be Veysberg] Three exc. from *Giul'nar* (premiere) Polovinkin, Piano Concerto (premiere)	**1933–4** (incomplete, up to March 1934) Shostakovich, Three mvts from *The Golden Age* Prokof'yev, Sinfonietta op. 5/48, Piano Concerto Nos 3 and 5, Symphony No. 4 op. 47 (in first version of 1929) Shteynberg, 'Turksib' Symphony Shebalin, 'Lenin' Symphony Myaskovskiy, Symphony No. 10 Entelis, 'War' Symphony Brusilovskiy, Symphony No. 2 Shcherbachev, Symphony No. 3
1934–5 (16 concerts available) Zhelobinskiy, Piano Concerto (premiere) Prokof'yev, Symphony No. 1, suite from *Lieutenant Kizhe* Knipper, Symphony No. 3 Chemberdzhi, Concert Suite Dzerzhinskiy, Piano Concerto Myaskovskiy, Symphony No. 14 (premiere)	**1934–5** (complete) Zhelobinskiy, Piano Concerto Prokof'yev, Symphony No. 3, Piano Concerto No. 1, *Egyptian Nights*, Four scenes from *Chout* Popov, Symphony No. 1 (premiere) Dzerzhinskiy, Piano Concerto Myaskovskiy, Symphony No. 6 Veysberg, excerpt from *Giul'nar* Yudin, Organ Concerto Gladkovskiy, Heroic Symphony Kabalevskiy, Piano Concerto Shcherbachev, *Groza*
1935–6 (five concerts available) Koval', Four Songs	**1935–6** (complete) Veysberg, Song of *Giul'nar* Veprik, *Songs and dances of the ghetto* Gayderov, Sinfonietta Dzerzhinskiy, Piano Concerto No. 2 Zhivotov, *Funeral Poem*, *Zapad*, Dance Suite

	Zaranek, Dance Suite Knipper, *Lyric Symphony* Koval', *Cursed Past* Polovinkin, overture *First of May* Chishko, 3 songs from *Battleship Potëmkin* Shostakovich, Symphony No. 1, suite from *The Bolt*, suite from *Balda*, Piano Concerto No. 1 Shcherbachev, 'Izhorsk' Symphony, excerpt from *Anna Kolosova*, suite from *Groza* Shtreyker, 'Women of the East' (first movement) Shebalin, Symphony No. 2
1936–7 (complete) Prokof'yev, *Russian Overture, Ala and Lolly*, suite from *Romeo and Juliet*, Piano Concerto No. 3, Symphony No. 1 Kabalevskiy, Piano Concerto No. 2 Veprik, *Song of Rejoicing* Myaskovskiy, Symphony No. 16 Zhelobinskiy, Dramatic Symphony Yudin, *Requiem in mem. Kirov* Chemberdzhi, Concert Suite Shebalin, Overture Vasilenko, Chinese Suite Shishov, 'Polevaya' Symphony Ivanov-Boretskiy, *Dniprovskiy Falls* Kreyn, *Spring Symphony* Aleksandrov, *Songs of the West* Glier, overture *Giul'nar* (prem) [*Dekada* of Georgian and Azerbaijanian music]	**1936–7** (data available from 5 March) Prokof'yev, *Russian Overture*, second suite from *Romeo and Juliet*, Piano Concerto No. 3, suite from *Chout*, Symphony No. 1 Kabalevskiy, Piano Concerto No. 2 Veprik, *Song of Rejoicing* Gedike, Trumpet Concerto Zhelobinskiy, Dramatic Symphony Duneyevskiy, excerpt from *Searching for Happiness* Shcherbachev, Suite from *Groza* Ivaniskin, Chuvash Symphony

to reclaim pre-Soviet Russian culture was not limited to music: as noted above, it was part of a seismic shift in Soviet culture that began around 1937 and continued for the rest of the Stalin period. As David Brandenberger and Kevin M. F. Platt explain in their introduction to the volume *Epic Revisionism*, which deals specifically with the canonization and glorification of pre-Soviet Russian figures at this time, the rise in importance of Russian Tsarist-era heroes came at the same time that early Soviet-era heroes were being discredited – Old Bolsheviks, military heroes from the Civil War, and even pre-Soviet peasant rebels like Yemel'yan Pugachev and Stepan Razin: 'As this cruel winnowing process [the purges] stripped the Soviet Olympus of its party activists and Red Army commanders, the prominence on the pantheon's constituents from the Russian national past rose dramatically.'[21] And as Stephanie Sandler notes in her chapter on the 1937 Pushkin celebrations in the same volume, the hysterical pitch of these national celebrations masked the state of terror which the nation itself had just been though: 'A historical experience of collective trauma lay just beneath the public performance of happiness and achievement required by the Pushkin jubilee in February 1937 ... it provided a blanket cover of optimism beneath which individual citizens suffered terrifying injustices.'[22]

Old Faces, New Scapegoats

It was largely this context that was the cause of a fresh wave of attacks on former RAPMovtsï in May 1937, led by the Committee's senior music bureaucrat Moisey Grinberg. In the spring of 1937 the leadership of their literary equivalent, RAPP, was attacked in the Writers' Union, and Grinberg swiftly moved to echo this in the Composers' Union.[23] In his article 'RAPMovskie perepevï' [RAPMovsky re-hashing], Grinberg attacks Anatoliy Groman's 1932 article on the *kuchka* and Chaykovskiy in *Proletarskiy muzïkant* for explaining the breakup of the *kuchka* in over-simplistic (and indeed, inaccurate) terms as a split between 'bourgeois liberals' and the 'muzhik democrat' Musorgskiy.[24] Cleverly pre-empting the imminent canonization of nineteenth-century Russian composers, Grinberg scoffs:

> What is written in this article about Glinka, the Conservatoires, Rimsky Korsakov, Borodin and Balakirev simply beggars description. We read that 'Glinka's nationalism is the broad concept of the Slavophiles', that the founding of the Conservatoires was one of the 'bourgeois reforms led by landowners supporting serfdom', that Borodin's In the Steppes of Central Asia was an 'idealization of the predatory politics of tsarism, in the interests of Russian capital' ... that Rimskiy-Korsakov's nationalism is of the 'Great Powers' character, and so on.[25]

This was precisely the kind of 'vulgar-sociology' that musicologists now rushed to scorn. The fact that Groman's subjects had been Russian composers really added insult to injury in 1937, since by this time, even the suggestion that any of them required such crude ideological categorization, still less open criticism, was made to look offensive, and Groman rushed to confess his errors (his article appeared in the very same issue, which at least gave him the right of reply).[26] Grinberg opportunistically ticked off Groman's 'crimes' in accordance with this new ideology: he accused members of the *kuchka* of being 'bourgeois', being politically in sympathy with the serf-owning classes, he grossly simplified Musorgskiy as a 'muzhik-democrat' and he neglected Chaykovskiy's importance. Grinberg opined that: 'To . . . illuminate anew the great legacy of Chaykovskiy means above all to stand against the vulgar sociology of RAPM's methods and their whole scheme of music history in 19th-century Russia.'[27] Groman's response is worth quoting at length, since it represents the terms in which those who had subscribed to proletarian ideological arguments in the late 1920s and early 1930s were now being forced publicly to recant:

> With regard to the national Russian character of Borodin and Rimskiy-Korsakov as a reflection of 'supreme power' [tsarist] and 'Slavophile narrow-mindedness', I was profoundly in error, and I admit that this was a vulgar simplification. I should have shown that the national folk char-acter of the kuchkists was, to them, of utmost value in the 1860s. I was also wrong in my assessment of the 'Eastern element' in the kuchka, seeing it merely as pure exoticism and again representative of this 'supreme power', and incorrectly interpreted the programme of Borodin's *Steppes*. In this I neglected the work of Stasov, who evaluated the folk music of the East highly. . . . I omitted the fact that both Borodin and Rimskiy had undertaken careful study of this folksong. Also, I should have shown that the way they used it (not counting a few uses of it as the exotic element) actually widened the folk basis of their work. It is no accident that the strongest Eastern composers – Paliashvili, Spendiarov – found this music to be a strong influence on them. In dividing Russian music between 'kulak' and 'peasant' music, RAPM put nearly every-thing in the 'kulak' bracket, fighting even the amateur workers' choirs who propagandized Russian folk song. By regarding Russian folk song as reflective of supreme-power chauvinism, RAPM then labelled folk music of other lands of the USSR as 'local nationalism'. Their campaign

set its face against the classical musical art of the USSR (opposing Paliashvili). And from this fundamentally wrong basis they evaluated such works as *Prince Igor*, *The Golden Cockerel*, etc. In closing I would like to share the rebuke Grinberg made about the leadership of the Composers' Union. It provides no encouragement for the study of our heritage, especially Russian music. We can't let this continue any further and hope that someone will write about these composers. We need a music conference for the study of Russian music, the sooner the better.[28]

By 1937 it was completely unnecessary to defend Russian nineteenth-century culture against RAPM: the organization had been dissolved for five years and had not gained significant influence in the post-1932 era. Russian nineteenth-century music was generously represented in the Philharmonias and opera houses, and Rimskiy-Korsakov, Borodin and Chaykovskiy certainly did not need Grinberg's intervention to be 'rehabilitated'. But in the tense atmosphere of 1937, those tasked with improving, investigating and 'unmasking' enemies in musical life required scapegoats, and Groman, as a former leader of RAPM, made a convenient target with his unfortunate attack on exactly those composers who were in the process of being glorified. As discussed in chapters One and Two, the *kuchka*, Chaykovskiy and their contemporaries had all been celebrated, performed and written about in the 1920s and early 1930s; their legacies had always been valued, even by many members of RAPM, but after 1937 they were placed beyond any criticism, no matter how mild. They were Russian: therefore they were *nashi* [ours] and held up as objects of intense national pride.

More dangerous attempts to revive attacks on RAPM in November 1937 – a very dark month for Soviet musicians, with Nikolay Zhilayev's arrest and a fresh wave of institutional purges – were quashed by senior composers who intervened to stop what could have been a full-scale witch-hunt, with tragic consequences.[29] Yet even as this terrifying moment passed without further incident, the musicologist Lev Kristiansen moved to attack RAPM again in 1938. Significantly, his anti-RAPM harangue was published in the same issue as Arnol'd Al'shvang's article on nineteenth-century Russian music which opens with the declaration 'Every true Soviet musician is rightly proud of the fact that he is the lawful heir of Glinka, Musorgskiy, Rimskiy-Korsakov, Chaykovskiy' and accuses RAPM and ASM of 'unlawfully' attempting to blacken their reputation in the pre-1932 years with 'reactionary theories'.[30] Kristiansen's article blames the same two trends in early

Soviet culture – those influenced by 'bourgeois modernism' and those on
the militant proletarian wing who followed 'pseudo-socialist "theories"' and
neglected Russian music because of their inability to see past their 'narrow
class understanding' of its composers.[31] This piece marks the latest point of
such attacks on RAPM: with new power structures and leaders in place after
Kerzhentsev was toppled from power in early 1938, Mikhail Khrapchenko
taking over as president of the Committee from 1939, and more importantly,
the pace of the purges at last beginning to ease, the situation within the
Composers' Union stabilized and the need to find scapegoats ebbed away.

The End of Internationalism?

As Simo Mikkonen has described in detail, Kerzhentsev, and with him
Shatilov, fell from grace in early 1938.[32] Kerzhentsev's replacement, Aleksey
Nazarov, did not keep his job for long, and it seems from the archival record
that this can only have been a good thing for musicians. In 1938 he called a
meeting at the Moscow Philharmonia very like the one chaired by
Kerzhentsev in 1936, where complaints and requests could be aired. But
when the conductor Aleksandr Gauk called for a wider range of Western
classics in the repertoire, so that Soviet composers might learn choral technique from Mozart, Beethoven and Handel, Nazarov pompously responded:
'Classical programmes were useful fifty or sixty years ago. They have no
Soviet content. When they [Soviet audiences] listen to such a programme
they think – have we or have we not had Soviet power for the past twenty
years? ... If the people go to a concert, they want to hear sounds that
chime with their own feelings. They seek, but do not find, those echoes
in worn out classical things.'[33] Nazarov was replaced by his own deputy,
Mikhail Khrapchenko, after just one year in his post, and immediately
Khrapchenko tried to recover some of what Soviet musical culture had lost
in the purges.

   Sometime in 1938, Khrapchenko wrote to Molotov and Sovnarkom to
request the resumption of invitations to distinguished foreign musicians.[34]
He pointed out that once authority for doing this fell from the Philharmonia's
hands (or those of the touring agency Gastrolburo) into those of the
Committee for Arts Affairs, not a single foreign musician had been invited
to the Soviet Union. Arguing that this was clearly an extreme response,
Khrapchenko wished to invite the following: Arturo Toscanini, Bruno
Walter, Otto Klemperer, Artur Rubinstein, Egon Petri, Robert Casadesus,

Yehudi Menuhin, Fritz Kreisler, Josef Szigeti, Pablo Casals, Lotte Lehmann, the Spanish conductor Pérez Casas, the American baritone Lawrence Tibbett and the American contralto Marian Anderson. Some had already toured the USSR just two or three years earlier. On the second copy of this letter in the file, in black ink is handwritten, diagonally over the page: 'Sebastian – conductor, Stiedry – conductor, Coates – conductor, Szenkar – conductor, Kleiber – conductor.'[35]

The Leningrad and Moscow Philharmonia records show that in 1936–7, Eugen Szenkar, Georges Sébastian, Erich Kleiber, Heinz Unger, Otto Klemperer, Fritz Stiedry and Ernest Ansermet were all working in the USSR but, as Khrapchenko observes, none of them returned the following season, nor were they replaced with other guest conductors. A vicious (and exceedingly lengthy) denunciation of Szenkar from anonymous art workers to the Ukrainian Committee for Arts Affairs in 1938 accused him of being an enemy of Stalin and a Trotskyist.[36] Unsurprisingly, he was not invited back to the Soviet Union, and this incident shows that foreign musicians could attract dangerous levels of hostility. The cancellation of contracts with foreign musicians also affected Fritz Stiedry and Otto Klemperer: in August 1937 officials told Stiedry that the contract he had signed with the Philharmonia in May was no longer valid and, in the conductor's own words, he was thus summarily 'kicked out of Russia' only four years after being forced to leave Germany. Klemperer's situation was slightly different: he had been appointed artistic director of the newly formed USSR State Symphony Orchestra (formed of the best players from the All-Union Radio and Moscow Philharmonia orchestras) which had been founded by Aleksandr Gauk in early 1936. Yet, as his biographer Peter Heyworth notes, Klemperer's appointment seems to have been cancelled in a piecemeal manner. When leaving the Soviet Union in 1936 – having conducted one performance already with the new orchestra – he made what he called a 'gentleman's agreement' to return for four weeks in the following year, even making a reservation for himself and his family to sail from New York to Leningrad on 28 April 1937. Yet while still in New York, he found his letters to Moscow were going unanswered; in early April he received a telegram explaining that the four-week visit had had to be reduced to two, but by then Klemperer had cancelled all his European commitments and could no longer travel to Moscow. On 4 January 1938 the Soviet authorities told Klemperer that they could not offer him any engagements, and thus Klemperer's association with the Soviet Union came to an abrupt end.[37]

But even without visiting musicians, Soviet musical life began to recover from the era of Kerzhentsev and Shatilov. From scheduling no Western music written after 1910 in the 1937–8 season, the Moscow Philharmonia put on a very unexpected programme the following year: in April 1939 they played a concert of contemporary French music consisting of Roussel's Fourth Symphony, Ravel's G major Piano Concerto, Honegger's *Pastorale d'été*, the finale of Elsa Barraine's First Symphony and Henri Sauveplane's symphonic suite *Jeanne d' Arc*.[38] Nothing so dramatic happened in Leningrad, where the Philharmonia very visibly increased its performances of Soviet music and special concerts for workers. But in the 1940–1 season, they cautiously began to reintroduce some contemporary Western music, even if by now it was not so new: Honegger's *Pacific 231* reappears in 1940, as does *Pulcinella* and Ravel's G major Piano Concerto. Once the Soviet Union was allied with Great Britain and America during the war, it once again became 'international', as will be seen in the next chapter. But in these lean years for international exchange, only a few chinks in the cultural armour were visible, chiefly through the friendly relations of Western composers with Soviet musicians via VOKS. The English composer Alan Bush was the main conduit for Anglo-Soviet musical exchange in the years between 1938 (the year of Bush's first Soviet visit) and 1941. Bush was certainly instrumental in arranging performances of new Soviet music in London, but despite regularly sending VOKS's music director, Grigoriy Shneyerson, generous parcels of his own music, Bush's music was hardly ever performed in the Soviet Union. It was still possible for foreigners who were sympathetic to communism and Soviet ideals to visit the Soviet Union in these years, but all such visits were arranged and monitored by VOKS; it is very likely that the single concert of contemporary French music was the result of a French cultural delegation (or even just a single composer) in 1938 or early 1939, but until evidence of such a visit has been found, this speculation cannot be proved.

Reinventing the Russian Musical Past

Of all the Russian composers celebrated in the late 1930s and early 1940s, Chaykovskiy occupied the prime position as the Number One Soviet favourite. Between 1934 – the year when the first of three volumes of his collected letters was published – and 1940, the year of his centenary, there were some very significant changes in Soviet policy that meant that, even as Chaykovskiy was being canonized, those engaged in the process were obliged to enact swift about-turns where necessary. As Andrey Budyakovskiy noted in his book on Chaykovskiy in 1935, the 1932 Resolution wrought dramatic changes in the composer's Soviet reception. Budyakovskiy recalled Mikhail Pekelis's article in *Muzïka i revoliutsiya* in 1928 which, though praising Chaykovskiy's music and his 'deep understanding of humanity', described him as 'the elegiac poet of the fading past now alien to us'.[39] In the RAPM years, he recalled, 'Chaykovskiy received the label of the ideologue of the dying Russian landowning class. His music, penetrating a deep tragic pathos and pessimism, was declaring war on the alien Soviet listener; its influence was corrupting.'[40] But in the post-1932 era, Budyakovskiy explains, 'The attitude towards our cultural heritage in general changed sharply; the question of how to shape the broadest, boldest, but no less critical basis for utilizing the whole musical heritage of the past was posed, and the vulgarized "totalizing" approach to the epoch of the creativity of individual composers was cast off.'[41]

One of the most fundamental ways of preserving heritage was through the publication of letters and other primary source documents. The collection of the composer's correspondence with Nadezhda von Meck, his patron between 1878 and 1890, was a major achievement, carried out by scholars working directly from archival sources. The three volumes were published in 1934, 1935 and 1936, the first with an introductory article by Pshibïshevskiy, the former director of the Moscow Conservatory.[42] As Richard Taruskin has noted, the editors state directly in this opening volume that Chaykovskiy was a homosexual. Indeed, the author of the introductory article, Pshibïshevskiy, was homosexual himself and would in fact be arrested for that very reason in 1934 – the year his essay was published – and given a three-year prison sentence.[43] Pshibïshevskiy here faces head-on the considerable difficulties in presenting Chaykovskiy – the loyal monarchist and political conservative – as acceptable to the Soviet reader. To begin with, the composer's close association with the Imperial Court was well known. He was especially close to Tsar Aleksandr III, and composed his 'Moscow' cantata for his coronation in 1881. What is more, Chaykovskiy went on record declaring his contempt for the proto-revolutionary organization *Narodnaya Vol'ya* [the People's Will] that had assassinated Aleksandr II and was not at all pleased when the activist Vera Zasulich was acquitted for her attempted murder of the St Petersburg governor Colonel Trepov in 1878.[44] Pshibïshevskiy, realizing that there was absolutely no chance of presenting Chaykovskiy as sympathetic to

revolutionary ideals in any way whatsoever, even goes so far as to compare
him unfavourably with Rimskiy-Korsakov, whose politics were far more
radical:

> In this specific class rootedness and ... the cold, almost negative atti-
> tude of Chaykovskiy towards Stasov and the Petersburg *kuchka* ... we
> see that clear expression of the ruling class's orientation towards the
> capitalist, 'Prussian' path of Russian development. At the time when
> Chaykovskiy in his letter to von Meck did not conceal his antipathy to
> Pisarev and Nekrasov (see his letter of 24 March 1878), Rimskiy-
> Korsakov in his 'Notes' wrote that 'the new spirit of the 1860s affected
> us.... We read ... John Stuart Mill, Belinskiy, Dobrolyubov and
> others. . . . In the meantime the Polish uprising began ... all my sympa-
> thies were towards Mordovin. Bakhteyarov, admiring Katkov, was not at
> all sympathetic [towards the rebels] and his convictions were not after
> my own heart. He is an ardent supporter of serfdom and a proud
> member of the landowning class.'[45] Just this one citation from Rimskiy-
> Korsakov's notes ... shows the difference in their world views between
> Chaykovskiy and the kuchkists.[46]

However, Pshibïshevskiy was an experienced writer on music, and knew
how to present great composers who did not fit neatly into the 'fellow-
traveller' mould to a Soviet readership. He compares the Chaykovskiy/
Rimskiy divide to that between Beethoven and Goethe: one a self-
proclaimed revolutionary, the other passive, even monarchist in his views:
'At the time when Goethe ... fled from German action towards castles in
the air and Hellenic beauty, Beethoven in his Ninth Symphony ... expressed
in music images that none of his contemporaries dared to give voice to,
excepting only Hölderlin in his "Death of Empedocles".'[47] This is an artful
angle to take, and proves fruitful: although Beethoven is clearly the favoured
revolutionary figure in Soviet historiography, Goethe was no less successful
in depicting the tribulations of his age. And that literary honesty, according
to no less an authority than Friedrich Engels, is the criterion by which all
literature should be judged, and not its tendentious character. His famous
letter to Margaret Harkness in April 1888, in which Engels specifically
states that the writer's opinions should take second place to a novel's social
realism, citing the monarchist Honoré de Balzac as an ideal example ('his
great work is a constant elegy on the inevitable decay of good society, his

sympathies are all with the class doomed to extinction') was published in the Soviet Union in 1932.[48] Engels's letter provided a convenient peg upon which to hang all sorts of literature and art: if social honesty was the one thing that mattered, not an artist's personal convictions, then there should be no limit to what Soviet critics could declare to be the valid heritage of the Soviet people. Chaykovskiy's reputation is effectively secured by it: like Goethe, he depicted a decaying world and he felt its oppressive sense of malaise and doom. Pshibïshevskiy makes exactly this point: Chaykovskiy was 'the creative voice of the tragedy of the doomed Russian ruling class . . . looking through the eyes of a dying class, he examined and rendered in musical form his environment and times, not in static but in dynamic form, in the tragic struggle of opposing principles, of "good versus evil".[49]

As Chaykovskiy's centenary year of 1940 approached, a committee was formed specifically to organize celebrations. The plan was approved by Stalin personally on 4 January 1940, and during that year a flurry of major publications hastened to cement his reputation as the foremost Russian composer of the Stalinist age.[50] They were all written in the immediate aftermath of the purges by writers who may well have counted themselves fortunate to have survived, and all would have been acutely aware of the veneration required of them. Most of the major books on the composer from 1940 – even those written by distinguished musicologists – are written as though addressed to children; bombastic and oversimplified in tone, they read as though the authors were addressing the Soviet reader at the level of political sloganeering through a megaphone. The major anniversary book celebrating Chaykovskiy's operas and ballets in the Leningrad former Mariinskiy Theatre (now named after Sergey Kirov) opened with a gushing paean to the composer that made it quite clear that Pshibïshevskiy-style arguments were now unnecessary:

The great family of peoples warmly united under the name of Lenin and Stalin, who love and cherish high art, pronounce with pride the name of the genius Chaykovskiy. All his life Chaykovskiy earned a wide popularity and was admired. All the more so in our own epoch are we grateful and constantly attentive to his great work . . . for there is not even a single public square in our great land which does not resound to his melodies. Every single symphonic collective wishes to perform Chaykovskiy's music with maximum expression. Any conductor considers that his creative development, as an interpreter of symphonic music, is far from complete without Chaykovskiy in his repertoire. Finally, none of our singers can tear themselves away from Chaykovskiy's operas. One can listen forever to Chaykovskiy's music. . . . In our theatres his operas invariably draw full houses. This is the reality of the understanding of Chaykovskiy that exists in our Soviet epoch. How might we explain this understanding? In the main, Chaykovskiy in all his works is deeply connected with folk roots [narodnïy]. His detailed study of western European musical culture constantly mixes with his own countless journeys where he took from them everything useful for a composer's technique but it would be utterly impossible to reproach him for merely borrowing, since Chaykovskiy fundamentally remained true to himself, in each one of his melodies gave the feeling of a deep sincere narodnïy spirit . . . and shaped them with tremendous power. Chaykovskiy specifically interests us in the area of musical theatre, having created such works that thrill anyone who hears them . . .

It is this world of suffering, deep humanity from its very essence, which, invested with complete musical and artistic form, stands before us as a living voice of reality because the suffering of each of Chaykovskiy's characters is above all vital and true. There is no exoticism, no excess, bombast, nothing forced or unnatural. In his operas, in contrast to Western-European opera, we are captivated not by orchestral beauty, or even the beauty of melody, or even the theatrical spectacle, but by their sheer humanity. . . . Deeply Russian in spirit, he equally identifies with the Georgian, the Tatar, Uzbek, Tadjik; all peoples understand him because his creativity penetrates their vital simplicity; he is close to all and captivates people, who find in him their own living image.

All theatres in the land, symphony orchestras, all musicians, singers, opera and chamber performers on this memorial day of 7 May, pay homage to our great beloved genius. Millions of recordings, across thousands of kilometres, convey this honour. The whole country resounds with Chaykovskiy's melodies.[51]

Bombastic as such writing was – and we should be acutely aware of how it must have felt for intelligent, trained musicologists to write like this – there are important messages here. First, Chaykovskiy is, though fully aware of Western techniques, presented as essentially another folk-orientated composer. His cosmopolitanism is not praised, but treated merely as an addendum to his rootedness in Russian folk culture. Second, the primary quality that Soviet writers would now draw from his operas was tragedy and suffering: this marked him out as both quintessentially humanitarian (even 'Shakespearean') and also underlined the unspoken assumption, *pace* Pshibïshevskiy, that the composer's age was itself tragic and 'doomed' in the spirit of Hölderlin's tragic play. Finally, Chaykovskiy's music is, 'though Russian', the heritage of every nation contained within the Soviet Union, and it speaks to and for all Soviet peoples. No Georgian, Tatar, Uzbek or Tadjik composer would in turn be expected to be hailed in such terms: the Stalinist embrace of cultures of the national republics had Russia firmly at its centre.[52]

Not all writing was quite this bland, although there is a clear consensus among the 1940 publications regarding these crucial points. Boris Asaf'yev took the opportunity to create critical distance between the newly canonized Chaykovskiy and his own previous championing of Russian modernism in the early Soviet period, associating himself firmly with the new image of the composer:

> Chaykovskiy was alien to any kind of symbolism (not without reason was his music so alien to the aesthetics of the epoch of Russian modernism), and always spoke of revealing concrete images in his musical drama-turgy, and in the struggle, stress and passion of his symphonic develop-ment, in the burning lyrics of his romances and instrumental chamber music. . . . Like Tolstoy, Chaykovskiy said of his own time that it was impossible to live. We, the happy generation of the great Stalin epoch, having given every gifted person all the possibilities to mature and grow to their full potential, we know and soberly consider the factors hindering Chaykovskiy's contemporaries in their creative strength . . .
>
> The best of Chaykovskiy's works – the themes of Romeo, Francesca, the Enchantress, Queen of Spades – are in their totality a terrible cry against the enslavement of the human spirit and consciousness, the cry of all great Russian contemporaries of Chaykovskiy's epoch. This comes not from a weak will, but from intensive striving for joy, for life and creativity.[53]

Asaf'yev's interpretation of Chaykovskiy's most prominent works as a 'terrible cry against the enslavement of the human spirit' owes much to the gist of Pshibïshevskiy's analysis. Yet a different emphasis can be found in Valerian Bogdanov-Berezovskiy's study of the operas and ballets. Bogdanov-Berezovskiy returns, albeit superficially, to the question of the composer's political orientation, but actually seems to refute Pshibïshevskiy's argument, which is now linked back to the discredited RAPM. In actual fact, both these sides of Chaykovskiy's creative personality were acknowledged in Soviet discourse of this time: whenever his music was tragic, this simply reflected the turbulence and injustice of the Tsarist era; when it was cheerful, it suited the official Soviet narrative that 'life has become more joyful'. Bogdanov-Berezovskiy comes back to the theme of the 'tragic Chaykovskiy' in time, but chooses to emphasize the positive aspects of his music:

> The tragic element in Chaykovskiy's creativity served as cause for an inaccurate picture of his music in the time of RAPM's 'revision of the classics', when he was listed in the category of decadent artists and called a 'singer of the declining class'. Such vulgarization and one-sided evaluation not only narrowed and impoverished the significance of Chaykovskiy's work as the greatest product of our national and world culture, but also misrepresented him. We know that in his own wonderful art Chaykovskiy, like his predecessor Glinka, or his contemporaries Musorgskiy and Rimskiy-Korsakov, was expressing the best hopes and expectations of the broadest and most progressive strand of Russian society, the Russian people [*narod*]. Of this with all certainty we can say that both the thematic and intonational content of his programmatic works (symphonies, overtures) are connected with the folk song source and the broad reality of the democratic intonations of his time.
>
> We cannot conceal Chaykovskiy's reactionary political views (as expressed in his letters and diary), nor their force and significance. . . . The reactionary mood of the time in which he lived, with its cult of individual freedom and religion, was in scandalous opposition to the reality of Tsarist Russia. We cannot forget that the period of most intense creativity of the composer was in the years of violent triumph of reaction. . . .
>
> Chaykovskiy did not turn away from those 'accursed questions' of his age, as some of his contemporaries did. He did not try to deny the torment of his own conflicted philosophical views that were typical of his epoch. He went head-first towards them. And this is characteristic: besides the tragic and sorrowful pages of his music Chaykovskiy was optimistic, full of life . . . In this sense there is very clearly an exceptional, ardent cult of Mozart's music, 'expressing a vital joy, healthy and precious' as Chaykovskiy himself wrote. We value in Chaykovskiy the sharp insight of the artist, and a clear realistic content in his art.[54]

What has really changed here from 1934? Not much in terms of real content, perhaps, but much in terms of sloganizing and harnessing the composer to present-day Stalinism. There is a deliberate stress on new terminology that was typical of the mature Stalin age: Chaykovskiy's music is deemed to be 'optimistic', 'vital', 'healthy', 'joyful' and 'realistic'. Bogdanov-Berezovskiy does not really refute Pshibïshevskiy's argument about reflecting the doomed landowning classes, but rather sweeps it aside in order to focus on the positives, and that could hardly be more typical of Stalinist criticism of this period. The celebrations of Chaykovskiy's music in the 1939–40 season form an exact musical counterpart to the glorification of Pushkin in 1937, and echo their rather chilling function as both emblematic of the over-arching superiority of Russian culture within the Soviet Union and also as a grand festive occasion that masked the terrifying sweep of the purges through Moscow and Leningrad's artistic circles. By 1940, no Soviet musi-cian would have dared to complain – even humorously – that there was too much Chaykovskiy played in Moscow and Leningrad. Calls for new Western music had vanished, and all Soviet musicologists and musicians participated in the public veneration of the great Russian composer.

Musorgskiy and the *Kuchka*

If the steady reinvention of Chaykovskiy during the 1930s proved chal-lenging for musicologists to keep pace with, Musorgskiy and his *kuchkist* colleagues offered a different set of problems, since the *kuchka* was not a homogeneous mass of composers with identical beliefs, and not all of them were equally palatable to Soviet writers at this time. As we have already seen, RAPM's writings on the *kuchka* (as represented by Anatoliy Groman's 1932 *Proletarskiy muzïkant* article) took the line that the *kuchka*'s split was caused by tension between 'bourgeois liberals' and the 'muzhik democrat' Musorgskiy. To this mindset, Borodin and Rimskiy-Korsakov sat uneasily with Musorgskiy, although that was largely because of the persistent Soviet presentation of Musorgskiy as a *narodnik* hostile to Tsarism and the aristoc-racy. While Chaykovskiy's image in the late 1930s was 'cleansed' of any details of his private views or associations that inconveniently subverted his new identity as honest chronicler of his times à la Engels, and composer of Russian folk-inflected music, such drastic steps were not necessary with Rimskiy-Korsakov. As a teacher, he had always been revered as the founding professor of composition in the St Petersburg Conservatoire, where his

teaching methods were still cherished by his son-in-law Maksimilian
Shteynberg. As a composer, he was also far less cosmopolitan by instinct
than Chaykovskiy, and his deep interest in Russian folk music was one of the
principal drivers of what became the 'Russian national style'. Moreover, as we
have seen, Rimskiy-Korsakov held far more radical political views than did
the ardent monarchist Chaykovskiy. Leningrad's musical leaders commem-
orated the year 1933 as the twenty-fifth anniversary of his death and held
a five-week festival devoted to him, spanning 13 May–21 June, during
which seven of his operas were performed, along with symphonic extracts
from two others [*Sadko* and *The Legend of the Invisible City of Kitezh*] and
his chamber works and songs. Lectures and exhibitions sat alongside
performances in the Leningrad Conservatory halls, the Malïy Theatre, the
Philharmonia Hall, in the music school named after the composer and in the
club 'Five-Year-Plan'. The brochure printed to accompany this festival sets
out Rimskiy-Korsakov's Soviet identity in very clear terms:

> In his own life and creative path Nikolay Andreyevich embodied the
> ideology of the bourgeois landowner [*oburzhuazivshegosya dvoryanstva*],
> who is conscious of the inevitability of the development of capitalism.
> The talent of Nikolay Andreyevich in responding to this particular stage
> in the historical evolution of the bourgeois-landowner class makes for us
> an important study of his creativity. The opposing side to this evolution
> finds itself in the expression in the fluctuations of Rimskiy-Korsakov
> between romanticism and realism, fable and history, fantasy and reality,
> the admiration of the old and the political focus of his satire.[55]

The authors are not trying to disguise Rimskiy-Korsakov as anything other
than what he was: a person of liberal, but certainly not revolutionary, views
that were typical of his class and era. But those views provided the 'liberal'
backdrop to the rise of the revolutionary movement in the late nineteenth
century, and Rimskiy-Korsakov's operas were now presented as ideological
resistance to the threat of capitalism. Accompanying the display of the
composer's work in the 1870s, the 1933 booklet comments on the rise of the
narodnik movement, the Slavophiles and the rise in interest in the ancient
folk culture of Russia ('folk tales, legends, bïlini, myths') in which Rimskiy-
Korsakov took a close personal interest. Finally, the authors draw attention
to the composer's modest revolutionary credentials and his experience of
Tsarist-era censorship over his last opera, *The Golden Cockerel*:

In the epoch of the 1905 revolution, Nikolay Andreyevich became accustomed to the wave of revolutionary, liberal-bourgeois protest and opposition to autocracy. Nikolay Andreyevich's dismissal from the Conservatoire because of his intervention in political matters called forth protests among the revolutionary-democratic intelligentsia.... His last opera, The Golden Cockerel, with its elements of satire against autocracy met with difficulties from the censor, and during the struggle [with the censor] Nikolay Andreyevich died.[56]

Although this brochure was written for a mass audience, and is demonstrably simplistic, avoiding technical discussion in favour of placing the composer's major works on a Marxist-Leninist revolutionary timeline, it nevertheless defines Rimskiy-Korsakov's mature Soviet identity, at least up to a point. Between this festival and the Stalinist purges, articles on Rimskiy-Korsakov did appear, but they were not, on the whole, tendentious or overly political. By 1938, of course, everything had changed and articles on the composer's approach to teaching, or other technical matters, were replaced by pieces heavily weighted towards the new trend of Russian nationalist ideology. Viktor Tsukkerman's article on Rimskiy-Korsakov's use of folk song concludes by reminding readers of the composer's own urban 'folk' song composed in 1905 (and a huge favourite with Shalyapin's audiences) 'Dubinushka':

> Although it is only small and not one of Rimskiy-Korsakov's best pieces, it is important to us that this great artist echoed the great events of his own time through his art ... he tuned the strings of his own glorious lyre [gusli] to another mode and played songs that were almost forbidden then, and played them not mournfully, but as they sounded long ago: cheerful and brilliant.[57]

This is highly romantic writing, blatantly intended to portray Rimskiy-Korsakov as proto-revolutionary, even subversive. By evoking the image of ancient Rus' with Rimskiy-Korsakov's gusli, echoing the songs of 'long ago', Tsukkerman also participates in the wider Soviet romanticism of Russia's past at this time. Sergey Eyzenshteyn's film Aleksandr Nevskiy (with score by Sergey Prokof'yev) was released in 1938, depicting the thirteenth-century invasion of the ancient city of Novgorod by the Teutonic Knights. Rimskiy-Korsakov's own historical epic (this time set in the sixteenth century, at the time of Ivan the Terrible) The Maid of Pskov was staged in a new production at the Bolshoy in January 1938, and Glinka's medieval epic *Ruslan and Liudmila* was also staged, again in a new production at the Bolshoy, in April 1937.

The upsurge in new, high-profile productions of Russian national opera continued apace in the last years of the decade. In February 1939, the Bolshoy staged the long-awaited Soviet premiere of Glinka's *Life for the Tsar* or, as it was usually known in the Soviet Union, *Ivan Susanin*, with a revised libretto commissioned from Sergey Gorodetskiy that removed its references to the Tsar.[58] Georgiy Khubov declared that it was:

> not possible to over-estimate the importance of this event . . . in this production Soviet musicians revealed anew the mighty genius of Glinka, in just the same way as Mendelssohn revealed the forgotten Bach in the severity and beauty of his 'Passions'. . . . The Soviet people have revived – in the true sense of the word – this great creation of national art at the very time when Western culture is enduring the most terrible, irreparable crisis and endless darkness.[59]

Khubov goes on to denounce the barbarism of the Third Reich, where Jewish composers were no longer played and where Mozart's *The Magic Flute* was 'grossly misinterpreted'.[60] 'Only in the Soviet Union', he boasted, is the concept of the Fatherland still 'a beautiful thing'. And in this context of supposedly untainted patriotism, Glinka's opera revival was, he argued, a very different phenomenon to the vulgar appropriation of 'true German music' in Nazi Germany. Now that the revised libretto focused attention away from the Russian monarchy and towards love for Russia in the abstract, *Ivan Susanin* was set to assume its rightful place as a Stalinist operatic icon alongside *Ruslan*, *Onegin*, *Boris* and other nineteenth-century Russian classics of the opera stage.

As both Marina Frolova-Walker and Marina Raku have shown, the saga of bringing *Ivan Susanin* back to the Bolshoy stage involved many different actors, possibly even including Stalin himself, though this has not been proven.[61] In April 1937, the Bolshoy conductor Samuil Samosud was interviewed by *Komsomolskaya pravda* about his work and the possibility of reviving *Ivan Susanin*. During the course of the interview, Samosud criticized *Susanin*'s monarchism and made clear that Glinka's opera could only be produced with a new text. The interview was printed on 20 April and, according to Marina Raku, on 9 May the set designer Pëtr Vil'yams informed Mikhail Bulgakov that it had been suggested to him (no doubt by Kerzhentsev) that Bulgakov should write the new *Susanin* libretto.[62] Bulgakov was an experienced librettist and was in fact at that very moment engaged in working with Boris Asaf'yev on a libretto for his forthcoming opera *Minin i Pozharskiy* which, owing to the pressing need to stage *Ivan Susanin*, ending up being shelved, much to Asaf'yev's frustration. However, Bulgakov had no choice but to comply. Despite no credit at all being publicly given to Bulgakov for the revisions to *Susanin*'s libretto – which was publicly announced as having been the work of Sergey Gorodetskiy, the stage designer Boris Mordvinov and Samosud – according to Bulgakova's diary, Bulgakov allegedly 'corrected every word' in Gorodetskiy's revised text, though of course this claim, exaggerated as it must surely be, has never been substantiated.[63] Gorodetskiy was indeed the author of the revised libretto, but Bulgakov evidently played a greater role in revising it than is usually realized – and his involvement was certainly not common knowledge at the time either.

The Bolshoy celebrated the centenary of Musorgskiy's birth in 1939 by staging a new production of *Khovanshchina*.[64] As discussed in Chapter One, Musorgskiy already had such a strong Soviet image as a proto-revolutionary *narodnik* that he did not require much Stalinist re-branding. However, in the hysterical climate of the purge years – and mass arrests were still being carried out in 1939 – Soviet critics repeatedly harped on his supposed dedication to 'truth' and depicting 'the people', and no resistance to this uniform portrait was possible. Khubov, once again, took it on himself to define Musorgskiy's Soviet identity in his *Sovetskaya muzïka* essay for the Bolshoy's production. Musorgskiy was, he writes, the 'brilliant helmsman of Russian art, the true pupil of Glinka and the great innovator of popular [*narodnïy*] music drama'.[65] Khubov pointedly draws a distinction between the 'real innovator' Musorgskiy – who stands as an ideal model for young Soviet composers to follow – and the figure once lauded in Soviet musical circles, and now banished from the opera stage altogether, Richard Wagner: 'Young Soviet composers should learn from our Musorgskiy, the great creator of "Boris" and "Khovanshchina". Above all, [they must learn] in the area of people's music drama from the creative innovations of Musorgskiy . . . which left Richard Wagner's operatic reforms far behind.'[66]

The musicologist Emilya Frid wrote a short book on Musorgskiy for the Leningrad Philharmonia in 1939, in which she firmly laid out his *narodnik* credentials, counterposing him with Glinka, Chaykovskiy, Rimskiy-Korsakov and Borodin as, in this respect, the 'first among equals' in a pantheon of nationalist greatness:

If Chaykovskiy in his own time with intense pathos defended the rights of a person to personal happiness, to free feeling, if Rimskiy-Korsakov cultivated an amazingly rich theme of folk fairy tale and legends, and if the wise optimist Borodin embodied in his own works the power of epic, the moral purity and wholesomeness of the Russian people, then the troubled, restless nature of Musorgskiy made him a singer of the people's [*narodnïy*] uprising, of the people's protest against social evil and injustice. All these artists served one general great cause – the interpretation in his own work of the different sides of the life of the Russian people. . . . From Musorgskiy to Glinka, there has been this hunger for peasant song, a deep assimilation of it as one organic song from which arises one's own musical language.

[Musorgskiy] denied that music was an end in itself but was rather subordinate to demands for the truthful representation of life and human feelings. . . . This isolated Musorgskiy from his fellow composers and contemporaries and was the source of his tragic isolation. But for us, Musorgskiy is an inalienable part of our own epoch, one of its clearest representatives, the incarnation in his own brilliant creations of the most acute questions of our contemporary age, the most cherished spirit and hope of the Russian people.[67]

While Musorgskiy himself is perhaps not really 'reinvented' here – Frid says little that would have surprised Stasov, after all – what has changed very dramatically are the aesthetic values bound up with this wholesale appropriation of nineteenth-century social issues. Logically, the image of Musorgskiy as one concerned with the classic 'accursed questions' of his era – Russian nationality, society, identity and the state – should render him a figure very much of the past – since what role could debating those questions possibly serve when the Soviet Union's attainment of socialism had already been declared by Stalin in 1936? There were not only no serfs to depict, downtrodden or otherwise, but the tenets of socialism realism did not admit dwelling on poverty and continuing social injustice under Stalin as a permissible aspect of contemporary art. Also notable is the extent to which the status of peasant culture – the old 'cult of the village' so despised in the 1920s – is now raised by its association with Russian nationalism.

An even more extreme stance was struck by Tsetsiliya Ratskaya in her substantial study of Musorgskiy published in the same year. Here, she seeks to align him more explicitly with two out of the three code words of socialist realism: *narodnost'* (variously, an evocation of Russian or Soviet folk culture, and/or obvious accessibility to a mass audience) and *ideynost'* (appropriate ideological content):[68]

> Musorgskiy was the leading representative of the living truthful and realistic tendency in musical art . . . [of the *kuchka*] . . . They [the *kuchka*] raised high the banner of the fight for *narodnost'*, for an ideological thematic. They were irreconcilable enemies of stagnation, routine and conservatism . . . Under the influence of the great revolutionary democrat Chernïshevskiy, his knowledge of the philosophers of the French materialists and his study of natural sciences Musorgskiy formulated his materialist world view.[69]

This clearly harks back to Pëtr Kogan's 1929 depiction of Musorgskiy as part of the nineteenth-century intellectual movements led by radical thinkers such as Chernïshevskiy and Dobrolyubov that would eventually underlie the social and political conditions which gave rise to the terrorist group *Narodnaya Vol'ya* who assassinated Tsar Aleksandr II and, ultimately, spawned Bolshevism. No other Russian composer could be so effortlessly appropriated as proto-revolutionary; and not only that, but aligned with those who attacked contemporary Soviet composers and artists for their alleged 'formalism' and lack of contact with the Soviet people. From this point until the end of the Stalin era (and in some quarters, well beyond that time) the national identity of these composers was set in stone; they could not be criticized in any way and, as the next chapter will show, during the post-war cultural repressions, they became pre-eminent over even the greatest Western icons like Bach, Handel and Beethoven. The Soviet 'Enlightenment' was well and truly over.

CHAPTER FIVE

FROM THE GREAT PATRIOTIC WAR TO THE ZHDANOVSHCHINA
1941–1953

From the signing of the Nazi–Soviet pact in August 1939 until 22 June 1941 – the day Nazi troops invaded Soviet territory – all anti-German rhetoric and talk of fascism, both in the Soviet music press and in documentary sources, vanished completely. How much of an impact this had on orchestral programmes is not easy to gauge, though the Leningrad Philharmonia offers the most startling change of direction, especially considering how quickly this followed the purges of the late 1930s. The season 1940–1 offers several surprises: the reappearance of *Pulcinella* and *Pacific 231* in the regular schedules indicates a definite leaning back towards the pre-purge years, even if not in any way German-related; but the most remarkable feature of this season is a series of four lectures on the following topics: twentieth-century modernism, the history of Western music, Russian music and Soviet music. Although there is no extant evidence to support this, the list of works selected for twentieth-century modernism strongly suggests the guiding hand of Sollertinskiy, who was the Philharmonia's artistic director at this time. It is not quite clear how the lectures were delivered; the orchestra itself probably did not take part, but it seems unthinkable that no musical illustration would have been given. Therefore it is likely that piano and piano/vocal reductions would have been used during the lectures. In the twentieth-century lecture, the speaker (again, very probably Sollertinskiy) covered the following works: Hindemith '1922' Suite, Schoenberg *Six Lieder* (1903), Poulenc *Mouvements perpetuels*, Milhaud *Brazilian Dances*, Casella *Tarantella*, three songs by Szymanowski and excerpts from *Wozzeck* and *Gurrelieder*.[1] The content of the lectures has not, to my knowledge, survived, but it is likely to have been at least semi-critical; though this, of course, would effectively be window-dressing for exposing Soviet audiences once again to music that had been declared 'decadent' since 1936. It is an astonishingly courageous step for an organization that had, only three years earlier, suffered a devastating investigation and purge, even if the personnel losses were less severe than in the Moscow Philharmonia.

The Moscow Philharmonia programmes are noticeably less enterprising than those in Leningrad during the years of the Nazi–Soviet pact, but there are still some noteworthy events. One was the appearance of the first foreign conductor for several years: Leo Blech, who had been exiled from Hitler's Germany and now worked in Latvia. There was a Moscow Bach premiere in March 1941 – the secular cantata *Der zufriedengestellte Aeolus*, BWV 205, which was played on early instruments (viola da gamba, viola d'amore and cello) and performed in a concert of 'monumental works' including the Bach–Gedike Toccata, Bach's D minor Piano Concerto and Handel's first organ concerto in G minor. This concert marks the last of the 'early music' concerts I have found in the Philharmonia programmes until the post-Stalin era. Another curiosity was Mahler's *Das Lied von der Erde*, played in the 1940–1 season; its performance indicates the extent to which he was regarded as an interesting, but safe, choice, even in 1941.

It is largely true to say that, with the dramatic exception of Eyzenshteyn's 1940 commission to stage *Die Walküre* at the Bolshoy (the production opened in November and ran till February 1941),[2] the signing of the Nazi-Soviet pact had no noticeable impact on programming, and there was certainly no echo of Nazi bans on Jewish composers. Only one event, in fact, looks significantly out of the ordinary, and even that was a far cry from a Nazi-inspired tribute: the Leningrad Philharmonia put on an all-German music concert in October 1940 featuring Franz Schreker's *Der Geburtstag der Infantin*, which was possibly the first time Schreker's music had been performed in Soviet Russia since his opera *Der Ferne Klang* had been performed in Leningrad in 1925, when there was also a Philharmonia concert dedicated to his music in Leningrad in October.[3] Celebrating Schreker's music was anything but sympathetic to Nazi cultural policies: it is quite certain, given their close contacts with Schreker's fellow German Jews like Otto Klemperer and Bruno Walter, that the Leningrad Philharmonia leadership knew that Schreker had been hounded from his position at the Berlin Academy of Music in 1932 by threats of violence from Nazi groups, and so including his music at this ostensibly pro-German concert was surely a subtle act of defiance. At the same concert, the audience heard an array of conventional German favourites of those years: excerpts from Wagner's operas (Walther's song from *Meistersinger*, Introduction and entr'acte to Act Three, *Lohengrin*, Lohengrin's story, *Tristan* Prelude and Liebestod, Wotan's Farewell) and Strauss's *Tod und Verklärung*; a few days later, there was a concert devoted to excerpts from *Der Ring*. On 13 May, practically on the eve of Nazi Germany's invasion of the Soviet Union, Nikolay Golovanov conducted another all-Wagner special concert in Moscow: the overtures to *Der fliegende Holländer* and *Tannhäuser*, Introduction and entr'acte to Act Three of *Lohengrin*, Lohengrin's story and duet of Lohengrin and Elsa, March and Wolfram's aria from *Tannhäuser*. The season 1940–1 was lavishly sprinkled with Johann Strauss concerts alongside Wagner, Austro-German classics and Bruckner; but at the same time, Mendelssohn and Mahler were still performed, and there is no indication that Germany's anti-Semitic cultural policies were being mirrored in the Soviet Union. As will be seen, although Wagner is diplomatically removed from orchestral programmes during the war, the same large-scale excerpts reappear very quickly afterwards in orchestral concerts from 1945 onwards.

After the Nazi invasion on 22 June 1941, the Soviet Union's newfound special relationship with Nazi Germany collapsed, and it found itself in an unexpected alliance with Great Britain and the United States. The effect of these new 'special relationships' on concert programming was not very significant – only a handful of Philharmonia concerts on English and American music were put on, some in Moscow, some in evacuation and some only on the radio – but perhaps more importantly, between 1942 and 1945, a large quantity of British music was sent to Moscow via diplomatic bags and, on one memorable occasion, in an army tank. The American Embassy in Moscow also arranged for scores to be sent over, usually in microfilm format, although archival records suggest that the influx of American scores and recordings – and the extent of musical exchange more generally – was considerably more modest in scale than that facilitated through the British Embassy. The joint effect of both Allies' cultural offerings to Soviet composers via VOKS, however, meant that composers and musicians had access to a body of music that was almost entirely new to them, albeit mostly rather conservative in nature. Soviet musicians were also sometimes able to hear radio broadcasts from London; where possible, concerts that the British Embassy and BBC particularly wished to be audible to Soviet listeners were made available through this channel, while for the wider Soviet public, the Radio Committee (whose music section was headed by Dmitriy Kabalevskiy) arranged for British music to be played on Soviet radio, using records sent over by the British Council via the Embassy.

Another major factor in the Philharmonias' repertoire during these years is the practical reality of their evacuation: the Moscow Philharmonia to Alma-Ata and the Leningrad Philharmonia to Novosibirsk. The most complete records of repertoire during evacuation are preserved in the Leningrad Philharmonia archive; very little – hardly anything at all – has survived in the Moscow Philharmonia archive. One of the most striking aspects of the Leningrad Philharmonia's wartime programmes during their evacuation is that Johann Strauss – whose ubiquity in their schedules between 1939 and 41 looks like a friendly nod to Nazi tastes – remains a firm fixture. A clear reason for this is that the evacuation programmes were orientated towards lighter and more popular works, and they included a lot of operatic extracts and arias, dances and smaller works in general. Johann Strauss was simply too popular to lose, even though Richard Strauss was definitely off the listings. Bruckner's Fourth Symphony, however, was played in the 1942–3 season and the orchestra even smuggled in Wagner's *Rienzi* overture in their first evacuation year. We do not, however, see any resurgence of European modernism during the evacuation, despite Sollertinskiy's continued influence until his premature death in 1944.

From the little that remains of the Moscow Philharmonia's wartime records (including concerts held in Alma-Ata, the Bolshoy Hall and the Chaykovskiy Hall), we know that there was an all-Rakhmaninov chamber concert in March 1942, showing that his Soviet canonization was under way before his death in 1943: his *Trio-élégiaque* No. 2, Vocalise, romances and Second Suite for two pianos op. 17 were all played in one evening in a special celebration of his music. After the massive celebrations of Chaykovskiy's anniversary year in 1940, the Moscow Philharmonia decided to celebrate him all over again in 1942, with a concert in May marking 102 years since his birth; the following year, his half-centenary (since his death in 1893) was celebrated with yet another cycle of his works. More modestly, but in the same season of 1943–4, the centenary of Rimskiy-Korsakov's birth was similarly marked with a concert of his orchestral works.

The Radio Committee Orchestra in Blockaded Leningrad, 1941–4

There are two comprehensive published accounts available of musical life in blockaded Leningrad: Andrey Kryukov's *Music broadcasts in Wartime*

Leningrad, and *Music in the Days of the Blockade*.[4] The Radio Committee Orchestra was the only remaining orchestra in Leningrad during the blockade (conducted by Karl Eliasberg) and it continued to broadcast for the entire duration of the blockade – an incredible achievement given the appalling conditions in the city, especially during the first terrible winter in which an estimated 1,500,000 Leningraders died of starvation and cold.[5] Eliasberg recalled that in mid-March 1943, when he saw the orchestra's membership list, the names printed in black were of players who had perished while those in red were still living. Of those names, only fourteen were found to be in a fit state for work. After this discovery, all surviving orchestral players were offered extra rations and a special canteen was opened for them. After a brave start to the season between September and December 1941, which included a symphonic cycle by Mozart and Beethoven, the orchestra had to cease performances by January 1942 owing to the weakened physical state of the musicians (and the deaths of several), and they did not resume playing until the spring of 1943; their main season did not start until 1 May that year. But from that short summer season, the repertoire they performed was impressively ambitious, including Chaykovskiy's Fifth and Sixth Symphonies, a special concert (evidently in a spirit of solidarity against the Nazis) of Norwegian music, including Grieg's Piano Concerto and Svendsen's Norwegian Rhapsody (number not given); and there were always the familiar selections of Russian and popular Western opera arias, short orchestral works, lighter dance pieces (Strauss, Chopin, Delibes) and songs.[6] In general, the Radio Committee Orchestra's repertoire was largely comprised of Russian and Western nineteenth-century classics, but they also played some new Soviet works, notably Shostakovich's 'Leningrad' Symphony (in August 1942), Khachaturyan's *Poem about Stalin* and a few arias and songs by other Soviet composers. We should never for a moment forget that these performances were incredible achievements of human endurance: three musicians died during rehearsals (which began in March) for the 'Leningrad' Symphony, and the physically weakened orchestra was only once able to gather enough strength to run through the whole work before the concert. Among the other non-Russian works they played during this first season were a medley of operatic and ballet excerpts: arias from Gounod's *Faust*, Delibes' Waltz from *Coppelia*, the gypsy chorus from *La Traviata*, gypsy dances from Albeniz's *Andalucian Wedding*, and Bizet's 'Habanera' from *Carmen*. Incredibly, in July 1942, there was a complete concert performance of *Carmen* in the Philharmonia's

Great Hall (conducted by the violinist Semën Arkin). How it was possible to gather together a large enough body of people strong and well enough (relatively speaking) to put on a production of a whole opera in a blockaded city is hard to imagine. Certainly, for the premiere of the 'Leningrad' Symphony a month later, extra rations were given to players, and some musicians, including several from other ensembles, including military bands, were even recalled from the trenches to play, so great was the propaganda value of the Leningrad premiere. Leningrad Radio broadcast the concert to German troops stationed just outside the city in an attempt to demoralize them (and, of course, to sustain the morale of Leningrad's own citizens at the same time).[7] Such an astonishing achievement testifies to the importance of musical culture in the city in maintaining a degree of morale in the face of appalling, and constantly deteriorating, conditions. Already, by December 1941 – only three months into the blockade – thousands of people were dying every day from hunger and cold; Shostakovich himself wrote to Isaak Glikman in February 1942 that hunger had driven the Leningraders to eat any surviving animals (including pets) during that first winter[8] and yet, in the midst of these horrors, Eliasberg's starving orchestra consoled their fellow citizens with music.[9] Unsurprisingly, their repertoire was as 'unpolitical' as it could possibly be – the focus was entirely on music's availability and the practical possibility of playing it at all (it was essential that the music not be too taxing to play, when the musicians were so physically weak) – and their emphasis on familiar classics met the needs both of the musicians themselves and on their audiences, who needed to play and hear music they knew and loved.

Allied 'Internationalism'

The impact of Soviet music – and of the 'Leningrad' Symphony in particular – on the musical life of Britain and America has been fairly well documented.[10] But little is known of the reciprocal impact on Soviet concert life as a result of opening channels of communication during the alliance. I have shown elsewhere how the British government was particularly anxious to foster good cultural relations with the Soviets, and the war offered the best opportunity during the whole of the Soviet era so far to acquaint Soviet audiences with British and American music.[11] Of course, technically there had been no barrier to this during the 1920s and mid-30s; but those who directed Soviet musical life had no discernible interest in British or

American music at that time, so performances of it were extremely rare events. Henry Cowell was the first American composer to visit the Soviet Union (in 1929), but his music was not played in the regular scheduled concerts of either of the Leningrad or Moscow Philharmonias, nor was that of any other American composer until the war years. As Elena Dubinets has shown, Cowell arranged for a series of exchange concerts between America and Soviet Russia in 1933, with three given in Moscow, two in Leningrad and one in Kiev, though she does not indicate what repertoire was played, or who played them.[12] Dubinets also mentions that on 2 June 2 1934 there was a broadcast of an American music concert in Moscow, organized by Cowell and VOKS, including music by Edward McDowell, Charles Ives, George Gershwin, Louis Grunberg, Aaron Copland, Walter Piston and Henry Cowell.[13] But certainly, the Leningrad and Moscow Philharmonia schedules do not feature any American orchestral music before 1942, when the next set of exchange concerts was arranged.

The impact made on Soviet musical life by individual musicians such as Cowell and, from England, Alan Bush (who visited in 1938 and 1939) still remains to be fully assessed; tracing the concerts of music that they brought is far from easy, because they were not usually played by the mainstream organizations that have substantial archival holdings. In his *Evening Moscow* review of the American music broadcast, Konstantin Kuznetsov observed that Cowell kept the Soviet Union well supplied with scores of new American music; if that was true, a less favourable assessment should probably be made of Alan Bush's contribution. According to the correspondence between Bush and Grigoriy Shneyerson, Bush did send scores after 1938, including Alan Rawsthorne's 'Pastoral' symphony and Concerto for String Orchestra, John Ireland's 'London' Overture and *These Things Shall Be*, and Benjamin Britten's *Ballad for Heroes* before 1941, so these items, at least, would have been available in the VOKS's music section score library for consultation.[14] But the scores that Bush sent over were overwhelmingly those of his own music which, with the exception of his 'Dance Overture', was never played by a major Soviet orchestra. Shneyerson was a loyal friend to Bush, writing enthusiastic reviews in *Sovetskaya muzïka* about his interest in the Soviet Union (Bush was a member of the Communist Party of Great Britain) and his work with the choral group he founded, the Workers Musical Association.[15] But even if he had wished to, Shneyerson could not persuade the Moscow Philharmonia to adopt Bush as a 'Soviet' composer: he remained a friend of the Soviet Union in Britain, but was generally kept at arms' length by the musical establishment within Russia itself, for reasons that are not explained in any source I have found. However, it would be unfair to point to Bush as any more neglected than Vaughan-Williams, Bliss or Elgar during this period: as I have already argued, before the Allied period, British music barely registered in Soviet musical discourse, which was wholly focused on European music (with nods – when considered timely – to certain branches of American music, most notably jazz). After 1948, Soviet orchestras had stopped playing British music again, and Bush's main contact, Shneyerson, was dismissed from his VOKS position, so Bush's neglect, if it can be called that, was circumstantial rather than a deliberate act. In fact, Bush suffered exactly the same fate as any other British or American 'fellow-traveller' composer in these years: his political views enabled him to travel to the Soviet Union and gain some acceptance there, but nothing more long-term.

A lack of Soviet interest in contemporary British and American music is indicated as early as 1931, when programme themes for the forthcoming Leningrad Philharmonia season are set out, carefully listing the song and dance music of Russia, Italy, Spain, France, Germany, Scandinavia and Poland, but without even a mention of British or American folk music.[16] Nor did any British musicians visit Moscow or Leningrad to perform in the Philharmonia seasons, who might have championed British music: America had sent the tenor Roland Hayes (1927–8) and the contralto Marian Anderson (1935–6), but they had not performed any American music: Anderson's recital, for example, featured Handel, Frescobaldi, Bach, Schubert, Donizetti and Sibelius, while Hayes sang entirely European repertoire, from Handel to Debussy, though he did include some Negro spirituals. However, there are a handful of English music performances, at least in Leningrad, in the 1920s and 1930s. The Russian-born (but of English parentage) conductor Albert Coates, who had worked as conductor of the London Symphony Orchestra (between 1919 and 1923), brought 'Mars' from Holst's *Planet Suite* to Leningrad in May 1927; Ernest Ansermet had brought the Purcell–Bliss arrangement *Suite of Songs and Dances for Strings* in May 1929 and Coates performed Elgar's *Enigma Variations* in the 1934–5 season, along with his own *Pickwick Suite*.[17] Arnold Bax, indeed, had visited Russia in 1910, though what music he performed there or left behind, if any, is not known.[18] But, so far as I have been able to tell, until Bush came and performed some of his own songs, together with piano reductions of the Lento and Scherzo (Nocturne) movements of Vaughan-Williams's 'London'

Symphony, John Ireland's 'London' Overture and his own 'Dance Overture' at a reception for foreign guests in Moscow in 1938, very little contemporary British music indeed had ever been heard in the Soviet Union, and I have not found any American music at all in the Moscow or Leningrad Philharmonia schedules during the 1920s and 1930s.[19]

At the start of the wartime alliance, then, the Soviet Union found itself in a quandary when VOKS wanted to put on concerts of English music. In 1942, the British Ambassador in Moscow (then Sir Stafford Cripps) wrote to William Walton to alert him to the lack of scores in the USSR and, from this point, various officials in the British Council and Foreign Office acted as agents between composers and music publishers in England and music organizations (and VOKS) in Moscow. The British Council, though they did not yet have a formal base in Moscow (only representatives within the British Embassy), worked with the Foreign Office to send over considerable numbers of scores during wartime, which they did via diplomatic bags, and individual composers sometimes sent generous quantities of their own scores. The Moscow Composers' Union also petitioned the British Council to send over more scores, and on one celebrated occasion, a package of thirteen orchestral scores[20] arrived in Moscow in April 1942 stuffed inside a tank. Unfortunately, the Moscow Philharmonia had already been evacuated to Alma-Ata, leaving no one left to play the music. Following mocking reports in the British press that the scores would be returned to England, the Foreign Office instructed that they instead be presented to the Moscow Conservatoire Library or to VOKS; in the end, the Conservatoire was the beneficiary.[21] The four years during which the British Embassy in Moscow worked together with the British Council in London and with VOKS in Moscow to bring British music of all kinds (classical, popular, light, music for children) to the Soviet Union saw a vast number of scores and gramophone records sent over, which were usually placed in the VOKS music library (which composers were able to use) and/or in the Composers' Union library, and sometimes in the conservatoires as well. But in the end, not very much of it was either performed in live concerts or broadcast, much to the disappointment of the British Foreign Office.

The first concert of British music (or 'English music' as it is always called in Soviet sources) took place in October 1942 in Kuybïshev, according to a Foreign Office report. The concert featured Vaughan Williams's 'London' Symphony, Delius's *Village Romeo and Juliet* (or, more likely, just the single orchestral interlude, 'Walk to the Paradise Garden'), Ireland's *Symphonic*

Rhapsody and Elgar's *Military March*.[22] The same month, the Radio Committee celebrated Henry Wood's seventy-fifth birthday by broadcasting his performances of Vaughan Williams's *Fantasia on Greensleeves* and Bach's Brandenburg Concerto No. 6.[23]

There were only three major orchestral concerts of English music and three of American music in the Moscow Philharmonia series between 1943 and 1946, all organized by VOKS. The first was on 25 May 1943, featuring John Ireland's 'London' overture, Vaughan Williams's *The Wasps* overture, Alan Bush's 'Dance Overture', several British folk songs and a Scottish dance arranged by Shostakovich, Bliss's march from the film score *Things to Come*, Elgar's *Enigma Variations* and his *Festive March*. The second concert, almost exactly a year later, featured Elgar's *Cockaigne* overture, three more folk songs arranged by Shostakovich, Vaughan-Williams's *Suite on English Folk Songs* and Christian Darnton's overture *Stalingrad*. In March 1945 (repeated in Moscow that November) the Science Workers' Orchestra gave a complete performance of Purcell's *Dido and Aeneas* (intended as a celebration of 250 years since Purcell's death, and probably using music from the Purcell Complete Edition sent over by the British Council in 1942), and the last of these friendly exchanges took place in May 1945, with Elgar's *Pomp and Circumstance* March No. 3, Vaughan-Williams's *Wasps* overture, more folk songs arranged by Shostakovich and Bliss's *Checkmate* suite.[24]

In May 1944, the first concert of Soviet and American music took place in Moscow, with Wallingford Riegger's Canon and Fugue, Samuel Barber's overture from *A School for Scandal*, three popular American songs (Stephen Foster, 'Swanee River', Jerome Kern, 'Smoke Gets in your Eyes', and George Gershwin, 'Love Came In'), together with Khachaturyan's Violin Concerto, Shaporin's aria from *Kulikovo's Field*, and excerpts from his cantata, *Battle for the Russian Land*. The following summer, in July, the newly opened Chaykovskiy Hall put on a second concert of American music, featuring both American and Soviet anthems, Roy Harris's *Ode to Friendship*, Wallingford Riegger's *March in Memoriam*, Gershwin's *Rhapsody in Blue* and excerpts from *Porgy and Bess*, Elie Siegmeister's *Ozark Set* and Barber's *Essay for Orchestra*. Finally, in June 1946, the third and last American music concert was put on in Moscow, featuring, again, both national anthems, George Antheil's Symphony No. 4, Gershwin's *Rhapsody in Blue*, Aaron Copland's *Two Pieces for Orchestra*, and a repeat performance of Siegmeister's *Ozark Set*.

Although none of the British or American music played during these years found a lasting place in concert repertoire during the late Stalin years, the cut-off after the war was not instantaneous. David Oystrakh was keen to perform the Elgar and Walton Violin Concertos, and he requested scores and parts directly through the British Embassy. He played both the Walton and Elgar concertos in the winter season of 1946–7, the Walton in Leningrad (under Kurt Sanderling) and the Elgar in Moscow as part of his 'Development of the Violin Concerto' series, with materials sent from the British Council via the diplomatic post from London.[25] After that there was emphatically no more British or American music in the schedules of either orchestra until after 1953. But even though it seems that no more music from former Allies entered the Soviet Union after 1946–7, far more had arrived than was represented in these concerts, and Soviet composers and musicians – even if only a select few – had access to a large body of scores and recordings as a result. When the Director of the Soviet Public Relations Division of the British Ministry of Information, Mr H. P. Smollett, visited Moscow in May 1944, he and the Embassy official George Reavey met with Kabalevskiy, Shneyerson and the VOKS official Lidiya Kislova. They requested more scores and recordings of English music and, on his return, Smollett saw to it that this request was met, choosing a selection based on their conversation: recordings of early English composers (John Dunstable, Thomas Arne, William Byrd, Henry Purcell), folk songs (English, Scottish, Irish, Welsh), modern music, light music (operetta), Arthur Bliss's Piano Concerto and several sets of Percy Scholes's 'History of Music' gramophone records and booklets, jazz (especially anything by Jack Hylton), war and popular songs. In addition to these Russian requests, Smollett and Reavey also sent *The Beggar's Opera*, some Gilbert and Sullivan, the score of Vaughan Williams's Violin Concerto and some Gracie Fields records. They also gave VOKS a set of the Purcell Society Complete Edition, which may have been used for the complete performances of *Dido* in 1945.

Restoring the Orthodox Church: The Return of Russian Sacred Music?

If the shift towards Russifying Soviet musical culture in the immediate pre-war years meant that Western repertoire took a back seat in concert schedules, then the onset of the Second World War further entrenched those cultural priorities. The deepening Russification of performance practice after around 1938 received a major boost from the Soviet Union's wartime alliance after the Nazi invasion of June 1941. One of the more unexpected

Figure 5.1: Programme of sacred music organized by the Moscow Patriarchate, 6 February 1945. The inscription reads 'In honour of members and guests of the Russian Orthodox Church'.

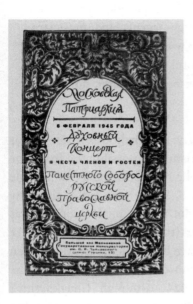
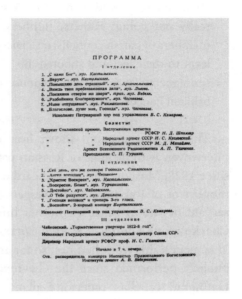

results of the invasion was Stalin's partial restoration of the Orthodox Church and re-election of the Moscow Patriarchate in September 1943; a programme of reopening churches was launched, and on 6 February 1945 the Moscow Patriarchate put on a concert of sacred music at the Moscow Conservatoire (Great Hall) featuring music by Aleksandr Kastal'skiy, Aleksandr Arkhangelskiy, Pavel Chesnokov, Rakhmaninov, Chaykovskiy, Dmitry Bortnyanskiy and others (see Figure 5.1).[26]

So far as I am aware, the only description currently available of this concert is in the memoirs of Nikolay Lyubimov, a notable translator and critic, who went to the concert. His account describes the attendance of priests, dressed in cassocks and carrying Orthodox pectoral crosses, bishops, foreign guests, literary figures, singers, musicians, representatives from the press, members of the Radio Committee, and employees of the publishing industries. He recalled the response during Chaykovskiy's 1812 Overture:

When the prayer *napev* 'Lord, save your people' sounded, all the priests, many of whom were probably hearing the overture for the first time, were transported with joy, and, their eyes glistening with tears, looked at each other and once more fixed their eyes and ears on the orchestra. Golovanov's conducting was inspired—he revealed all of his Russian, Orthodox soul. And then the orchestra finished playing. Lord, then it really got going! Fathers, mothers, church regents and musicians, members of parish councils, officials—in a word, everyone in the hall— leapt to their feet and shouted 'Bis!' [encore] I never witnessed such a spontaneous and heartfelt response either before or after, nor such a brilliant concert as that again.[27]

This moving account shows how closely the Orthodox Church was interwoven with feelings of Russian patriotism. For possibly the first time since 1928, Moscow audiences heard a public live performance of a single movement of Rakhmaninov's *Vespers* (No. 5, 'Lord, now lettest thou thy servant depart in peace'). Another important revival in this concert was Chaykovskiy's *Liturgy of St John Chrysostom* (the single movement No. 11 'It is meet'): this work had not, so far as I have been able to ascertain, been publicly performed since the Glavrepertkom censors struck it from the Leningrad capella's repertoire plans in 1924. Although Chaykovskiy's secular 'Moscow' Cantata would be given its Soviet premiere in October 1947 (Moscow Philharmonia), his *Liturgy* – like Rakhmaninov's *Vespers* – would not be revived for the rest of the Stalin period, and this single movement is the only documented performance during the Stalin years. Another event, which at the time combined with these others to give the impression that performances of Russian sacred music might now be revived, was the founding, in 1944, of the Moscow Choral School as a continuation of the old Leningrad Capella School. Largely staffed by ex-Church singers, the School's director was the Leningrad Capella's former conductor, Aleksandr Sveshnikov. Although it was not openly acknowledged during the Soviet period, Sveshnikov worked as a church precentor before 1917 and had received his diploma from the former Imperial Capella.[28] But it would have been utterly impractical to reject such a wealth of professional experience on the basis of anti-clericalism, and so the church background of many Choral School staff was inevitable.

It has long been assumed that the reason for Stalin's unexpected show of tolerance for the Church was a combination of gratitude (for the Church's rallying calls and financial support during the war) and expediency (exploiting the Church as an agent of Russian nationalism during the war).[29]

Recent research by Steven Miner, however, has revealed that further motivations for Stalin's apparently conciliatory attitude lay in the hope of Western financial and military aid. Religious persecution under the Bolsheviks had been a point of concern with Western nations since the end of the Civil War. Stalin's biographer Dmitry Volkogonov argued that in the months leading up to the Tehran Conference, Stalin went on a charm offensive in order to clear the ground for opening a second military front in Europe. Also, according to Miner, the 'prominence in organizations supporting material assistance for the USSR of sympathetic Western church leaders, such as the so-called Red Dean of Canterbury, Hewlett Johnson, persuaded Stalin to make the "publicity gesture" of restoring the Moscow Patriarchate'.[30] Furthermore, it seems that Stalin planned to use the Orthodox Church to 'Russify' the citizens of recently annexed states such as the Baltics, Bessarabia and Poland, where Catholicism was the dominant religion, as well as to reinforce the re-assimilation of Soviet citizens who had been living under German occupation. Therefore, the re-emergence of the Orthodox religion in Soviet life after 1943 was – at least up to a point – largely driven by a mixture of political and tactical expediency. But on another level, it sat well with the deepening Russification of Soviet cultural life that had already begun in the late 1930s. As the friendly exchanges of the allied period trickled to a standstill, Soviet musicians and musicologists were forced to turn their gaze inwards, firmly close all windows opened to the West, and focus on reviving Russian national pride. Though church music did not play any further role in public musical life during the Stalin period, the foundations were nonetheless being laid for its resurrection in the Khrushchev era, when Sveshnikov's protégé, Aleksandr Yurlov, and Sveshnikov himself, would rediscover old Russian sacred music, and kick-start its 'renaissance' (albeit a gradual and cautious one) in the 1960s.[31]

The 'Rehabilitation' of Rakhmaninov

Although Rakhmaninov's music was not hugely popular during the first two decades of the Soviet era, there was no sustained period of time when his music was seriously neglected. There were several performances of his operas in the early 1920s: the first Soviet staging of *Aleko* was in Petrograd in 1921, with Shalyapin (conducted by Emil Kuper), and *The Miserly Knight* was also staged in the same year. Along with other major composers, Rakhmaninov was honoured with a jubilee event when an auspicious date was due, this time to mark fifty years since his birth, in 1923, with the Petrograd Malïy Theatre giving performances of his cantata *Spring* as well as *Aleko* and *The Miserly Knight*. There were further performances of *Aleko* both in Leningrad and Moscow in 1927, 1929 (Moscow Conservatoire) and 1935 – though this last was admittedly not in a major opera theatre but was rather an amateur performance by the Perm' railway workers' club.[32] *Francesca de Rimini* had to wait until 1940, when the All-Union Radio Committee orchestra gave a concert performance, but starting from 1944, the opera was performed more frequently. Apart from banning the Leningrad capella from singing his *Vespers* after 1928, there was no public campaign against Rakhmaninov until RAPM began to attack him in 1931 – or, more specifically, his choral work on verses by Edgar Allen Poe, *The Bells*, as described in Chapter Two.

Though vicious in its portrayal of him as a 'White-émigré', the campaign to discredit Rakhmaninov and to force the Philharmonias to remove *The Bells* from their repertoires was limited in its success. Certainly, we do not find *The Bells* or any other work by Rakhmaninov listed in Leningrad and Moscow Philharmonia programmes in the two seasons immediately after the March 1931 conference, where the proposal to excise his music from public performance was put forward, but this minor 'success' for RAPM was short-lived owing to the April 1932 Resolution which stripped them of their power. Nevertheless, Rakhmaninov's acceptance into the Soviet concert canon was relatively slow during the 1920s and 1930s: in the 1932–3 season the Leningrad Philharmonia performed his Second Symphony (February 1933); Albert Coates brought the new Fourth Piano Concerto to Moscow in January 1935 and in November 1935 the Moscow Philharmonia played *The Isle of the Dead* and *Three Russian Songs* op. 41. After the document discussed in Chapter Three was (presumably) circulated in 1937 in which Rakhmaninov is once more described as a 'White-émigré', *The Bells* is certainly not heard again for two seasons, though his piano concertos remained in the Philharmonias' repertoire. *The Bells* was restored in the Moscow 1939–40 season, and remained a standard repertoire piece from that time onwards.

Although Rakhmaninov's piano concertos and works for solo piano were regarded by Soviet pianists as an essential component of their repertoire and never came under threat, less well-known works would be revived only as the composer's Soviet image was boosted further during the war. This happened for three major reasons: first, Rakhmaninov was now an

American citizen, and received the same kind of cordial, fraternal interest from the Soviet Union that other American composers and musicians received during the alliance. The single fact of being an émigré did not count against Rakhmaninov in these years any more than it did against Sergey Kusevitskiy, Jascha Heifetz or Aleksandr Grechaninov – all of whom were favourably discussed in documents from the Committee on Arts Affairs. Second, Rakhmaninov had, like his fellow émigrés Heifetz and Kusevitskiy, given benefit concerts for Russian troops during the war, and this was enormously appreciated. The third major factor in his rehabilitation was the composer's approaching seventieth birthday in March 1943. Rakhmaninov's former Russian friends and colleagues, together with students from the Moscow Conservatoire, the State Museum of Musical Culture and VOKS, sent congratulatory telegrams wishing him many long years of health and success. It was in the middle of this flurry of greetings that Soviet musicians heard the shocking and unexpected news that he had died.[33] Less than a week after his death on 23 March, the Moscow Philharmonia held a memorial concert in his honour, although this was almost certainly originally planned as a birthday concert. Glier's review of the concert served as a warm and generous obituary for his old colleague, and he stressed how, during the war, Rakhmaninov had 'proved himself to be a Russian patriot' by giving benefit concerts for the Soviet Union.[34]

It was only at this point that a really full-scale embrace of Rakhmaninov in Soviet music took place. He had retained his repertoire position, it is true; but he had not yet been celebrated in the same way as other Russian composers like Glinka, Chaykovskiy or members of the *kuchka* had been, and there were as yet no Soviet-era monographs on his music. It would probably be too strong to call this semi-neglect, given the consistency with which his orchestral music was performed, but there is no doubt that, after 1943, there was a determined effort to bring Rakhmaninov into the Russian classical fold. After the 1923 Leningrad jubilee celebration, no special event had been held for him, but for his seventieth birthday two decades later, the State Museum of Musical Culture (later named the Glinka Museum) held a major exhibition in his honour, featuring all the materials relating to his life and performance history in Russia that they could lay their hands on. Rakhmaninov himself contributed to the exhibition by sending over records of his works.[35] The exhibition booklet opens with an essay by the musicologist Ol'ga Levasheva in which Rakhmaninov's status is left in no doubt: 'Rakhmaninov was a leading Russian composer-symphonist who

continued the traditions of Chaykovskiy.'[36] Given Chaykovskiy's unim-
peachable status in Soviet musical life, this is an accolade that signals a
point of no return: clearly, those involved in bringing Rakhmaninov back
to the forefront of Soviet musical life clearly did not expect any further
changes in the composer's image.

This upsurge in interest also had an impact on the programming of
Rakhmaninov's more obscure works. His *Spring* cantata, set to texts by
Nikolay Nekrasov in 1902, had already been played in Leningrad in the
1933–4 season, and, as detailed above, it had been performed in 1923 for his
fiftieth birthday jubilee, but it was not played again by either of the
Philharmonias apart from that single 1933–4 performance. However, after
his death it was revived and performed in Leningrad in the 1945–6 season,
alongside two other post-war Russian choral revivals: Chaykovskiy's secular
cantata *Moscow* had its Soviet premiere in 1947 and Sergey Taneyev's *St John
of Damascus* had its post-war revival in 1950.[37] The State Museum of Musical
Culture established a Rakhmaninov *fond* in their archival holdings in 1945,
and a new chapter in Soviet studies on Rakhmaninov was signalled by Igor
Belza's book on the composer, published in 1946.[38]

The wartime collection *Sovetskaya muzïka: sbornik statey* [Soviet music:
collected articles] devoted a whole issue to Rakhmaninov in 1945, and this
source provides a useful gauge of how some Soviet critics tiptoed around the
question of his emigration. Rakhmaninov, who was himself from the landed
gentry class, left Russia in the December following the Bolshevik Revolution
in October 1917. Taking only the most essential belongings, the composer
and his family fled by sledge to Helsinki, and spent a year giving concerts
there and in other Scandinavian countries before sailing for America in 1918.
Or, as Grigoriy Shneyerson delicately put it, the composer 'left Scandinavia
for America'; the fact that he had deliberately left Bolshevik Russia the
previous year in seriously straitened circumstances is, of course, too uncom-
fortable a fact to mention.[39] Konstantin Kuznetsov more bravely mentions
the *Vespers*, commenting favourably on its 'instrumental vocal effects' but
inevitably says nothing about its sacred content.[40] He also says nothing about
Rakhmaninov's decision to leave Bolshevik Russia in 1917, but that is not at
all surprising: this fact is essentially a negative one in the composer's Soviet
biography and, in the wake of his death and the satisfaction of being able to
write freely about him and his importance to Russian music, Soviet musicologists were hardly likely to rake up anything that could be construed as
problematic. A more accurate, if again partial, picture of Rakhmaninov's

emigration is given two years later by Anatoliy Solovtsov in his monograph on the composer. It is worth quoting Solovtsov at some length, because this extract shows how important it was not merely to state that Rakhmaninov was a great Russian composer in the traditions of Chaykovskiy – though that was a vital starting point – but also to strongly underline his patriotism and his interest even in Soviet culture, though the author has so little to base this last claim on that he is reduced to making much out of pitifully little:

> The Moscow period in Rakhmaninov's life ended in 1917. At the end of this year he left for a Scandinavian tour. At the end of 1918 he travelled to the United States of America. Rakhmaninov never returned to his homeland. But we know that his thoughts returned to the place of his birth. We know, for example, that he constantly collected and read books and journals that came from Russia. Soviet music never fell from his sphere of interest. He willingly listened to records of Soviet songs, including songs of the Red Army. People close to him say that Rakhmaninov thought highly of many Soviet songs. We know that Rakhmaninov believed in and loved Russian culture. . . . Rakhmaninov remained Russian and a foreigner [in America]. His love for the motherland was woken fully, as is well known, by the Patriotic War.[41]

Thus Rakhmaninov's emigration becomes no longer an embarrassing fact of his biography, but a cause for his own personal sadness and sense of loss for his homeland. This, indeed, was something to celebrate after a fashion. But leaving aside the issue of how to deal with Rakhmaninov's abrupt departure from Bolshevik Russia, there were other issues at stake following the composer's death. It is probably true to say that the Soviet Union felt under considerable pressure at that time to ensure that Rakhmaninov would be remembered and celebrated first and foremost in Russia, rather than in America. This pressure initially came from the creation in New York, in early 1944, of the Rachmaninoff Memorial Fund, an organization founded by the composer's widow Nadezhda as honorary president, Horowitz as president, Kusevitskiy as chair of the Artists' Advisory Committee and Olin Downes as chair of the executive committee. Its inaugural statement contained several phrases embarrassing to the Soviet Union: 'In the years of revolution [Rakhmaninov's] sensitive mind would not come to peace with Russia. But when the monstrous, soul-destroying evil fell upon the land of his fathers, he did not isolate himself. . . . The

Soviet Union, which had previously banned his music, reciprocated by instituting festivals in his honor. ... Rachmaninoff, despite his previous politican [sic] differences with the land of his birth, contributed large sums from the receipts of his concerts to the Russian War Relief.'[42] The inaccurate charge that the Soviet Union had banned his music was evidently not left unchallenged, for Olin Downes subsequently retracted this statement and wrote to the Soviet Ambassador in Washington (Vladimir Bazïkin) to inform him.[43] The Soviets' cabled response to the Fund's establishment was courteous and positive, but it is easy to discern a proprietorial note behind the polite phrases: 'Rachmaninoff's music and his genius inspired executancy is highly appreciated by and profoundly moves all soviet lovers of musical art and this means millions of people in composers birthland.'[44] A later cabled response from VOKS to the Fund's intention to start a piano competition where the winner would tour the Soviet Union after touring America, was even more defensive:

> we would ask directors this fund take into consideration fact that all concrete questions of contests tour trips etcetera can be discussed and decided only after war ends ... for your information we advise herewith of certain measures being affected in ussr to perpetuate memory rachmaninoff ... special volumes articles dedicated to rachmaninoff will shortly appear ... in march will be given first performance newly found four hand arrangement rachmaninoffs first symphony ... score of symphony is being restored ... rachmaninoffs works are regularly performed at concerts and by radio.[45]

Two further anecdotes remain with regard to Rakhmaninov's relationship with Soviet Russia, both during the composer's lifetime. In late December 1942, a senior Soviet diplomat in Washington (Vladimir Bazïkin) contacted Rakhmaninov to ask for scores and parts for his Third Symphony and Fourth Piano Concerto, for performance in the Soviet Union. Charles Foley, Rakhmaninov's New York publisher, arranged to send the symphony, and the concerto when it was ready (the final, third version was not yet printed in 1942) on hire, but mentioned that a fee would be due by the receiving party. When Bazïkin questioned this (since Rakhmaninov was a Russian composer), Foley countered by observing that the Soviet Union did not intend to pay Rakhmaninov royalties for the performance because he was classed as a foreigner. Thus Bazïkin assumed that, as a native Russian,

Rakhmaninov's music could be performed without a hire fee, but at the same time did not offer any royalty payments because these were never paid to foreign composers.[46] In the end, it seems that the modest fee Foley requested ('on average ten dollars per performance' for the hire – he does not give a sum for the performance rights) was paid, because the Third Symphony was performed in Moscow on 28 October 1945 and his Piano Concerto No. 4 was played in a special concert of Rakhmaninov's music on 2 November 1945, with two new editions, both prepared by Pavel Lamm: the *Scherzo* and symphonic poem *Prince Rostislav*. Because of the question of hire and performance fees, however, neither the Third Symphony nor the Piano Concerto No. 4 became Soviet repertoire pieces: after this concert, they were not played again within the chronological limits of this study. In general, after 1945 there is a dip in the performance of Rakhmaninov's music, not because he fell out of favour, but simply because the urgency associated with celebrating him had passed.

The second anecdote is that Rakhmaninov, taking advantage of the newly opened channels of communication with Russia, made a request through the New York Soviet Embassy (through V. A. Fedyushin) to Vladimir Kemenov for the return of three scores which he had left behind in Russia: *The Miserly Knight*, *Francesca da Rimini* and his *All-night Vigil*. It is not clear whether they were original autographs, manuscript copies or simply printed scores.[47] The initial request was made on 7 January 1942 and by June that year a response had still not arrived, promoting a second, more abrupt request: 'Please send the following scores for the composer S. Rakhmaninov: 1. *The Miserly Knight*, 2. *Francesca da Rimini*, 3. *All-Night Vigil*.'[48] There is no record that any of these scores were returned, at least not in the composer's lifetime, although Boosey and Hawkes published scores of all three works after 1947, suggesting that either they were sent, thus giving Western publishers the opportunity to reprint them, or that they were available already and Rakhmaninov had wanted his original copies back.

The 'Iron Curtain' Descends: 1944–7

As the war drew to a close, it was not clear either to Western powers or even to certain levels of the Soviet government how post-war cooperation might continue. One of the best sources for assessing Soviet attitudes to cultural exchanges with their former allies in the post-war era is the file of the Committee on Arts Affairs which, until 1948, was still headed by Mikhail

Khrapchenko. Because foreign governments and arts organizations were not always aware of the correct procedures for making cultural approaches, when they were met with prolonged silence it was easy to assume that invitations had gone into some kind of bureaucratic black hole, or that they were being stonewalled deliberately. But examination of Khrapchenko's files gives a very different picture. A surprising number of Western invitations were positively received, and Khrapchenko himself made further inquiries as to how some of them might proceed. The undeniable fact that almost none ever took place, however, points the finger of blame not at the arts bureaucrats themselves but rather at Stalin, whose swift retreat from Allied cooperation once the war was over meant a change of cultural policy so stark that it took the relevant government departments some time to catch up. Indeed, it has not yet been proven how pre-planned Stalin's move into what became known as the 'cold war' actually was. His dislike of post-war changes of leadership (Truman in America, Attlee in Great Britain), combined with the alarming knowledge that America had the atom bomb while the Soviet Union did not, did nothing to improve relations on the cultural front. As I have argued elsewhere, the British government plainly expected cultural cooperation to continue in the Soviet Union after the war – even going so far as to plan a British Council cultural centre in Moscow for language teaching, film screenings and so on – but initially, at least, so did Soviet organizations like VOKS, whose entire *raison d'être* had been to foster cordial relations with Western powers.[49] Yet after the post-war carving up of Europe, where vast swathes of formerly occupied territories were handed over to the Soviet Union and Soviet influence in Eastern Europe produced communist governments across what came to be known as the Soviet bloc, the Soviet Union itself emerged as a modern superpower, vastly richer and more powerful than, for example, Great Britain, whose own empire was rapidly crumbling. Where once the Soviet Union had regarded fostering good relations with Western cultural figures as important for its international prestige, it now set itself up in opposition to the West as a newly empowered empire, with new satellite states to command and control. The importance of cultural relations with the West was downgraded as the opportunities offered by their new Soviet neighbours took shape and ultimately held out the attractive prospect of showcasing Soviet culture as superior to that of their former allies.

I have shown elsewhere that ambitious plans to bring the Bolshoy Ballet to London – starting as early as 1941 and finally coming to nought in

1946 – were originally conceived by officials in the British Ministries of Economic Warfare and from the Russian Department of the Ministry of Information as a propaganda strategy to bring Soviet citizens 'out of their ring-fence' to experience 'normal' life in Britain.[50] Further proposals to invite the Bolshoy came from John Maynard Keynes (Covent Garden) in 1944 and the private impresario firm Hyde Productions in 1946, both of whom offered to pay full Russian travel and living expenses. Keynes's invitation was sponsored by the British Council, who promised to underwrite the tour up to 10,000 pounds costs. When the proposal first arrived on Khrapchenko's desk in November 1944, his response was enthusiastic:

> The Committee for Arts Affairs of the USSR considers it possible and valuable to send for exhibition in London artists of the Bolshoy ballet of the USSR. The best popularization abroad of Soviet theatrical art would be valuable to show in London a few ballet spectacles – Swan Lake, Don Quixote, Romeo and Juliet and Gayane . . . Our best artists may take part in the trip to London – Ulanova, Lepeshinskaya, Dudinskaya, Sergeyev, Chabukiani, Messerer and the conductor Feyer, the balletmaster Lavrovskiy and the set designer Pëtr Vilyams.[51]

The proposal got no further during wartime: when the Soviet Ambassador in London, Fëdor Gusev (who had brokered the original invitation) was contacted by Anthony Eden in March 1945 to see how the invitation had been received, Gusev contacted his superiors and, a week later, told Eden that wartime conditions made such a trip impractical. But once the war was over, and Hyde Productions' invitation came to Khrapchenko's notice in February 1946, there seemed no obvious barrier to accepting the British terms, especially given their financial generosity. Khrapchenko contacted the Director of the Bolshoy Ballet and asked for his opinion. It was only then – when the Bolshoy had set out its own demands and preconditions – that Khrapchenko realized the plan was completely out of the question. The Bolshoy demanded that over 250 personnel should go (not counting the orchestra, who were too busy to travel), that new staging and sets were required because of the different proportions of the Bolshoy stage and that of Covent Garden and that all material costs must be met by the inviting organization. Certainly, neither Covent Garden nor Hyde Productions had expected such a large troupe, and the costs would have been phenomenally high. Khrapchenko sent a polite note to the British, declining their invitation but offering them the Ensemble of Folk Dance of the USSR under the direction of Igor Moiseyev, who had just toured in Czechoslovakia, Hungary, Yugoslavia and Romania.[52] Even that trip did not take place, although correspondence on the subject between the Central Committee members Andrey Vïshinskiy and Georgiy Malenkov shows that Vïshinskiy was in favour of the tour, and his letter mentions that Molotov had also recommended it.[53] Despite this high-level support, Vïshinskiy's formal request to Malenkov – for the Central Committee of the Communist Party to resolve this question – evidently received an unfavourable reply.

Khrapchenko's file reveals that he was far more positive about American proposals than about British ones, and there were several reasons why this may have been so. First, there is the question of relative familiarity: several distinguished musicians who had left Russia after 1917 were now living in America and their international status was well known to him. Second, the Americans were not as fixated as the British seemed to be on bringing Soviet musicians out of their country: they were just as interested in visiting the Soviet Union themselves, and this not only made the prospect of a tour easier (because the Americans would take the lion's share of organizational matters), but it also reduced any chance of adverse propaganda from the West, and removed the risk of defection.[54] One of the earliest proposals from America, however, came not from a high-profile performer but from the elderly composer Aleksandr Grechaninov, who had written to his friend Glier of his homesickness and wish to visit. Glier had passed this letter on to VOKS, and it was a colleague from their American section, Zarubin, who wrote sympathetically to Khrapchenko:

> The composer Grechaninov, who is living in the USA, has written to Glier: 'in 1944 I will be 80 years old. If my homeland would make me the gift of performing my "Dobrïniya", then I would definitely come home, where my heart still is.' The workers at our Embassy in America have recommended that we explore all possibilities of granting Grechaninov's wishes. Apart from that, it is desirable to send him greetings and to write an article about him and put on a concert of his works. On the orders of Comrade Dekanozov I ask your opinion about all this and to consider Grechaninov's wishes in the USSR.[55]

Khrapchenko's response was wholly positive, and as a result, a concert for Grechaninov celebrating his eightieth birthday was put on in Moscow in

October 1944, where his Symphony No. 4 op. 102 (1927) received its Soviet premiere alongside his beloved opera *Dobrïniya Nikitich*. Grechaninov never did return to Russia, but it seems that hearing about the suffering endured by the Russian people during the war increased his feelings of homesickness and wish to reconnect with his own culture; happily, the final years of friendly collaboration with America allowed Russians to respond in kind. His birthday was marked by many friendly greetings from Soviet composers and musicians dated after this concert, so evidently Grechaninov was unable to travel.[56] The same homesickness was probably not suffered by the violinist Jascha Heifetz who had left Russia in 1917 as revolution was breaking out and, apart from a single Soviet tour in April 1934, never returned. Between 1941 and 1945 Heifetz travelled worldwide all over the front line playing for American troops, in tour after gruelling tour. It is unsurprising, therefore, that when Khrapchenko sent his rather peremptory message in May 1944 to Vladimir Kemenov, the president of VOKS, stating bluntly that 'The Committee on Arts Affairs considers it valuable to request a tour in the USSR with the violinist Jascha Heifetz. His visit to the USSR is desirable if timed with the winter concerts of Oct–Nov 1944' the file does not record a response. In May–June 1944 Heifetz was undertaking another United States Organization tour in Europe and was probably not in a position to reply, if indeed he ever received the invitation. A more promising proposal went to VOKS in October 1944 from the senior diplomat Vladimir Bazïkin in Washington, asking for permission for the American composer Roy Harris to visit the Soviet Union. Khrapchenko's file holds an evaluation of Harris as a friend of the Soviet Union who had dedicated his Fifth Symphony (the first movement of which was performed in Moscow in October 1944) to the Soviet people, but all the same, Khrapchenko does not respond enthusiastically. What he does seem keen on, however, is a visit by musicians who strike him as more impressively famous:

> In connection with your question about the possibility of a visit to the USSR by leading American musicians we have concluded: the Committee on Arts Affairs considers it extremely valuable to have a tour to the USSR by the conductors Arturo Toscanini, Sergey Kusevitskiy, Leopold Stokowski, Otto Klemperer and the pianist Vladimir Horowitz, the violinists Jascha Heifetz, Yehudi Menuhin and the singer Lily Pons. We do not consider it valuable for the composer Roy Harris and the balletmaster Leonid Massine to visit at the present time.[57]

This is a roll call of big names; the political allegiances of the individuals count for nothing when compared to their international status, while a self-declared friend of the Soviet Union like Harris seems to have been insufficiently famous for Khrapchenko seriously to consider inviting him. The only demonstrable fruit of this correspondence is that Yehudi Menuhin did indeed tour to the Soviet Union in November 1945: he was, so far as I have been able to discover, the only major artist from an Allied nation to do so in this period. Horowitz was certainly invited, but could not come, though his telegram expressed the wish to be re-invited for the next season.[58]

Khrapchenko's ambition to lure Kusevitskiy back to Russia was revived in 1946, when the Boston Symphony Orchestra proposed an exchange visit with Yevgeniy Mravinskiy. Mravinskiy was to visit Boston and conduct Kusevitskiy's orchestra (planned for December 1946) as a reciprocal visit for that of Kusevitskiy and the Boston Symphony to Moscow in September that year. The original request had come from the President of Trustees of the Boston Symphony Orchestra, Anny B. Cabat, to the Soviet Ambassador in Washington on 26 February 1946. Mravinskiy was invited entirely at the orchestra's expense and the orchestra also proposed to fund their own Soviet tour, offering to stay anywhere they were told to and even to use any airline. Though Khrapchenko responded positively, neither trip ever took place, meaning that a veto must have come from higher in the command chain. A similar offer had already been made by the conductor of the Los Angeles Symphony Orchestra, Alfred Wallenstein, who in December 1944 asked permission to bring the orchestra to Moscow for a concert 'dedicated to the idea of peace and friendship between the Soviet Union and USA'.[59] Wallenstein proposed to fund the entire tour himself, with the aid of box-office receipts, and suggested for his programme Shostakovich's Seventh Symphony, a selected American work and 'a musical work dedicated to peace and friendship between the USSR and USA'. Correspondence between the NKID's American section head S. Tsarapkin and Khrapchenko shows that both the NKID and Committee on Arts Affairs regarded the proposal favourably as a significant boost to strengthening cultural relations between the USSR and America – something that was evidently seen as eminently desirable on the Soviet side, at least at this level of bureaucracy. There is no record that the trip took place, but the fact that Wallenstein's offer was appreciated and taken seriously adds to this body of evidence proving that blocks to post-war cultural exchange often came from the highest political levels and that cultural organizations only learned of the changes in policy at a much later stage.

Perhaps the most intriguing of all the proposals made between 1942 and 1946 was a request in April 1946 that, unusually, originated from two Soviet organizations: Leningrad's Malïy and Moscow's Stanislavskiy theatres. Both wished to perform George Gershwin's *Porgy and Bess* and requested, via VOKS, that they be sent performing parts. *Porgy* was known in the Soviet Union, partly through the concert of American and Soviet music in Moscow in July 1945, where excerpts from the opera were performed alongside his *Rhapsody in Blue*.[60] But by that time, Moscow audiences had had a chance to hear the whole work, because at some point before 25 April, the opera was given a complete concert performance in Moscow, possibly by the Bolshoy, though the Bolshoy's official records do not include this event.[61] Shneyerson had written a long article on *Porgy* in *Sovetskaya muzïka* in 1946, in which he quoted extensively from the score, suggesting that at least the VOKS library owned a copy.[62] In many ways, the opera was eminently suitable for a Soviet audience: it was, as Gershwin himself claimed, a 'folk opera' that celebrated the culture of a poor black fishing settlement in South Carolina. The Soviet Union still prided itself on its acceptance of multi-ethnic cultures, especially in comparison with American society. Kemenov's letter to Khrapchenko set out the reasons why they could do nothing to facilitate these requests: when VOKS had put the matter before their legal consultant in their New York Embassy, they learned that the lack of copyright protection for foreign authors in the Soviet Union would mean trouble with the current owners of its copyright, the Dramatists' Guild of America. As a result, *Porgy* could only be heard in the Soviet Union in concert performance. Fearing protests in America if they pressed ahead with a stage performance, Kemenov explained to Khrapchenko that they would not be able to proceed with the opera unless the law was changed, or they got formal permission.[63] That was, sadly, the end of the line for *Porgy* on the Soviet stage until the famous American tour to Leningrad in 1955 immortalized by Truman Capote, who travelled with the company, first in the *New Yorker* and then in his short book, *The Muses Are Heard*.[64]

As we have seen, the channel of musical exchange between Britain and the Soviet Union was as lively during wartime as was humanly possible, with the British Council and Foreign Office working with VOKS to exchange scores and recordings for performance and broadcast, and during these years the VOKS music library – and by extension other music libraries such as that of the Moscow and Leningrad Conservatoires and Composers'

Union – all benefited from the influx of new scores. But as diplomatic relations became strained and Churchill made his 'Iron curtain' speech in March 1946, musicians, cultural officials and government ministers in Britain and America perceived an encroaching hostility that threatened all that they had carefully built up during the war years. Yet it is clear from papers relating to VOKS and Khrapchenko's Committee for Arts Affairs that Soviet officials were also keen to maintain friendly cultural relations during this transitional period. As we have seen, Khrapchenko seems to have been swayed largely by prestige, taking major artists and organizations seriously and freely disregarding others who struck him as less important. VOKS, however, was more intimately involved with exchange work at all levels and hoped to emerge from the fruitful wartime years a stronger, not weaker, organization. In particular, it wished to avoid a repetition of the purges that saw some of its most active officials arrested and charged with espionage on account of their contact with foreigners. But by mid-1945, VOKS had serious concerns about the Soviet government's post-war commitment to fostering cultural exchanges with its former allies. In what with hindsight appears a total misreading of the way Stalin's post-war international policies were heading, Aleksandr Karaganov, a member of the VOKS presidium, wrote to Molotov in September 1945 with a serious complaint and request:

In 1944 and 1945 VOKS and the Committee for Arts Affairs sent abroad several workers in Soviet culture, scholars, writers, architects, artists, painters. The presentation of these workers of Soviet culture in Finland, Romania, Czechoslovakia, Bulgaria, Yugoslavia, Poland and Austria caused a great social resonance and effectively aided the propaganda of Soviet culture in those lands. However up to now we have not sent any group to the USA or England. Hence there has been organization of presentations of Soviet artists and cultural workers in a series of European countries, including those allied to Germany during the war, while at the same time we negatively replied to invitations from lands which were *our* main allies in the war with Germany. Up to now new, numerous invitations to Soviet cultural workers have been received. For example, the National Council of American–Soviet Friendship invited a delegation from VOKS, including scholars, composers, painters, artists and writers. The composers Prokof'yev and Shostakovich have received personal invitations from Sergey Kusevitskiy. The National Council invited the Red Army Ensemble of Song and Dance, the Ensemble of Folk Dance and a group of ballet artists to tour the USA. Many similar invitations have come from England. The rejection of all these invitations at the same time as our groups of artists are going to neighbouring European lands may give an undesirable impression . . . in the USA and England. And, apart from that, we urgently stress that we should utilize trips by Soviet cultural workers for activities of cultural connections with these countries. In connection with this summary, I consider the following valuable: 1) To send to the USA a) the ballet troupe of the Bolshoy Theatre to give performances of Swan Lake and Raymonda, b) a delegation from VOKS of comrades Shostakovich, Shokolov, Kukrïniksï (Kupryanov, Krïlov, Sokolov) . . . The delegation's director would be the President of VOKS, Comrade V. S. Kemenov. 2) To send to England an artistic brigade, the structure of the brigade to be determined with the Committee for Arts Affairs and a group of cultural workers including the composer Kabalevskiy, the writer K. [Konstantin] Simonov, the sculptor V. [Vera] Mukhina, the film director S. [Sergey] Gerasimov and the academic Vavilov.[65]

Karaganov's proposal was followed up by a wealth of information charting the activities of VOKS and the Society for Cultural Relations (with USSR) in Britain, all of which was circulated at the highest levels of the Central Committee. His request was in vain: both Karaganov and Kemenov misread the way in which Soviet foreign policy was moving, though they were hardly alone even among high-ranking Soviet bureaucrats in that.

Whether or not what followed was prompted by such appeals is not known, but in or before February 1947, the Central Committee ordered an investigation of VOKS's work, co-ordinated by Molotov. Kemenov submitted a report to Molotov, detailing the exponential increase in VOKS's work between 1940 and 1946. In 1940, it had representatives in just six countries; by 1946 this number had grown to fifty-four. International societies for cultural relations with the Soviet Union numbered twenty-four in 1940 and over 4,000 in 1946, while the 800-strong membership in 1940 had swelled to over three million by 1946. Kemenov also reminded Molotov that as recently as November 1945, VOKS had been asked to broaden the scope of its work by two Central Committee members: Andrey Vïshinskiy and Georgiy Aleksandrov.[66] However impressive Kemenov's achievements during wartime undoubtedly were, documents from the Kremlin issued in early 1947 show that the work of VOKS was being scrutinized, ostensibly in a drive to cut their extravagant spending. Certainly, the orders do not read as though Stalin wished to liquidate VOKS – after all, it was a valuable propaganda facilitator – but it is impossible to judge, at this distance, how fairly made the accusations of financial mismanagement really were. L. Mekhlis wrote directly to Stalin on 9 July 1948, listing the main findings of the recent financial audit. Charges levelled at Kemenov and his staff included over-lavish and illegal payments to 'private individuals and inter-mediaries' who were perceived as benefiting unfairly from State largesse, and a large sum of money (over a million roubles) wasted on producing a journal that never went to press (*Sovetskaya kul'tura*).[67] Mekhlis's longer report (of the same date) to the Council of Ministers goes into more detail regarding over-payments to the State music publishers, Muzgiz, in which Shneyerson was directly implicated. More seriously, perhaps, Mekhlis and Kemenov accused Shneyerson of misrepresenting Soviet music by sending abroad works that were, according to the audit, of poor quality, thereby not only wasting State funds in propagating worthless music, but also giving a poor impression of Soviet musical creativity. This report contains a state-ment by Kemenov, in which he blames Shneyerson outright for nefarious practices that he had been unaware of:

> Undoubtedly, my opinion is that Shneyerson's activities were suppressed too late. In the opinion of members of the Presidium and workers in accounts, who processed the finance documents, Shneyerson's notions regarding pay seemed to be completely out of control, and the result of this was a wasteful squandering of resources that went unremarked upon by the VOKS Presidium and became known only after Goscontrol revealed it. Apart from that, notwithstanding the categorical ban by the VOKS Presidium to send abroad any musical work without the approval of the music section of the VOKS Presidium, Shneyerson fraudulently proceeded without them, organizing for dispatch abroad music by unknown composers, whose work is in no way representative of the achievements of Soviet music.[68]

With memories still fresh of the tragic fate of the former VOKS presi-dent Aleksandr Arosev in 1938,[69] it is hardly surprising to find Kemenov fighting for survival at this time. The VOKS audit was unquestionably the cause of his abrupt about-turn with regard to Soviet foreign policy towards

Western culture. From July 1947 the signal from the Soviet Union to the West was very clear: an ideological line was drawn between Soviet and Western art, in terms reverting sharply to earlier, pre-war Soviet rhetoric of Western 'decadence' and 'bourgeois decay'.[70] In an aggressive speech at the Polytechnical Museum, Moscow on 9 July 1947, when his organization was undergoing investigation, Kemenov delivered the first public blow to Anglo-American-Soviet cultural relations, denouncing Western art as 'anti-humanistic', and its belief in 'art for art's sake' symptomatic of the decline of the capitalist world.[71] The speech's closing paragraph summed up the new position perfectly:

> A valuation of Russian and Soviet art will help to see all the contradic-
> tions of bourgeois art. It was the leading art in the war, and will remain
> so in the post-war period. It was born in different conditions from the
> art of America and Western Europe. Soviet culture – national in form,
> socialist in content – is destined to serve the people. It does serve them,
> and from them it derives its strength, and therefore it will remain eter-
> nally healthy and bright, and it has no need to turn for its themes to
> schizophrenics, it has no need to bow down before decaying bourgeois
> culture; on the contrary, the eyes of progressive people throughout the
> world are turned towards Soviet art, since Soviet art expresses the ideas
> of new democratic morality.[72]

From this point on until after Stalin's death in March 1953, cultural exchanges with the Soviet Union's former Allies were non-existent. Despite Kemenov's efforts, he lost his position in 1948, though fortunately did not suffer any worse fate. Khrapchenko, too, lost his job as part of the sweeping reforms initiated in January–February 1948 by the post-war investigation of Soviet music commonly known as the *Zhdanovshchina* after the Minister of Culture who had already led similar investigations into literature and art in 1946, Andrey Zhdanov.

Background to the *Zhdanovshchina*

Kiril Tomoff has argued persuasively that what music historians have taken as an inevitable continuation of the *Zhdanovshchina* from literature and art into music was, in fact, not planned at the time Zhdanov's post-war cultural reform began.[73] This view is supported by Zhdanov's own claim at the

January 1948 meeting of Soviet music workers: 'It has required a discussion in the Central Committee of the Party for the comrades to discover the fact that this regime [the Composers' Union] has its negative side. However that may be, before the conference not one of them thought of changing the state of affairs in the Union of Composers.'[74] Rather, Tomoff argues, and Zhdanov also implies, it was infighting within the music world that precipitated the events of January–February 1948, which saw the six leading names in Soviet music – Shostakovich, Prokof'yev, Myaskovskiy, Khachaturyan, Shebalin and Popov – denounced and selections of their works placed on a blacklist.[75] The selection of banned works was peculiarly arbitrary and, since it contained works that were already never played such as Popov's First Symphony (effectively banned since its premiere in 1934) and Prokof'yev's 1947 'Flourish, Mighty Land', seems to have been a mixture of raking up past sins and dragging along whatever more recent 'failures' came to mind. Banning Shostakovich's 1943 Piano Sonata No. 2, for instance, instead of his radically avant-garde Sonata No. 1 (1926) would be funny if it had not happened in such a traumatic context; likewise, choosing Myaskovskiy's attempt to please Stalin, his cantata *Kremlin by Night*, rather than his modernistic Thirteenth Symphony (1933), looks almost deliberately perverse. The singling out of Igor Belza – really more a musicologist than composer – shows that there is also an element here of punishing figures who had friendly connections with Western composers; Belza had published an article in 1943 on English music.[76] The Central Committee's 'Protocol No. 62' from 26 January 1948 concerning the leadership of the Composers' Union and of the Committee on Arts Affairs shows that the priorities at this stage were to dismiss Khrapchenko and replace him with the hard-liner art critic and Central Committee member Polikarp Lebedev, and to dismiss Khachaturyan, Muradeli and Atovm'yan from the organizational committee (Orgkomitet) of the Composers' Union and replace them with Khrennikov, Asaf'yev, Koval' and Zakharov; other Soviet composers shortly to be included in the list of disgraced names (Shostakovich, Myaskovskiy, Shebalin, Popov) were not mentioned anywhere at this stage.[77] Asaf'yev (who died in January 1949) was to have become the new President of the Composers' Union, and also of the music section of the Stalin Prize Committee, with Khrennikov as his deputy (those selected by the Politburo to serve alongside them on the Prize Committee were the former Leningrad capella conductor Aleksandr Sveshnikov, Gol'denveyzer, Shaporin, and the minor composer Anatoliy Novikov). However, accusations levelled at the Orgkomitet in this protocol inescapably imply that the shortcomings in the Composers' Union leadership were the shared responsibility of each member, and thus implicated Shostakovich and Myaskovsky, who were also Presidium members:

> the Orgkomitet was turned into a hotbed of convicted formalist parties, anti-people tendencies in Soviet music, thereby doing serious damage to its development. The Orgkomitet not only did not facilitate the expansion of creative discussions, criticism and self-criticism amid Soviet composers, but quite the reverse: they cultivated an alien Soviet social disposition, suppressing criticism and self-criticism and assisting the unrestrained eulogizing of works by a small group of composers.[78]

Thus by the time the main three-day February conference of Soviet composers and musicians led by Zhdanov took place, those who later assumed power had already been elected and very probably already knew of this themselves.

But as Leonid Maksimenkov has shown, Stalin already had a file of complaints from the public relating to Soviet music, dating back to March 1947 – well before he attended Muradeli's ill-fated opera. One of the earliest documents mentioned in the ensuing report 'Letters and declarations received by Stalin' was a letter from a professional violinist based in Odessa, M. E. Gol'dshteyn, complaining to Stalin on the subject of 'incomprehensible music':

> I regard myself as a well enough educated musician to understand the niceties of compositional technique; however, for all the strength of my musical perception, a series of works by our best composers remain incomprehensible to me. They sometimes create the impression that I am listening, not to music, but to a mathematical calculation, the purpose of which is to show how clever the composer is to combine different voices in works with definite themes, disregarding whether or not it sounds false or unpleasant – the author does not trouble over that.
>
> What must it be like for the listener who is not musically prepared? They indeed have to be forced to listen to such musical stunts, to be deprived of their own senses, their own artistic-musical perceptions. To such listeners they say that such and such a work is written by a master and they are required to simply believe it. . . . Among the creators of

these inaccessible works I would like to name composers such as Prokof'yev, Shostakovich, Shebalin and such younger composers as follow these masters. In our land, the art of music has become accessible to the whole Soviet people, who genuinely love and respect those working in music. In such conditions it is incomprehensible to find music in collections of works, in which any clear melody or transparency is absent. We often learn new works to perform written for violin and among them I have found some that are absolutely incomprehensible to the listener – they are exhausted by them, they don't respond with any emotion to them.

I think that the fault for this lies not with the listener, but with the composer.

One of the reasons for this, it seems to me, is the necessity to search for the break between composers and listeners. The greatest composers of the 18th and 19th centuries adorned their works with popular melodies, songs and dances from folklore, which you can hear in symphonies and operas. Glinka said that 'music is created by the people; we, the composers, merely arrange it'.

Where, in the symphonies and chamber music of Shostakovich or Prokof'yev, can we find popular songs, or the intonations of popular song? I think, very rarely indeed.[79]

Some of these phrases or ideas are recognizable from Zhdanov's own speech to the Central Committee of the Communist Party in January 1948 – the reference to Glinka's famous remark and the allusion to a 'break' between composers and audiences stand out particularly strongly.[80] But letters from the public formed only a small part of the growing brief against Soviet composers. As Tomoff, Maksimenkov and Vlasova have all shown, one of the *agents provocateurs* behind the scenes in 1948 was none other than the Moscow Conservatoire professor, the distinguished pianist Aleksandr Gol'denveyzer.

'Weary of False Notes': The Gol'denveyzer Affair

Vlasova speculates that Gol'denveyzer's grudge against his colleagues dated back to when he was displaced by Shebalin as Director of the Moscow Conservatoire in 1942 while evacuated to Saratov, allegedly for reasons of old age and inability to carry out his duties. There is no evidence that

Shebalin sought this position; in fact, Vlasova shows that the starting point was actually an ugly anti-Semitic attack on Gol'denveyzer and other Jewish musicians by the Agitprop head, Georgiy Aleksandrov to the secretariat of the Central Committee, Andrey Andreyev, Malenkov and Aleksandr Shcherbakov, entitled 'On the selection and nomination of cadres in art' on 22 August 1942.[81] It was after this complaint had been passed to Khrapchenko and his Committee that Khrapchenko took the decision to relieve Gol'denveyzer of his duties as Director and replace him with Shebalin. But Vlasova also speculates that Gol'denveyzer's grudge against Shebalin and the Conservatoire had other, more immediate, causes: in the spring of 1947, the Committee on Arts Affairs sent Shebalin and the conductor Nikolay Golovanov to Italy, intending to forge links with Italian vocal teachers who might then visit the Soviet Union. Gol'denveyzer wrote to M. Suslov of the Central Committee on 8 January 1948 – two days before the three-day conference began – to complain about the plan, pointing out a precedent from the late 1920s and 1930s in which he felt he had been vindicated. As Gol'denveyzer describes it: 'I alone stood up against the continuous invitations to the USSR of the foreign pianists Godovsky, Petri, Cortot and others, in the capacity of professors of our Conservatoire . . . I was accused of countless mortal sins: obscurantism, chauvinism, envy etc.' But, he triumphantly claims, the success of young Soviet pianists in international competitions proved him right: though it was undeniable that the West had many distinguished pianists, Russia's own traditions were, in his view, superior by far.[82] Gol'denveyzer's xenophobia provided the Central Committee with an authoritative musical source for an impending attack: in Vlasova's words, his letter was 'consonant with the needs of the time'.[83]

It seems from the archive record that, on 19 January 1948, *after* the three-day music workers' conference, Gol'denveyzer sent Zhdanov another document, this time a long essay entitled 'Questions on the musical front'. Zhdanov sent it on to his fellow Central Committee colleagues Dmitriy Shepilov, Pëtr Pospelov and Polikarp Lebedev with a view to meeting in order to discuss it.[84] The purpose of the essay was clearly to undermine the authority of the leading names in Soviet music by claiming that ordinary people could not understand it; that its cacophonous modernism alienated the listener and that it was the duty of Soviet composers to follow in the spirit of Glinka, the *kuchka* and Chaykovskiy in writing music that was 'born from folk song and dance'.[85] In addition to criticizing individual Soviet composers, Gol'denveyzer turned his dissatisfaction upon

Soviet musical organizations: Muzgiz, the Composers' Union and the Philharmonias:

> The leading Moscow and Leningrad Philharmonias, in their attitudes to performing works by Soviet composers, completely fulfil directives from the very same heads of the Composers' Union. Those works that are not of their kind – non-conformist [*inakomïslyashchiye*] – are hardly ever played. Works of the Russian classics are played incompletely and often carelessly. Glazunov is hardly ever played, we rarely hear Borodin's symphonies ... from Rimskiy-Korsakov's instrumental works we hear only Shcheherazade. Arenskiy's fine First Symphony is not performed, nor are Lyapunov's Piano Concerti. I could continue this list for a long time. The works of Western classics are unsystematically played. ... Haydn's symphonies and quartets, each year inspire listeners with joy, but are hardly ever played in our concerts; we hear very little of Mozart, Schubert; alien to us are Mendelssohn's and Schumann's symphonies which are hardly ever heard.[86]

There is a strong echo here of the anonymous 1937 document described in Chapter Three, which voices a similar dissatisfaction with the infrequency of performances of Borodin, Glazunov, Rimskiy-Korsakov and Arenskiy. It is certainly possible that a similar harangue by Gol'denveyzer had provided at least a starting point for that document, which officials in the Committee for Arts Affairs then used to give their own directive musical authority. Though unquestionably distinguished, Gol'denveyzer was also bigoted and resentful, and believed himself to be insufficiently respected by the Soviet musical elite. These qualities made him the ideal 'go-to' person for the Central Committee in preparing their case against Soviet music: he was a completely reliable source of grudges, complaints and vox populi sentiments about the evils of modern music.

In the copy of this essay preserved in Molotov's personal files, certain phrases are heavily underlined, as though marked out for use in the final Resolution of the Central Committee of the Communist Party 'On Muradeli's Opera "The Great Friendship"' which was published in *Pravda* on 11 February 1948.[87] The underlined passages include remarks that modern music 'goes beyond the boundaries of all harmonic logic' and that its sounds were 'more suitable as the expression of the ideological degeneration of Western culture, of fascism, than they are of the healthy type of

Russian, Soviet, man'.[88] Though I have not been able to ascertain whether this essay was sent to Zhdanov any earlier than 19 January (and thus could be regarded as a commission, designed to aid Zhdanov in formulating his own position), it is very noticeable that Gol'denveyzer's claim that modern music is not 'normal' or 'healthy' chimed with a major plank of Zhdanov's attack: 'This [formalist] trend exchanges natural, beautiful, human music for music that is false, vulgar and often purely pathological.'[89] Most fundamentally, both Gol'denveyzer and Zhdanov harp on the notion that the composers of the past – the 'classics' – wrote for the people (and not for themselves or for 'aesthetes'), in comprehensible language derived from national folk music and dance and that modern composers have forgotten the listener and derived their inspiration not from folk culture but from the rotten, decaying culture of the bourgeois West. In Zhdanov's words:

> Soviet composers have two major issues to address. The chief one is to develop and perfect Soviet music. The other is to protect Soviet music against penetration by elements of bourgeois decay. We must not forget that the U.S.S.R. is now the true preserver of the musical culture of mankind just as she is in all other fields, too, a stronghold of human civilization and culture against bourgeois corruption and cultural decay.[90]

In the end, Gol'denveyzer's letter and essay probably provided some useful material for Zhdanov, but he cannot be blamed for the ensuing events of February 1948, where the colleagues he denounced were dismissed from their posts and their music banned.[91] The ensuing personnel changes in the Composers' Union, the Moscow Conservatoire and in the Committee on Arts Affairs (which ended up being subsumed into Agitprop) were dramatic but, in some cases at least, short-lived: Shebalin would return to teach in the Conservatoire, as would Shostakovich, and Khachaturyan had also resumed his teaching career by 1951.

The End of Internationalism: Late Stalinist Stagnation

If Kemenov's July 1947 speech had signalled the new Soviet cultural foreign policy, the *Zhdanovshchina* cemented it for the rest of the Stalin period. As we have seen, the Central Committee possessed several documents (some unsolicited, some probably commissioned) that compared Soviet music unfavourably with the 'classics', both Russian and Western. Ironically, Soviet composers – some wholly products of Soviet society and culture – are at this point effectively deemed less *nashi* [ours] than their pre-revolutionary forebears, Western as well as Russian. By 1948, the leading names in Soviet music found themselves cast in the role of copying bourgeois Western 'individualists', 'formalists' and decadents. Effectively, they were tarnished with the same brush as Western modernists like Schoenberg, Hindemith and other Soviet musical bogeymen of the late 1930s and post-war 1940s, although Zhdanov took care to frame his criticisms in terms of undue deference and admiration towards 'decadent' Western contemporary music, rather than accusing Soviet composers themselves of decadence. The faults of Western composers, in other words, were inevitable and incorrigible; whereas Soviet composers, if they turned to the right path (socialist realism and nationalism), could still be saved.

Groundwork for this new position on Soviet versus Western art took place well before January 1948, as is evident from the date of Kemenov's speech and the freeze on cultural relations after 1947, which, as we have seen, came from the highest ranks of the Central Committee, and almost certainly from Stalin personally. But for music, its clearest statement comes in Zhdanov's January 1948 Central Committee speech (repeated in his February speech to composers). Much has already been written on the *Zhdanovshchina*, and I will not repeat here what has already been said, except to observe the key pointers laid out in this speech relating to the classics and to the concept of internationalism, which ended up directing musical policy not only in the Soviet Union, but also across the whole Soviet bloc after 1948. First, as we have seen, in Zhdanov's speech the 'classics' constituted both Western and Russian composers, but there is a strong emphasis on nineteenth-century Russian traditions. While in the wake of the 'Muddle Instead of Music' article in *Pravda*, Handel, Bach, Mozart and Haydn were frequently invoked as models to follow, in 1948 Zhdanov does not mention a single non-Russian composer by name; he simply lumps them together as 'classical music':

> We will take as our example attitudes towards the classical heritage. There is no indication whatever that the afore-mentioned composers [those of the 'formalist' type] have their roots in the classical tradition, and not one of them can claim to be continuing the heritage of classical music. . . . Any listener will tell you that the works of Soviet composers

of the formalist type sound nothing like classical music. Classical music is characterized by its truthfulness and realism, its ability to unite brilliant artistic form with the profoundest content, and to combine the highest technical achievement with simplicity and clarity.[92]

Where Zhdanov did mention some Western names, he was quoting directly from the nineteenth-century critic Aleksandr Serov: 'A. N. Serov was profoundly right when he said that "but for the eternally beautiful in art . . . we would have no love neither for Homer, Dante and Shakespeare, nor for Raphael, Titian and Poussin, nor for Palestrina, Handel and Gluck".'[93] Zhdanov took great care, however, to name individually every single front-rank Russian composer of the mid- to late nineteenth century and to hold each and every one of them up as a model of what the 'Soviet *kuchka*' should be. The same exclusivity is found in *Sovetskaya muzïka*'s response to the conference in the article 'The Classics Speak', published in the same issue as Zhdanov's January 1948 speech to the Central Committee.[94] This article printed a selection of letters and writings by composers from the *kuchka*, Chaykovskiy and the critics Prince Odoyevskiy, Stasov, Laroche and Serov, with the obvious intention of underlining their love for Russian culture and their suspicion of certain Western developments (such as, for example, Wagner's operas). The 'classics' now were definably Russian; Western composers would accompany them by implication, but would be kept at a lower profile.

Zhdanov's speech quickly became the basis for a new orthodoxy based around the assertion that nineteenth-century Russian composers inherited the humanism of Bach, the heroism of Handel and the Austro-German classical tradition, while cleverly avoiding the pitfalls of superficiality and pretentiousness that lay in wait for their Western colleagues. Glinka, the *kuchka* and Chaykovskiy were, in Zhdanov's new construction of internationalism, 'international' at the same time as profoundly 'national': they were educated and well travelled, and that was a good thing, but their music was 100 per cent Russian, uncorrupted by foreign influences. This, of course, was not true at all, and the very notion that Glinka and Chaykovskiy were not significantly influenced by their European contemporaries and forbears is absurd, but the assertion became the new mantra in Stalin-era music historiography after 1948. Zhdanov's argument redefines internationalism so that it no longer denotes participation in international trends but becomes merely a willingness to share one's own national culture:

Those who believe that the flowering of national music – whether Russian music or that of the other peoples of the Soviet Union – means that art becomes less international, are profoundly mistaken. Internationalism in art does not spring from a basis of impoverishment of national art. On the contrary, internationalism grows where national culture flourishes. . . . One cannot be international in art without being a true patriot of one's own country.[95]

In the new post-1948 historiography, not only did nineteenth-century Russian composers forge their own unique style and were not beholden in any way to Western influences, but nineteenth-century Russian critics were also the first to point out what was most valuable, and what was least successful, in the music of their Western forbears and contemporaries.

A useful source of gauging how Zhdanov's speech was absorbed into late Stalinist musicology is a short book, *Russian Musicians on Western Music*, by the musicologist Isabella Abezgauz. At the time it was published (1950), she was a twenty-seven-year-old postgraduate student at the Moscow Conservatoire under Tamara Livanova, teaching in the junior department of the Conservatoire. Both her professional position and her advisor are of especial importance when considering the line she took with her first major publication.

Livanova had never been one of those who supported Western contemporary music, although her primary area of expertise at this time was nevertheless Western, rather than Russian, music. By 1948 she had written several works on Western eighteenth-century music, including a major study of Bach. In January 1948, she had petitioned Zhdanov directly, perhaps seeing, as did Gol'denveyzer, a chance for revenge on her colleagues, by whom she felt marginalized and unfairly treated. Vlasova reveals that, after Livanova had publicly criticized Roman Gruber's book, *The History of Musical Culture* for its 'highly disreputable' and 'harmful' positive line on Western music, she felt victimized by colleagues who admired Gruber's work and found her comments inappropriate. Khrapchenko had even recommended it for a Stalin Prize and this, too, she resented because his wife worked as Gruber's assistant and therefore she believed he was not able to consider the book without bias. After the Zhdanov Decree, Khrapchenko lost his position, but Livanova was one of those selected to replace the existing Stalin Prize committee, together with a number of other composers and critics who emerged from 1948 with more power than they had had before.[96] In short, Livanova was someone for whom the new historical orthodoxy post-1948 in all probability came as second nature, and no student of hers in the period between 1948 and 1953 could be expected to deviate from the narrow line set out by Zhdanov; rather, Abezgauz's work suggests that she was part of a new generation of post-1948 musicologists who actively built on the foundations of the Zhdanov Decree.

Abezgauz begins by asserting Russians' superior appreciation of J. S. Bach, insinuating, *pace* Zhdanov's accusations of Western 'formalism' that, in the West, issues of form and technique were of greater interest than expression, whereas Russians were not primarily concerned with formalistic matters but were instead naturally inclined to value the 'deep humanism' that they found in his music.[97] Russian musicians were also, she claims, the first to point out Handel's heroism, to reveal the ideology behind Gluck's opera reforms and the first to explain Haydn's role in the development of the symphony, among a host of other achievements. But even these claims pale into insignificance beside her bald assertion that nineteenth-century Russian operas were simply better than those written anywhere else:

> Gluck, like Mozart, did not find any deserving heirs in the West during the 19th century. Russian musicians understood him far better, having created their own high quality operatic works, their own opera classics, which had no equal anywhere in the world.[98]

Indeed, she argues, it was through Russian opera masterpieces such as *Khovanshchina*, *Boris Godunov*, *Pskovityanka* and *Ivan Susanin* that Russian composers 'were able to expose with utmost clarity the false historicism of French "grand" opera, its pseudo-folk nature and its superficial brilliance'.[99] In her construction of the 'superficial French', Abezgauz dismisses almost the whole of French grand opera – including those written on major literary themes – with the added authority of no less a figure than Aleksandr Serov (who was writing specifically about Gounod's *Faust* at the time): '"Othello", "Romeo and Juliet" – they have been cut to shreds in a librettist's workshop in order to serve as canvases to solfeggio and costumes.' *Faust* itself, Serov declared, was simply a 'dramatic-musical pretence of the untalented French'.[100] Yet despite Abezgauz's selection of negative quotations, she could not entirely deny that Russian composers and writers had often admired their Western contemporaries. Indeed, since major opera composers such as Gounod and Bizet still regularly appeared in Bolshoy schedules, there was nothing to be gained in slandering them too harshly. What she needed to balance was the degrees of success and influence: it was important to select only a few Western composers as truly great, while laying stress on how it took the perspicacity of Russian musicians to see through the superficial mannerisms of the others, even the ones whose operas were still appearing at the Bolshoy. Thus Verdi is praised as a great realist and reformer, but it was Russian musicians, Abezgauz claims, who valued his 'impetuousness' and 'energy' amid the general malaise of shallowness.[101] Likewise, it was Chaykovskiy who predicted the worldwide success of *Carmen*, while at around the same time, Musorgskiy furiously dismissed Saint-Saëns' *Samson and Delilah*: 'We don't need such music . . . damn it all to hell with its lies *e tutti quanti* . . . give us living thoughts, living speech and living people.'[102] *Carmen* was a perennial Soviet classic, while *Samson* had not been staged at the Bolshoy since 1919, so although Saint-Saens' orchestral works were still performed by the Philharmonias, his opera was a safe target, even if attacked only indirectly through Musorgskiy's words. The remaining elephant in the room at this point is, of course, Wagner, and here the compliments are so back-handed as to be deliberately dismissive: 'Chaykovskiy, Serov and Stasov considered Wagner to be primarily a symphonist . . . the direct descendant of Beethoven and Schumann.' As an opera composer, Abezgauz informs her readers, Wagner was regarded in Russia as less successful: Chaykovskiy found his characters unrealistic and his subject-matter lacking in human feeling.[103] In fact, Abezgauz ends the section on Wagner with the most vicious comment Chaykovskiy ever made about him, in a letter to Taneyev: 'Can it really be that this pretentious, heavy-handed and untalented rubbish will be enjoyed by future generations, as we now enjoy the Ninth Symphony? If so, it's a terrible prospect.'[104] She does not elaborate on, confirm or deny Chaykovskiy's remarks – he himself was of course absolutely beyond criticism – but simply lets them stand as food for thought for her readers.

It is not surprising, in view of such publications, to find that after 1948 the opera schedules were dominated by Russian operas, with only a very select few Western works remaining in the repertoire. Between 1941 (when Eyzenshteyn's *Die Walküre* was still running) and 1953, no Wagner opera was performed at the Bolshoy, while, from 1948, those Western operas remaining in the Bolshoy's repertoire – *Carmen*, *Barber of Seville*, *Rigoletto*, *Aida*, *La Traviata*, Gounod's *Romeo and Juliet* and *Faust*, *Madam Butterfly*,

Lakmé and *Don Giovanni* – simply continued seamlessly as a stream of uncontroversial favourites from the pre-war era. In fact, *Carmen*, Gounod's *Faust* and *Romeo and Juliet*, *Lakmé*, *Aida* and *The Barber of Seville* had been in the Bolshoy's repertoire since the 1920s. What is missing, from 1941 onwards, is any Wagner, any Richard Strauss or – it goes without saying – any Western opera written in a modernist style.[105]

Wagner Revisited and New Soviet Music

If he was still banished from the opera stage, Wagner was emphatically not barred from the concert hall in the post-war years: as soon as the Moscow Philharmonia resumed their regular series back in the capital in 1944–5 (full records available only from the 1945–6 season), the old pre-war Wagner favourites immediately reappeared: Introduction to Act Three of *Lohengrin*, the *Prelude and Liebestod* from *Tristan*, excerpts from *The Ring* ('Siegfried's Journey', 'Forest Murmurs', 'Funeral March') and the overtures. After January 1948 there was less Wagner in the Philharmonia programmes, but only once – in the year 1949–50 – does he disappear altogether. Whether this is due to any hostility towards Wagner seems unlikely – Mravinskiy included excerpts from *Tannhäuser* in his Wagner/Brahms concert in November 1948 – so in all probability, Wagner was not *non grata* but simply squeezed out owing to the dominance of other kinds of repertoire. Indeed, in the 1952–3 season the Moscow Philharmonia held four all-Wagner concerts to celebrate seventy years since the composer's death, with all the old pre-war favourites, including the whole of the first act of *Meistersinger*. In effect, the situation with Wagner in the post-war Stalin years was the same as between around 1935–41: his operas were not staged, but sizeable parts of them remained core orchestral repertoire.

As Tomoff has shown, from the summer of 1949 the Composers' Union had an increased level of influence over the Philharmonias' programming. From the summer of 1948, the Moscow Philharmonia had to submit programmes for the future concert season to the Composers' Union, a sign that it had become a lot more powerful in shaping the capital's musical life. As Tomoff argues:

> It [the Composers' Union] cast itself as the authoritative interpreter of the Central Committee resolution's ramifications in the realm of music performance. The Secretariat claimed that the Philharmonic had never

adequately popularized compositions by Soviet composers, and its concert plans for the 1948–9 season did nothing to remedy that past oversight.[106]

Thereafter, the Composers' Union Secretariat formed a commission of three Union leaders and a Philharmonia member to draft new concert series properly representing Soviet new music. Yet it would be a mistake to assume that new Soviet music was now at the forefront of the Philharmonias' scheduling. If we look at the season 1950–1, new Soviet music is no more in evidence than it had been even before the 1937 purge. To offer a representative year and season, if we refer back to Table 4.1 in Chapter Four, the Moscow Philharmonia had performed fifteen Soviet works in the 1933–4 season, including three premieres, and in 1936–7 eighteen, plus a *dekada* of Georgian and Azerbaijanian music. In 1950–1 the total number of Soviet works performed by the same orchestra was higher, but these included by now quite old works, such as Myaskovskiy's Fifth Symphony (1918), Romances on verses by Lermontov (1935–6), Gedike's 1928 *Prelude for Strings* and Prokof'yev's *Romeo and Juliet* suite. If we count only Soviet works composed since 1936 (which presumably was the major concern of the Composers' Union in 1948, since living composers benefited from royalties), Table 5.1 below shows that there are a total of fourteen played in the 1950–1 season, including seven in a special concert devoted to new Soviet music:

Table 5.1: Soviet music performed in the Moscow Philharmonia season 1950–1

Tat'yana Nikolayeva, Piano Concerto No. 1
Nikolay Myaskovskiy, Symphony No. 21
Shostakovich, 'Slava' (from *The Fall of Berlin*)
Lev Knipper, Symphony No. 11
Vano Muradeli, *Path to Victory*
Yuriy Shaporin, aria from *Kulikovo's Field*
Kara Karayev, *Leyli and Majnun*
20/12/50: special concert of new Soviet works: Aleksandr Kholminov, *Slava to Stalin*, Naumov, songs, David L'vov-Kompaneyets, cantata *Russian song*, Sulkhan Tsintsadze, Piano Concerto, German Galïnin, *Epic Poem*, Rustem Yakhin, Piano Concerto, Ashraf Abbasov, *Cantata about Stalin*

This does not denote a dramatic rise in the performance of new Soviet works from the norm during the early to mid-1930s, during the very years when the Philharmonias were accused of playing too little of it. Now the Composers' Union had the power to assess whether enough was being played, they actually seemed content with the same levels of exposure as the Philharmonias had independently judged to be reasonable long before anyone forced their hand. Repertoire listings of the music occupying the rest of the Philharmonia programmes contain no surprises: there is the usual mixture of nineteenth- and early twentieth-century Russian music and Western classics, including Bach's B Minor Mass, symphonies and concerti by the major nineteenth-century French and Austro-German composers, including Brahms, Liszt, Mendelssohn, Berlioz, Saint-Saëns and Debussy, and works by Scandinavian and East European composers such as Grieg, Dvořák, Smetana, Chopin, Karlowicz, early Panufnik, Kodály, Laszlo-Erkel and, once in November 1951, Bartok's *Hungarian Peasant Songs*. As a result of the enlarged Soviet bloc, music from Poland, Czechoslovakia, Hungary and Romania began to appear in the Philharmonia programmes, often conducted by visiting musicians from those countries, though this aspect of Soviet programming lies slightly outside the thematic and chronological limits of this study. While it is certainly true that the orchestral programmes show absolutely no new Western music whatsoever, the modest acceptance of composers like Bartok, Kodály and Panufnik offered Soviet audiences a particular, folk-inspired brand of 'contemporary' music (though Bartok's *Hungarian Peasant Songs* were originally composed in 1918 and so can hardly be regarded any longer as 'contemporary') along-side that of Soviet composers. Also, some established post-1910 Western works were retained, such as Ravel's *Boléro*, *Daphnis* and *Tzigane*, and his Piano Concerto for the left hand (Leningrad and Moscow); the visiting Italian conductor Willi Ferrero rather daringly conducted Salome's Dance in Leningrad in February 1952 and Sibelius's Fifth Symphony was also played in Leningrad in the 1952–3 season (conducted by Kurt Sanderling). But there is no escaping the fact that, compared with the dazzling interna-tionalism of the late 1920s and the mid-1930s, Leningrad and Moscow Philharmonia programmes in the late Stalin era are marked by a dull conservatism, an extreme anti-Western attitude towards most twentieth-century art, and a firm entrenchment of older Western and Russian classics.

One of the saddest aspects of this post-1948 insularity is the sheer stale-ness of musical life in the two Russian capitals. It is not that the music left in

Soviet concert programmes was in any way at fault – the staleness came precisely from their familiarity and too-frequent recycling at the expense of hearing new repertoire. After 1917, the new audiences who flooded the concert halls and music clubs were there to hear music that was already very familiar to the Russian educated classes. But when it was being heard for the first time by new social groups, this, too, added a genuine excitement to those who devoted their energies to sharing works like Beethoven's symphonies, Mozart's Requiem and Schubert's songs. Because the 1920s – when the groundwork for this 'sharing' activity was laid – were characterized by such a wide spectrum of musical experience, from Avraamov's *Symphony of Sirens* and Roslavets's works to Davidenko's mass songs, these classics simply took their place alongside new music of all kinds, and were not held up to Soviet composers as models of expressive clarity in the way they would be after 1936. Even after 1936, there was still a real sense of achievement, even excitement, in performing Handel's oratorios and marketing them to the Soviet public as pinnacles of democratic, even proto-revolutionary, art. Yet when, after the sudden influx of new British and American music during the war, composers found the doors to the West slammed shut, their realization that they were doomed to be cut off from the Western world and its post-war developments must have been incredibly frustrating, all the more so as the critical narratives around Soviet musical life were obliged to adhere to the crushing limitations of the Zhdanov doctrine. Even the 'novelties' of the 1920s and 1930s – the revivals of Bach and Handel – and the later marketing of the Romantic Requiems and secular cantatas by Chaykovskiy, Rakhmaninov and Taneyev had either vanished or turned sour when audiences realized that this (alongside approved Soviet repertoire) was more or less all they were ever going to hear.

Attitudes to the West in Post-war Soviet Scholarship

One of the most regular sources of information on both Soviet music abroad and new Western works during the late 1930s and 1940s was Grigoriy Shneyerson's column in *Sovetskaya muzïka*, 'Chronicle of Musical Life Abroad', or simply 'Abroad' [*Za rubezhom*], as the column was called before 1941. Shneyerson did not go abroad to review concerts, but rather collected press reviews of contemporary music concerts abroad sent to him through VOKS and, where possible, matched them up with scores and/or recordings that he had available in Moscow; then he would collate all his information in a 'report' that was usually not much more than a summary of live reviews. Publication of the journal ceased for the war, though, and so all that we have for the period 1941–5 is his article in the issue for May 1941. That issue contains quotations from reviews of American performances of new works by two composers long since banished from Soviet concert programmes: Milhaud (his First Symphony, 1939) and Schoenberg (his Violin Concerto, 1936). Milhaud's symphony was played in Chicago to celebrate his fiftieth birthday and both reviews cited by Shneyerson – in *Musical America* and *Modern Music* – were positive, if not ecstatic, describing its pastoral tone (the first movement was subtitled 'Pastorale') and the 'religious' mood of the third movement. The American audience at Schoenberg's Violin Concerto greeted the work with 'sparse applause and laughter', with one woman actually shouting 'Ridiculous!' After this, Shneyerson reports, the conductor (Stokowski) asked for the woman to be taken out of the concert hall, and gave an impassioned speech in defence of new music.[107] Shneyerson makes no personal comment or evaluation, but it is worth noting that he felt able to repeat the positive reports of Milhaud's symphony, and even if he told his readers about the poor reception of Schoenberg's concerto, he at least repeated his source's information about Stokowski's defence.

By 1946 Shneyerson's passive-positive tone has changed. In November that year, *Sovetskaya muzïka* published his lengthy review of the Paris 1945–6 season, drawn from his own knowledge of scores sent to Moscow and from Parisian press reviews. After the liberation of Paris, musical life in the city not only resumed, but burst into a newly enriched flowering of world culture, with visiting conductors from America (Rudolph Dunbar) and England (Thomas Beecham) playing alongside Charles Munch and other leading European conductors in a festival of contemporary music showcasing Soviet, American, British, Polish, French, Belgian, Finnish and even Chinese contemporary music. Predictably, Shneyerson dwells proudly on the high status of Soviet music, as represented in the performances of music by Shostakovich and Prokof'yev, but his evaluation of Olivier Messiaen's music is worth repeating here, because it shows very clearly the direction in which the official Soviet musical attitude to music of the West in the post-war period was moving:

If we are to judge by the few compositions that we have in Moscow, and from press cuttings from French music criticism, there is no doubting the creative gifts of this composer or of his significant mastery. However, it is not just this that has given Messiaen his exceptional status, as noted above; it is not only this that can explain the atmosphere of admiration and exaggerated ecstasy surrounding his music and personality in French musical circles and in the public. Messiaen is a prophet of individualism, at the very breaking point of expression. He has enveloped his work in a dense cloud of mysticism, of the Catholic religion that inspires him. Messiaen's artistic position is essentially deeply reactionary.[108]

Yet not every Western composer, even in the post-war Soviet era, drew forth ideological criticism. In February 1947, Shneyerson reviewed Bohuslav Martinů's threnody dedicated to the Czech village of Lidice. In 1942, every single adult male from the village was shot and its women and children sent to concentration camps before the village itself was razed to the ground by Nazi troops in a savage reprisal for the assassination of Reinhardt Heydrich. The vast majority of the 105 children rounded up were then murdered in gas chambers; after the war, only seventeen of Lidice's children were still living. Martinů's *Memorial to Lidice* was composed the following year, and was performed by the Leningrad Philharmonia on 9 April 1947 and by the Moscow Philharmonia in December, so Shneyerson's article was not a concert review but rather a preview for the approaching Leningrad premiere, made possible by the fact that the score had recently arrived in Moscow. Martinů is warmly introduced right from the start as 'one of the leading representatives of the progressive artistic Western intelligentsia, whose creative work is indissolubly linked with the life and spiritual questions of his own people'.[109] This is a stronger statement than it might first appear, and to understand its implications we have to look back at Shneyerson's repeated definition of 'progressive' in his French music review, by which he means music that is connected with life, lofty ideas and speaks to the broad masses of the people: in other words, Soviet music. Music like Messiaen's, by contrast, is not progressive in Shneyerson's view but actually regressive, or rather 'reactionary', because it tries to avoid such content. His chief criticism of *Memorial to Lidice*, which he otherwise praises warmly, is that it displays insufficient emotional anguish; but this does not lead Shneyerson into making any unflattering comparison between Soviet and 'Western' composers; although Martinů is by now living in America (since 1941), he is discussed here as a Czech and a 'sensitive artist-patriot'.[110] And, since Czechoslovakia was now part of the

Soviet bloc, and Czech composers and musicians were a newly introduced feature of post-war Soviet musical life, even an émigré Czech (so long as he composed in a relatively conservative idiom) was still sufficiently Czech to merit Soviet approval. That approval would not last long – Martinů's music began to be attacked in Czechoslovakia after the communists took power there in 1948 and after these two performances, neither *Lidice*, nor any other work by Martinů, appears in Philharmonia schedules.[111]

A year later, during the critical month of February 1948, Shneyerson's attitude shows a further hardening towards the West. His article 'American musical engineering' was a scathing attack on the music theorist and composer Joseph Schillinger, the Russian émigré who had made his home in America after 1917 and had died in 1943 after a pioneering career as a teacher (including of George Gershwin). His concluding words perfectly sum up the post-*Zhdanovshchina* attitude to the 'degenerated art of the capitalist world': 'Thus one of the most persuasive examples of the negation of musical art serves to bring home to us the widespread phenomenon in America of "rationalized" methods of composition and the obsession of American composers with soulless musical engineering.'[112] It is especially sad to see Shneyerson attacking the very same American composers whose music he had warmly greeted in Moscow at the VOKS concerts of Allied music: Elie Siegmeister (a personal friend of Shneyerson's), Roy Harris and Aaron Copland. Even these talented composers, he asserts, were infected with 'empty formalistic contrivance, false "novelty", addressing only a narrow circle of "epicures", devoid of healthy ideological-emotional content.'[113]

Of course, Shneyerson's writings must be seen in context. In January 1948, which is presumably the month when he was writing this article, he must have feared that his job was at risk (he was dismissed on 2 February 1948) and he was being investigated for alleged financial mis-dealings. Those found guilty of similar charges in the pre-war purges had been arrested and, in some cases, shot. To begin with, the music scandals of 1948 looked like a repetition of 1936–7 and there was no way of knowing, at any point during the proceedings as they unfolded, that they would not spiral into something equally serious. Whatever his personal convictions, it is certain that Shneyerson was now desperately trying to save himself from further repercussions by aligning himself firmly with Zhdanov's aesthetic position. That is not to say that we can be sure he did not mean what he wrote in every case: in particular, his words on Messiaen come across as genuine, since he is still able to consider him extremely talented, and he does not embark on a wholesale rejection of degenerate Western art in his review of the Paris season. But of course, between publishing that report and the later 1948 piece, several crucial things had affected Shneyerson's professional world: his VOKS superior, Kemenov, had made his anti-Western speech in 1947; by January 1948 Zhdanov's speech at the January Central Committee conference had been published and it was clear that a serious and very fundamental change in the Soviet government's attitude to the West had taken place. That left people like Shneyerson especially vulnerable, since in the last round of devastating repressions between 1936 and 1939, the VOKS chief Aleksandr Arosev had been shot for espionage. To add to the already dangerous cocktail, Shneyerson – who was not, at this time, a Party member – was married to a Jew and may himself have been half-Jewish. His early VOKS records identify him as Russian, but married to a Jew; however, Kemenov's final report on him in June 1948 openly identifies him as both non-Party and Jewish.[114] Shneyerson's VOKS reports had always commented on his lack of interest and knowledge in political affairs (he was a fully trained musician, pianist and talented linguist) and identified this as a major reason why he had not been promoted to a more senior position in the organization. Now, in 1948, Shneyerson looked politically very insecure indeed, and it is no wonder that he now applied himself to putting as much distance between himself and his former Western friends as possible. The old fear of associating with foreigners returned with a vengeance, and those VOKS employees who had worked so hard during the war years to bring about a rich fraternal culture of Allied–Soviet cultural exchange were now potentially on the front line of post-war reprisals, not knowing what form those reprisals might take. It is hardly surprising, then, to see other Soviet critics fearfully queuing up behind Shneyerson at this time to express their disgust at Western degeneracy: the distinguished musicologist Iosif Rïzhkin published a piece on Schoenberg as the 'liquidator of music' in 1949;[115] while Izrail' Nest'yev published a harshly critical piece on Gavriil Popov – still being used as a formalist scapegoat fourteen years after the banning of his First Symphony – entitled 'In Thrall to Bourgeois Modernism'.[116] It was a desperately sad end to the hopes of the wartime alliance, when musicians on both sides had expressed sincere delight in each other's music and equally sincere hopes of a post-war culture of further co-operation and friendship. Whatever 'thaw' there had been between 1941 and 1947 was now over: already, by March 1946 Churchill had delivered his 'Iron Curtain' speech, and the ensuing Cold War began to cast its chill over the remnants of allied friendship. From January 1948 it was clear that hostility to the West had returned with a vengeance; Soviet musical culture not only was set back to the repressed climate of the late purge years 1939–40, but was even more restricted than it had been before the war, when enthusiasm for music of the European Enlightenment was still delivering new musical experiences in Moscow and Leningrad.

The process of rediscovering the old had thus come to an end, and cultural channels to the West would not be reopened until after Stalin's death in March 1953, which very quickly paved the way for the resumption of international cultural agreements, exchanges and an influx of new European and American music into the Soviet Union. This happened partly courtesy of the Warsaw Autumn Festival and the often-private gifts of scores to Soviet composers and musicians from their Western colleagues, but partly (if less radically) out in the open, in the Philharmonia programmes. After the 'thaws' of Khrushchev's era (he was ousted in 1964), the Soviet Union would never return to the deep insularity of these post-war years: changes could be infuriatingly slow, hampered, doubtless unnecessarily, for years by over-cautious or hostile bureaucrats and powerful musical figures. But Russian musical life was never again as limited as it was between 1948 and 1953, when windows to the West were bolted shut and the word 'cosmopolitan' was either a term of abuse or a description of someone at risk of imminent arrest.

CONCLUSION

It was during the thirty-six years of Soviet concert programming under Lenin and Stalin – the period 1917–53 – that the process of building a uniquely Soviet musical identity was most conscious and most beholden to the vagaries of individual tastes, cultural fashions, power struggles and, lying behind it all, the more intensive forces of political strategizing. Though changes in arts personnel and shifts in the balance of power could produce very dramatic consequences – indeed, could mean the difference between life and death for music workers during the repressions – Soviet musical life in the elite institutions of the Philharmonias and in the Bolshoy (and to a lesser degree, in the Leningrad Capella) proceeded ponderously, seeming at times curiously immune to extreme changes in cultural climate, in particular that of the 'Cultural Revolution' years. Indeed, exactly what music offended whom and why is not always as predictable a matter as we might think. For example, the practice of inviting foreign conductors and musicians to the Philharmonias during the New Economic Policy of the mid-1920s, and programming the contemporary European music that they brought with them, seems to have been acceptable even to the militant proletarians, since the trend proceeded without serious interruption right through the 'Cultural Revolution' and only dwindled in the mid- to late 1930s, by then due to quite different forces. Likewise, pressure to programme more nineteenth-century Russian music in the second half of the 1930s was merely adding proportional weight to something the Philharmonias did already, though of course the concurrent drop in performance of Western modernist music was forced upon them. Equally, we should not assume, where a given musical trend has obvious political drivers, that its proponents were insincere in their public support. For instance, it is highly likely that the upsurge in Western Baroque and early classical music programmed in 1935 onwards benefited from a mutual wish on behalf of both arts bureaucrats and musicians to 'reclaim' Bach and Handel from the Nazis, demonstrate Soviet cultural superiority and introduce Soviet audiences to first-rate operatic and choral music all at the same time. After 1936, the aggressive canonization of these, and other, composers (both Western and nineteenth-century Russian), became an effective stick with which to browbeat Soviet composers, whose music was deemed less appealing to the people than that of their classical forbears. Yet even during the purges of the late 1930s, it is not clear that much of the 'heroic' classical music demanded of the Philharmonias would not have been programmed in any case, or that the enthusiasm critics like Sollertinskiy showed for Handel and Bach, or indeed Berlioz and Verdi, was anything other than utterly sincere. Paradoxically, this whole episode seems to have been an instance where official policy and musicians' personal tastes came together in a strikingly productive and mutually congenial way.

However, it must be remembered that, even if there is little or no documentary evidence to show that the Philharmonias' repertoire committees came under attack, it is highly likely (and after 1936 inevitable) that they did their best to self-regulate in order to avoid censure. Bans did not often come in the form of handed-down directives, but that does not mean that whole swathes of repertoire did not have to be scrupulously avoided. How concert repertoire was shaped during these years meshes tightly with trends in new Soviet music, and the exclusion of Western and Russian modernist repertoire was a key element in the shaping both of older music's reception (bringing 'safe' Western music of the past to the fore to offset the effect of closing the door on new foreign music) and the creation of new Soviet works. And, of course, ultimately – no matter how persuasively we might argue that new Soviet music of the mid- to late 1930s meshed with more conservative tonal styles of New Deal America, Britain and Europe – we must remember that the key difference between the Soviet Union, Britain and America (leaving aside Europe for the moment) was that, while America and Britain had experimental composers like Henry Cowell and Elizabeth Lutyens, all musical avant-gardism in the Soviet Union had been stamped out. International parity of style is not evidence of willing conformity.

In terms of directly striving to shape mass taste, the evidence is surprisingly scanty, considering the effort expended on bringing art music to the mass listener. Precious few audience surveys have been preserved in the Philharmonia archives and, as we saw in Chapter One, records of the individual voices of workers and peasants expressing their private opinions of music are few and far between. By the 1930s, the sheer scale of amateur music-making, together with hugely ambitious enterprises like Olympiads and collective farm festivals, testifies to the energy and commitment of thousands upon thousands of amateur musicians, though we should not accept without question their much-vaunted success in the Soviet press of those years, especially where collective farm festivals were concerned.[1] Ironically, it could probably be said that, in the end, mass participation in art music (as opposed to folk music, mass song or popular music) fulfilled the aims not of RAPM or of later bodies like the Committee on Arts Affairs, but rather those of the earliest propagandists – the pre-revolutionary musicians who taught music to workers and attendees of the People's Houses and special Conservatoire classes. That is, art music did not demonstrably 'mould' the Soviet listener in any appreciable ideological way; but it did offer them a form of education and entertainment that was not easily accessible to many of them before 1917. Some of the most burning issues of the 1920s and 1930s – how to regard music of the past, the culture of the pre-revolutionary village, Russian folk music and, in particular, Russian and Western sacred music – lose much of their potency in the post-war era, as Soviet musical life settled into a routine of folk choirs and established classics. They only raise their heads again in the 1960s, when, for example, Russian sacred music was cautiously 'rediscovered' by Sveshnikov and his former students and when American touring ensembles began introducing Soviet audiences to sacred music from the medieval period and to 'authentic' performance practice of Renaissance and Baroque music – thus prompting younger composers like Arvo Pärt and Al'fred Shnitke to echo those new sounds in their own music, as well as inspiring Andrey Volkonskiy to form his 'Madrigal' ensemble in 1965.[2]

The question of whether Western composers and major works were truly 'appropriated' as opposed to merely performed in the Soviet Union is not a straightforward one. Certainly, music writers did, from the very beginning, seek to market classical music, whether Russian or Western, to an audience that was recognized as being quite new – that of the 'mass listener' who was now invited to share high culture with the middle classes. Whether those early attempts to persuade Soviet listeners that the composers whose names meant little or nothing to them could be viewed through a 'revolutionary' lens constitute true appropriation is doubtful. But when in the mid-1930s we see a palpable shift towards a very deliberate canon-building – taking masterpieces of the past with a particularly monumental character, and underpinning their performance by press articles and programme booklets that argued powerfully for their reinterpretation as benchmarks of the Enlightenment progress towards socialism – then that is something quite different. Such a consciously adoptive process can be read as a genuine attempt to appropriate another culture with quite specific intentions: canon-building, discrediting cultural enemies (Nazi Germany in particular) and claiming high cultural status for oneself via that culture's alleged unique appreciation of those artworks. That the values trumpeted in some of these press articles and booklets were standard tropes of good Soviet citizenship – selfless dedication to the collective, physical courage, steadfast commitment to a cause, strength and heroism – almost goes without saying: in this loaded context, Handel's oratorios could be seen almost as propaganda works. But it is much harder to discern such classically 'Soviet' values in the Bach Passions, or indeed in Mozart's *The Magic Flute* regarding which, as we have seen, Sollertinskiy's roll call of Enlightenment values most certainly did not match up with those of his own age, namely, 'tolerance, Enlightenment philosophy, European humanism and liberalism'.[3] That he wrote those words in 1938, at the height of the Stalinist repressions, is particularly striking, and perhaps shows another level at which the 'appropriation' of classics of the European Enlightenment could actually serve as a parallel narrative that implicitly pointed out the failures and flaws in Soviet society. If so, it was not a narrative that gained any significant presence; for though Sollertinskiy was an influential and popular speaker and writer, there was no shortage of others like Georgiy Khubov and Tamara Livanova who would actively downplay or deny any elements in the music they described which seemed at odds with Soviet values. Thus both vehemently denied the religious content of Bach and Handel's music and sought to market it as purely dramatic, revealing above all the human passions, struggles and triumphs that were the essence of dramatic realism and so offering little or no resistance to the demands for socialist realism made on Soviet composers.

Where Russian composers were concerned, Chaykovskiy and, to a lesser degree, Glinka, were the ones in most need of re-branding in the late 1930s. Both demonstrably monarchist and conservative in their views, they were nonetheless far too valuable to reject and so became the focus of assiduous attempts both to overwhelm Soviet audiences with their greatness (as seen in the Chaykovskiy centenary publications of 1940), and to suppress biographical knowledge that might run counter to prevailing Soviet ideology (such as Glinka's European training, Chaykovskiy's homosexuality, or his repeated exposure to European culture). This is still an appropriation of sorts, feeding directly into precisely the same cultural and political concerns as that of Bach and Handel: canon-building and claiming high cultural status, in terms of both Russia's past and its present (showing its sophistication in accepting all great art of the past, supposedly regardless of its ideological content). From the late 1930s we see the start of the freezing over in relations with Western democracies that would, after their forced wartime alliance, be resumed with redoubled hostility after 1945, and the glorification of Russian composers at this time was an early signal of this policy change, regardless of its deferral between 1941 and 1945.

Ultimately, we can pose the question of whether or not Stalinist musical canon-building resulted in a kind of 'museum culture', where, once established, artefacts languished in a state of critical torpor, accepted and described with increasingly standardized language but never displaced, challenged or refreshed by alternative perspectives. I would argue that a wholly static culture of that sort never quite arrived: the creation of the Stalinist musical 'museum' was certainly well under way in the 1930s but, as we have seen, works like the Passions and Handel oratorios, which at one time seemed canonic, quickly turned out to be expendable, and by 1948, the loud praise for Western classics like Mozart, Beethoven and Gluck that was typical of the 1936–7 years had been entirely replaced with praise for nineteenth-century Russians. Though after 1948, concert programmes do become more insular in terms of Western music (and indeed of the type of music played, no matter from whence it came), the regular visits from musicians within the newly Sovietized Eastern Europe – and indeed from Finland, which was accepted in these years as a friendly state with which cultural exchange could be made – meant that Finnish, Polish, Hungarian, Romanian and Czech music occupied a more prominent role in concert schedules that it had done previously, so audiences were not entirely deprived of novelty. Added to this, the names of Soviet composers on Philharmonia schedules begin to look more familiar to twenty-first-century readers: names of the Shostakovich students Kara Karayev, Boris Chaykovskiy and Yuriy Levitin begin to appear alongside other talented Soviet composers like Nikolay Peyko, Otar Taktakishvili, Andria Balanchivadze and Levko Revutskiy and, of course, Shostakovich and his Soviet contemporaries like Prokof'yev, Myaskovskiy and Khachaturyan, whose music gradually began to be played again (after its brief ban in 1948) as early as April 1949.[4] Even between 1948 and 1953, then, the Philharmonia schedules are not as feeble and dull as might be thought. A great deal of music was kept out but, on the other hand, there was a regular supply of new Soviet music brought in, and in this sense, Soviet audiences had access to a lot of 'new music', even if their diet was a restricted one. If Soviet musical culture can be viewed as a 'museum' at all, it was one with very active curators, able deftly to replace Bach with Glinka, Wagner with Chaykovskiy and Stravinsky with Szymanowski as required. Though never entirely static, it was most certainly carefully controlled and monitored and in that sense, was a true microcosm of the society it served.

BIOGRAPHIES

Andreyev, Andrey Andreyevich (1895–1971). Member of the Communist Party from 1914, member of the Politburo from 1932 to 1952, on the secretariat of the Communist Party between 1935 and 1946.

Ansermet, Ernest (1883–1969). Swiss conductor, especially associated with the music of Stravinsky in the 1920s and 1930s. He founded the Orchestre de la Suisse Romande in 1918. He toured the Soviet Union in 1927–8, bringing with him the newest works by Stravinsky, and visited again in 1936–7.

Arkad'yev, Ivan Petrovich (1872–1946). Conductor and minor composer; graduate of St Petersburg Conservatoire. Worked as opera conductor in Odessa 1920–3 and was a professor and rector of the Odessa Conservatoire. He moved back to Leningrad in 1923 and specialized in amateur work, including conducting the opera group at the 'Red Triangle' factory.

Arkad'yev, Mikhail Pavlovich (1896–1937). Narkompros and Rabis official, first chair of Moscow branch of Composers' Union from 1932–3. Director of the Moscow Art Theatre 1936–7; dismissed on 5 June 1937, arrested soon afterwards and shot in September the same year.

Asaf'yev, Boris Vladimirovich (1884–1949). Often wrote under his pseudonym Igor Glebov in the 1920s. The most distinguished and prolific of all Soviet musicologists under Lenin and Stalin, he was also a successful ballet composer.

Bogdanov-Berezovskiy, Valerian Mikhaylovich (1903–71). Contemporary and friend of Shostakovich at the Leningrad Conservatoire, where he graduated in composition. He composed several operas, symphonies and orchestral works but was far better known as a musicologist and critic.

Braudo, Yevgeniy Maksimovich (1882–1939). A former student of Max Reger, musicologist and music critic.

Bubnov, Andrey Sergeyevich (1883–1940). Commissar of the Red Army; successor to Lunacharskiy as head of Narkompros in 1929. Arrested in 1937 and later executed.

Bukharin, Nikolay Ivanovich (1888–1938). An Old Bolshevik and close associate of both Lenin and Stalin, Bukharin opposed some of Stalin's reforms and his fate from that time would be a drawn-out process of punishment and reward until his arrest in 1937. He was charged with treason in a major show trial in 1938, after which he was shot.

Chelyapov, Nikolay Ivanovich (1889–1938). Chair of the Moscow branch of the Composers' Union, 1933–7. Editor of *Sovetskaya muzïka* from 1933 to 1937. A non-musician, Party bureaucrat and administrator, he was arrested and later executed in the wake of the attacks on Shostakovich and the resulting mêlée in the Composers' Union.

Chemodanov, Sergey Mikhaylovich (1888–1942). Musicologist specializing in Western classical and romantic repertoire, especially during the 1920s, when his interest in Marxist theories of history and their transference to music laid foundations for later writers in the 1930s such as Georgiy Khubov.

Chulaki, Mikhail Ivanovich (1908–89). Composer, teacher, director of Leningrad Philharmonia between 1937 and 1939 (he replaced Isay Renzin), then its artistic director. Had a successful Soviet career. Member of Party from 1943. Graduated from Leningrad Conservatoire in 1931. Taught at Moscow Conservatoire from 1948 until 1989. Director of Bolshoy Theatre 1955–70.

Davidenko, Aleksandr Aleksandrovich (1899–1934). One of the best-known mass song composers during the proletarian era and a leading member of RAPM.

Dzerzhinskiy, Ivan Ivanovich (1909–78). Member of Communist Party from 1942. Composer of the opera *The Quiet Don* (after Mikhail Sholokhov's novel), which (with Shostakovich's help) was premiered in 1935, eliciting personal praise from Stalin. Despite limitations as a composer, he had a successful Soviet career, writing further operas and several film scores.

Fried, Oskar (1871–1941). The first foreign conductor to work in post-1917 Russia, Fried came to conduct the Petrograd Philharmonia in the 1922–3 season and settled in the Soviet Union permanently in 1934, after leaving Nazi Germany.

Gauk, Aleksandr Vasil'yevich (1893–1963). Soviet conductor who graduated from Glazunov's composition class at the Petrograd Conservatoire. He began his career in the Leningrad Theatre of Opera and Ballet but is better known as an orchestral conductor. He worked with the Leningrad Philharmonia between 1930 and 1934.

Ginzburg, Semën L'vovich (1901–78). Graduate of the Petrograd Institute for Arts History and professor of music history at the Leningrad Conservatoire. Active member of the ASM in the 1920s and frequent contributor to progressive music journals from that period.

Gnesin, Mikhail Fabianovich (1883–1957). Graduate of the St Petersburg Conservatoire and student of Rimskiy-Korsakov, Gnesin was closely involved with musical activities for workers both before and after 1917. From 1923 to 1935 he taught at the Gnesin State Music Institute (founded by his sisters in 1895), becoming its director in 1945, and was professor of composition at the Moscow Conservatoire during the same period.

Gol'denveyzer, Aleksandr Borisovich (1875–1961). Pianist and founding member of the pre-revolutionary People's Conservatoire in Moscow. Briefly Director of Moscow Conservatoire (1939–42) and professor there from 1906 until his death. Prominent critic of Western modernism in the 1930s and 1940s.

Gorodinskiy, Viktor Markovich (1902–59). Graduate of St Petersburg Conservatoire from Lev Nikolayev's piano class. Musicologist and editor; head of arts section of the Central Committee 1935–7.

Grinberg, Matias Markovich (1896–1977). Pianist and musicologist, editor of journal *Muzïka i revoliutsiya* (ORKiMD) in the 1920s, and on music board of *Sovetskoe iskusstvo* from 1932 to 1938; music inspector of Glaviskusstvo Narkompros in 1931.

Grinberg, Moisey Abramovich (1904–68). Artistic director of Moscow Philharmonia between 1958 and 1968. Party member from 1930. One-time head of Muzgiz and, from 1938, replaced Shatilov as head of the music section of the Committee on Arts Affairs. Deputy Artistic Director of Music in Nemirovich-Danchenko Theatre; on editorial board of *Sovetskoe iskusstvo*.

Groman-Solovtsov, Anatoliy Aleksandrovich (1898–1965). Musicologist, pianist and graduate of Moscow Conservatoire and student of Mikhail Ivanov-Boretskiy. He was a music critic and member of RAPM from 1926 to 1932 and, after 1932, worked as editor on *Sovetskaya muzïka* and at Muzgiz. His articles were variously signed A. Groman, Solovtsov, Groman-Solovtsov, A. G., or even Hans Sachs. His particular interests were in Russian and Soviet music as well as the music of Chopin. He taught music history briefly at the Moscow Conservatoire between 1933 and 1935.

Gruber, Roman Il'yich (1895–1962). Musicologist and colleague of Boris Asaf'yev, Gruber taught at the Leningrad Institute for Arts History as well as at the Leningrad Conservatoire and translated several important German musicological works into Russian and wrote monographs on Handel and Wagner.

Gusman, Boris Yevseyevich (1892–1944). Head of repertoire and deputy director of Bolshoy Theatre 1929–30; member of Committee for Arts Affairs.

Ivanov-Boretskiy, Mikhail Vladimirovich (1874–1936). Soviet musicologist and former student of Rimskiy-Korsakov. Professor and founder of the musicology faculty of the Moscow Conservatoire in 1922.

Kemenov, Vladimir Semënovich (1908–88). Art historian and critic. Director of VOKS from 1940 until March 1948.

Kerzhentsev, Platon Mikhailovich (1881–1940). Chair of Radio Committee and first chair of the Committee for Arts Affairs 1936–8. Dismissed in 1938 from his post as chair, he was not arrested and continued in minor administrative roles until his death.

Khrapchenko, Mikhail Borisovich (1904–86). Chaii of Committee for Arts Affairs, 1939–48 and vice-chair under Nazarov from 1938. He lost his position in 1948 in the row over Muradeli's opera *The Great Friendship* and continued his career in more modest academic positions. Two years before his death in 1986, Khrapchenko was awarded the title 'Hero of Socialist Labour' and the Order of Lenin.

Khubov, Georgiy Nikitich (1902–81). Soviet musicologist and critic, editor of *Sovetskaya muzïka*, 1932–9, and its chief editor, 1952–7. During the war he worked as music editor for the All-Union radio and was a member of the Moscow Composers' Union Secretariat from 1952 to 1957.

Klemperer, Otto (1885–1973). German conductor and friend of Gustav Mahler, he was forced to leave Nazi Germany in 1933, after which he settled in America. He toured several times to the Soviet Union in the late 1920s and 1930s, where he was friendly with Shostakovich and Sollertinskiy.

Klimov, Mikhail Georgiyevich (1881–1937). Choral conductor, former student of Rimskiy-Korsakov and graduate of the St Petersburg Conservatoire. He was director of the Soviet-era incarnation of the former Imperial capella in Petrograd–Leningrad from 1917 until his death.

Kol'tsov, Mikhail Efimovich (1890–1940). Journalist, editor of *Ogonëk*; closely involved with foreign writers as head of Foreign Commission of the Writers' Union. He was executed in 1940.

Kon, Feliks Yakovlevich (1864–1941). Former revolutionary and director of Glaviskusstvo and the Narkompros Arts Section between 1930 and 1932. The Moscow Conservatoire briefly carried his name during that period.

Korev, Semën Isaakovich (1900–1953). Musicologist, member of RAPM, deputy director of Moscow Philharmonia 1931–2.

Kremlëv, Yuliy Anatol'yevich (1908–1971). Soviet musicologist and composer; student of Boris Asaf'yev and Mariya Yudina at the Leningrad Conservatoire. He was an extremely prolific scholar and author of monographs on Russian and Western composers.

Krïlova, Sarra Alekseyevna (1894–1988). Member of RAPM, co-author with her then husband Lev Lebedinskiy of a number of highly political writings on music, but also a critic in her own right.

Kulyabko, Nikolay N. (1894–?). Director of Moscow Philharmonia in the mid- to late 1930s, dismissed in Shatilov's investigation in 1937. He was a graduate of the Gnesin School, a student of Nikolay Zhilayev and a long-standing friend of the family of Marshal Mikhail Tukhachevskiy, whom he first recommended for entry into the Communist Party in 1918. Kulyabko was arrested in the purge of the Philharmonia but survived his sentence and lived at least long enough to write a short memoir of Tukhachevskiy in 1957, following his rehabilitation.

Kuper, Emil Al'bertovich (1877–1960). A Russian-born conductor of English parentage, Kuper was a major figure in Russian and early Soviet musical life, conducting what became known as the Leningrad Philharmonia until his emigration in 1924.

Kuznetsov, Konstantin Alekseyevich (1883–1953). Graduate of Heidelberg University and composition student of Max Reger. He began teaching at Moscow University in 1912 and later taught at the Moscow Conservatoire.

Lamm, Pavel Aleksandrovich (1882–1951). The most distinguished Soviet editor of his generation, Lamm was responsible for restoration work on Musorgskiy's operas, producing new editions of *Boris Godunov* and *Khovanshchina*. He was a close friend of Nikolay Myaskovskiy and Boris Asaf'yev.

Lebedinskiy, Lev Nikolayevich (1904–1992). Member of Communist Party from 1919. One of the leading and most vocal members of RAPM, Lebedinskiy turned to a quieter career in folk music after 1932 and became one of Shostakovich's more unlikely friends.

Livanova, Tamara Nikolayevna (1909–1986). Member of Communist Party from 1948. A former student of Mikhail Ivanov-Boretskiy, she graduated from the Moscow Conservatoire and taught musicology there between 1932 and 56.

Lunacharskiy, Anatoliy Vasil'yevich (1875–1933). Old Bolshevik colleague of Lenin's and Commissar of Education. Strong supporter of the arts after 1917 and active writer and public speaker; his liberalism made him a target in 1929, when he was sacked and demoted to a diplomatic post.

Martïnov, Ivan Ivanovich (1908–1974). Soviet musicologist; author of monographs on Ravel, de Falla, Shostakovich and others.

Mel'nikov, Pëtr Ivanovich (1867–1940). Major Russian opera conductor, director of Latvian National Opera (1922–33) and Kulyabko's deputy at the Moscow Philharmonia, dismissed by Kerzhentsev in 1937. He was a specialist in nineteenth-century Russian opera, but also conducted European works and conducted at La Scala, Milan, between 1932 and 1940.

Meyerkhol'd, Vsevolod Emil'yevich (1874–1940). Member of Communist Party from 1918. One of the greatest theatrical innovators of the last century, Meyerkhol'd pioneered the acting technique known as 'biomechanics' and was active in the creation of a revolutionary theatre. After speaking out against the crippling restraints of socialist realism in 1939, he was arrested and later tortured and shot in prison.

Mosolov, Aleksandr Vasil'yevich (1900–1973). Born into an educated *intelligentsia* family, Mosolov travelled widely in Europe during his childhood, then volunteered for Red Army service in the civil war. He studied composition under Glier and Myaskovskiy at the Moscow Conservatoire, graduating in 1925. After a promising start to his career as one of the most interesting and cosmopolitan young Soviet composers, Mosolov felt so constrained by the encroaching doctrine of socialist realism that he wrote to Stalin asking for permission to leave the Soviet Union. When this was not granted, his career began to go downhill and he was expelled from the Composers' Union in 1936 for alleged drunkenness. He was later arrested in 1937 but his eight-year penal sentence was transmuted to a five-year exile from Leningrad, Moscow and Kiev. After the war Mosolov returned to live in Moscow.

Myaskovskiy, Nikolay Yakovlevich (1881–1950). One of the most distinguished Soviet composers of the early Soviet period. He was a close friend and colleague of Boris Asaf'yev, Pavel Lamm and Sergey Prokof'yev, with whom he exchanged a lively and warm correspondence during the younger composer's years abroad. His style was mostly rather conservative, though he composed two very modernist works: the Tenth and Thirteenth Symphonies (1927, 1933), which never gained acceptance during Myaskovsky's lifetime.

Nazarov, Aleksey Ivanovich (1905–1968). Chair of Committee for Arts Affairs 1938–9; temporary replacement for Kerzhentsev in 1938.

Neygauz, Genrikh Gustavovich (1988–1964). Pianist and Professor of piano at the Moscow Conservatoire. In 1941 he was arrested and spent eight months in the Lubyanka for refusing to be evacuated. From 1944 he resumed his teaching duties in Moscow.

Ossovskiy, Aleksandr Vyacheslavovich (1871–1957). Musicologist and critic and specialist in eighteenth-century Western music; director of Leningrad Philharmonia's artistic department, 1933–6.

Popov, Gavriil Nikolayevich (1904–1972). Talented composer and contemporary of Shostakovich, he turned away from modernism after his First Symphony was banned in 1934 and composed in a more conservative style thereafter.

Pshibïshevskiy, Boleslav Stanislavovich (1892–1937). Member of Communist Party 1920–33. Director of Moscow Conservatoire 1929–31. Arrested on charge of homosexuality in the early 1930s (probably in 1933, when his membership of the Party was revoked) and sent to forced labour for three years on the Belomor–Baltic Canal. After his release, he was again arrested in 1937 on a false espionage charge and executed. He was rehabilitated in 1956.

Rayskiy, Nazariy Grigor'evich (1876–1958). Distinguished operatic tenor and pedagogue. Professor of the Moscow Conservatoire, director of the Moscow Philharmonia 1933–4.

Renzin, Isay Mikhailovich (1903–1969). Director of Leningrad Philharmonia 1935–7. Pianist, student of Mariya Yudina and Lev Nikolayev, graduate of Leningrad Conservatoire. He was reportedly one of those who persuaded Shostakovich to cancel the premiere of his Fourth Symphony and was one of the four pianists to perform in *Les Noces* in Leningrad in 1928, with Mariya Yudina, Gavriil Popov and Dmitry Shostakovich. He founded the Piano Faculty at the Petrozavodsk Conservatoire, where he worked until his death in 1969.

Roslavets, Nikolay Andreyevich (1881–1944). One of the most radical of early Soviet composers, Roslavets composed using a form of serial technique that he invented himself, but in a manner different from Schoenberg. He worked as a censor at Glaviskusstvo in the 1920s, edited the music workers journal *Rabis* and was bitterly opposed by the musicians of RAPM, who finally managed to have him removed from any professional position in 1930. Until the end of his life, Roslavets was not admitted to the Composers' Union and never obtained a professional post in music. He was probably saved from further punishment by suffering a serious stroke in 1939, after which he lived as an invalid until his death.

Sabaneyev, Leonid Leonidovich (1881–1968). Well-known music critic in pre-revolutionary St Petersburg who continued his career there until his emigration in 1926.

Sanderling, Kurt (1912–2011). German conductor who left Nazi Germany to work in the Soviet Union in 1936. After initially working with the All-Union Moscow Radio Orchestra, he became joint principal conductor of the Leningrad Philharmonia with Yevgeniy Mravinskiy, a position he held until 1960.

Sébastian, Georges (1903–1989). Hungarian-born conductor of French parentage who worked as conductor of the All-Union Moscow Radio Orchestra 1931–7. After holding several posts in America, he returned to Europe after the war and resumed his career in France.

Sergeyev, Aleksey Alekseyevich (1899–1958). Member of RAPM, choral conductor and editor of the short-lived journal *Muzïkal'naya nov'* [Musical virgin soil]. He left RAPM for ORKiMD during the brief split between with two groups.

Shatilov, Sergey Sergeyevich (1901–?). Member of Communist Party from 1918. An economist by training, he rose through various committees and took up a leading role in the music administration of the Committee for Arts Affairs under Kerzhentsev. He led investigations of Conservatoires, Philharmonias and other music institutions in 1937 and was responsible for approving lists for dismissal and proposing replacements. In March 1938, after Kerzhentsev's downfall, he left his post.

Shaverdyan, Aleksandr Isaakovich (1903–1954). Graduated as a composer from the Leningrad Conservatoire, but turned to musicology and music journalism. From 1926 he was affiliated with RAPM and edited their journals *Proletarskiy muzïkant* and *Za proletarskuyu muzïku*. He worked as a music editor for the All-Union Radio Committee between 1928 and 1936 and later acted as editor and consultant for *Sovetskoe iskusstvo* and *Izvestiya* and, after the war, as repertoire consultant for the Bolshoy Theatre.

Sherman, Nikolay Samoylovich (1896–?). Pianist and professor at the Moscow Conservatoire from 1922; member of RAPM and member of Committee for Arts Affairs 1936–9.

Shneyerson, Grigoriy Mikhaylovich (1900–1982). Graduate of Leningrad Conservatoire who worked as a professional pianist, writer and music bureaucrat, including work for the Red Army. He spoke several European languages (English, French, German and Italian) and worked for VOKS between 1942 and 1948 as head of their music section. He was investigated as part of the 1947 purge of VOKS and lost his job there in February 1948.

Shteynpress, Boris Solomonovich (1908–1986). Graduate of Moscow Conservatoire from Konstantin Igumnov's piano class; active in RAPM circles from 1926 while still a student. He taught Western music history at Sverdlovsk Conservatoire, returning to Moscow in 1938, where he worked as an editor on the Soviet Encyclopaedia, a job he returned to after the war.

Shul'gin, Lev Vladimirovich (1890–1968). Member of Communist Party from 1917. Composer, founding member of RAPM, then founding member of ORKiMD. Head of propaganda department of Muzgiz from 1921 to 1933.

Sollertinskiy, Ivan Ivanovich (1902–1944). Distinguished linguist and polymath, who began as a literature specialist and attended Mikhail Bakhtin's meetings in Vitebsk. From around 1928 he turned his attention to musical life, played a leading role in the Leningrad Bruckner–Mahler society and in the Leningrad Philharmonia, where he was both a popular pre-concert lecturer and a key figure in their repertoire section. After the purge of the institution in 1937, he was appointed artistic director and he also lectured in music history at the Leningrad Conservatoire. He was Shostakovich's closest friend until his sudden death from a heart attack in 1944.

Stiedry, Fritz (1863–1968). Austrian conductor and former student of Mahler at the Vienna Opera, who left Nazi Germany in 1933 to take up a post as chief conductor of the Leningrad Philharmonia which he held until 1937. He moved to America in 1937, where he championed new music, especially by his compatriot Arnold Schoenberg.

Sveshnikov, Aleksandr Vasil'yevich (1890–1980). Choral conductor who directed the Leningrad Capella between 1937 and 1941 and gave the Soviet premiere of Bach's *Magnificat*. After 1948 he was given the position of rector at the Moscow Conservatoire, which he held until 1975.

Szenkar, Eugen (1891–1977). Hungarian conductor who toured extensively in the Soviet Union. He was a distinguished opera conductor, holding positions in Prague, Budapest, and later in major German opera houses.

After leaving Nazi Germany in 1933, he worked as a conductor in Moscow, and taught Kiril Kondrashin at the Conservatoire. He left the Soviet Union after a campaign against him in 1937, but pursued a successful career thereafter, eventually returning to Germany in 1949.

Unger, Heinz (1895–1965). German conductor and Mahler enthusiast who began working in the Soviet Union as early as 1924, later exclusively with the Leningrad Radio Orchestra up to 1937. His memoir of those years, *Hammer, Sickle and Baton* (London, 1939) gives a frank account of the difficulties and pressures of working in that environment. After 1937 he worked in various European countries before finally settling in Toronto, where he continued his conducting career right up until his death.

Yezhov, Nikolay Ivanovich (1895–1940). Head of NKVD 1936–8; overseer of the big political show trials and the mass purges of the late 1930s, which have sometimes been referred to as the *Yezhovshchina*. He was arrested in 1939 and shot in 1940.

Yudina, Mariya Veniaminovna (1899–1970). One of the greatest Soviet pianists of her generation, a contemporary of Shostakovich at the Leningrad Conservatoire and a close friend and associate of Mikhail Bakhtin.

Zhilayev, Nikolay Sergeyevich (1881–1938). Musicologist, worked at Moscow Conservatoire 1926–37 (with a three-year break between 1930 and 1933). Arrested and later executed in connection with his friendship with Mikhail Tukhachevskiy.

NOTES

Introduction

1. Indeed, Western scholars have only very recently begun to think of early Soviet culture in terms of 'appropriation' at all, and that particular zeitgeist has undoubtedly been shaped by a much wider conceptualization of the phenomenon of cultural borrowing or transfer. Musicologists have been very active in this field, with important studies on the German and Nazi reception and 'appropriation' of Mozart and Verdi, but also studies of less overtly politicized borrowing. See Katharine Ellis's *Interpreting the Musical Past* (New York: Oxford University Press, 2005), Erik Levi's *Mozart and the Nazis: How the Third Reich Abused a Cultural Icon*, New Haven and London: Yale University Press, 2011; Gundula Kreutzer, *Verdi and the Germans: From Unification to the Third Reich*, Cambridge: Cambridge University Press, 2010; and Annegret Fauser and Mark Everist, eds, *Music, Theatre and Cultural Transfer: Paris 1830–1914*, University of Chicago Press, Chicago, 2009.
2. Cited in Stephen Moller-Sally, *Gogol's Afterlife. The Evolution of a Classic in Imperial and Soviet Russia*, Evanston, IL: Northwestern University Press, 2002, 145.
3. Cited in David Brandenberger, *National Bolshevism: Stalinist Mass Culture and the Formation of Modern Russian National Identity, 1931–1956*, Cambridge, MA: Harvard University Press, 2002, 78 and n. 8.
4. Cited in Moller-Sally, *Gogol's Afterlife*, 145.
5. This is the term used by Hans Günther in his *Der sozialistische übermensch: M. Gor'kij und der sowjetische Heldenmythos*, Stuttgart: J. B. Metzler, 1993.
6. See Catriona Kelly, *Refining Russia: Advice Literature, Polite Culture and Gender from Catherine to Yeltsin*, New York: Oxford University Press, 2001, especially 278–311. See also Vera Dunham, *In Stalin's Time: Middleclass Values in Soviet Fiction*, Durham and London: Duke University Press, 1990. As Dunham explains, the social meaning of *kul'turnost'* covered a wide range of social conduct from polite behaviour in public to a broad embrace of middle-class values that, in the post-war era especially, came to be synonymous with what she calls 'a refurbished, victorious, conservative force in Soviet postwar life, embodying a slick decorum and a new kind of self-righteousness, stable, prudent, heavy'.
7. Evgeny Dobrenko, trans. Jesse M. Savage, *The Making of the State Reader. Social and Aesthetics Contexts of the Reception of Soviet Literature*, Stanford, CA: Stanford University Press, 1997, 2.
8. *Rabochiy i teatr*, 1932, no. 4, 'Protiv gnilogo liberalisma na muzïkal'nom fronte' [Against rotten liberalism on the musical front], 3.
9. Günther, *Der sozialistische übermensch*.

10. Gumilëv – the first husband of the poet Anna Akhmatova – was arrested and shot by the Cheka in 1921 on a fabricated charge of plotting to restore the monarchy.
11. Alexandra Tolstoy, *Out of the Past*, New York: Columbia University Press, 1981.
12. Régis Debray, 'Socialism: A Life-Cycle', *New Left Review*, 46, July–August 2007, 12.
13. Katerina Clark, *Moscow: The Fourth Rome. Stalinism, Cosmopolitanism and the Evolution of Soviet Culture, 1931–1941*, Cambridge, MA: Harvard University Press, 2011.
14. Jiří Smrž, *Symphonic Stalinism. Claiming Russian Musical Classics for the New Soviet Listener, 1932–1953*, Berlin: Lit Verlag, 2011, 104–27. Tragically, Smrcž died in 2006 before he could prepare his doctoral dissertation for publication and it was published posthumously thanks to Thomas Lahusen and Peter H. Solomon Jr. Smrcž's approach differs from my own in that he traces the processes whereby Soviet writers identified Chaykovskiy and other nineteenth-century Russian composers as proto-Soviet in their thinking, passionately aligned with progressive social and political trends but prevented from full development by the regressive political order of their time.
15. See especially Rebecca Mitchell, 'Nietzsche's Orphans: Music and the Search for Unity in Revolutionary Russia, 1905–1921', PhD diss., University of Illinois at Urbana-Champaign, 2011.
16. This is according to the memoir of the conductor Aleksandr Gauk, who reported that Sollertinskiy worked with him on repertoire under the aegis of GOMETs (State Ministry of Estrada and Circuses) between 1925 and 1933. See L. P. Gauk, R. V. Glezer and Ya. I. Mil'shteyn, eds, *Aleksandr Vasil'evich Gauk. Memuarï, izbrannïe stat'i, vospominaniya sovremennikov* [Aleksandr Vasil'yevich Gauk. Memoirs, collected essays, recollections of his contemporaries], Moscow: Sovietskiy kompozitor, 1975, 76.

Chapter 1: Propagandizing the Classics, 1917–1929

1. See Alexander Grechaninov, *My Life*, trans. N. Slonimsky, New York: Coleman-Ross, 1952, and Maxim Gorky, *Chaliapin. An Autobiography as told to Maxim Gorky*, trans. and ed. Nina Froud and James Hanley, London: Columbus Books, 1988.
2. Yekaterina Vlasova, *1948 god v Sovetskoy muzïke* [The Year 1948 in Soviet Music], Moscow: Klassika XXI, 2010, 8. Presumably describing a different – more successful – meeting, Boris Schwarz lists Asaf'yev, Karatïgin and Shcherbachëv among those who responded to Lunacharskiy's public call in *Pravda* on 1 December 1917. See Boris Schwarz, *Music and Musical Life in Soviet Russia, 1917–1981*, enlarged edn, Bloomington, IN: Indiana University Press, 1983, 13.
3. Lynn M. Sargeant, 'High Anxiety: New Venues, New Audiences, and the Fear of the Popular in Late Imperial Russian Musical Life', *19th-Century Music*, vol. 35, no. 2, Fall 2011, 97.
4. Sargeant notes that, working alongside *zemstva*, these People's Houses were also established by branches of the tellingly named Guardianship of Popular Sobriety. Sargeant, 'High Anxiety', 99.
5. Ibid., 99–100.
6. Cited in Rebecca Mitchell, 'Nietzsche's Orphans: Music and the Search for Unity in Revolutionary Russia 1905–1921', PhD diss., University of Illinois at Urbana-Champagn, 2011, 67.
7. Gorky, *Chaliapin*, 191.
8. See Anthony Phillips, trans. and ed., *Sergey Prokofiev Diaries, vol. 3, 1924–1933. Prodigal Son*, London: Faber and Faber, 2012. Shostakovich would emerge as a major new talent only in 1926, with the premiere of his First Symphony in a performance sponsored by the Leningrad Association of Contemporary Music (LASM, *Leningradskaya assotsiatsiya sovremennoy muzïki*), conducted by Nikolay Mal'ko. For details of Myaskovskiy's relationship with Universal Edition, see Olesya Bobrik, *Venskoe izdatel'stvo 'Universal Edition' i muzïkantï iz sovetskoy Rossii* [The Viennese publisher 'Universal Edition' and musicians from Soviet Russia], St Petersburg: N. A. Novikova publishers, 2011.

9. These documents first appeared in Andrey Artizov and Oleg Naumov, *Vlast i khudozhestvennaya intelligentsiya: dokumentï TsK RKP (b) – VKP (b) – VChK – NKVD o kul'turnoy politike, 1917–1953* [Power and the artistic intelligentsia: documents on cultural politics from the Central Committee of the Russian Communist Party (Bolsheviks) 1917–1953], Moscow: 'Demokratiya', 1999, 31–3. All the materials are available in English in the volume containing many of their key findings, Katerina Clark and Evgeny Dobrenko, with Andrei Artizov and Oleg Naumov, *Soviet Culture and Power: A History in Documents*, New Haven and London: Yale University Press, 2007, 23–31.

10. See Nikolai Malko, *A Certain Art*, New York: William Morrow, 1966, 8–9.

11. Stanislav Ponyatovskiy, *Orkestr Sergeya Koussevitskogo*, Moscow: 'Muzïka', 2008, 3.

12. Ibid., 229–94.

13. For a detailed account of Georgiy Rimskiy-Korsakov's activities and an excellent study of this early phase of experimental music in the Soviet Union, see Lidia Ader, 'Mikrotonovaya muzïka v Evrope i Rossii v 1900–1920-e godï' [Microtonal music in Europe and Russia in the 1900–1920s], PhD diss., St Petersburg Conservatoire, 2013, and 'Microtonal Storm and Stress: Georgy Rimsky-Korsakov and Quarter-Tone Music in 1920s Soviet Russia', *Tempo*, 63 (2009), 27–44.

14. Igor Glebov, ed., *Proshloe russkoy muzïki. Materialï i issledovaniy vol. 1 P. I. Chaikovskiy* [Russian music of the past. Materials and research. Vol. 1, P. I. Chaykovskiy], Petrograd, 1918, reprinted Petersburg, Kinoizdatel'stvo 'Ogni', 1920.

15. Ibid., 10–11.

16. For a clear account of these events, see Marina Frolova-Walker and Jonathan Walker, *Music and Soviet Power, 1917–1932*, Woodbridge: Boydell Press, 2012, 86–90.

17. Marina Raku, *Muzïkal'naya klassika v mifotvorchestve sovetskoy epokhi* [Musical classicism in the mythology of the Soviet epoch], Moscow: Novoe literaturnoe obozrenie, 2014, 568.

18. Ibid., 571.

19. See Richard Taruskin, 'Who Speaks for Musorgsky?', in Taruskin, *Musorgsky. Eight Essays and an Epilogue*, Princeton, NJ: Princeton University Press, 1993, 8.

20. ORKiMD = *Obyedineniye Revolyutsionnïkh Kompozitorov i Muzïkal'nïkh Deyateley* [association of revolutionary composers and music workers], founded 1924, merging with RAPM (*Rossiskaya assotsiatsiya proletarskikh muzïkantov*, or Russian association of proletarian musicians) in 1929.

21. Yefim Vilkovir, 'M. P. Musorgskiy', *Muzïka i revoliutsiya*, 1926, no. 5, 4.

22. Ibid., 5.

23. See Taruskin, 'Musorgsky versus Musorgsky', in Taruskin, *Musorgsky*, 206–7.

24. Yevgeniy Braudo and Andrey Rimskiy-Korsakov, *Boris Godunov Musorgskogo* [Musorgskiy's Boris Godunov], Moscow and Leningrad: Kino-pechat', 1927.

25. Braudo and Rimskiy-Korsakov, *Boris Godunov Musorgskogo*, 8.

26. Taruskin, 'Sorochinski Fair Revisited', in *Musorgsky*, 385.

27. Braudo and Rimskiy-Korsakov, *Boris Godunov Musorgskogo*, 12.

28. For the best available account in English of Musorgskiy's Soviet-era harnessing to the identity fashioned for him by Stasov, see Taruskin, 'Musorgskiy versus Musorgskiy'.

29. Viktor Belyayev, Igor' Glebov, Pavel Lamm et al., *Musorgsky: Boris Godunov. Stat'i i issledovaniya* [Musorgskiy: Boris Godunov. Articles and research], Moscow: Gosudarstvennaya Akademiya Khudozhestvennikh Nauk, muzïkal'naya sektsiya, 1930.

30. This was the term given to a new class of intellectuals from non-landowning or aristocratic backgrounds, who went on to play important roles in Russian culture and intellectual life in the 1860s and '70s.

31. P. S. Kogan, 'Sotzial'niy portret Musorskogo' [A social portrait of Musorgskiy], in Belyayev et al., *Musorgskiy: Boris Godunov*, 1. I am assuming that the author was Pëtr Kogan, a specialist on Belinskiy and other nineteenth-century writers, a former member of the Moscow Philharmonic Society (who moved to St Petersburg in 1909 and hence probably knew musicians there) and who, after 1917, became rector of the Moscow

State University. In 1929 he would have been fifty-seven and a sufficiently senior figure to command the opening pages of such an important volume. His authorship would also account for the heavy weighting – untypical of musical writing of this time – towards nineteenth-century Russian thinkers and writers. If he was the author, as seems likely, then his article set the tone for Musorgskiy scholarship a decade later, when this way of writing about the composer became standard.

32. Ibid., 4.
33. Albrecht Gaub, 'Mikhail Glinka as Preached and Practiced in the Soviet Union Before and After 1937', *Journal of Musicological Research*, 22, 2003, 101–34.
34. Marina Raku has examined the libretto for this revised version of Glinka's opera in the music library of the Bolshoy Theatre. For an excellent discussion of this and of Glinka's Soviet-era reception, see Raku, *Muzïkal'naya klassika*, 452–563.
35. Igor Glebov, 'Nash dolg' [Our duty], in Glebov, ed., *Proshloe russkoy muzïki*, 7.
36. Maureen Perrie, 'The Terrible Tsar as Comic Hero. Mikhail Bulgakov's *Ivan Vasil'evich*', in David Brandenberger and Kevin M. F. Platt, *Epic Revisionism. Russian History and Literature as Stalinist Propaganda*, Madison, WI: University of Wisconsin Press, 2006, 151.
37. Konstantin Kuznetsov, *Glinka i ego sovremenniki* [Glinka and his contemporaries], Moscow: Gosudarstvennoe izdatel'stvo, muzïkal'niy sektor, 1926; Nikolay Strel'nikov, *Glinka. Opït kharakteristiki* [Glinka. Characteristics of his style], Moscow: Gosudarstvennoe izdatel'stvo, 1923.
38. Strel'nikov, *Glinka*, 22.
39. Ibid., 37.
40. However, see Raku's discussion of Glinka's reception at this time, including some of Strel'nikov's less flattering remarks about the 'decline' of Glinka's talent towards the end of his life, and of Konstantin Kuznetsov's claim (in 1929) that his music echoed the heritage of the pre-revolutionary gentry (Raku, *Muzïkal'naya klassika*, 454–63). I would argue, though, that both writers were far more positive than negative about Glinka.
41. See Yelena Bronfin, *Muzïkal'naya kul'tura Petrograda pervogo poslerevolyutsionnogo pyatiletiya 1917–1922* [The musical culture of Petrograd in the first five years after the revolution], Leningrad: Sovetskiy kompozitor, 1984, 44.
42. Simon Dreyden, 'Na volye revoliutsii' [At the will of the revolution], *Sovetskaya muzïka*, 1966, no. 4, 11–20.
43. Quoted in Dreyden, 'Na volye revoliutsii', 19.
44. Sergey Chemodanov, 'Muzïka i teoriya istoricheskogo materializma' [Music and the theory of historical materialism], *Muzïkal'naya nov'* [Musical virgin soil], 1923, no. 1, 15–16.
45. Ibid.
46. Anon., *Zhizn' iskusstva* [Life of art], 18 December 1923, 13.
47. *Moscow Workers' Gazette*, no. 32, 9 February 1927, preserved in press cuttings from Klimov's notebook, National Library of St Petersburg, manuscript department, f. 1127, op. 8332, ed. khr. 28, l. 32.
48. Anton Tsenovskiy, review in *Trud* [Labor], 12 February 1927, preserved in ibid.
49. *Izvestiya TsIK SSSR*, 1927. Month, issue number and page unknown. Preserved in ibid.
50. The critic Viktor Gorodinskiy later made this comparison in his article 'Etyud o Bakhe' [Study on Bach], *Sovetskoe iskusstvo*, 11 April 1935, 2.
51. See Vladimir Muzalevskiy, *Mikhail Georgevich Klimov. Ocherk zhizni i tvorcheskoy deyatel'nosti* [Mikhail Georgevich Klimov. On his life and work], Leningrad: Sovetskiy kompozitor, 1960, 46–7.
52. Staged not on the Bolshoy main stage but on the 'filial stage'. The music director was Mikhail Ippolitov-Ivanov and the premiere date was 26 November. Prior to that performance *Figaro* had not been performed at the Bolshoy since 1868. The new production was repeated on the filial stage in 1927, 1928, 1929, 1930 and 1931 – the only one of Mozart's operas to be staged by the Bolshoy for the whole period 1917–32. *Figaro* was re-launched in a new Bolshoy production in 1936 and staged thereafter every season until 1942.

53. Igor Glebov, 'Motsart i sovremennost' [Mozart and the present], *Sovremennaya muzïka*, 1927, no. 5, (no. 25), 55–9.

54. Ibid.

55. Quoted in H. C. Robbins-Landon, *Beethoven*, Thames and Hudson, London, 1970, 118.

56. Sergey Chemodanov, 'O Betkhoven i sovremennost'' [On Beethoven and the present day], *Muzïkal'naya nov'*, 1923, no. 2 (30 November), 16.

57. Anatoliy Lunacharskiy, 'Velikie sëstrï' ['Great Sisters'], *Muzïka i revoliutsitya*, 1926, no. 1, 16.

58. See the Moscow Conservatoire house journal *Muzïkal'noe obrazovanie* [Music Education] 2, nos 1–2 (1927) for serious scholarly articles including a facsimile of Sketchbook no. 4, the ORKiMD (Obedineniye revoliutsionnïkh kompozitorov i muzïkal'nikh deyateley, or Association of revolutionary composers and music workers) journal *Muzïka i revoliutsiya*, 1927, no. 3 for more political articles, and the ASM (Assotsiatsiya sovremennoy muzïki, or Association for Contemporary Music) journal *Sovremennaya muzïka*, 1927, no. 21 for reports of Beethoven-related ASM concerts and lectures.

59. Yevgeny Braudo, 'Betkhoven-grazhdanin' ['Beethoven-Citizen'], *Muzïka i revoliutsiya*, 1927, no. 3, 22–3.

60. Anatoliy Lunacharsky, 'Romantika', *Muzïka i revoliutsiya*, 1928, no. 10, 5.

61. Mikhail Pekelis, 'Frants Shubert', *Muzïka i revoliutsiya*, 1928, no. 10, 8.

62. Ibid., 12.

63. Mikhail Ivanov-Boretskiy, 'E.T.A. Gofman'' [E.T.A. Hoffmann], *Muzïkal'noe obrazovanie*, 1926, no. 1, 15.

64. Mikhail Cheremukhin, 'K voprosu o putyakh sovetskoy muzïki' [On the question of the path for Soviet music], *Sovetskaya muzïka*, 1933, no. 5, 24.

65. Mikhail Ivanov-Boretskiy, 'Revoliutsionnïe khorï Shumana' [Schumann's revolutionary choruses], *Muzïkal'noe obrazovanie*, 1930, no. 2, 16–19.

66. Rosamund Bartlett, *Wagner and Russia*, Cambridge: Cambridge University Press, 1995, 259.

67. Aleksandr Blok, 'Iskusstvo i revoliutsiya' [Art and revolution], *Izvestiya*, 1919, no. 223, 24 August, 1–2. The essay is reprinted in his collected works; see Aleksandr Blok, *Sobranie sochinenii* [Collected works], vol. 6, Moscow: Sovremennik, 1979, 228–32, where the date of writing is given as 1918.

68. Bartlett claims that *Parsifal* was the first Wagner opera to be performed in the Soviet Union. I have not been able to verify this, though Fedorov's excellent record of Bolshoy Theatre productions shows that there, at least, the first Soviet-era Wagner opera was *Das Rheingold* (1918) and *Parsifal* was never performed. See Bartlett, *Wagner and Russia*, 311–13 and Konstantin Kuznetsov, 'Dirizhër Vagnera' [Wagner the conductor], in Emil Kuper, *Stat'i, vospominaniya, materialï* [Emil Kuper, articles, reminiscences, materials], Moscow: Sovetskiy kompozitor, 1988, 49–75, and V. V. Fedorov, *Repertuar Bol'shogo teatra SSSR, 1776–1955* [Repertoire of the Bolshoy theatre in the USSR, 1776–1955], New York: Norman Ross Publishing, 2001.

69. For a fuller account of Wagner's reception in the Soviet Union, see Pauline Fairclough, 'Wagner Reception in Stalinist Russia', in Luca Sala, ed., *The Legacy of Richard Wagner*, Speculum Musicae, Turnhout: Brepols Publishers, Centro Studia Opera Omnia Luigi Boccherini, 2012, 309–26.

70. Yevgeny Braudo, 'Ob ekspressionizme v muzïke' [On Expressionism in Music], *Muzïkal'naya letopis* [Music Chronicle], 1922, no. 2, 150.

71. Ibid.

72. Viktor Belyayev, 'Myaskovskiy, Gedike i Aleksandrov', *Sovremennaya muzïka*, 1924, no. 8, 19–20. ASM = Assotsiatsiya sovremennoy muzïki [Association for Contemporary Music].

73. Ibid.

74. Anon., *Sovremennaya muzïka*, 1924, no. 1, 22.

75. Yevgeniy Braudo, 'Leningradskaya muzïkal'naya zhizn'' [Leningrad's musical life], *Muzïkal'naya nov'*, 1924, no. 4, 31 Jan, 31.

76. Anon., *Zhizn' iskusstva* 28 December 1926, 21.

77. Ivan Sollertinskiy, *Gustav Maler*, Leningrad: Triton, 1932. For a detailed discussion of Sollertinskiy, see Pauline Fairclough, 'Mahler Reconstructed: Sollertinskiy and the Soviet Symphony', *Musical Quarterly*, 85/2, 2001, 367–90.
78. Yevgeniy Dukov, 'Vlast kak muza muz: otechestvennïy opït' ['Power as muse of the mus: our national experience', in Yevgeniy Dukov, ed., *Mezhdu obshchestvom i vlast'yu: massovïe zhanrï ot 20-x k 80-m godam XX veka* [Between society and power: mass genres from the 1920s to 1980s], Moscow: 'Indrik', 2002, 15.
79. Ibid.
80. Musical members of the Beethoven Society, in alphabetical order as follows (not complete list): Aleksandr Aleksandrov, Boris Asaf'yev, Yevgeniy Braudo, Nadezhda Bryusova, Sergey Chemodanov, Aleksandr Gedike, Aleksandr Glazunov, Reyngol'd Glier, Aleksandr Gol'denveyzer, Konstantin Igumnov, Mikhail Ippolitov-Ivanov, Mikhail Ivanov-Boretskiy, Georgiy Konius, Boris Krasin, Aleksandr Krein, Viktor Kubatskiy, Konstantin Kuznetsov, Lev Lebedinskiy, Anatoliy Lunacharskiy, Nikolay Mal'ko, Nikolay Myaskovskiy, Genrikh Neygauz, Pavel Novitskiy, Lev Oborin, Aleksandr Ossovskiy, Vyacheslav Suk, Lev Tseitlin, Boris Yampol'skiy, Boleslav Yavorskiy. Source: RGALI, f. 645, op. 1, ed. khr. 7, l. 95. Vlasova lists other members outside the musical community, including Marshal Mikhail Tukhachevskiy and the diplomat Maksim Litvinov. See Vlasova, *1948 god*, 98. Vlasova, consulting archival documents from earlier in 1930 in GARF, observes correctly that the Beethoven Society was required to merge with the All-Russian workers' music society 'Music for the Masses' and to give them all their materials; this was the first stage in its closure, but after that it was completely closed and its materials and remaining funds passed straight to Narkompros. See ibid., l. 99.
81. RGALI, f. 645, op. 1, ed. khr. 7, l. 99.
82. RGALI, f. 645, op. 1, ed. Khr. 457, l. 206.
83. RGALI, f. 645, op. 1, ed. khr. 457, ll. 209–10. Vlasova notes that the Society was formed on the instigation of Narkompros. She also lists Mikhail Gnesin, Sergey Vasilenko, Aleksandr Gol'denveyzer, Nikolay Zhilayev, Konstantin Igumnov, Nikolay Myaskovskiy, Lev Oborin, Pavel Lamm, Aleksandr Kreyn and Dmitriy Kabalevskiy among its professional members. See Vlasova, *1948 god*, 101. RSFSR = *Rossiyskaya Sovetskaya Federativnaya Sotsialisticheskaya Respublika* [Russian Soviet Federation of Socialist Republics].
84. See S. K. Kvostin, 'Iz muzïkal'noy zhizni Leningrada (Obshchestvo vagnerovskogo iskusstva, 1920-e godï)' [From Leningrad's musical life (the Society for Wagner's Art in the 1920s)], in Tamara Livanova, ed., *Iz proshlogo sovetskoy muzïkal'noy kul'turï* [From the Past of Soviet Musical Culture], vol. 3, Moscow: Sovetskiy kompozitor, 1982, 231–7.
85. Ivan Yershov had declined Cosima Wagner's invitation to sing at Bayreuth precisely because he did not wish to re-learn his roles in German.
86. See Neil Edmunds, *The Soviet Proletarian Music Movement*, Bern: Peter Lang, 2000, and Amy Nelson, *Music for the Revolution: Musicians and Power in Early Soviet Russia*, Pennsylvania: Pennsylvania State University Press, 2004. See also Robin La Pasha, 'Amateurs and enthusiasts: folk music and the Soviet state on stage in the 1930s' in Neil Edmunds, ed., *Soviet Music and Society Under Lenin and Stalin: the Baton and Sickle*, London and New York: Routledge Curzon, 2004, 123–47, though her chapter deals exclusively with the 1930s.
87. In addition to the publications given above, see also Lynn M. Sargeant, *Harmony and Discord: Music and the Transformation of Russian Cultural Life*, New York: Oxford University Press, 2011.
88. TsGALI f. 279, d. 101. The questionnaires come from a concert in Kislovodsk in 1938; evidently a tour concert, probably given over the summer.
89. Edmunds, *The Soviet Proletarian Music Movement*, 126. See also V. Ilin, *Iskusstvo millionov. Iz istorii muzïkal'noy samodeyatel'nosti Petrograd-Leningrad* [Art of the millions. From the history of amateur music-making], Leningrad: Muzïka, 1967, 101. Ilin notes that they also performed Bizet's *Carmen* in 1930 at the Leningrad Conservatoire, with the student orchestra.

90. M. Dmitr'yev, 'Mechtaem o simfonicheskom orkestre' [We dream of a symphony orchestra], *Muzïka i bït*, no. 4 (August) 1927, 13.
91. Nikolay Mal'ko, 'O "diletantakh" i liubitelyakh' [On 'dilettantes' and music lovers], *Muzïka i bït*, no. 2, June 1927, 1–2.
92. *Rabis* (Rossiyskiy professional'nïye soiuz rabotnikov iskusstv, or Russian professional union of art workers) was the journal of the art workers' trade union.
93. Ilin, *Iskusstvo millionov*, 106.
94. Anon., *Muzïka i revoliutsiya*, no. 10, 1928, 41.
95. Ibid.
96. B. Valeryanov, 'Opera v klube' [Opera in the club], *Rabochiy i teatr*, 17 June 1928, 14.
97. Nikolay Roslavets, 'Kul't-rabota Vserabisa' [Cultural work of Vserabis], *Vestnik rabotnikov iskusstv* [Bulletin of art workers], 1920, nos 2–3, 47.
98. 'D', 'O simfonicheskikh kontsertakh rabochikh' [On symphony concerts for workers], *Rabochiy zritel'* [The worker-listener], no. 4, 22 January 1924, 10.
99. Lev Kaltat, 'Zametki o Sofilé' [Notes on Sofil], *Proletarskiy muzïkant*, 1929, nos 7–8, 13.
100. Ibid.
101. Ibid, 19.
102. Anton Tsenovskiy, ' "Mï" i "oni" ' [Them and us], *Rabochiy i teatr*, 1 December 1924, 7.
103. A. S., 'Razgovor v rabochem klube' [Conversation in a workers' club], *Muzïka i revoliutsiya*, 1926, no. 1, 22–3.
104. N. V. Mirov, 'Dukhovïe rabochie orkestrï-kruzhki' [Workers' orchestral groups], *Muzïka i revoliutsiya*, 1927, nos 5–6, 8.
105. M. Korotkov, 'Leningradskaya muzïkal'naya samodeyatel'nost'' [Leningrad's amateur music scene], *Rabochiy i teatr*, 21 February 1931, 16.
106. N. Kudryatsev, 'Kak ozdorovit muzïkal'niy repertuar klubov' [How to improve club music repertoire], *Proletarskiy muzïkant*, 1929, no. 4, 29.
107. Sergey Novitskiy, 'Shto delat'?' [What is to be done?], *Muzïka i revoliutsiya*, 1929, no. 4, 35–6.
108. A. Koposov, 'O rukoviditelyakh klubnïkh muzïkal'nïkh kruzhkov' [On the leadership of club music groups], *Muzïka i revoliutsiya*, 1929, nos 7–8, 5.
109. V. F., 'O voennikh orkestrakh' [On military bands], *Proletarskiy muzïkant*, 1929, no. 6, 32.
110. Note, however, that there were pro-Soviet *chastushki* and even Stalinist *chastushki*. As a song form it was not suppressed per se, but its urban and flippant nature was far removed from the proletarian mass song that RAPM supported.
111. Cited in Suzannah Lockwood Smith, 'Soviet Arts Policy, Folk Music, and National Identity: The Piatnitskii State Russian Folk Choir, 1927–1945', PhD dissertation, University of Minnesota, 1997, 66. For details of the persecution of the choir and the repression of peasant and folk culture during the early 1930s, see especially 69–84.
112. Cited in ibid, 66.
113. Igor Glebov, 'Muzïka goroda i derevni' [Music of town and country], *Muzïka i revoliutsiya*, 1926, no. 3, 6.
114. P. Yarkov, 'Muzïka v derevnye. Pis'mo krest'yanina' [Music in the village. A letter from a peasant], *Muzïka i revoliutsiya*, 1926, no. 1, 42.
115. Smith, 'Soviet Arts Policy', 71.
116. This was the very same Zakharov whose crude attacks on Soviet composers would be preserved for Western readers in Alexander Werth's *Musical Uproar in Moscow*, the English-language partial translation of proceedings of the infamous conference of musicians presided over by Andrey Zhdanov in February 1948. See Alexander Werth, *Musical Uproar in Moscow*, London: Turnstile Press, 1949.
117. The programmes for the two chamber concerts were: (25 March 1928) Glinka songs, Dargomïzhskiy: songs from Act One of *Rusalka*, Rubinstein: Piano Trio, 'Canzonetta' from the Cello Sonata, songs; (22 April 1928) Chopin: Piano Trio, Nocturne, 'Lithuanian Song', Grieg: Violin Sonata, songs, Liszt: 'La Campanella', Nocturne. See Roman Gruber, 'Kak slushaet muzïku rabochaya auditoriya' [How a workers' audience listens to music], *Muzïka i revolyutsiya*, 1928, no. 12, 12.

118. Ibid.
119. Ibid.
120. Ibid., 14.
121. Ibid., 15.
122. Sarra Krïlova and Lev Lebedinskiy et al., *Rabochie o literature, teatre i muzïke* [Workers on literature, theatre and music], Leningrad: 'Prïboy', 1926, 68. For an entertaining and perceptive English-language account of this book and the issues it raises, see Evgeny Dobrenko, 'The Disaster of Middlebrow Taste, or, who "invented" socialist realism?', in Thomas Lahusen and Evgeny Dobrenko, eds, *Socialist Realism Without Shores*, Durham and London: Duke University Press, 1997, 135–64.
123. Krïlova et al., *Rabochie o literature*, 73–4.
124. Cited in Vlasova, *1948 god*, 41.
125. Krïlova et al., *Rabochie o literature*, 75.
126. Ibid., 80.
127. Note here that even the most militant of RAPM's activists, Krïlova and Lebedinskiy, at this point supported the performance of Russian folk song.
128. Ibid., 81.
129. For an excellent account of the rivalry between Roslavets and the militant proletarian activists of RAPM, see Frolova-Walker and Walker, *Music and Soviet Power*, 100–17.
130. Krïlova et al., *Rabochie o literature*, 94.
131. See Lev Lebedinskiy, 'Kontsertnaya rabota v rabochey auditorii' [Concert works for workers], *Proletarskiy muzïkant*, 1929, no. 2, 9.
132. My source for this is RGALI f. 2922 (Moskovskaya Gosudarstvennaya filarmoniya), op. 1. Opening notes. The *fond* only has files for mass work starting from 1933, for the concert (club) bureau from 1939 and planning from 1936, making it impossible to research this aspect of their activities in the 1920s. The Chaykovskiy concert hall was opened in 1946.
133. The Leningrad Philharmonia had its own library and archive from its inception, in which all programmes are still kept, and there are very few gaps in their records. Other documents, such as minutes of meetings, plans, posters and official documents relating to the Philharmonia are stored in TsGALI. The Moscow Philharmonia's programmes are stored in RGALI and mostly present a full record after 1937.
134. Sollertinskiy's record is reproduced in Lyudmila Mikheyeva, *Pamyati I. I. Sollertinskogo. Vospominaniya, materialï, issledovaniya* [In memory of I. I. Sollertinskiy. Recollections, materials, research], Leningrad: Sovetskiy kompozitor, 1978, 244–6.
135. The table does not include details of Prokof'yev's visit to the Soviet Union in early 1927. The best account of this is now to be found in Phillips, *Sergey Prokofiev Diaries*.
136. What this work actually was is not quite certain; the *Konzertmuzik* for Viola and Orchestra was still being written (it would be completed only in 1930), yet 'Viola Concerto' here cannot mean *Kammermusik No. 5*, since this is listed separately.
137. Though this work falls outside the 1910 cut-off date, I included it because Berg was one of the major European modernists represented in Leningrad in the 1920s.
138. It is not quite clear what this work was, but it might have been the 1921 arrangement of Purcell, *Set of Act Tunes and Dances*.
139. In 1920 the Mariinskiy was renamed GATOB (State Academic Theatre of Opera and Ballet).
140. Schwarz, *Music and Musical Life*, 64–5.
141. Ibid., 65.
142. V. Bogdanov-Berezovskiy and A. Aldanov, 'Kontsertï Ansermet' [Ansermet's concerts], *Rabochiy i teatr*, 2 June 1929, 10. The music Ansermet performed was as follows (spread over three concerts): Debussy's *La Mer* and *L'Après-midi d'un faune*, Prokof'yev's *Chout*, Honegger's *Rugby*, de Falla's *L'amour sorcier*, Bach's Brandenburg No. 1, Bliss's Suite for Strings, Ravel's *La Valse*, Stravinsky's *Petrushka* (1925 version), *L'Histoire*, *Oedipus Rex* (with capella) and *Rite of Spring*.

143. See the editorial 'Dovesti do kontsa s nepmanskoy muzïkoy' [Let us bring an end to Nepman music], *Za proletarskuyu muzïku*, 1930, no. 9, 1–3.

144. Anatoliy Groman-Solovtsov and V. Voloshnikov, 'Betkhoven v ispolnenii dvukh germanskikh dirizherov' [Beethoven as performed by two German conductors], *Za proletarskuyu muzïku*, February–March 1932, 36–8.

145. Anatoliy Groman, 'Bela Bartok', *Proletarskiy muzïkant*, 1929, no. 1, 38.

146. The Leningrad Capella was independent from the Leningrad Philharmonia, even though its director, Mikhail Klimov, held directorial posts in the Philharmonia.

147. Anon., 'O "sovremennoy muzïke"' [On 'contemporary' music], *Proletarskiy muzïkant*, 1926, no. 6, 6–7.

148. Anon., '"Levïy" flang sovremennoy muzïki' [The 'left' wing of contemporary music], *Muzïka i revoliutsiya*, 1927, no. 1, 6. I have used Marina Frolova-Walker and Jonathan Walker's translation: see Frolova-Walker and Walker, *Music and Soviet Power*, 188–92.

149. S. A. Liberson, 'Sumerki muzïkal'nogo tvorchestva' [The twilight of musical creativity], *Muzïka i revoliutsiya*, 1927, nos 7–8, 8.

150. This was the name given to the group of Moscow-based Conservatoire teachers who formed their own faction in January 1924. They were committed to educational work among workers and students who could not afford a Conservatoire education.

151. Cited in Frolova-Walker and Walker, *Music and Soviet Power*, 231.

152. Aleksandr Veprik, 'O "levoy" i "pravoy" muzïke i o zadachakh sovetskikh kompozitorov' [On 'left' and 'right' in music and on the tasks of Soviet composers], *Muzïka i revoliutsiya*, 1929, no. 2, 16.

153. Anon., '"Industrializm" i "narodnichestvo" v muzïke' [Industrialism and folk-ism in music], *Muzïka i revoliutsiya*, 1928, no. 3, 5.

154. ORKiMD, 'Nash protest' [Our protest], *Muzïka i revoliutsiya*, 1928, nos 5–6, 43.

155. They had been merged briefly under Narkompros but from July 1922 the capella was independent. Records show that a merger was again broached in the summer of 1941, but was vigorously opposed by the capella management. See TsGALI f. 77, op. 2, d. 242, ll. 4–7. Its independence probably saved it from the purge that followed the Committee on Arts Affairs investigation of the Philharmonia in late 1937, which resulted in several arrests. When the capella's turn came to be investigated in 1941, its affairs were judged to be in good order. See ibid, l. 3. The investigation seems to have taken place actually during the first few months of the war: by the time the report was sent to the Committee on Arts Affairs (September 1941) the capella had already been evacuated to Kirov.

156. A complete list of pre- and post-revolutionary repertoire up to 1957 is given in D. V. Tkachev and I. L. Gusin, *Leningradskaya akademicheskaya kapella imeni M. I. Glinki* [The Leningrad academic Glinka capella]. Leningrad: 1957, 139–61.

157. Nadezhda Sheremet'yeva gives the location as *Dom raboch-krestiyanskiy armii* [House of the worker-peasant army] but Vladimir Muzalevskiy gives the title as *Dom krasnoy armii* [House of the Red Army]. See Nadezhda Sheremet'yeva, *M. G. Klimov. Dirizhër Leningradskiy akademicheskoy kapellï* [M. G. Klimov. Director of the Leningrad academic capella], Leningrad: Muzïka, 1983, 19, and Muzalevskiy, *Mikhail Georgevich Klimov*, 14.

158. The concert was reviewed in *Izvestiya*, 21 February 1918. See Sheremet'yeva, *M. G. Klimov*, 20–1.

159. They performed many other smaller sacred works, including sacred songs and motets by Lassus, Palestrina and Bach, in addition to early Russian liturgical music (from the fourteenth century onwards). After 1932, when the proletarian organizations that campaigned against religious music were dissolved, the capella again performed Russian liturgical music for a brief period until around 1935–6.

160. See Bronfin, *Muzïkal'naya kul'tura Petrograda*, 48. Mozart's Requiem was performed twenty-three times by the capella between 1922 and 1924; see Sheremet'yeva, *M. G. Klimov*, 86.

161. The programme is preserved in the Glinka Museum, in the personal papers of the Moscow Conservatoire professor Mikhail Ippolitov-Ivanov. See GTsMMK fund 2

(Ippolitov-Ivanov), file 5784. It seems that Klimov's usual practice in the 1930s was to perform the Passions in Russian; the anniversary concert of the St John Passion in May 1935 was sung to a new translation, but I have not been able to verify whether the 1923 St Matthew Passion was sung in German or Russian. Given the impact it apparently had on audiences, it was probably sung in Russian.

162. A. Anisimov, *Repertuar akademicheskoy kapellï* [Repertoire of the academic capella], Moscow: Muzgiz, 1958, 46.

163. Sheremet'yeva, *M. G. Klimov*, 32. Glavprofobr and Glavnauka were created in January 1922 as discussions about Glavrepertkom's charter and location in Narkompros were still ongoing. They were the interim censorship organs before Glavrepertkom took on the responsibility of inspecting repertoire plans.

164. Sheremet'yeva, *M. G. Klimov*, 32.

165. Ibid., 32–8 and 70.

166. Quoted in ibid., 79.

167. Ibid.

168. See Nelson, *Music for the Revolution*, 152 and 125–54 for a very useful concise summary of Narkompros's activities at this time. Nelson is wrong, however, in asserting that the capella only sang Rakhmaninov's *All-Night Vigil* once; they performed it almost annually until 1928.

169. See Sheremet'yeva, *M. G. Klimov*, 37.

170. *Zhizn' iskusstva* [Life of Art], 45 (1925). Cited in Muzalevskiy, *Mikhail Georgievich Klimov*, 21.

171. Cited in ibid., 46.

172. See RGALI fund 645 (Glaviskusstvo and Narkompros) inventory 1, file 524, 55. The document is signed by the secretary of Glavrepertkom, Sokolov.

173. The director of the Respublika choir and Aleksandr Sveshnikov's pupil, Aleksandr Yurlov, first discovered this repertoire in the 1950s. See Ushkarov, Veprintsev and Buneyeva in Irina Marisova, ed., *Aleksandr Yurlov*, Moscow: Sovetskiy kompozitor, 1983, 65 and 103–8. All remember the upsurge in interest in Russian choral music of the sixteenth and seventeenth centuries and how Yurlov was a passionate advocate of this repertoire very early on. Sveshnikov finally recorded Rakhmaninov's *All-Night Vigil* with Melodiya in 1965.

174. See RGALI fund 645 inventory 1 file 524, 71. Leningrad Philharmonia records show that the Verdi Requiem was the work the capella and Philharmonia opted to retain.

175. Ibid., 55.

176. Ibid., 25.

Chapter 2: Cultural Revolution, Repertoire Politics and the Classics

1. For a detailed discussion of scholarship relating to this term and its uses, see Michael David-Fox, 'What is Cultural Revolution?' *Russian Review*, vol. 58, no. 2, 1999, 181–201.

2. Katerina Clark and Evgeny Dobrenko, *Soviet Culture and Power: A History in Documents*, New Haven and London: Yale University Press, 2007, 50.

3. At the All-Union conference on amateur art music in Moscow 1930, delegates passed a resolution to lobby GOMETs and other organizations for a ban on Utësov's music. RGALI, f. 645 op. 1 ed. khr. 344, l. 16.

4. For a good summary of the founding of ASM and its initial activities, see Boris Schwarz, *Music and Musical Life in Soviet Russia, 1917–1981*, enlarged edn, Bloomington, IN: Indiana University Press, 1983, 49–54.

5. Marina Frolova-Walker, and Jonathan Walker, *Music and Soviet Power 1917–1932*, Woodbridge: Boydell Press, 2012, 204.

6. Yekaterina Vlasova, *1948 god v Sovetskoy muzïke* [The Year 1948 in Soviet Music], Moscow: Klassika XXI, 2010.

7. Lev Lebedinskiy, 'O zhivïkh muzeyakh' [On living museums], *Za proletarskuyu muzïku*, 1931, no. 6, 8–9.
8. Ibid., 9.
9. RGALI f. 645 op. 1, ed. khr. l. 339.
10. RGALI f. 645, op. 1, ed. khr. 126, l. 52.
11. RGALI f. 645, op. 1, ed. khr. 336, l. 18.
12. Robert Pel'she had been Chair of Glavrepertkom from 1925 to 1926 and edited the arts paper *Sovetskoe iskusstvo*.
13. RGALI f. 645, op. 1, ed. khr. 336, ll. 152–4.
14. RGALI f. 645, op. 1, ed. khr. 336, l. 61. Lunacharskiy handed in his resignation from Narkompros two months after the conference.
15. RGALI f. 645, op. 1, ed. khr. 344, l. 12.
16. RGALI, f. 645, op. 1, ed. khr. 344, l. 138v.
17. Régis Debray, 'Socialism: A Life-Cycle', *New Left Review*, 46, July–August 2007, 13.
18. TsGALI f. 279 op. 1 d. 46, l. 3.
19. Paul Bekker, *Die Sinfonie von Beethoven bis Mahler* (1918), trans. into Russian by Roman Gruber as *Simfoniya do Betkhoven do Malera*, Leningrad: Triton, 1926; Igor Glebov, *Russkaya muzïka ot nachala XIX stoletiya* [Russian Music from the beginning of the nineteenth century], Leningrad and Moscow: Muzgiz, 1930; Lev Lebedinskiy, *O proletarskoy massovoy pesne* [On proletarian mass song], Moscow: Glaviskusstvo, 1929; Semën Korev, *Muzïka i sovremennost'* [Music and the contemporary age], Moscow: Muzgiz, 1928.
20. RGALI, f. 645 op. 1, ed. khr. 333, ll. 3–4.
21. RGALI f. 645 op. 1, ed. khr. 333, l. 21.
22. Ibid., l. 67.
23. Ibid., l. 38.
24. Partnering works were Polovinkin's Symphony No. 1 (1929) and his overture 'The First of May' (1930). The concert was conducted by the Russian Mark Shneyderman.
25. Ibid., l. 11.
26. See Chapter One, note 136.
27. Strictly speaking, Berg's songs should not be included in the table, but Berg was such an important figure to those championing European modernism that I felt not listing them would mean an important musical event was bypassed.
28. See Chapter One, n. 138.
29. Probably Kammermusik No. 7.
30. Frolova-Walker and Walker, *Music and Soviet Power*, 284.
31. Ibid., 292–3.
32. RGALI, f. 645 op. 1, ed. khr. 344, ll. 21–2.
33. See for example Viktor Vinogradov, *Protiv tserkovshchinï v muzïke* [Against the church in music], Moscow: State Music Publishers, 1931, and G. Anisimov, 'Na bor'ba s tserko-vshchinoy v muzïke' [On the struggle with the church's influence in music], *Za proletar-skuyu muzïku*, 1932, no. 6, 6–9, where the writer indignantly quotes from the 1927 plenum of the All-Union Society of Evangelical Christians, who reported seven Evangelical choirs in Leningrad. Religion, along with the so-called 'kulaks' (rich peasants) was a target of the Cultural Revolution, which extended the attacks upon priests and worshippers that Lenin had initiated, but informal small-scale meetings of worshippers were never fully stamped out. The toleration of this Soviet 'Christian Union' typified the more liberal years of the New Economic Policy (approximately 1921–8).
34. RGALI f. 645 (Glavisskustvo), op. 1, ed. khr. 121, ll. 87–8.
35. 'Muzrabotnik', 'Za sotsialisticheskoe nastuplenie v muzïke' [Towards a socialist offensive in Music], *Rabochiy i teatr*, 2 June 1929, 8.
36. Works in this category range from Glinka's 'Lullaby' to songs by the RAPM composers Davidenko and Koval'.
37. This programme consisted of the following works: Vasiliev-Buglay, 'The priest-worker lives by swindling', 'The Harvest'; Beliy, 'Godless Work'; Krasev, 'Glorious marvel';

Krosov, 'Time to die'; Korchmarëv, 'An invisible thread', 'About the Deacon'; Pototskiy, 'Conversation of Two Bells'; Linyeva, 'A happy wake'; Sokolov, 'They Say There are Stars in the Sky'. Russian National Library, manuscript department. Fond 1127 (Klimov), ed. khr. 26, work plan 1931–2.

38. See Russian National Library, manuscript department. Fond 1127 (Klimov), op. 26.
39. RGALI f. 645 op. 1 ed. khr. 505, l. 73.
40. RGALI f. 645 op. 1 ed. khr. 505, l. 53.
41. RGALI f. 645 op. 1 ed. khr. 505, l. 68.
42. RGALI f. 645 op. 1 ed. khr. 505, l. 77. Korev's report is undated in the file, but was probably written in late 1930 (late November or December), because he refers to the investigation into the societies as being in the autumn of this year (i.e. 1930).
43. Ibid., l. 94v. Narkomvnudel is the NKVD.
44. RGALI, f. 645, op. 1, ed. khr. 457, l. 203.
45. Ibid., l. 206.
46. Ibid., ll. 202–3.
47. Vlasova, *1948 god*, 101.
48. RGALI f. 645 op. 1 ed. khr. 505, l. 81.
49. Ibid.
50. RGALI f. 645 op. 1 ed. khr. 505, l. 69.
51. Anon, 'Ozdorovit' muzïkal'nuyu obshchestvennost'' [Making music societies healthier], *Rabochiy i teatr*, 12 March 1930, 11.
52. Shostakovich, speech at Vseroskomdram meeting, 18 December 1931. RGALI f. 2954 op. 1 ed. khr. 176, l. 111. Davidenko's opera was a one-act work staged in 1931.
53. The letter is discussed, and partially quoted, in Frolova-Walker and Walker, *Music and Soviet Power*, 315–16.
54. Anon., 'Protiv gnilogo liberalisma na muzïkal'nom fronte' [Against rotten liberalism on the musical front], *Rabochiy i teatr*, 1932, no. 4, 3.
55. Vladimir Iokhel'son, 'Muzïkal'niy front i reshenie partii' [The Musical Front and the Party's Decision], *Rabochiy i teatr*, 1932, no. 16, n. p.

Chapter 3: Internationalism, Modernism and the 'Stalinist Enlightenment', 1932–1941

1. For a clear account of how Chelyapov's fall and subsequent arrest and execution was engineered by Kerzhentsev's committee, see Simo Mikkonen, '"Muddle Instead of Music" in 1936', in Pauline Fairclough, ed., *Shostakovich Studies 2*, Cambridge: Cambridge University Press, 2010, 231–48. Note especially that Kerzhentsev – with astonishing hypocrisy – accused Chelyapov of sheltering former RAPMovtsï within the Composers' Union. Mikkonen rightly surmises that this was a convenient rather than honest charge: a flurry of public criticism against former RAPMovtsï did take place at this time but they were not, in fact, the real targets. Kerzhentsev's aim was simply to blame Chelyapov for alleged 'failings', probably in a bid to cement his own authority, and that of his new Committee, at a tense time following the public criticism of Shostakovich's opera *Lady Macbeth*.
2. See anon., 'Sumbur vmesto muzïki: ob opere Ledi Makbet Mtsenskogo uyezda' [Muddle instead of music: on the opera 'Lady Macbeth of Mtsensk], *Pravda*, 28 January 1936, 3, and 'Baletnaya fal'sh' [Balletic falseness], *Pravda*, 6 February 1936, 3. Leonid Maksimenkov initially suggested that the author of both articles was Platon Kerzhentsev (see Leonid Maksimenkov, *Sumbur vmesto muzïki: stalinskaya kul'turnaya revoliutsiya, 1936–1938* [Muddle instead of music: the Stalinist cultural revolution 1936–1938], Moscow: Yuridicheskaya kniga, 1997, 88–112) but a later publication has demonstrated that the author was the *Pravda* staff writer David Zaslavskiy. See Yevgeniy Yefimov, *Sumbur vokrug 'sumbura' i odnogo'malen'kogo zhurnalista'* [Muddle around a 'muddle' and one 'minor journalist'], Moscow: 'Flinta', 2006.
3. For the best available account of how Bukharin was slowly hunted down by Stalin in a process of demoralization that actually began as early as 1933, see Roy Medvedev's

chapter 'The Murder of Bukharin' in Zhores A. Medvedev and Roy A. Medvedev, *The Unknown Stalin*, trans. Ellen Dahrendorf, London: I. B. Tauris, 2006, 265–96.

4. VOKS (Vsesoiuznoe obshchestvo kul'turnoy svyazi s zagranitsey) was formed in 1925 specifically for the purpose of fostering friendly cultural relations with non-Soviet countries, effectively as the 'soft power' arm of the Comintern (Communist International, which existed from 1919 to 1943), which had directly political aims, including the overall control of international communist parties.

5. Katerina Clark, *Moscow: The Fourth Rome. Stalinism, Cosmopolitanism and the Evolution of Soviet Culture, 1931–1941*, Cambridge, MA: Harvard University Press, 2011, 10–11.

6. There was a series of decrees from 1926 to 1929 inhibiting contact with foreigners and admission of foreign artists to the USSR. In 1926 Soviet citizens returning from higher education abroad had to pass tests on Soviet society; in 1927 a decree ordered 'a strict cutback in foreign trips'; in 1928 a commission was set up to scrutinize hiring of foreign art-workers in the USSR and in 1929 it was decreed that those sent on foreign trips must not alter the route of their journeys. See Matthew Cullerne Bown, *Art Under Stalin*, New York: Holmes and Meier, 1991, 61.

7. David L. Hoffmann, *Cultivating the Masses: Modern State Practices and Soviet Socialism, 1914–1939*, Ithaca and London: Cornell University Press, 2011, 279, and Nicolas Werth, 'The Mechanism of a Mass Crime: The Great Terror in the Soviet Union 1937–1938', in Robert Gellately and Ben Kiernan, eds, *The Specter of Genocide: Mass Murder in Historical Perspective*, New York: Cambridge University Press, 2003, 219.

8. For a good English-language account of this, see Alexander Werth, *Musical Uproar in Moscow*, London: Turnstile Press, 1949.

9. Pavel Veys, 'O zhurnale "Proletarskiy muzïkant"' [On the journal 'Proletarian musician'], *Sovetskaya muzïka*, 1933, no. 1, 133.

10. Lev Kaltat and David Rabinovich, 'V boyakh za nasledstva' [Fighting for a heritage], *Sovetskaya muzïka*, 1933, no. 3, 7–40.

11. Ibid., 12.

12. See especially the meteoric success of the popular songwriter Isaak Dunayevskiy in the mid-1930s (especially in his soundtracks for Grigoriy Aleksandrov's films *Vesëliye rebyata* and *Tsirk*) and the revival of Leonid Utësov's jazz career. From being hounded by RAPM in 1930, after 1932 Utësov became one of the most successful entertainers of his day.

13. See Sheila Fitzpatrick, 'The Lady Macbeth Affair', in Fitzpatrick, *The Cultural Front: Power and Culture in Revolutionary Russia*, Ithaca and London: Cornell University Press, 1992, 202–3.

14. For the best available account of this process, see Simo Mikkonen, *Music and Power in the Soviet 1930s: A History of Composers' Bureaucracy*, Lewiston, Queenston and Lampeter: The Edwin Mellen Press, 2009, 321–68.

15. Clark, *Moscow: The Fourth Rome*, 22–3.

16. The best English-language account of this can be found in Ludmila Stern, *Western Intellectuals and the Soviet Union, 1920–40: From Red Square to the Left Bank*, London and New York: Routledge, 2007.

17. Nailya Safiullina, 'The Canonization of Western Writers in the Soviet Union in the 1930s', *The Modern Language Review*, vol. 107, no. 2, April 2012, 559–84.

18. Andre Gide, *Return from the USSR*, New York: Alfred A. Knopf, 1937; translation of *Retour de l'URSS*, 1936. Available from Internet Archive: https://archive.org/details/returnfromtheuss010214mbp, accessed 03/03/2014.

19. Safiullina, 'The Canonization of Western Writers', 573.

20. For discussion of many of these events, see Clark, *Moscow: The Fourth Rome*, especially chapters 4 and 5.

21. Valerian Bogdanov-Berezovskiy, review, *Rabochiy i teatr*, 1934, no. 6, 10–11.

22. Boris Schwarz, *Music and Musical Life in Soviet Russia, 1917–1981*, enlarged edn, Bloomington, IN: Indiana University Press, 1983, 134. Cowell had visited the Soviet Union in 1929; for this, and details of his later correspondence with Grigoriy Shneyerson,

see Elena Dubinets, 'Pervootkrïvatel' novoy muzïki' [The Groundbreaker of new music], *Muzïkal'naya akademiya*, no. 3, 2003, 196–205 and 'Henry Cowell and Russia: Connections and Influences', unpublished ms. I am grateful to Elena Dubinets for allowing me to see this article.

23. Ivan Sollertinskiy, *Rabochiy i teatr*, 1935, no. 7, 13–14. The capella went through a bad patch between around 1935–38, because its director Mikhail Klimov was seriously ill (he stopped conducting in 1935 and died the following year). In the late 1930s, when it began reviving Handel oratorios and Bach's *Magnificat*, it was being conducted by Aleksandr Sveshnikov.

24. For details, see Caroline Brooke, 'The Development of Soviet Music Policy 1932–1941', PhD diss., University of Cambridge, 1998, 147–8.

25. For a good account of musical life under Mussolini, see Alexandra Wilson, *The Puccini Problem*, Cambridge: Cambridge University Press, 2007. For accounts of musical life in Nazi Germany, see: Erik Levi, *Music in the Third Reich*, London: Palgrave MacMillan, 1996; Michael Haas, *Forbidden Music: the Jewish Composers Banned by the Nazis*, New York and London: Yale University Press, 2013; Nikolaus Bacht, ed., *Music, Theatre and Politics in Germany. 1848 to the Third Reich*, Farnham: Ashgate, 2006; and Michael Kater, *Composers of the Nazi Era. Eight Portraits*, New York: Oxford University Press, 2002.

26. Note that Fritz Stiedry was appointed Chief Conductor of the Leningrad Philharmonia in 1933, so strictly speaking is no longer a 'visitor'.

27. Untypically, programme data for this season is for the most part not contained in dated programmes, but only in a repertoire list. Therefore it is not possible to see (with a few exceptions) what repertoire was performed when in the season, or what was not played after January 1936. It is conceivable that Berg, Milhaud and Honegger were scheduled and then dropped, but I have not been able to establish this.

28. Data for the 1932–3 season is missing entirely.

29. Note, though, that Oskar Fried and Kurt Sanderling were both appointed to permanent positions in the Soviet Union. Sanderling moved from the Moscow Radio Orchestra to the Leningrad Philharmonia in 1936, while Fried worked at both the Tblisi Opera and at the Moscow Radio Orchestra.

30. It is highly likely that all these conductors also worked in Leningrad that season. The same works the other way around for years when the Moscow records are incomplete: the presence of just a few names in the Moscow programmes in years like 1934–5 does not mean that those working in Leningrad avoided the Soviet capital. Usually, it is safe to assume that visiting musicians and conductors worked in both cities.

31. RGALI f. 962, op. 3, ed. khr. 68, l. 10.

32. Ibid.

33. RGALI f. 962 op. 10 ed. khr. 15. 1936. l. 98 'Secret' To N. Yezhov and A. Andreyev from Kerzhentsev, 2/7/36.

34. Clark, *Moscow: The Fourth Rome*, 25.

35. See Pauline Fairclough, 'Don't Sing it on a Feast Day: The Reception and Performance of Western Sacred Music in Soviet Russia, 1917–53', *Journal of the American Musicological Society*, vol. 65/1, 2012, 71–116. The Requiem had been performed first by Klimov in the Leningrad Philharmonia's 1928– 9 season, and this seems to have been its Soviet premiere.

36. Yevgeniy Braudo, *Sovetskoe iskusstvo*, 17 April 1935, 4.

37. 'Musician', *Sovetskoe iskusstvo*, 23 December 1935, 3.

38. Anon., programme note for Verdi's Requiem, Leningrad: Leningrad Philharmonia, 1937, 5.

39. Ivan Sollertinskiy, 'Iuda Makkabey' [Judas Maccabeus], *Leningradskaya pravda*, 22 April 1939, 3.

40. Sollertinskiy, programme note to *Judas Maccabeus*, 8 February 1939, 15, Russian National Library, f. 451, d. 849.

41. Sollertinskiy, 'Georg Gendel'. 250 let dniya rozhdeniya' [George Handel. 250 years since his birth], *Izvestiya*, 27 February 1935, 2.

42. Roman Gruber, *Gendel'* [Handel], Leningrad: Izdanie nauchno-issledovatel'skogo institute iskusstvoznaniya [Institute of Arts History], 1935, 107–8.

43. See Erik Levi, *Mozart and the Nazis: How the Third Reich Abused a Cultural Icon*, New Haven and London: Yale University Press, 2011, and Pamela Potter, 'The Politicization of Handel and His Oratorios in the Weimar Republic, the Third Reich, and the Early Years of the German Democratic Republic', *The Musical Quarterly*, vol. 85/2, 2001, 311–41.

44. Viktor Gorodinskiy, *Sovetskoe iskusstvo*, 11 April 1935, 4.

45. Sollertinskiy, 'Iogann Sebastian Bakh. K 250-letiu co dniya rozhdeniya' [Johann Sebastian Bach. On the 250th anniversary of his birth], *Izvestiya*, 21 March 1935, 2.

46. Tamara Livanova, *Muzïkal'naya klassika XVIII veka* [Musical classicism of the 18th century], Leningrad: Muzgiz, 1939, 107.

47. Ibid.

48. Ivan Martïnov, I. S. Bakh 'Magnifikat' [J. S. Bach's 'Magnificat'], Moscow: Moscow State Philharmonia, 1935, 3.

49. Georgiy Khubov, *I. S. Bakh. Opït kharakteristiki* [J. S. Bach. Characteristics of his style], Moscow: Muzgiz, 1937, 151–2. The word *meshchanin* simply denotes a member of the petit-bourgeoisie, but Khubov's implication goes further to denote a person who is well-off, politically passive, socially complacent and not a member of the intelligentsia.

50. Georgiy Khubov, programme note for St Matthew Passion and B Minor Mass, Leningrad: Leningrad Philharmonia, 1935, 10.

51. Ibid., 22.

52. Ibid., 30.

53. V. N. Bakheyeva and A. N. Kotlyaredskiy, *Magnifikat I. S. Bakha* [J. S. Bach's Magnificat], Leningrad: Leningrad Philharmonia, 1939, 14.

54. The Leningrad Philharmonia had programmed the St Matthew Passion for the 1940–1 season as the opening work of their first subscription series. Their records for that year begin only in November, but it seems likely that the performance went ahead, making that concert the last hearing of the St Matthew Passion until well into the post-Stalin period. The St John Passion was performed in Leningrad under Kurt Sanderling in the 1954–5 season, which was the first time it had been performed there since 1935.

55. For a detailed discussion of the fate of sacred music in this period, see Fairclough, 'Don't Sing it on a Feast Day'.

56. Semën Ginzburg, *Muzïka v muzee* [Music in the museum], Leningrad: State Hermitage, 1934, 22.

57. Ibid., 7–8.

58. The Hermitage's collection of historic instruments was partly photographed and listed in Ginzburg, *Muzïk v muzee*. It included a three-keyboard clavecin, a clavichord, a 'Giraffe' fortepiano, a double-ended Pleyel grand piano (for duet playing), a viola da gamba and cello, a viola d'amore, a Stradivarius violin and pochetti violins, a lute, lyre-guitar, flutes, recorders of all sizes, bagpipes, serpent and organ.

59. Semën Ginzburg, *Sluzhanka-gospozha* [La Serva Padrona], Leningrad: State Hermitage, 1933, 11.

60. Boris Shteynpress, 'Ob instrumental'nom tvorchestve Motsarta [On Mozart's instrumental music], *Sovetskaya muzïka*, 1935, no. 6, 58.

61. Ibid., 44–5.

62. Ivan Sollertinskiy, *Volshebnaya fleyta Motsarta* [Mozart's Magic Flute], Leningrad: Leningrad Philharmonia, 1938, 11–13.

63. Ibid., 32.

64. Ibid., 17.

65. Ibid., 32.

66. Yuliy Kremlëv, *Volfgang Motsart. Kratkiy ocherk zhizni i tvorchestva* [Wolfgang Mozart. A short study of his life and work]. Leningrad: Triton, 1935, 38.

67. Aleksandr Shaverdyan, *Simfonii Betkhovena* [Beethoven's symphonies], Moscow: Moscow Philharmonia, 1936, 26.

68. Ibid., 26–7.
69. Ibid., 26.
70. Igor Glebov, 'Petrogradskie Kuranti' [Petrograd chimes], *K novïm beregam*, 1923, no. 3, 42.
71. Sollertinskiy, 'O puti Rikharda Vagnera' [On the path of Richard Wagner], *Rabochiy i teatr*, 1933, nos 4–5, 4.
72. Ibid.
73. Ibid.
74. This is, of course, rather problematic when Wagner never gave a specific anti-capitalist interpretation of the *Ring*. However, Soviet writers would have drawn on remarks in his writings and letters to make their case for such a reading; a particularly useful one was his letter to Liszt of October 1854, in which Wagner writes that the world was 'fundamentally evil . . . it belongs to *Alberich*: no one else!' Cited in Bryan Magee, *Wagner and Philosophy*, London: Allen Lane, The Penguin Press, 2000, 40.
75. Dmitriy Gachev, 'Vagner i Feyerbakh' [Wagner and Feuerbach], *Sovetskaya muzïka*, 1934, no. 7, 61–2.
76. D. Baksan, 'Nasledstvo Vagnera' [Wagner's legacy], *Izvestiya*, 18 September 1937, 3.
77. Vladimir Iokhel'son, 'Tvorcheskaya diskussiya v Leningrade' [The creative discussion in Leningrad], *Sovetskaya muzïka*, 1936, no. 4, 13.
78. Genrikh Neygauz, 'O prostote v iskusstve' [On simplicity in music], *Sovetskoe iskusstvo*, 17 February 1936, 1. This article was published eleven days after the second of *Pravda*'s critical articles concerning Shostakovich's music.
79. Popov's ambitious First Symphony was completed in 1932 and premiered in March 1935. It was immediately banned for apparently 'reflecting the ideology of hostile classes'; though Sollertinskiy and others fought successfully to overturn the ban, it was never performed again in Popov's lifetime. See Zarui Apetyan, *Gavriil Popov. Iz literaturnogo naslediya: stranitsï biografii* [Gavriil Popov. Pages of a biography from his literary legacy], Moscow: Sovetskiy kompozitor, 1986, 260–1.
80. Anon., '*Klassicheskaya muzïka v strane sovetov*' [Classical Music in the Land of the Soviets], *Sovetskoe iskusstvo*, 5 February 1936, 1. The speed with which this article appeared after Shostakovich was publicly criticized, and the fact that it is anonymous raises suspicions that the author was either involved in behind-the-scenes discussions with the Committee for Arts Affairs, or directly commissioned to write the article by someone in that organization.
81. Konstantin Kuznetsov, 'Etiudï o Gluk' [Studies on Gluck], *Sovetskaya muzïka*, 1937, no. 12, 94–100.
82. Aleksandr Shaverdyan, 'Mozart's Requiem' [*Rekviem Motsarta*], *Sovetskoe iskusstvo*, 25 June 1939, 4.
83. For example, 1938 marked the thirtieth anniversary of Rimskiy-Korsakov's death, and 1944 the centenary of his birth.

Chapter 4: Turning Inwards: The Rise of Russian Nationalism, 1937–1941

1. David Brandenberger, *National Bolshevism: Stalinist Mass Culture and the Formation of Modern Russian National Identity, 1931–1956*, Cambridge, MA: Harvard University Press, 2002, 8–9.
2. Cited in ibid., 95.
3. I have not been able to track down Lazarenko's, Smirnov's and Nikolayev's first names, probably because they did not play a sufficiently distinguished role in Soviet culture to have been included in any dictionary or encyclopaedia. Lazarenko's initials are given as M. L. in L. G. Grigor'yev and Ya. M. Platek, *Moskovskaya Gosudarstvennaya Filarmoniya* [Moscow State Philharmonia], Moscow: Sovetskiy kompozitor, 1973, 118, but I have not been able to identify his full name.
4. Tukhachevskiy was implicated in an alleged plot to assassinate Stalin and was shot in June 1937. See Caroline Brooke, 'The Development of Soviet Music Policy 1932–1941', PhD diss., University of Cambridge, 1998, 185.

5. For Kerzhentsev's angry reply to Molotov, defending himself against the trio's accusations, see RGALI f. 962 op. 10 ed. khr. 24, l. 161. A copy of this letter is available on the Russian Radio Liberty website: http://www.svoboda.org/content/transcript/24199717.html, accessed 20/05/2014.

6. By the end of the purges, Stalin was the only remaining 'Old Bolshevik' associate of Lenin's in the Central Committee.

7. For Kulyabko's statement, referring both to his own rehabilitation and to Tukhachevskiy's, see http://www.e-reading.co.uk/chapter.php/96194/5/Marshal_Tuhachevskiii.html. Accessed 02/02/2014.

8. See RGALI f. 962 op. 3 ed. khr. 434. Stenographic report of May 1938 Philharmonia meetings. Moisey Grinberg denounced Lazarenko as 'a person of corrupted morals and vulgar attitudes' with 'a hostile attitude to the Philharmonia'.

9. Anon., 'Filarmonicheskie dela' [Philharmonia affairs], Sovetskoe iskusstvo, 25 January 1938, 4.

10. Ya. Chernov, 'V Vetoshnom pereulke' [In Vetoshniy lane], Sovetskoe iskusstvo, 18 February 1938, 4.

11. This is according to Grigor'yev and Platek, Moskovskaya Gosudarstvennaya Filarmoniya, 118.

12. The online encyclopaedia 'Slovari' (http://slovari.yandex.ru) claims that Chulaki was the Philharmonia's Director between 1937 and 1939, but in fact he was dismissed as Director in January 1938 and retained only the office of Deputy Artistic Director. See TsGALI f. 962 op. 3 ed. khr. 190, l. 22.

13. I have not been able to trace this person, nor discover what happened to Renzin or his deputy in 1937–8. Both may well have been arrested, but no clear record of this survives in Philharmonia sources. Renzin went on to found the Piano Faculty at the Petrozavodsk Conservatory and occupied this position until his death in 1969. Mikhail Chulaki, however, enjoyed a successful career as a teacher at the Moscow Conservatoire and was Director of the Bolshoy Theatre from 1955 until 1970.

14. TsGALI f. 279, op. 1, d. 83, l. 107.

15. See Yuriy Veprik, 'Proshloye i nastoyashcheye' [Past and present], in Leningradskaya Gosudartsvennaya Ordena Trudovogo krasnogo znameni filarmoniya: stat'i, vospominaniya, materialï [Leningrad State Order of Red Banner of Labour Philharmonia: articles, recollections, materials], Leningrad: Muzïka, 1972, 30.

16. RGALI f. 962 op. 3 ed. khr. 190, ll. 47–50 and ed. khr. 215, 41–4.

17. RGALI f. 962 op. 3 ed. khr. 215, ll. 53–8, unattributed and undated. The document is five single-sided, A4 sides long (typescript).

18. Ibid., l. 56.

19. Ibid., l. 57.

20. Sollertinskiy, address at February 1935 conference, published in Sovetskaya muzïka, 1936, no. 6, 29.

21. David Brandenberger and Kevin M. F. Platt, Epic Revisionism. Russian History and Literature as Stalinist Propaganda, Madison, WI: University of Wisconsin Press, 2006, 11.

22. Stephanie Sandler, 'The 1937 Pushkin Jubilee as Epic Trauma', in ibid, 195.

23. Among the charges levelled at the defunct proletarian writers' group RAPP (Rossiskaya assotsiatsiya proletarskikh pisateley, or Russian Association of Proletarian Writers) between 1936 and 1938 was their use of 'vulgar sociology' as a canonization tool. This particular criticism was transferred seamlessly to the musical sphere at the same time.

24. Anatoliy Groman-Solovtsov was on the leadership of RAPM at least from May 1928. His name is often abbreviated to 'Groman' or 'Solovtsov'.

25. Moisey Grinberg, 'RAPMovskie perepevï' [RAPMovsky re-hashing], Sovetskoe iskusstvo, 11 May 1937, 3.

26. Anatoliy Groman, 'Istoriya Russkoy muzïki i RAPM' [The history of Russian music and RAPM], Sovetskoe iskusstvo, 11 May 1937, 5.

27. Grinberg, 'RAPMovskie perepevï', 3.

28. Groman, 'Istoriya Russkoy muzïki', 5.
29. See Simo Mikkonen, *Music and Power in the Soviet 1930s: A History of Composers' Bureaucracy*, Lewiston, Queenston and Lampeter: The Edwin Mellen Press, 2009, 330.
30. Arnol'd Al'shvang, 'Narodnost' v Rossiyskoy klassicheskoy muzïke' [Folk qualities in Russian classical music], *Sovetskaya muzïka*, 1938, no. 5, 5.
31. Lev Kristiansen, 'Likvidirovat' ostatki RAPMovshchini' [To finish off the remnants of the rapmovshchina], *Sovetskaya muzïka*, 1938, no. 5, 9–14.
32. See Mikkonen, *Music and Power*, 363.
33. RGALI f. 962 op. 3 ed. khr. 432, l. 25.
34. Sovnarkom = Council of People's Commissars [*Sovet narodnïkh kommissarov*].
35. RGALI f. 962 op. 3 ed. khr. 367. ll. 1719, 'To the Council of Sovnarkom, USSR, Comrade Molotov'. The letter is undated but as Khrapchenko is obviously looking ahead to the 1938–9 season, it seems likely that it dates from early 1938. However, Mikkonen, who has examined copies of similar documents in GARF, claims that Khrapchenko's two appeals were made on 15 September and 26 November respectively. Mikkonen also points out that Nazarov had been the first to appeal to Molotov to reinstate the practice of inviting foreign artists, making Khrapchenko's letter a follow-up request. Replies have not been located, but it is clear that none of these appeals was successful. See Mikkonen, *Music and Power*, p. 366, n. 1209. Caroline Brooke also refers to the RGALI copy of this letter but assumes that invitations were issued and not taken up (Brooke, 'The Development of Soviet Music Policy', 142, n. 9). However, we simply do not yet know how Molotov responded to these requests and no evidence has yet come to light to show that any of these musicians were invited.
36. RGALI f. 962 op. 10 ed. khr. 24, ll. 10–11. Caroline Brooke mentions this episode in her article 'Soviet Musicians and the Great Terror', *Europe–Asia Studies*, vol. 54, no. 3, 2002, 403–4.
37. Peter Heyworth, *Otto Klemperer: His Life and Times vol. 2: 1933–1973*, Cambridge: Cambridge University Press, 1996, 70–71.
38. All of these composers apart from Ravel were affiliated with the 'Fédération musicale populaire' (FMP), an organization with close ties to pro-Soviet intellectual circles in France during the late 1930s. Roussel was the Fédération's first president up until his death in 1937. Honegger, Barraine and Sauveplane were all involved in FMP-sponsored events celebrating the idea of 'music for the people' during this time. The FMP was also part of a broader organization grouped under the 'Maison de la Culture', an entity that included the *Association des écrivains et artistes révolutionnaires*, many of whom had ties with and/or strong sympathies to French Communist, and by extension Soviet, politics and cultural circles. I am grateful to Professor Christopher Moore for this information (personal communication, 21 August 2014). See Christopher Moore, 'Socialist Realism and the Music of the French Popular Front', *The Journal of Musicology*, 25/4, Fall 2008, 473–502.
39. Andrey Budyakovskiy, *P. I. Chaykovskiy. Simfonicheskaya muzïka* [P. I. Chaykovskiy. Symphonic music], Leningrad, Leningradskaya filarmoniya, 1935, 18.
40. Ibid.
41. Ibid., 18–19.
42. By the time this volume was published, it is possible that Pshibïshevskiy was already in the Gulag, where he was sent after Stalin's reversal of the homosexuality laws and his subsequent arrest. His Party membership was revoked in 1933 and he received a three-year sentence before being arrested again in 1937. He was shot in August that year.
43. Richard Taruskin, 'Pathetic Symphonist', in Taruskin, *On Russian Music*, Berkeley, CA: University of California Press, 2008, 83. Taruskin notes that by 1940, the year of Chaykovskiy's centenary celebrations, mentioning this fact was a punishable offence and a new edition of his correspondence published that year, containing some frank letters to Modest, was confiscated and its editors (the same team that published the von Meck letters) were sacked (Taruskin, ibid.).

44. Colonel Trepov aroused anger in Russian liberal circles after his brutal flogging of a political prisoner who refused to remove his cap in the colonel's presence.

45. P. A. Mordovin and A. E. Bakhtyarov were associates of Rimskiy-Korsakov in the 1860s. Mordovin sympathized with the Polish rebels, and this caused discord with Bakhtyarov, who held more reactionary views. Mikhail Katkov was a prominent writer in the Russian media whose hostile views towards the Polish rebellion made him extremely popular.

46. Boleslav Pshibïshevskiy, Introduction to V. A. Zhdanov and N. T. Zhegin, eds, *P. I. Chaykovskiy. Perepiska s N. F. fon-Mekk tom 1, 1876–1878* [P. I. Chaykovskiy. Correspondence with N. F. von Meck, Volume 1], Moscow and Leningrad: 'Akademiya', 1934, xii–xiii.

47. Ibid. Friedrich Hölderlin's play was written between 1798 and 1800 and, according to David Farrell Krell, is 'a meditation on the rise and fall of civilizations and historical epochs within the "ferment of time"'. See *The Death of Empedocles. A Mourning-Play*, trans. with introduction, notes and analysis by David Farrell Krell, New York: State University of New York, 2009, 170.

48. See www.marxists.org/archive/marx/works/1888/letters, accessed 20/05/2014, for the complete correspondence between Engels and Harkness. This letter was published in the Soviet Union in the collection *Literaturnoe nasledstvo* [Literary heritage], vol. 2, Moscow: 1932 and republished in the collection *Marks i Engels o literature* [Marx and Engels on literature], Moscow: 1933.

49. Pshibïshevskiy, Introduction to Zhdanov and Zhegin, *P. I. Chaykovskiy*, xiv.

50. See Leonid Maksimenkov, *Muzïka vmesto sumbura: kompozitorï i muzïkantï v strane sovetov 1917–1991* [Music instead of muddle: composers and musicians in the land of the Soviets 1917–1991], Moscow: Rossiya XX vek. Documents, 2013, 208–9. Maksimenkov notes that the decision to put up a monument to the composer (which still stands in front of the Moscow Conservatory) was taken by the Politburo on 5 May 1940 – just two days before his centenary. Along with this, there was to be a complete edition of his works (a task that is still incomplete), a gift of student stipends for composers in his name at the conservatoires in Moscow, Leningrad, Kiev and Tblisi, a Moscow street was to be named after him and a major celebration was to be held on 7 May at the Bolshoy Theatre.

51. 'Sto let, 1840–1940' [100 years, 1840–1940], in N. A. Shuvalov, ed., *P. I. Chaykovskiy na tsene teatra operï i baleta im. S. M. Kirova (b. Mariinskiy)* [P. I. Chaykovskiy on the stage of the Kirov Theatre of Opera and Ballet (formerly the Mariinskiy)], Leningrad: Izdatel'stvo Leningradskogo gos. Ordna Lenina Akademicheskogo teatra operï i baleta im. S. M. Kirov, 1941, 9–12.

52. This ran counter to earlier Soviet ideology, which was hostile to nationalism as an essentially bourgeois political force. But from the late 1930s, this began to change: as Gerhard Simon has noted, 'Before World War II, Russian nationalism was used only to a limited extent to substantiate Soviet patriotism. Nevertheless, all-Soviet chauvinism grew to phenomenal dimensions even then.... On March 13 1938 the Central Committee and the Council for People's Commissars resolved to introduce compulsory Russian classes in all non-Russian schools in the Union Republics and Autonomous Republics.' Gerhard Simon, trans. Karen Forster and Oswald Forster, *Nationalism and Policy Toward the Nationalities in the Soviet Union. From Totalitarian Dictatorship to Post-Stalinist Society*, Westview Special Studies on the Soviet Union and Eastern Europe, Oxford: 1991, 150–52.

53. Boris Asaf'yev, *Pamyati Pëtra Il'icha Chaykovskogo 1840–1940* [In memory of Pëtr Il'ich Chaykovskiy], Leningrad and Moscow: Muzgiz, 1940, 24–5.

54. Valerian Bogdanov-Berezovskiy, *Opernoe i baletnoe tvorchestvo Chaykovskogo* [Chaykovskiy's operas and ballets], Leningrad and Moscow: Iskusstvo, 1940, 6–9.

55. *N. A. Rimskiy-Korsakov i ego vremena. Kratkiy putevoditel' po vïstavke v russkom muzee* [N. A. Rimskiy-Korsakov and his epoch. A short tour around the exhibition in the Russian museum], Leningrad: Komitet po chestvovaniyu pamyati N. A. Rimskogo-Korsakova, 1933, 4.

56. Ibid., 11.
57. Viktor Tsukkerman, 'Rimskiy-Korsakov i narodnaya pesnya' [Rimskiy-Korsakov and folk song], *Sovetskaya muzïka*, 1938, nos 10–11, 127.
58. The premiere date was 21 February 1939, with a libretto advertised as having been reworked by the Soviet poet and writer Sergey Gorodetskiy, Boris Mordvinov (the stage director of the production) and Samuil Samosud (the conductor). Mikhail Bulgakov's involvement in the libretto revision was not mentioned, but, as will be seen, he was closely involved with it.
59. Georgiy Khubov, 'Ivan Susanin', *Sovetskaya muzïka*, 1939, no. 2, 34.
60. Khubov does not enlarge on this comment, but he may have had in mind Mathilde Lüdendorff's 1936 book *Mozarts Leben und gewaltsamer Tod* [Mozart's life and violent death] which laid the blame for the composer's death at the door of a conspiracy between the Jews, the Jesuits and the Freemasons. See Erik Levi, *Mozart and the Nazis: How the Third Reich Abused a Cultural Icon*, New Haven and London: Yale University Press, 2011, 35–9. In fact, as Levi demonstrates, Hitler personally refused to sanction revising the libretto to *The Magic Flute*, merely indicating that Masonic symbols should be removed from productions, so it is far from clear what Khubov is referring to here.
61. The idea of Stalin's involvement was mooted by the Norwegian musicologist Jon-Roar Bjørkvold in 1983. See Marina Raku, *Muzïkal'naya klassika v mifotvorchestve sovetskoy epokhi* [Musical classicism in the mythology of the Soviet epoch], Moscow: Novoe literaturnoe obozrenie, 2014, 486. For discussion of Gorodetskiy's 1937 article discussing the forthcoming production in *Sovetskoe iskusstvo*, see ibid.
62. See ibid., 503. *Dnevnik Yeleni Bulgakovoy* [Yelena Bulgakova's diary] can be accessed online: www.imwerden.info/belousenko/books/memoirs/Bulgakova_Dnevnik.htm, accessed 30/08/2014. I thank Marina Frolova-Walker for alerting me to this link.
63. Yelena Bulgakova, *Dnevnik Yeleni Bulgakovoy*, 373. Raku provides a detailed account of the opera's revival in 1939: see *Muzïkal'naya klassika*, 507–23. See also Albrecht Gaub, 'Mikhail Glinka as Preached and Practiced in the Soviet Union Before and After 1937', *Journal of Musicological Research*, 22, 2003, 101–34, and Marina Frolova-Walker, 'The Soviet opera project: Ivan Dzerzhinsky vs. *Ivan Susanin*', *Cambridge Opera Journal*, vol. 18/2, 2006, 181–216. Frolova-Walker gives a superb account of *Ivan Susanin's* revival based on archival records including Sergey Gorodetskiy's file in RGALI, noting crucial changes in the plot, chronology and even location.
64. The production premiere was on 25 November 1939. The opera had previously been staged in 1928 at the Bolshoy. The opera was performed on both occasions in Rimskiy-Korsakov's edition: a revised version was commissioned by the conductor Boris Khaykin in the 1950s, who asked Shostakovich to re-orchestrate the opera and add parts that Rimskiy-Korsakov had removed, but which were now published in Pavel Lamm's edition. See Laurel Fay, *Shostakovich: A Life*, New York: Oxford University Press, 2000, 210.
65. Georgiy Khubov, 'K novïm beregam' [Towards new shores], *Sovetskaya muzïka*, 1939, no. 4, 21.
66. Ibid., 25.
67. Emilya Frid, *Modest Petrovich Musorgskiy*, Leningrad: Leningrad Philharmonia, 1939, 39.
68. *Partiinost'*, or party-mindedness, the third ingredient as defined at the Writers' Congress in 1934, was, of course, impossible to apply to artists of the past.
69. Tsetsiliya Ratskaya, *M. P. Musorgskiy. K stoletiyu so dnya rozhdeniya (1839–1939)* [M. P. Musorgskiy. On the centenary of his birth], Moscow and Leningrad: Muzgiz, 1939, 3–4.

Chapter 5: From the Great Patriotic War to the Zhdanovshchina, 1941–1953

1. Leningrad Philharmonia archive, folder 1940–1.
2. For details, see Rosamund Bartlett, *Wagner and Russia*, Cambridge: Cambridge University Press, 1995, 271–82.
3. Works performed were: his Chamber Symphony (1916), Five Songs (1923) and the Introduction to *Die Gezeichneten* [The marked ones].

4. Andrey Kryukov, *Muzïka v efire voennogo Leningrada* [Music broadcasts in wartime Leningrad], St Petersburg: Kompozitor, 2005; *Muzïka v dni blokadï* [Music in the days of the blockade], St Petersburg: Kompozitor, 2002.
5. Kryukov, *Muzïka v efire*, 88–9.
6. Ibid., 94–5.
7. See Laurel Fay, *Shostakovich: A Life*, New York: Oxford University Press, 2000, 133.
8. See Isaak Glikman, trans. Anthony Phillips, *Story of a Friendship. The Letters of Dmitry Shostakovich to Isaak Glikman*, London: Faber and Faber, 2001, 8. Also see the diary of Kseniya Matus, a musician in the Radio Committee orchestra before and during the blockade, reproduced in Kryukov, *Muzïka v efire*, 342–50.
9. For comprehensive listings of music played in blockaded Leningrad, see Kryukov, *Muzïka v dni blokadï*.
10. See for example, Christopher Gibbs, 'The Phenomenon of the Seventh', in Laurel Fay, ed., *Shostakovich and his World*, Princeton, NJ: Princeton University Press, 2004, 59–105 and Pauline Fairclough, 'The "Old Shostakovich": Reception in the British Press', *Music and Letters*, vol. 88/2, 2012, 266–96.
11. See Pauline Fairclough, 'From Détente to Cold War', in Pauline Fairclough, ed., *Twentieth-Century Music and Politics: Essays in Memory of Neil Edmunds*, Farnham: Ashgate, 2013, 37–56.
12. Elena Dubinets, 'Pervootkrïvatel' novoy muzïki' [The Groundbreaker of new music], *Muzïkal'naya akademiya*, no. 3, 2003, 200–2.
13. Henry Cowell, 'Igraya kontserti v Moskve' [Performances in Moscow], trans. Elena Dubinets, *Muzïkal'naya akademiya*, no. 3, 2003, 211 (note 15).
14. See Pauline Fairclough and Louise Wiggins, 'Friendship of the Musicians: Anglo-Soviet Musical Exchanges 1938–1948', in Simo Mikkonen and Pekka Suutari, eds, *Art and Diplomacy: East–West Cultural Interactions and the Cold War*, Farnham: Ashgate, 2016.
15. See Grigoriy Shneyerson, review of Bush's Piano Concerto (premiered in London) in *Sovetskaya muzïka*, 1938, no. 6, 106–8 and his general profile of Bush in issue 1938, no. 9, 86–7.
16. TsGALI f. 279, op. 1, d. 46, l. 38.
17. The *Enigma Variations* received what was probably its Soviet, even Russian, premiere under Sergey Kusevitskiy in Moscow, sometime in November–December 1918, in the Theatre of K. N. Nezlobin.
18. See letter to Bax preserved in GARF f. 5238 (VOKS) op. 15 d. 23, l. 9, which mentions his 1910 visit.
19. See *Sovetskaya muzïka* 1938, no. 12, 76–8 for Kuznetsov's review. This choice of repertoire seems to have influenced the first of the English music concerts held in Moscow during the war, since Bush's 'Dance Overture' was played again at that concert (25 May 1943).
20. The scores were: 'Theme of Reconstruction' from Bliss's *Things to Come*, Purcell Trumpet Voluntary, Vaughan Williams's *Fantasia on Greensleeves*, Delius's 'Walk to the Paradise Garden' and 'Serenade' from *Hassan*, John Ireland's 'Mai Dun' and *Forgotten Rite*, Peter Warlock's *Capriol Suite*, Stanford's *Irish Rhapsody*, Gilbert and Sullivan's *Iolanthe* and Alexander Mackenzie's *Britannia Overture*. NA FO 6166.
21. NA, FO370/654.
22. NA, FO370/675.
23. Ibid.
24. Shostakovich's folk-song arrangements 'Eight British and American Folksongs' were published in the *New Collected Works*, vol. 149, Moscow: DSCH, 2009.
25. NA, FO924/279.
26. The programme from this concert, a copy of which was very kindly given me by Edward Morgan, provides a precious example of a documented concert of Russian sacred music during these years. Though the late Soviet practice of performing this repertoire in churches offers the possibility that this was an ongoing part of Soviet 'unofficial' musical life, the lack of documentation means that it is not generally possible to trace other such concerts. I thank Marina Frolova-Walker for drawing my attention to this practice.

27. Nikolay Lyubimov, *Neuvyadaemïy svet. Kniga vospominaniy* [Everlasting light. A Memoir], 2004. Cited in V. V. Perkhin, *Deyateli russkogo iskusstva M. B. Khrapchenko, predsedatel' Vsesoiuznogo komiteta po delam iskusstv aprel' 1939 – yanvar' 1948* [President of the All-Union Committee on Arts Affairs, April 1939–January 1948: M. V. Khrapchenko: statesman of Russian art], Moscow: Nauka, 2007, 70. As Perkhin notes (p. 69), the concert must have been approved by Mikhail Khrapchenko and the Committee for Arts Affairs (and indeed also at a higher level than that), though no archival evidence has yet been found to show how it was discussed behind the scenes.

28. See Mikhail Shtangrud, 'History of Moscow State Choral College from 1944 through 1991', DMA diss., Thornton School of Music, University of Southern California, 2006, 43. I am grateful to Marina Rakhmanova for the information concerning Sveshnikov's diploma.

29. Tatiana A. Chumachenko, *Church and State in Soviet Russia: Russian Orthodoxy from World War II to the Khrushchev Years*, Armonk, NY: M. E. Sharpe, 2002, 50 and 58.

30. Steven Merritt Miner, *Stalin's Holy War: Religion, Nationalism and Alliance Politics, 1941–1945*, Chapel Hill: University of North Carolina Press, 2003, 8.

31. For a brief outline of these events, see Pauline Fairclough, 'Don't Sing it on a Feast Day: The Reception and Performance of Western Sacred Music in Soviet Russia, 1917–53', *Journal of the American Musicological Society*, vol. 65/1, 2012.

32. My source is Ye. Varvatsi, 'Operï Rakhmaninova na Sovetskoy stsene' [Rakhmaninov's operas on the Soviet stage], in Igor Belza, ed., *S. V. Rakhmaninov*, Moscow: All-Russian Theatre Society, 1947, 184.

33. GARF f. 5283 op. 14 d. 126.

34. Reyngol'd Glier, 'Vïdayushchiysya russkiy kompozitor' [A distinguished Russian composer], *Izvestiya*, 31 March 1943, 4.

35. GARF f. 5283 op. 14 d. 126, l. 20. Rakhmaninov wrote to Yekaterina Alekseyeva, the Museum's Director, on 28 January 1942 regretting that he could not provide her with the oil painting and sculpture of himself that she had asked for because, as he put it, 'If they still exist at all, then I certainly do not have them.' From this we must assume that the composer was forced to leave them behind when he left the country in 1917, after which they evidently disappeared.

36. Ol'ga Levasheva, opening essay in the collection *S. V. Rakhmaninov Katalog vïstavki* [S. V. Rakhmaninov, exhibition catalogue], Moscow: Iskusstvo, 1945, 8.

37. This work had been in the Leningrad Philharmonia's repertoire in the early 1920s; it was revived in the post-1932 era (in Moscow in October 1934, alongside his *Oresteia*), and in Leningrad in 1940. After that it disappears until October 1950.

38. Igor Belza, *S. V. Rakhmaninov*, Moscow and Leningrad: Muzgiz, 1946.

39. S. Rakhmaninov, trans. with introduction by Grigoriy Shneyerson, 'O Russkom narodnom muzïkal'nom tvorchestve', *Sovetskaya muzïka: sbornik statey*, Moscow: Muzgiz, 1945, 52.

40. Konstantin Kuznetsov, 'Tvorcheskaya zhizn' S. V. Rakhmaninova', in ibid., 45.

41. Anatoliy Solovtsov, *S. V. Rakhmaninov*, Moscow and Leningrad: Muzgiz, 1947, 35–6.

42. GARF f. 5283 op. 14 d. 126, l. 69.

43. Ibid., l. 68. In the official statement released in America, this claim is not made, and all the negative statements regarding the composer's attitude to the Soviet Union were also removed. See the New York Philharmonia archive online, http://archives.nyphil.org/index.php/artifact/b08e8bfd-51c6-4a05-8c19-a64d383c6849, accessed 20/12/2014.

44. The telegram was signed by every conceivable significant name in Soviet music: Myaskovskiy, Shostakovich, Khachaturyan, Glier, Asaf'yev, Shaporin, Kabalevskiy, Konstantin Igumnov, Gol'denveyzer, Lev Oborin, Vladimir Sofronitskiy, David Oystrakh, Nikolay Golovanov, Aleksandr Gedike, Mravinskiy and the VOKS president Kemenov. Prokof'yev's name was added upon his return to Moscow from his holidays. GARF f. 5283 op. 14 d. 126, ll. 111 and 89.

45. Ibid., l. 96.

46. GARF, f. 5283 op. 14 d. 126, ll. 15–17.

47. *Francesca de Rimini* and *The Miserly Knight* were reprinted by Boosey and Hawkes in 1947.
48. GARF f. 5283 op. 14, d. 126, ll. 3, 6.
49. See Fairclough, 'Détente to Cold War' for a more detailed discussion.
50. See ibid., 46.
51. RGALI f. 962 op. 10, ed. khr. 64, l. 17.
52. RGALI f. 962 op. 10, ed. khr. 86, ll. 49–52.
53. RGASPI f. 17 op. 125 ed. khr. 637, letter of 18 April 1946, l. 74.
54. Strictly speaking, defection was largely a post-Stalinist phenomenon, enabled by greater freedoms for Soviet artists to travel abroad. But nonetheless, it should be recalled that the Soviet Union had lost several of its best artists this way in the 1920s, including Glazunov and Mal'ko, both of whom went abroad ostensibly only to tour and never returned. In contrast to those musicians who left the Soviet Union during the initial upheaval of the Revolution or Civil War years (Rakhmaninov, Kusevitskiy, Heifetz, Auer and many others), the unofficial departures of Glazunov and Mal'ko for the West constitute true defections.
55. RGALI f. 962 op. 10 ed. khr 64 ll. 69.
56. GARF f. 5283 op. 14 d. 205.
57. RGALI f. 962 op. 10 ed. khr. 64, l. 23.
58. GARF f. 5283 op. 14 d. 427 l. 18.
59. RGALI f. 962 op. 10 ed. khr. 64, ll. 8–9.
60. *Porgy and Bess*, though a box-office flop on Broadway in 1935, had recently been revived on Broadway (in 1942) and subsequently toured in Copenhagen (1943) and Zurich (1945).
61. See letter from Shneyerson to Elie Siegmeister of 25 April 1945, where he informs him that *Porgy and Bess* has recently been given a complete concert performance. GARF f. 5283 op. 14, d. 205, l. 113. Concert performances are not included in the listings compiled by Fedorov (V. V. Fedorov, *Repertuar Bol'shogo teatra SSSR, 1776–1955* [Repertoire of the Bolshoy theatre in the USSR, 1776–1955], New York: Norman Ross Publishing, 2001). The concert performance is also mentioned in a report sent to the British Foreign Office by a New Zealand official, Mr Sanley, 'Some Notes on Cultural Activities in the Soviet Union'. The Foreign Office did not take any interest in the report because of the absence of British composers represented in it ('apart from Purcell and Gershwin [*sic*!]') and the report even carries a piqued memo from the senior Foreign Office official Thomas Brimelow noting that, notwithstanding the Russians' desire for records of English music during wartime, the only fruit of it was two concerts of English music and a few radio broadcasts. See NA, FO924/480. A review in the *New York Times* (17 June 1945, Section Two, 4:3) states that it was given 'last month' by the Stanislavskiy Opera Players and the chorus of the Moscow Theatrical Society in the House of Actors in Moscow. Shostakovich, who evidently attended the event, pronounced it 'magnificent'. Clearly, there is some mismatch of information here, unless Shneyerson was actually referring to an earlier performance (meaning that there were two in 1945). I thank Erik Levi for drawing my attention to this review.
62. Grigoriy Shneyerson, 'Porgi i Bess', *Sovetskaya muzïka*, 1946, nos 5–6, 89–96.
63. RGALI, f. 962 op. 10, ed. khr. l. 102.
64. Truman Capote, *The Muses Are Heard*, Melbourne, London and Toronto: Heinemann, 1957.
65. RGASPI f. 17 op. 125 ed. khr. 371 l. 131.
66. RGASPI f. 82 op. 2, d. 1013, l. 15.
67. RGASPI f. 82 op. 2, d. 1013, l. 25.
68. RGASPI f. 82 op. 2, d. 1013, l. 62.
69. Arosev was arrested in the *Yezhovshchina* in July 1937 and was shot on 10 February 1938.
70. The first of Andrey Zhdanov's Resolutions on Soviet culture was issued in the previous year, 1946. For details of the background to this event, see Katerina Clark and Evgeny Dobrenko, *Soviet Culture and Power: A History in Documents*, New Haven and London: Yale University Press, 402–25.

71. For the Foreign Office's responses to this speech, and a full transcript, see NA FO371/66413.
72. Ibid.
73. Kiril Tomoff, *Creative Union: The Professional Organization of Soviet Composers, 1939–1953*, New York: Cornell University Press, 2006, 124.
74. Zhdanov, concluding speech at the conference of Soviet music workers, February 1948, in *Andrey Zhdanov on Literature, Music and Philosophy*, London: Lawrence & Wishart, 1950, available online at http://www.revolutionarydemocracy.org/archive/zhdanovlit.htm#music, accessed 20/05/2014.
75. The list of banned works was produced on 5 March 1948 and ran as follows: Shostakovich: Symphonies Nos 6, 8 and 9, Piano Concerto [No. 1], Octet, Piano Sonata No. 2, Romances on Verses by English Poets, *Aphorisms*; Prokof'yev: Symphonic Suite 'The Year 1941', Ode to the end of the war, Festive Poem, Cantata for the 30th anniversary of the October Revolution [best known in English as 'Flourish Mighty Land'], Ballad of a Youth, *Pensées*, Piano Sonata No. 6; Myaskovskiy: 'Kremlin by Night' cantata, 'Pathetic overture'; Khachaturyan: Symphony-Poem for orchestra and organ; Shebalin: Symphony No. 3, Violin Concerto; Popov: Symphonies Nos 1 and 3, *Divertissement*, Violin Concerto. Those by composers other than the 'big six' that were also banned were as follows: Aleksander Kreyn: Symphony No. 2; Samuil Feynberg: Piano Concerto No. 3; Leonid Polovinkin: Symphonies Nos 8 and 9; Igor Belza: Symphonies Nos 1–3, *Anchar*, Romances on verses of Pushkin and Shakespeare; Nikolay Peyko: Romances on verses by Chinese poets, Romances on verses by American poets; Moysey Vaynberg: 'Welcome' Overture, Festive Ode, Sixth Quartet, Shakespeare Sonnets; Yuriy Levitin: Festive Overture, Piano Concerto, Quintet for flute, violin, clarinet, cello and piano. RGALI, f. 963 op.3, ed. khr. 2007, ll. 84–9.
76. Igor Belza, 'O tvorcheskikh napravleniyakh v sovremennoy angliyskoy muzïke' [On creative directions in contemporary English music], *Sovetskaya muzïka. Sbornik statey*, vol.1, Muzgiz, 1943, 68–72. Leonid Maksimenkov has shown that Belza's name was added after the initial draft resolution was made, not later than 2 February 1948, and even then was added to the list of critics rather than composers. Leonid Maksimenkov, *Muzïka vmesto sumbura: kompozitorï i muzïkantï v strane sovetov 1917–1991* [Music instead of muddle: composers and musicians in the land of the Soviets 1917–1991], Moscow: Rossiya XX vek. Documents, 2013, 295. In 1948 Belza, along with Daniil Zhitomirskiy and Lev Mazel', was labelled a 'formalist critic'. See D. G. Nadzhafov and Z. S. Belousova, *Stalin i kozmopolitanizm. Dokumentï Agitprop TsK KPSS 1945–1953* [Stalin and cosmopolitanism. Documents from agitprop of the Central Committee of the Communist Party of the Soviet Union, 1945–1953], Moscow: Mezhdunarodnïy fond 'Demokratiya', 2005, 538.
77. Nadzhafov and Belousova, *Stalin i kozmopolitanizm*, 149–50.
78. Ibid., 149–50.
79. Maksimenkov, *Muzïka vmesto sumbura*, 256.
80. See Zhdanov's January 1948 speech, presented at a meeting of the Central Committee of the Communist Party convened to discuss Soviet musical affairs. It was published in *Sovetskaya muzïka* 1948, no. 1, 14–26. The reference to Glinka is on p. 18, and comments on the divorce between composers and their public (though a continuous theme throughout the speech) can be found on p. 24.
81. Yekaterina Vlasova, *1948 god v Sovetskoy muzïke* [The Year 1948 in Soviet Music], Moscow: Klassika XXI, 2010, 248.
82. RGASPI f. 17, op. 125, ed. khr. 636, l. 5.
83. Vlasova, *1948 god*, 247.
84. Ibid., 250.
85. RGASPI f. 17 op. 125 ed. khr 636, l. 11.
86. Ibid., l. 25.
87. The Resolution of 10 February is published in full in Nadzhafov and Belousova, *Stalin i kozmopolitanizm*, 159–64.

88. RGASPI f. 17 op. 125 ed. khr. 636, l. 13.

89. Address of A. A. Zhdanov, *Sovetskaya muzïka*, 1948, no. 1, 17.

90. Ibid, 25.

91. Of course, not all the music by all the composers listed was banned; but such was the fear of reprisal that Moscow Philharmonia listings for the 1948–9 season feature no music at all by any of the listed composers (not just the main six) until April 1949, when a Soviet cultural delegation including Shostakovich had already represented the Soviet Union at the Cultural and Scientific Conference for World Peace, held in the Waldorf Hotel in New York between 25 and 27 March 1949. By that time the blacklist had been revoked by Stalin personally, and so it was once again safe to perform music by these composers, even if only a very selected body of their work. There is just one exception to the ban in this period: Khachaturyan's Hymn 'Glory to the Komsomol' was performed in Moscow in October 1948.

92. A. A. Zhdanov, ibid., 18.

93. Ibid., 23.

94. 'Govoryat klassiki' [The classics speak], *Sovetskaya muzïka* 1948, no. 1, 29–52.

95. Address of A. A. Zhdanov, *Sovetskaya muzïka*, 1948, no. 1, 20.

96. Maksimenkov, *Muzïka vmesto sumbura*, 288.

97. Isabella Abezgauz, *Russkie muzïkantï o muzïke zapada* [Russian musicians on Western music], Moscow: Muzgiz, 1950, 6.

98. Ibid., 8.

99. Ibid., 47.

100. Ibid., 50.

101. Ibid., 45.

102. Ibid., 51–2.

103. Ibid., 55.

104. Ibid., 58.

105. *Salome* was in the Bolshoy's repertoire in the 1920s, but *Samson and Delilah* had not been performed since 1919.

106. Tomoff, *Creative Union*, 204.

107. Grigoriy Shneyerson, 'Khronika zarubezhnoy muzïkal'noy zhizni' [Chronicle of musical life abroad], *Sovetskaya muzïka*, 1941, no. 5, 108.

108. Grigoriy Shneyerson, 'Muzïkal'naya Frantsiya' [Musical France], *Sovetskaya muzïka*, 1946, no. 11, 98.

109. Grigoriy Shneyerson, 'Boguslav Martinu – Lidice', *Sovetskaya muzïka*, 1947, no. 2, 102.

110. Ibid., 103.

111. Martinů came under attack after 1948 from the musicologist Zdeněk Nejedlý, who later became Minister of Culture. See Aleš Březina, 'McCarthy's America and Communist Czechoslovakia', in Michael Brim Beckerman, ed., *Martinů's Mysterious Accident: Essays in Honor of Michael Henderson*, New York: Pendragon Press, 2007, 67, n. 18.

112. Grigoriy Shneyerson, 'Amerikanskaya muzïkal'naya inzheneriya' [American musical engineering], *Sovetskaya muzïka*, 1948, no. 2, 167.

113. Ibid., 161.

114. GARF, f. 5283, op. 28, d. 1452, ll.14.

115. Iosef Rïzhkin, 'Arnol'd Shenberg – likvidator muzïki' [Arnold Schoenberg – the liquidator of music], *Sovetskaya muzïka*, 1949, no. 8, 97–103.

116. Izrail' Nest'yev, 'B plenu burzhuaznogo modernizma' [In thrall to bourgeois modernism], *Sovetskaya muzïka*, 1948, no. 10, 16–23.

Conclusion

1. For an account of these, see Robin LaPasha, 'Amateurs and Enthusiasts. Folk Music and the Soviet State on Stage in the 1930s', in Neil Edmunds, ed., *Soviet Music and Society Under Lenin and Stalin. The Baton and Sickle*, London: Routledge Curzon, 2004, 123–47.

2. For further discussion of these visits, see Pauline Fairclough, 'Don't Sing it on a Feast Day: The Reception and Performance of Western Sacred Music in Soviet Russia, 1917–53', *Journal of the American Musicological Society*, vol. 65/1, 2012, 109–11 and, especially, Peter Schmelz, *Such Freedom, if Only Musical: Unofficial Soviet Music During the Thaw*, New York: Oxford University Press, 2009.

3. Ivan Sollertinskiy, *Volshebnaya fleyta Motsarta* [Mozart's Magic Flute], Leningrad: Leningrad Philharmonia, 1938, 17.

4. While the Moscow and Leningrad schedules are not generously stocked with music by Shostakovich, Prokof'yev, Myaskovskiy and Khachaturyan between 1948 and 1953, the safest works – Shostakovich's Fifth Symphony, the Cello and Violin Concertos of Myaskovsky and Khachaturyan – were already being played in the second half of the 1948–9 season (Moscow Philharmonia). However, I do not wish to overstate their 'rehabilitation': in the 1948–9 season, Shostakovich's Fifth was the only Shostakovich work performed in the Moscow Philharmonia Bolshoy Hall programmes; in 1949–50, no Shostakovich was played at all in that series other than his *Song of the Forests* and there was not a single work performed by Prokof'yev, Khachaturyan, Shebalin or Myaskovskiy apart from extracts from Khachaturyan's *Gayane*. The following season (1950–1) programming starts to look more normal, with the orchestra playing Myaskovskiy's Symphony No. 21, Shostakovich songs from *The Fall of Berlin*, Prokof'yev's First and Third Piano Concerti, *Romeo and Juliet* suite (number unspecified) and his First Symphony. It seems certain, in short, that the 'blacklist' was lifted not just for Shostakovich but also for his four compatriots in 1949, but that orchestras exercised extreme caution in allowing music by those five composers in the years immediately following the 1948 ban.

SELECT BIBLIOGRAPHY

Books

Abezgauz, Isabella, *Russkie muzïkanti o muzïke zapada* [Russian musicians on Western music], Moscow: Muzgiz, 1950

Anisimov, A., *Repertuar akademicheskoy kapelli* [Repertoire of the academic capella], Moscow: Muzgiz, 1958

Anon., *N. A. Rimskiy-Korsakov i ego vremya. Kratkiy putevoditel' po vïstavke v russkom muzee* [N. A. Rimskiy Korsakov and his epoch. A short guide to the exhibition in the Russian museum], Leningrad: Komitet po chestvovaniyu pamyati N. A. Rimskogo-Korsakova, 1933

—, *Rekviem Verdi*, Leningrad: Leningrad Philharmonia, 1937

—, *S. V. Rakhmaninov. Katalog vïstavki* [S. V. Rakhmaninov, exhibition catalogue], Moscow: Iskusstvo, 1945

Apetyan, Zarui, *Gavriil Popov. Iz literaturnogo naslediya: stranitsï biografii* [Gavriil Popov. Pages of a biography from his literary legacy], Moscow: Sovetskiy kompozitor, 1986

Artizov, Andrey, and Oleg Naumov, *Vlast i khudozhestvennaya intelligentsiya: dokumentï TsK RKP (b) – VKP (b) – VChK – NKVD o kul'turnoy politike, 1917–1953* [Power and the artistic intelligentsia: documents on cultural politics from the Central Committee of the Russian Communist Party (Bolsheviks) 1917–1953], Moscow: 'Demokratiya', 1999

Asaf'yev, Boris, *Pamyati Pëtra Il'icha Chaykovskogo 1840–1940* [In memory of Peter Il'ich Chaykovskiy], Leningrad and Moscow: Muzgiz, 1940

Bacht, Nikolaus, ed., *Music, Theatre and Politics in Germany. 1848 to the Third Reich*, Farnham: Ashgate, 2006

Bakeyeva, V. N., and A. N. Kotlyaredskiy, *Magnifikat I. S. Bakha* [J. S. Bach's Magnificat], Leningrad: Leningrad Philharmonia, 1939

Barenboym, L., *Iz istorii sovetskogo muzïkal'nogo obrazovaniya* [From the history of Soviet musical education], Leningrad: Muzïka, 1969

Bartlett, Rosamund, *Wagner and Russia*, Cambridge: Cambridge University Press, 1995

Bassin, Mark, and Catriona Kelly, *Soviet and Post-Soviet Identities*, Cambridge: Cambridge University Press, 2012

Beckerman, Michael Brim, ed., *Martinů's Mysterious Accident: Essays in Honor of Michael Henderson*, New York: Pendragon Press, 2007

Bekker, Paul, *Die Sinfonie von Beethoven bis Mahler* (1918), trans. into Russian by Roman Gruber as *Simfoniya do Betkhoven do Malera*, Leningrad: Triton, 1926

Belyayev, Viktor, Igor Glebov, Pavel Lamm et al., *Musorgskiy: Boris Godunov. Stat'i i issledovaniya* [Musorgskiy: Boris Godunov. Articles and research], Moscow: Gosudarstvennaya Akademiya Khudozhestvennikh Nauk, muzïkal'naya sektsiya, 1930

Belza, Igor, *S. V. Rakhmaninov*, Moscow and Leningrad: Muzgiz, 1946

Belza, Igor, ed., *S. V. Rakhmaninov*, Moscow: All-Russian Theatre Society, 1947

Berlyand, Ye, *Motsart*, Leningrad and Moscow: Muzgiz, 1948

Blok, Aleksandr, *Sobranie sochinenii* [Collected works], vol. 6, Moscow: Sovremennik, 1979

Bobrik, Olesya, *Venskoe izdatel'stvo 'Universal Edition' i muzïkanti iz sovetskoy Rossii* [The Viennese publisher 'Universal Edition' and musicians from Soviet Russia], St Petersburg: N. A. Novikova Publishers, 2011

Bogdanov-Berezovskiy, Valerian, *Opernoe i baletnoe tvorchestvo Chaykovskogo* [Chaykovskiy's operas and ballets], Leningrad and Moscow: Iskusstvo, 1940

Bown, Matthew Cullerne, *Art Under Stalin*, New York: Holmes and Meier, 1991

Brandenberger, David, *National Bolshevism: Stalinist Mass Culture and the Formation of Modern Russian National Identity, 1931–1956*, Cambridge, MA: Harvard University Press, 2002

—, and Kevin M. F. Platt, *Epic Revisionism. Russian History and Literature as Stalinist Propaganda*, Madison, WI: University of Wisconsin Press, 2006

Braudo, Yevgeniy, *Iogann Sebastiyan Bakh* [Johann Sebastian Bach], Petersburg: Svetozar, 1922

—, *Svad'ba Figaro* [Marriage of Figaro], Moscow: Muzgiz, 1938

—, and Andrey Rimskiy-Korsakov, *Boris Godunov Musorgskogo* [Musorgsky's Boris Godunov], Moscow and Leningrad: Kino-pechat', 1927

Bronfin, Yelena, *Muzïkal'naya kul'tura Petrograda pervogo poslerevolyutsionnogo pyatiletiya 1917–1922* [The musical culture of Petrograd in the first five years after the revolution], Leningrad: Sovetskiy kompozitor, 1984

Budyakovskiy, Andrey, *P. I. Chaykovskiy. Simfonicheskaya muzïka* [P. I. Chaykovskiy. Symphonic music], Leningrad, Leningradskaya filarmoniya, 1935

Burnett, Leon, and Emily Lygo, eds, *The Art of Accommodation. Literary Translation in Russia*, Bern: Peter Lang, 2013

Capote, Truman, *The Muses Are Heard*, Melbourne, London and Toronto: Heinemann, 1957

Chumachenko, Tatiana A., *Church and State in Soviet Russia: Russian Orthodoxy from World War II to the Khrushchev Years*, Armonk, NY: M. E. Sharpe, 2002

Clark, Katerina, *Moscow: The Fourth Rome. Stalinism, Cosmopolitanism and the Evolution of Soviet Culture, 1931–1941*, Cambridge, MA: Harvard University Press, 2011

—, and Evgeny Dobrenko, with Andrei Artizov and Oleg Naumov, *Soviet Culture and Power: A History in Documents*, New Haven and London: Yale University Press, 2007

Cowell, Henry, 'Igraya kontsertï v Moskve' [Performances in Moscow], trans. Elena Dubinets, *Muzïkal'naya akademiya*, no. 3, 2003, 205–12

Dams, V., trans. from German by Lev Mazel, *F. Mendel'son-Bartoldi*, Moscow: Muzgiz, 1930

Davidson, Pamela, *Cultural Memory and Survival. The Russian Renaissance of Classical Antiquity in the Twentieth Century*, UCL SSEES Inaugural Lecture Series, 21 May 2009

Davies, Sarah, *Popular Opinion in Stalin's Russia. Terror, Propaganda and Dissent, 1934–1941*, Cambridge: Cambridge University Press, 1997

Dobrenko, Evgeny, trans. Jesse M. Savage, *The Making of the State Reader. Social and Aesthetics Contexts of the Reception of Soviet Literature*, Stanford, CA: Stanford University Press, 1997

—, trans. Jesse M. Savage, *The Making of the State Writer. Social and Aesthetics Origins of Soviet Literary Culture*, Stanford, CA: Stanford University Press, 2001

—, trans. Jesse M. Savage, *Political Economy of Socialist Realism*, New Haven and London: Yale University Press, 2007

Dorontchenkov, Ilia, ed., trans. Charles Rougle, *Russian and Soviet Views of Modern Western Art. 1890s to Mid-1930s*, Berkeley, CA: University of California Press, 2009

Druskin, Mikhail, and Yakov Druskin, *Strasti po Matfeiyu I. S. Bakha* [Bach's St Matthew Passion], Leningrad: Leningrad State Philharmonia, 1941

Dubinets, Elena, 'Pervootkrïvatel' novoy muzïki' [The groundbreaker of new music], *Muzïkal'naya akademiya*, no. 3, 2003, 196–205

Dukov, Yevgeniy, ed., *Mezhdu obshchestvom i vlast'yu: massovïe zhanrï ot 20-x k 80-m godam XX veka* [Between society and power: mass genres from the 1920s to 1980s], Moscow: 'Indrik', 2002

Dunham, Vera S., *In Stalin's Time. Middleclass Values in Soviet Fiction*, Durham and London: Duke University Press, 1990

Edmunds, Neil, *The Soviet Proletarian Music Movement*, Bern: Peter Lang, 2000

—, ed., *Soviet Music and Society Under Lenin and Stalin: the Baton and Sickle*, London and New York: Routledge Curzon, 2004

Fairclough, Pauline ed., *Shostakovich Studies 2*, Cambridge: Cambridge University Press, 2010

—, ed., *Twentieth-Century Music and Politics: Essays in Memory of Neil Edmunds*, Farnham: Ashgate, 2013

Fairclough, Pauline and Louise Wiggins, 'Friendship of the Musicians: Anglo-Soviet Musical Exchanges 1938–1948', in Simo Mikkonen and Pekka Suutari, eds, *Art and Diplomacy: East-West Cultural Interactions and the Cold War*, Farnham: Ashgate, 2016

Fay, Laurel, *Shostakovich: A Life*, New York: Oxford University Press, 2000

—, ed., *Shostakovich and his World*, Princeton, NJ: Princeton University Press, 2004

Fedorov, V. V., *Repertuar Bol'shogo teatra SSSR, 1776–1955* [Repertoire of the Bolshoy theatre in the USSR, 1776–1955], New York: Norman Ross Publishing, 2001

Fishman, N. L., ed., *Iz istorii sovetskoy Betkhovenniani* [From the history of Soviet Beethoveniana], Moscow: Sovetskiy kompozitor, 1972

Fitzpatrick, Sheila, *The Cultural Front: Power and Culture in Revolutionary Russia*, Ithaca and London: Cornell University Press, 1992

Frid, Emiliya, *Modest Petrovich Musorgskiy*, Leningrad: Leningrad Philharmonia, 1939

Froese, Paul, *The Plot to Kill God. Findings from the Soviet Experiment in Secularization*, Berkeley, CA: University of California Press, 2008

Frolova-Walker, Marina, and Jonathan Walker, *Music and Soviet Power 1917–1932*, Woodbridge: Boydell Press, 2012

Gauk, L. P., R. V. Glezer and Ya. I. Mil'shteyn, eds, *Aleksandr Vasil'yevich Gauk. Memuarï, izbrannïe stat'i, vospominaniya sovremennikov* [Aleksandr Vasil'yevich Gauk. Memoirs, collected essays, recollections of his contemporaries], Moscow: Sovetskiy kompozitor, 1975

Gellately, Robert, and Ben Kiernan, eds, *The Specter of Genocide: Mass Murder in Historical Perspective*, New York: Cambridge University Press, 2003

Gentile, Emilio, trans. Keith Botsford, *The Sacralization of Politics in Fascist Italy*, New York: Harvard University Press, 1996

Gershkovich, Yevgeniya, and Natalya Semënova, *Stalin's Imperial Style*, Moscow: Trefoil Press, 2006

Gide, Andre, *Return from the USSR*, New York: Alfred A. Knopf, 1937

Ginzburg, Semën, *Sluzhanka-gospozha* [La Serva Padrona], Leningrad: State Hermitage, 1933

—, *Muzïka v muzee* [Music in the Museum], Leningrad: State Hermitage, 1934

Glebov, Igor, ed., *Proshloe russkoy muzïki. Materialï i issledovaniya vol. 1 P. I. Chaikovskiy* [Russian music of the past. Materials and research. Vol. 1, P. I. Chaykovskiy], Petrograd, 1918, reprinted Petersburg, Kinoizdatel'stvo 'Ogni', 1920

Glebov, Igor, *Russkaya muzïka ot nachala XIX stoletiya* [Russian Music from the beginning of the nineteenth century], Leningrad and Moscow: Muzgiz, 1930

Glikman, Isaak, trans. Anthony Phillips, *Story of a Friendship. The Letters of Dmitry Shostakovich to Isaak Glikman*, London: Faber and Faber, 2001

Gol'denveyzer, Aleksandr B., *Vospominaniya* [Memoirs], Moscow: Deka, 2009

Gorky, Maxim, *Chaliapin. An Autobiography as told to Maxim Gorky*, trans. and ed. Nina Froud and James Hanley, London: Columbus Books, 1988

Grigor'yev, L. G., and Ya. M. Platek, *Moskovskaya Gosudarstvennaya Filarmoniya* [Moscow State Philharmonia], Moscow: Sovetskiy kompozitor, 1973

Grosheva, Ye., *Bolshoy Teatr* [Bolshoy Theatre], Moscow: 1978

Gruber, Roman, *Richard Vagner*, Moscow: 1934

—, *Asis i Galeteya Gendelya* [Handel's Acis and Galatea], Leningrad: Leningrad Philharmonia, 1934

—, *Gendel'* [Handel], Leningrad: Izdanie nauchno-issledovatel'skogo institute iskusstvoz-naniya [Institute of Arts History], 1935

Günther, Hans, *Der sozialistische übermensch: M. Gor'kij und der sowjetische Heldenmythos*, Stuttgart: J. B. Metzler, 1993

Haas, Michael, *Forbidden Music: the Jewish Composers Banned by the Nazis*, New Haven and London: Yale University Press, 2013

Halfin, Igor, *From Darkness to Light: Class, Consciousness and Salvation in Revolutionary Russia*, Pittsburgh: Pittsburgh University Press, 2000

Heyworth, Peter, *Otto Klemperer: His Life and Times vol. 2: 1933–1973*, Cambridge: Cambridge University Press, 1996

Hoffman, David L., *Stalinist Values. The Cultural Norms of Soviet Modernity, 1917–1941*, Ithaca and London: Cornell University Press, 2003

—, *Cultivating the Masses: Modern State Practices and Soviet Socialism, 1914–1939*, Ithaca and London: Cornell University Press, 2011

Hölderlin, Friedrich, *The Death of Empedocles. A Mourning-Play*, trans. with introduction, notes and analysis by David Farrell Krell, New York: State University of New York, 2009

Ilin, V., *Iskusstvo millionov. Iz istorii muzïkal'noy samodeyatel'nosti Petrograd-Leningrad* [Art of the millions. From the history of amateur music-making], Leningrad: Muzïka, 1967

Kalinin, S. S., *Pamyati Aleksandra Vasil'evicha Sveshnikova* [In memory of Aleksandr Vasil'evich Sveshnikov], Moscow: Muzïka, 1998

Kater, Michael, *Composers of the Nazi Era. Eight Portraits*, New York: Oxford University Press, 2002

Kelly, Catriona, *Refining Russia: Advice Literature, Polite Culture and Gender from Catherine to Yeltsin*, New York: Oxford University Press, 2001

Kharlamov, Yuriy, *Skazka o tsare Saltane* [The Tale of Tsar Saltan], Leningrad: Leningrad State Academic Theatre (Kirov), 1937

Khubov, Georgiy, *I. S. Bakh. Opït kharakteristiki* [J. S. Bach. Characteristics of his style], Moscow: Muzgiz, 1937

Khubov, Georgiy, *I. S. Bakh. Strasti po Matfeiu i Messa h-moll* [J. S. Bach. St Matthew Passion and B Minor Mass], programme note for St Matthew Passion and B Minor Mass, Leningrad: Leningrad Philharmonia, 1935

Korev, Semën, *Muzïka i sovremmenost'* [Music and the contemporary age], Moscow: Muzgiz, 1928

Kremlëv, Yuliy, *Volfgang Motsart. Kratkiy ocherk zhizni i tvorchestva* [Wolfgang Mozart. A short study of his life and work], Leningrad: Triton, 1935

Krïlova, Sarra, and Lev Lebedinskiy et al., *Rabochie o literature, teatre i muzïke* [Workers on literature, theatre and music], Leningrad: 'Prïboy', 1926

Kryukov, Andrey, *Muzïka v efire voennogo Leningrada* [Music broadcasts in wartime Leningrad], St Petersburg: Kompozitor, 2005

—, *Muzïka v dni blokadï* [Music in the days of the blockade], St Petersburg: Kompozitor, 2002

Kuper, Emil, *Stat'i, vospominaniya, materialï* [Emil Kuper, articles, reminiscences, materials], Moscow: Sovetskiy kompozitor, 1988

Kuznetsov, Konstantin, *Glinka i ego sovremenniki* [Glinka and his contemporaries], Moscow: Gosudarstvennoe izdatel'stvo, muzïkal'niy sektor, 1926

Lahusen, Thomas, and Evgeny Dobrenko, eds, *Socialist Realism Without Shores*, Durham and London: Duke University Press, 1997

Lebedinskiy, Lev, *O proletarskoy massovoy pesne* [On proletarian mass song], Moscow: Glaviskusstvo, 1929

Levi, Erik, *Music in the Third Reich*, London: Palgrave MacMillan, 1996

Levi, Erik, *Mozart and the Nazis: How the Third Reich Abused a Cultural Icon*, New Haven and London: Yale University Press, 2011

Livanova, Tamara, *Muzïkal'naya klassika XVIII veka* [Musical classicism of the 18th century], Leningrad: Muzgiz, 1939

—, ed., *Iz proshlogo sovetskoy muzïkal'noy kul'turï* [From the Past of Soviet Musical Culture], vol. 3, Moscow: Sovetskiy kompozitor, 1982

Lunacharskiy, Anatoliy, ed. Grigoriy Bernandt, *V mire muzïka* [In the world of music], Moscow: Sovetskiy kompozitor, 1958

Luukanen, Arto, *The Party of Unbelief. The Religious Policy of the Bolshevik Party, 1917–1929*, Helsinki: Finnish Historical Society, 1994

Magee, Bryan, *Wagner and Philosophy*, London: Allen Lane, The Penguin Press, 2000

Maksimenkov, Leonid, *Sumbur vmesto muzïki: stalinskaya kul'turnaya revoliutsiya, 1936–1938* [Muddle instead of music: the Stalinist cultural revolution 1936–1938], Moscow: Yuridicheskaya kniga, 1997

Maksimenkov, Leonid, *Muzïka vmesto sumbura: kompozitorï i muzïkantï v strane sovetov 1917–1991* [Music instead of muddle: composers and musicians in the land of the Soviets 1917–1991], Moscow: Rossiya XX vek. Documents, 2013

Malko, Nikolai, *A Certain Art*, New York: William Morrow, 1966

Marisova, Irina, ed., *Aleksandr Yurlov*, Moscow: Sovetskiy kompozitor, 1983

Martïnov, Ivan, I. S. Bakh 'Magnifikat' [J. S. Bach's 'Magnificat'], Moscow: Moscow State Philharmonia, 1935

Medvedev, Zhores A., and Roy A. Medvedev, *The Unknown Stalin*, trans. Ellen Dahrendorf, London: I. B. Tauris, 2006

Mikheyeva, Liudmila, *Pamyati I. I. Sollertinskogo. Vospominaniya, materialï, issledovaniya* [In memory of I. I. Sollertinskiy. Recollections, materials, research], Leningrad: Sovetskiy kompozitor, 1978

Mikkonen, Simo, *Music and Power in the Soviet 1930s: A History of Composers' Bureaucracy*, Lewiston, Queenston and Lampeter: The Edwin Mellen Press, 2009

Miner, Steven Merritt, *Stalin's Holy War: Religion, Nationalism and Alliance Politics, 1941–1945*, Chapel Hill: University of North Carolina Press, 2003

Moller-Sally, Stephen, *Gogol's Afterlife. The Evolution of a Classic in Imperial and Soviet Russia*, Evanston, IL: Northwestern University Press, 2002

Muzalevskiy, Vladimir, *Mikhail Georgevich Klimov. Ocherk zhizni i tvorcheskoy deyatel'nosti* [Mikhail Georgevich Klimov. On his life and work], Leningrad: Sovetskiy kompozitor, 1960

Nadzhafov, D. G., and Z. S. Belousova, *Stalin i kozmopolitanizm. Dokumentï Agitprop TsK KPSS 1945–1953* [Stalin and cosmopolitanism. Documents from agitprop of the Central Committee of the Communist Party of the Soviet Union, 1945–1953], Moscow: Mezhdunarodnïy fond 'Demokratiya', 2005

Nelson, Amy, *Music for the Revolution: Musicians and Power in Early Soviet Russia*, Pennsylvania: Pennsylvania State University Press, 2004

Paperny, Vladimir, trans. John Hill and Roann Barris, *Architecture in the Age of Stalin: Culture Two*, Cambridge: Cambridge University Press, 2002

Perkhin, V. V., *Deyateli russkogo iskusstva M. V. Khrapchenko, predsedatel' Vsesoiuznogo komiteta po delam iskusstv aprel' 1939 – yanvar' 1948* [President of the All-Union Committee on Arts Affairs, April 1939–January 1948: M. V. Khrapchenko: statesman of Russian art], Moscow: Nauka, 2007

Phillips, Anthony, trans. and ed., *Sergey Prokofiev Diaries, vol. 3, 1924–1933. Prodigal Son*, London: Faber and Faber, 2012

Plamper, Jan, *The Stalin Cult. A Study in the Alchemy of Power*, New Haven and London: Yale University Press, 2012

Ponyatovskiy, Stanislav, *Orkestr Sergeya Kusevitskogo*, Moscow: 'Muzïka', 2008

Rakhmaninov, S., trans. with introduction by Grigoriy Shneyerson, 'O Russkom narodnom muzïkal'nom tvorchestve', *Sovetskaya muzïka: sbornik statey*, Moscow: Muzgiz, 1945, 52

Raku, Marina, *Muzïkal'naya klassika v mifotvorchestve sovetskoy epokhi* [Musical classicism in the mythology of the Soviet epoch], Moscow: Novoe literaturnoe obozrenie, 2014

RAPM, *Voprosï natsional'noy muzïki* [Questions of national music], Moscow: Muzgiz, 1931

Ratskaya, Tsetsiliya, *M. P. Musorgskiy. K stoletiyu so dnya rozhdeniya (1839–1939)* [M. P. Musorgskiy. On the centenary of his birth], Moscow and Leningrad: Muzgiz, 1939

Sargeant, Lynn M., *Harmony and Discord: Music and the Transformation of Russian Cultural Life*, New York: Oxford University Press, 2011

Sala, Luca, ed., *The Legacy of Richard Wagner*, Speculum Musicae, Turnhout: Brepols Publishers, Centro Studia Opera Omnia Luigi Boccherini, 2012

Sarkisov, O. S. and Fomin, V. S., Leningradskaya gosudarstvennaya ordena trudovogo krasnogo znameni filarmoniya. Stat'i. Vospominaniya. Materialï. Leningrad: Muzïka, 1972

Schmelz, Peter, *Such Freedom, if Only Musical: Unofficial Soviet Music During the Thaw*, New York: Oxford University Press, 2009

Schwarz, Boris, *Music and Musical Life in Soviet Russia, 1917–1981*, enlarged edn, Bloomington, IN: Indiana University Press, 1983

Shaverdyan, Aleksandr, *Simfonii Betkhovena* [Beethoven's symphonies], Moscow: Moscow Philharmonia, 1936

Sheremet'yeva, Nadezhda, *M. G. Klimov. Dirizhër Leningradskoy akademicheskoy kapellï* [M. G. Klimov. Director of the Leningrad academic capella], Leningrad: Muzïka, 1983

Shneyerson, Grigoriy, *Sovremennaya Amerikanskaya muzïka* [Contemporary American music], Moscow: State Philharmonia, 1945

—, *Sovremennaya Angliiskaya muzïka* [Contemporary English music], Moscow: State Philharmonia, 1945

—, *Muzïka na sluzhbe reaktsii* [Music serving reaction], Moscow and Leningrad: Muzgiz, 1950

Shteynpress, Boris, *Klassicheskaya muzïka* [Classical music], Moscow: State publishing for radio, 1935

Shuvalov, N. A., ed., *P. I. Chaykovskiy na tsene teatra operï i baleta im. S. M. Kirova (b. Mariinskiy)* [P. I. Chaykovskiy on the stage of the Kirov Theatre of Opera and Ballet (formerly the Mariinskiy)], Leningrad: Izdatel'stvo Leningradskogo gos. Ordena Lenina Akademicheskogo teatra operï i baleta im. S. M. Kirov, 1941

Simon, Gerhard, trans. Karen Forster and Oswald Forster, *Nationalism and Policy Toward the Nationalities in the Soviet Union. From Totalitarian Dictatorship to Post-Stalinist Society*, Westview Special Studies on the Soviet Union and Eastern Europe, Oxford: 1991

Smrž, Jiří, *Symphonic Stalinism. Claiming Russian Musical Classics for the New Soviet Listener, 1932–1953*, Berlin: Lit Verlag, 2011

Sollertinskiy, Ivan, *Gustav Maler*, Leningrad: Triton, 1932

—, *Zhak Offenbakh*, Leningrad: State Academic Malïy Opera Theatre, 1933

—, *Romantizm: ego obshchaya i muzïkal'naya estetika* [Romanticism: its general and musical aesthetics], Moscow: Muzgiz, 1962

—, *Volshebnaya fleyta Motsarta* [Mozart's Magic Flute], Leningrad: Leningrad Philharmonia, 1938

Solovtsov, Anatoliy, *S. V. Rakhmaninov*, Moscow and Leningrad: Muzgiz, 1947

Stern, Ludmila, *Western Intellectuals and the Soviet Union, 1920–40: From Red Square to the Left Bank*, London and New York: Routledge, 2007

Strel'nikov, Nikolay, *Glinka. Opït kharakteristiki* [Glinka. Characteristics of his style], Moscow: Gosudarstvennoe izdatel'stvo, 1923

Tarkhanov, Alexei and Kavtaradze, Sergei, *Stalinist Architecture*, London: Laurence King, 1992

Taruskin, Richard, *Musorgsky. Eight Essays and an Epilogue*, Princeton, NJ: Princeton University Press, 1993

—, *On Russian Music*, Berkeley, CA: University of California Press, 2008

Tkachev, D. V. and Gusin, I. L., *Leningradskaya akademicheskaya kapella imeni M. I. Glinki* [The Leningrad academic Glinka capella], Leningrad: 1957

Tolstoy, Alexandra, *Out of the Past*, New York: Columbia University Press, 1981

Tomoff, Kiril, *Creative Union: The Professional Organization of Soviet Composers, 1939–1953*, New York: Cornell University Press, 2006

Unger, Heinz, *Hammer, Sickle and Baton. The Soviet Memoirs of a Musician*. London: The Cresset Press Ltd, 1939

Vaynkop, Yuriy, *Betkhoven i ego tvorchestvo* [Beethoven and his work], Leningrad: Triton, 1934

Vinogradov, Viktor, *Protiv tserkovshchinï v muzïke* [Against church style in music], Moscow: State Music Publishers, 1931

Vlasova, Yekaterina, *1948 god v Sovetskoy muzïke* [The Year 1948 in Soviet Music], Moscow: Klassika XXI, 2010

Werth, Alexander, *Musical Uproar in Moscow*, London: Turnstile Press, 1949

Wilson, Alexandra, *The Puccini Problem*, Cambridge: Cambridge University Press, 2007

Yefimov, Yevgeniy, *Sumbur vokrug 'sumbura' i odnogo'malen'kogo zhurnalista'* [Muddle around a 'muddle' and one 'minor journalist'], Moscow: 'Flinta', 2006

Yufit, A. Z., *Sovetskii teatr* [Soviet theatre], Leningrad: 1978

Zhdanov, Andrey, *Andrey Zhdanov on Literature, Music and Philosophy*, London: Lawrence & Wishart, 1950

Zhdanov, V. A., and N. T. Zhegin, eds, *P. I. Chaykovskiy. Perepiska s N. F. fon-Mekk tom 1, 1876–1878* [P. I. Chaykovskiy. Correspondence with N. F. von Meck, Volume 1], Moscow and Leningrad: 'Akademiya', 1934

Articles and Theses

Al'shvang, Arnol'd, 'Narodnost' v Rossiskoy klassicheskoy muzïke' [Folk qualities in Russian classical music], *Sovetskaya muzïka*, 1938, no. 5, 5

Anisimov, G., 'Na bor'ba s tserkovshchinoy v muzïke' [On the struggle with the church's influence in music], *Za proletarskuyu muzïku*, 1932, no. 6, 6–9

Anon., 'Dovesti do kontsa s nepmanskoy muzïkoy' [Let us bring an end to Nepman music], *Za proletarskuyu muzïku*, 1930, no. 9, 1–3

—, 'O "sovremennoy muzïke"' [On 'contemporary music'], *Proletarskiy muzïkant*, 1926, no. 6, 6–7

—, '"Levïy" flang sovremennoy muzïki' [The 'left' wing of contemporary music], *Muzïka i revoliutsiya*, 1927, no. 1, 6

—, 'Betkhoven v ispolnenii dvukh germanskikh dirizherov' [Beethoven performed by two German conductors], *Za proletarskuyu muzïku*, February–March 1932, 36–8

—, 'Dovesti do kontsa bor'bu nepmanskoy muzïki' [Finishing off the struggle against NEPman music], *Za proletarskuyu muzïku*, 1930, no. 9, 1–3

—, 'Ozdorovit' muzïkal'nuyu obshchestvennost'' [Making music societies healthier], *Rabochiy i teatr*, 12 March 1930, 11

—, 'Protiv gnilogo liberalisma na muzïkal'nom fronte' [Against rotten liberalism on the musical front], *Rabochiy i teatr*, 1932, no. 4, 3

—, 'Boykot muzïke beloemigranta Rakhmaninova' [Boycott the music of the White-émigré Rakhmaninov], *Za proletarskuyu muzïku*, 1931, no. 5 (15), 6

—, 'Vserossiskaya muzïkal'naya konferentsiya' [All-Russian music conference], *Proletarskiy muzïkant*, 1929, no. 4, 3–12

—, '"Industrializm" i "narodnichestvo" v muzïke' [Industrialism and folk-ism in music], *Muzïka i revoliutsiya*, 1928, no. 3, 5

—, 'Sumbur vmesto muzïki: ob opera Ledi Makbet Mtsenkogo uyezda' [Muddle instead of music: on the opera 'Lady Macbeth of Mtsensk'], *Pravda*, 28 January 1936, 3

—, 'Baletnaya fal'sh' [Balletic falseness], *Pravda*, 6 February 1936, 3

—, 'Klassicheskaya muzïka v strane sovetov' [Classical Music in the Land of the Soviets], *Sovetskoe iskusstvo*, 5 February 1936, 1

—, 'Filarmonicheskie dela' [Philharmonia affairs], *Sovetskoe iskusstvo*, 25 January 1938, 4

—, 'Govoryat klassiki' [The classics speak], *Sovetskaya muzïka*, 1948, no. 1, 29–52

Ansari, Emily, '"Masters of the President's Music": Cold War Composers and the United States Government', PhD diss., Harvard University, 2009

Artamonova, Elena, 'Between Tradition and Modernity: Sergei Vasilenko and His Unknown Works for Viola and Piano', PhD diss., University of London, 2014

Asmus V., 'Muzïkal'naya estetika filosofkogo romantizma' [Musical aesthetics of philosophical romanticism], Sovetskaya muzïka, 1934, no. 1, 52–71

Baksan, D., 'Nasledstvo Vagnera' [Wagner's legacy], Izvestiya, 18 September 1937, 3

Belyayev, Viktor, 'Myaskovskiy, Gedike i Aleksandrov', Sovremennaya muzïka, 1924, no. 8, 19–20

Belza, Igor, 'O tvorcheskikh napravleniyakh v sovremennoy angliyskoy muzïke' [On creative directions in contemporary English music], Sovetskaya muzïka. Sbornik statey, vol. 1, Muzgiz, 1943, 68–72

Bogdanov-Berezovskiy, Valerian, and A. Aldanov, 'Kontsertï Ansermet' [Ansermet's concerts], Rabochiy i teatr, 2 June 1929, 10

Bogdanov-Berezovskiy, Valerian, 'O rabote Leningradskogo muzïkal'nogo veshchaniya' [On the work of the Leningrad musical broadcaster], Sovetskaya muzïka, 1934, no. 12, 69–77

Braudo, Yevgeniy, 'Betkhoven-grazhdanin' [Beethoven-Citizen], Muzïka i revoliutsiya, 1927, no. 3, 22–3

—, 'Leningradskaya muzïkal'naya zhizn'' [Leningrad's musical life], Muzïkal'naya nov', 1924, no. 4, 31 January, 31

—, 'Ob ekspressionizme v muzïke' [On Expressionism in Music], Muzïkal'naya letopis [Music Chronicle], 1922, no. 2, 150

Brooke, Caroline, 'The Development of Soviet Music Policy 1932–1941', PhD diss., University of Cambridge, 1998

—, 'Soviet Musicians and the Great Terror', Europe-Asia Studies, vol. 54, no. 3, 2002, 403–4

Bruk, M., 'Shubert i ego pesni' [Schubert and his songs], Za proletarskuyu muzïku, no. 16 (26), 1931, 6–12

Chemodanov, Sergey, 'Muzïka i teoriya istoricheskogo materializma' [Music and the theory of historical materialism], Muzïkal'naya nov' [Musical virgin soil], 1923, no. 1, 15–16

—, 'O Betkhovene i sovremennost'' [Beethoven and the present day], Muzïkal'naya nov', 1923, no. 2, 14–16

Cheremukhin, Mikhail, 'K voprosu o putyakh sovetskoy muzïki' [On the question of the path for Soviet music], Sovetskaya muzïka, 1933, no. 5, 23–30

Chernov, Ya., 'V Vetoshnom pereulka' [In Vetoshniy lane], Sovetskoe iskusstvo, 18 February 1938, 4

'D', 'O simfonicheskikh kontsertakh dlya rabochikh' [On symphony concerts for workers], Rabochiy zritel' [The worker-listener], no. 4, 22 January 1924, 10

David-Fox, Michael, 'What is Cultural Revolution?', in Russian Review, vol. 58, no. 2, 1999, 181–201

—, 'The Fellow-Travelers Revisited: The Cultured West through Soviet Eyes', Journal of Modern History, 75, no. 2, June 2003, 300–35

Debray, Régis, 'Socialism: A Life-Cycle', New Left Review, 46, July–August 2007, 5–28

Digonskaya, Ol'ga, 'Dmitriy Rogal'-Levitskiy – Ya ne stremilsya k "silnïm mira sego"' [Dmitriy Rogal'-Levitskiy – I didn't strive for a 'strong world of my own'], Muzïkal'naya akademiya, 1998, nos 3–4, 159–76

Dmitr'yev, M., 'Mechtaem o simfonicheskom orkestre' [We dream of a symphony orchestra], Muzïka i bït, no. 4 (August), 1927, 13

Dreyden, Simon, 'Na volye revoliutsii' [At the will of the revolution], Sovetskaya muzïka, 1966, no. 4, 11–20

Druskin, Mikhail, 'Repertuar i ispolniteli simfonicheskie kontsertï filarmonii' [Repertoire and performance of symphonic repertoire in Philharmonia concerts], Sovetskoe iskusstvo, no. 32, 1933, 2

—, 'Muzïkal'no-lektsionnaya rabota v Leningrade' [Music-lecture work in Leningrad], Sovetskaya muzïka, 1935, no. 11, 93–4

Druzhinina, Ye, 'Kak Mosfil obsluzhivaet rabochego slushatelya' [How Mosfil serves the worker listener], *Sovetskaya muzïka*, 1934, no. 7, 71–2

Dubinets, Elena, 'Pervootkrïvatel' novoy muzïki' [The Groundbreaker of new music], *Musïkal'naya akademiya*, no. 3, 2003, 196–205

V. F., 'O voennikh orkestrakh' [On military orchestras], *Proletarskiy muzïkant*, 1929, no. 6, 32

Fairclough, Pauline, 'Mahler Reconstructed: Sollertinskiy and the Soviet Symphony', *Musical Quarterly*, vol. 85/2, 2001, 367–90

—, 'The "Old Shostakovich": Reception in the British Press', *Music and Letters*, vol. 88/2, 2012, 266–96

—, 'Don't Sing it on a Feast Day: The Reception and Performance of Western Sacred Music in Soviet Russia, 1917–53', *Journal of the American Musicological Society*, vol. 65/1, 2012, 71–116

Frolova-Walker, Marina, 'The Soviet opera project: Ivan Dzerzhinsky vs. *Ivan Susanin*', *Cambridge Opera Journal*, vol. 18/2, 2006, 181–216

Gachev, Dmitriy, 'Vagner i Feyerbakh' [Wagner and Feuerbach], *Sovetskaya muzïka*, 1934, no. 7, 61–2

Gaub, Albrecht, 'Mikhail Glinka as Preached and Practiced in the Soviet Union Before and After 1937', *Journal of Musicological Research*, 22, 2003, 101–34

Glebov, Igor, 'Mozart and Sovremennost' [Mozart and the present], *Sovremennaya muzïka* 1927, no. 5 (no. 25), 55–9

—, 'Muzïka goroda i derevni' [Music of town and country], *Muzïka i revoliutsiya*, 1926, no. 3, 6

—, 'Petrogradskie Kurantï' [Petrograd chimes], *K novïm beregam*, 1923, no. 3, 42

Glier, Reyngol'd, 'Vïdaushchiysya russkiy kompozitor' [A distinguished Russian composer], *Izvestiya*, 31 March 1943, 4

Glumov, A., 'Lelio', *Sovetskaya muzïka*, 1934, no. 2, 44–50

Gorodinskiy, Viktor, 'Etyud o Bakhe' [Study on Bach], *Sovetskoe iskusstvo*, 11 April 1935, 2

Grinberg, Moysey, 'RAPMovskie perepevï' [RAPMovsky re-hashing], *Sovetskoe iskusstvo*, 11 May 1937, 3

Groman, Anatoliy, 'Bela Bartok', *Proletarskiy muzïkant*, 1929, no. 1, 36–8

—, 'Istoriya Russkoy muzïki i RAPM' [The history of Russian music and RAPM], *Sovetskoe iskusstvo*, 11 May 1937, 5

Groman-Solovtsov, Anatoliy, and V. Voloshinov, 'Betkhoven v ispolnenii dvukh german-skikh dirizhërov' [Beethoven as performed by two German conductors], *Za proletarskuyu muzïku*, nos 4–5 (38–9) 1932, 36–8

Gruber, Roman, 'Kak slushaet muzïku rabochaya auditoriya' [How a workers' audience listens to music], *Muzïka i revoliutsiya*, 1928, no. 12, 12

—, 'Bakh i Gendel'' [Bach and Handel], *Sovetskaya muzïka*, 1935, no. 3, 5–29

Iokhel'son, Vladimir, 'Muzïkal'niy front i reshenie partii' [The Musical Front and the Party's Decision], *Rabochiy i teatr*, 1932, no. 16, n. p.

Iokhel'son, Vladimir, 'Tvorcheskaya diskussiya v Leningrade' [The creative discussion in Leningrad], *Sovetskaya muzïka*, 1936, no. 4, 13

Ivanov-Boretskiy, Mikhail, 'E.T.A. Gofman'' [E.T.A. Hoffmann], *Muzïkal'noe obrazovanie*, 1926, no. 1, 15

—, 'Dz'oakino Rosini' [Gioacchino Rossini], *Proletarskiy muzïkant*, 1930, no. 7 (15), 19–26

—, 'Revoliutsionnïe khorï Shumana' [Schumann's revolutionary choruses], *Muzïkal'noe obrazovanie*, 1930, no. 2, 16–19

—, 'Ot operï k oratorii' [From opera to oratorio], *Sovetskaya muzïka*, 1935, no. 3, 30–7

Kal'tat, Lev, 'Zametki o Sofil'e' [Notes on Sofil], *Proletarskiy muzïkant*, 1929, nos 7–8, 13

—, and David Rabinovich, 'V boyakh za nasledstvo' [Fighting for a heritage], *Sovetskaya muzïka*, 1933, no. 3, 7–40

Kelly, Catriona, 'Socialist Churches: Heritage Preservation and "Cultic Buildings" in Leningrad, 1924–1940', *Slavic Review*, Vol. 71, no. 4, 2012, 792–823

Khubov, Georgiy, 'Ivan Susanin', *Sovetskaya muzïka*, 1939, no. 2, 34

—, 'K novïm beregam' [Towards new shores], *Sovetskaya muzïka*, 1939, no. 4, 21

Kiprianov, V., 'Ot yablochka k Betkhovenu' [From yablochka to Beethoven], *Rabochiy i teatra*, no. 10, 1937, 3

Koposov, A., 'O rukovoditelyakh klubnïkh muzïkal'nïkh kruzhkov' [On the leadership of club music groups], *Muzïka i revoliutsiya*, 1929, nos 7–8, 5

Korotkov, M., 'Leningradskaya muzïkal'naya samodeyatel'nost" [Leningrad's amateur music scene], *Rabochi i teatr*, 21 February 1931, 16

Koval', Marian, 'Mavra Stravinskogo' [Stravinsky's Mavra], *Proletarskiy muzïkant*, 1929, no. 3, 33–5

Koval', Marian, 'Aleko M. G. K.' [Aleko in the Moscow State Conservatoire], *Proletarskiy muzïkant*, 1929, no. 3, 35–6

Kovnatskaya, Lyudmila, '"Vagnerovskie golosa" v Sankt-Peterburge. Razocharovanie i nadezhdï' ['Wagnerian voices' in St Petersburg. Disappointments and hopes], *Muzïkal'naya akademiya*, 1994, no. 3, 133–4

Kristiansen, Lev, 'Likvidirovat' ostatki RAPMovshchini' [To finish off the remnants of the rapmovshchina], *Sovetskaya muzïka*, 1938, no. 5, 9–14

Kudryatsev, N., 'Kak ozdorovit muzïkal'niy repertuar klubov' [How to improve club music repertoire], *Proletarskiy muzïkant*, 1929, no. 4, 29

Kuznetsov, Konstantin, 'Etiudï o Gluke' [Notes on Gluck], *Sovetskaya muzïka*, 1937, no. 12, 94–100

LaPasha, L. Robin C., 'From Chastushki to Tchaikovsky: Amateur Activity and the Production of Popular Culture in the Soviet 1930s', PhD diss., Duke University, 2001

Lebedinskiy, Lev, 'Kontsertnaya rabota v rabochey auditorii' [Concert works for workers], *Proletarskiy muzïkant*, 1929, 2, 9

—, 'O zhivikh muzeyakh' [On living museums], *Za proletarskuyu muzïku*, 1931, no. 6, 8–9

Liberson, S. A., 'Sumerki muzïkal'nogo tvorchestva' [The twilight of musical creativity], *Muzïka i revoliutsiya*, 1927, nos 7–8, 8

Lovell, Stephen, 'Broadcasting Bolshevik: The Radio Voice of Soviet Culture, 1920s–1930s', *Journal of Contemporary History*, 2013, no. 48, 78–97

Lunacharskiy, Anatoliy, 'Velikie sëstrï' ['Great Sisters'], *Muzïka i revoliutsitya*, 1926, no. 1, 16

— 'Romantika', *Muzïka i revoliutsiya*, 1928, no. 10, October, 3–6

—, 'Sotsial'nie istoki muzïkal'nogo iskusstva' [Social sources of musical art], *Proletarskiy muzïkant*, 1929, no. 4, 12–20

—, 'Novie puti operï i baleta' [New steps in opera and ballet], *Proletarskiy muzïkant*, 1930, no. 5 (13), 4–6

Maddox, Steven, 'These Monuments Must Be Protected! The Stalinist Turn to the Past and Historic Preservation during the Blockade of Leningrad', *Russian Review*, 70, 2011, 608–26

Makar'in, Aleksandr, and Rafael Suslovich, 'Izuchayte rabochego zritelya!' [Study the working listener!], *Rabochiy i teatr*, 27 October 1925, no. 43, 5.

Mal'ko, Nikolay, 'O "diletantakh" i liubitelyakh' [On 'dilettantes' and music lovers], *Muzïka i bït*, no. 2, June 1927, 1–2

Mirov, N. V., 'Dukhovïe rabochie orkestrï-kruzhki' [Workers' orchestral groups], *Muzïka i revoliutsiya*, 1927, nos 5–6, 8

Mitchell, Rebecca, 'Nietzsche's Orphans: Music and the Search for Unity in Revolutionary Russia, 1905–1921', PhD diss., University of Illinois at Urbana-Champagn, 2011

Moore, Christopher, 'Socialist Realism and the Music of the French Popular Front', *The Journal of Musicology*, 25/4, Fall 2008, 473–502

'Muzrabotnik', 'Za sotsialisticheskoe nastuplenie v muzïke' [Towards a socialist offensive in Music], *Rabochiy i teatr*, 2 June 1929, 8

Nadol'skiy, D., 'Muzïka v goscapella' [Music in the State capella], *Rabis*, 15 March 1926, 10

Nest'yev, Izrail', 'V plenu burzhuaznogo modernizma' [In thrall to bourgeois modernism], *Sovetskaya muzïka*, 1948, no. 10, 16–23

Neygauz, Genrikh, 'O prostote v iskusstve' [On simplicity in music], *Sovetskoe iskusstvo*, 17 February 1936, 1

Novitskiy, Sergey, 'Shto delat'?' [What is to be done?], *Muzïka i revoliutsiya*, 1929, no. 4, 35–6

ORKiMD, 'Nash protest' [Our protest], *Muzïka i revoliutsiya*, 1928, nos 5–6, 43

Pekelis, Mikhail, 'Frants Shubert', *Muzïka i revoliutsiya*, 1928, no. 10, 7–15

Potter, Pamela, 'The Politicization of Handel and His Oratorios in the Weimar Republic, the Third Reich, and the Early Years of the German Democratic Republic', *The Musical Quarterly*, vol. 85/2, 2001, 311–41

Ratskaya, Tsetsiliya, 'Voprosï metodiki kontsertno-lektsionnoy rabotï' [Questions of methods of concert-lecture work], *Sovetskaya muzïka*, 1935, nos 7–8, 121–7

Remezov, I., 'Massovaya rabota s rabochim zritelem v Bol'shom teatre' [Mass work with worker-listeners at the Bolshoy Theatre], *Sovetskaya muzïka*, 1934, no. 4, 94–7

Rïzhkin, Iosef, 'Arnol'd Shënberg – likvidator muzïki' [Arnold Schoenberg – the liquidator of music], *Sovetskaya muzïka*, 1949, no. 8, 97–103

Roslavets, Nikolay, 'Nash muzïkal'niy front' [Our musical front], *Rabis*, 5 December 1925, 2–3

—, 'Kul't-rabota Vserabisa' [Cultural work of Vserabis], *Vestnik rabotnikov iskusstv* [Bulletin of art workers], 1920, nos 2–3, 46–8

A. S., 'Razgovor v rabochem klube' [Conversation in a workers' club], *Muzïka i revoliutsiya*, 1926, no. 1, 22–3

Safiullina, Nailya, 'The Canonization of Western Writers in the Soviet Union in the 1930s', *The Modern Language Review*, vol. 107, no. 2, April 2012, 559–84

Sargeant, Lynn M., 'High Anxiety: New Venues, New Audiences, and the Fear of the Popular in Late Imperial Russian Musical Life', *19th-Century Music*, vol. 35, no. 2, Fall 2011, 93–114

Shaverdyan, Aleksandr, 'Mozart's Requiem' [*Rekviem Motsarta*], *Sovetskoe iskusstvo*, 25 June 1939, 4

Shlifshteyn, Semën, 'O rabote Moskovskoy filarmonii' [On the work of the Moscow Philharmonia], *Sovetskaya muzïka*, 1934, no. 9, 45–9

Shneyerson, Grigoriy, 'Alan Bush', *Sovetskaya muzïka*, 1938, no. 9, 86–7

—, 'O Russkom narodnom muzïkal'nom tvorchestve', *Sovetskaya muzïka: sbornik statey*, Moscow: Muzgiz, 1945

—, 'Porgi i Bess', *Sovetskaya muzïka*, 1946, nos 5–6, 89–96

—, 'Khronika zarubezhnoy muzïkal'noy zhizni' [Chronicle of musical life abroad], *Sovetskaya muzïka*, 1941, no. 5, 108

—, 'Muzïkal'naya Frantsiya' [Musical France], *Sovetskaya muzïka*, 1946, no. 11, 95–100

—, 'Boguslav Martinu – Lidice', *Sovetskaya muzïka*, 1947, no. 2, 102

—, 'Amerikanskaya muzïkal'naya inzheneriya' [American musical engineering], *Sovetskaya muzïka*, 1948, no. 2, 167

Shtangrud, Mikhail, 'History of Moscow State Choral College from 1944 through 1991', DMA diss., Thornton School of Music, University of Southern California, 2006

Shteynpress, Boris, 'Ob instrumental'nom tvorchestve Motsarta [On Mozart's instrumental music], *Sovetskaya muzïka*, 1935, no. 6, 58

Smith, Suzannah Lockwood, 'Soviet Arts Policy, Folk Music, and National Identity: The Piatnitskii State Russian Folk Choir, 1927–1945', PhD dissertation, University of Minnesota, 1997

Sollertinskiy, Ivan, 'Iuda Makkabey' [Judas Maccabeus], *Leningradskaya pravda*, 22 April 1939, 3

—, 'Georg Gendel'. 250 let so dnya rozhdeniya' [George Handel. 250 years since his birth], *Izvestiya*, 27 February 1935, 2

—, 'I. S. Bakh. K 250-letiu so dniya rozhdeniya' [Johann Sebastian Bach. On the 250th anniversary of his birth], *Izvestiya*, 21 March 1935, 2

—, 'O puti Rikharda Vagnera' [On the path of Richard Wagner], *Rabochiy i teatr*, 1933, nos 4–5, 4

Swift, Megan, 'The Bronze Horseman Rides Again: The Stalinist Reimaging of Alexander Pushkin's Mednyi vsadnik, 1928–53', *Russian Review*, 72, 2013, 24–44

Tiulin, Yu, 'Kristallizatsiya tematizma v tvorchestve Bakha' [Crystallization of themes in Bach's work], *Sovetskaya muzïka*, 1935, no. 3, 38–54

Tretyakova, Yelena, 'Rabochie-krest'yanskomu zriteliyu zhelaten?' [What does the worker-peasant listener really want?], *Muzïkal'naya akademiya*, 1994, no. 3, 131–2

Tsenovskiy, Anton, '"Mï" i "oni"' [Them and us], *Rabochiy i teatr*, 1 December 1924, 7

Tsukkerman, Viktor, 'Rimskiy Korsakov i narodnaya pesnya' [Rimskiy Korsakov and folk song], *Sovetskaya muzïka*, 1938, nos 10–11, 104–27

Valerianov, B., 'Opera v klube' [Opera in the club], *Rabochiy i teatr*, 17 June 1928, 14

Veprik, Aleksandr, 'O "levoy" i "pravoy" muzïke i o zadachakh sovetskikh kompozitorov' [On 'left' and 'right' in music and on the tasks of Soviet composers], *Muzïka i revoliutsiya*, 1929, no. 2, 16

Veys, Pavel, 'O zhurnale "Proletarskiy muzïkant"' [On the journal 'Proletarian musician'], *Sovetskaya muzïka*, 1933, no. 1, 133

Vilkovir, Yefim, 'M. P. Musorgskiy', *Muzïka i revoliutsiya*, 1926, no. 5, 4

Vinogradov, V., 'Protiv tserkovshchinï v muzïke' [Against the church in music], *Za proletarskuyu muzïku*, 1931, nos 17–18 (27–8), 9–18

Vlasova, Yekaterina, 'Nachalo tridsatikh godov' [At the beginning of the 1930s], *Muzïkal'naya akademiya*, no. 2, 2008, 81–8

Yarkov, P., 'Muzïka v derevnye. Pis'mo krest'yanina' [Music in the village. A letter from a peasant], *Muzïka i revoliutsiya*, 1926, no. 1, 42

Zhitomirskiy, Daniil, and N. Makeyev, 'Kruzhok VAPM i predpriyati' [The VAPM circle and its work], *Za proletarskuyu muzïku*, 1931, no. 2 (12), 11–18.

Zhitomirskiy, Daniil, 'Mifologiya "klassvogo" iskusstva' [The myth of 'class art'], *Muzïkal'naya akademiya*, 1993, no. 2, 144–54

INDEX